Handling the Medical Claim

An 8-Step Guide on "How-To" Correct and Resolve Claim Issues

Handling the Medical Claim

An 8-Step Guide on "How-To" Correct and Resolve Claim Issues

Catherine Cochran

CRC Press
Taylor & Francis Group
Boca Raton   London   New York

CRC Press is an imprint of the
Taylor & Francis Group, an **informa** business

A PRODUCTIVITY PRESS BOOK

CRC Press
Taylor & Francis Group
6000 Broken Sound Parkway NW, Suite 300
Boca Raton, FL 33487-2742

© 2013 by Taylor & Francis Group, LLC
CRC Press is an imprint of Taylor & Francis Group, an Informa business

No claim to original U.S. Government works

Printed in the United States of America on acid-free paper
Version Date: 20120808

International Standard Book Number: 978-1-4398-5624-6 (Paperback)

Library of Congress Cataloging-in-Publication Data

Cochran, Catherine.
   Handling the medical claim : an 8-step guide on "how to" correct and resolve claim issues / Catherine Cochran.
     p. ; cm.
   Includes bibliographical references and index.
   Summary: "Packed with forms, charts, and illustrative examples, this book supplies step-by-step guidance for practice administrators and managers on how to bill and collect on claims for services provided in a physicians' office. It covers the CMS-1500 claim form, obtaining patient and insured information, submission of claims, accounts receivable, and collections. The book provides an understanding of the entire process to help you address issues before they become problems"--Provided by publisher.
   ISBN 978-1-4398-5624-6 (pbk. : alk. paper)
   I. Title.
   [DNLM: 1. Clinical Coding. 2. Practice Management. 3. Insurance Claim Reporting. W 80]

  651.5'04261--dc23   2011043468

Visit the Taylor & Francis Web site at
http://www.taylorandfrancis.com

and the CRC Press Web site at
http://www.crcpress.com

Contents

Acknowledgments

I would like to take this time to first give a special thanks to my husband, Rodney, and my son, Chris, for making this possible. My life has been put on hold for quite some time. I dedicated a lot of my time to writing this book, which meant spending my weekends on the computer. Both have been very understanding and very supportive by pulling the extra load. I want to say thank you and I love you both.

I wish to thank my parents for their encouragement and support. I want to give a special thank you to a couple of special friends, Vickie Coleridge and Helen Jones. Both of them always asked me how my book was coming along and provided me with so many compliments. When I completed my book, they could not have been any happier for me.

I would like to recognize and acknowledge my boss, Lisa Burcher, who helped me by letting me rearrange my work schedule so I had more time to complete this book. She always gave me the support I needed and wanted to be one of the first to read my book.

Finally, I would like to thank Don Karecki, who at the time was the owner and publisher of K&M Publishing, Inc., who made this all possible. When I first began this journey, I sent out twenty to thirty letters asking if anyone would be interested in publishing my book; his was the only response I received. He has been with me throughout this whole process since day one.

Also many thanks go out to my senior editor with CRC Press, Taylor & Francis Group, Kristine Mednansky, for all her endless patience and support throughout the past year. The last several months were especially rough, but she never gave up on me and always had a kind word.

I am very grateful to the Lord above for helping me through some difficult times and giving me the courage to finish. He provided me with a lot of patience, good health, and pushed me when I wanted to quit.

Introduction

When a doctor sees a patient, how does that doctor's office know exactly what to bill? How does that doctor get paid? If a service or procedure that was provided is denied, how does that doctor's office know what to do to get that patient's insurance company to pay?

To answer these questions, and to have an understanding of how a doctor is paid for each service provided to a patient, you have to know the whole process. *Handling the Medical Claim: An 8-Step Guide on "How To" Correct and Resolve Claim Issues* explains, from beginning to end, how a service provided in a physician's office is billed and how reimbursement is collected.

To understand the process, I will begin with some basic good practice management skills. Every office must learn how to delegate specific job duties. Depending on the size of the doctor's office or clinic, your duties may be divided up by job description or departments. In a large group clinic, different departments may be set up as follows: front office (includes patient data entry and appointments), medical records, transcription, triage/nurses station, administrative, and billing departments. The front office consists of appointments and patient data entry. The billing department includes a receipt poster (who enters the payment), charge entry and coders (who capture all the charges), and a billing representative, collector, or billing clerk (who researches and resolves claim issues). The credentialing officer maintains insurance contracts as well as licenses and certifications for all the providers in the clinic. This position can be handled by an administrative assistant or by the billing department. Each department has specific duties, and I have outlined those duties based on the responsibilities each department has for a specific part of the claim. Through my years of experience, I have worked in the front office, coding, medical and insurance terminology, and billing and collections areas. Depending on your position in the office, you have a hand in gathering information that in one way or another involves the handling of a medical claim.

I have divided this book into five chapters that describe the processes necessary to bill charges and obtain reimbursement for services provided in a physician's office. Chapter 1 discusses the CMS-1500 claim form (CMS stands for Centers for Medicare and Medicaid Services). Chapter 2 covers obtaining patient and insurance information (patient data entry). Chapter 3 discusses the submission of the claim (charge entry). Chapter 4 covers the processing of an allowed claim (accounts receivable), and Chapter 5 considers claims that cannot be processed or are denied claims (collections).

Chapters 2 through 5 are divided into eight major steps. Each of those eight steps is then broken into specific parts. Each part is linked from one section to another section of the book. For example, in Chapter 5, Step 8, Unit II, Part B, Section 2, 2a is linked to Section 6, 6b and then it is linked to Unit III, Part A, Section 1, 1d. I will provide you with a description and/or explanation of what that part consists of as well as the importance and understanding of how each part affects the claim. A very important thing to remember is that different insurance companies require different information on the claim form. If the proper information is not on the claim it will be returned or denied. See Step 6 for more details.

For a physician or provider of service to bill for charges, the physician's office must submit the charges to the patient's insurance company. To do so, the office uses the CMS-1500 claim form. Facilities, such as hospitals, use the UB-04 or CMS-1450 claim form. In this book we will focus on the CMS-1500 claim form, and will link the information in each chapter to the claim form itself.

In Chapter 1, "The CMS-1500 Claim Form," I have divided the claim form into two sections, the upper half and the lower half. The upper half pertains to patient and policyholder information; the lower half pertains to the type of service provided, who provided that service, and where the service was provided (office, hospital, etc.).

Chapter 2, "Patient Data Entry (Steps 1, 2, and 3)," covers the first three steps; Step 1 covers setting up the doctor's schedule and reviewing the different appointment types; Step 2 covers the patient's chart, medical documentation, and forms; Step 3 covers patient registration, which includes patient information, guarantor, and policyholder and insurance information.

In Chapter 3, "Charge Entry (Steps 4, 5, and 6)," the next three steps are reviewed. Step 4 covers the actual appointment itself, where the service took place, who provided the service, and the patient complaint (diagnosis). Step 5 covers the different types of coding systems used for billing charges. Step 6 covers how a claim is formatted and different ways a claim can be filed. It is important to remember that when new procedure and billing code books are published, you must make sure that you are using the most current codes for services rendered; always check for new codes and deletions.

Chapter 4, "Accounts Receivable (Step 7)," covers Step 7, how a claim is adjudicated. This chapter discusses how a claim is processed, how a service or procedure is approved, and the different types of reimbursement fees. We will also go over an explanation of benefits (EOB) and what the American National Standards Institute (ANSI) reason codes mean. It is important to remember to print out new fee schedules at the beginning of the year and mid-year to ensure that you will have the correct fee allowances.

Chapter 5, "Collections (Step 8)," covers Step 8, what to do when a claim is rejected or denied. You will learn how to correct a claim, how to appeal a denied claim, and how to handle patient balances. I will also show you where and how to obtain claim requirements and coverage determinations. I have also laid out, as a medical billing specialist, what your daily work duties entail so you will learn how to become organized and prioritize your work.

I will provide you with case examples and a step-by-step guide to resolving a claim issue. This process involves looking at the denied EOB, determining what step in the chapter will help you find your answer, and then being able to link your findings to the box number on the claim form to which the problem pertains. This will provide you with an understanding of the whole picture so that you will know what you need to do to correct the problem.

The last section of the book includes an overview of the revenue cycle and the importance of keeping cash flow moving. I have highlighted opportunities for increasing revenue and ways to avoid losing money.

With the information in this book, you will be able to work in any physician's office or clinic department and be a very important asset to that organization.

About the Author

Catherine Cochran has more than sixteen years of experience in the medical office field, including front office and business office operations in small and large clinics. Her knowledge and experience ranges from patient data entry, charge entry, receipt posting, to billing and working on medical claims.

Her decision to write this book came about several years ago. Many coworkers commented that she was a good teacher and always provided help and information. As a result, she decided to pass on her knowledge and experience to new students and medical billing representatives.

Catherine's career began in October 1995 when she first enrolled in a medical terminology class at Rose State College, followed by a medical transcriptionist and insurance filing and coding class at DeMarge College. She began her career as a business office manager for two oral surgeons in June 1996 and in 1999 transferred to the billing department, where she became an insurance billing clerk. In 2000 she went to work for a billing company, where she became a receipt poster as well as an accounts receivable (A/R) representative. In July 2005, when the company she worked for moved out of state, she decided to take a different direction and went to work for a large insurance company paying claims as a claims examiner. This position lasted until March of 2006 when she returned to claim submission activities. She has been working for the same company since 2006 as a billing specialist. During this time she has gained experience in charge entry, patient data entry, and posting of receipts.

Catherine, her son Chris, and her husband Rodney have lived in the small town of McLoud, Oklahoma, since 1992. Rodney is retired from the US Navy. Today, Catherine works as a medical billing specialist for a large clinic, but she plans to start her own business as an independent billing consultant and learn about medical billing from the hospital side.

Chapter 1

The CMS-1500 Claim Form

Contents

Unit I: Introduction

Different Types of Claim Forms

There are three different kinds of claim forms: the professional paper claim form, the institutional paper claim form, and the dental paper claim form.

The professional paper claim form is called the CMS-1500 (08/05); CMS stands for Centers for Medicare and Medicaid Services (see Figure 1.1). It is used in a physician's office or by medical suppliers for the purpose of billing charges for services rendered. Previously, it was referred to as the HCFA-1500 (12/90); and HCFA stands for Health Care Finance Administration. The institutional paper claim form is called the CMS-1450, but is also referred as the UB-04, which replaced the UB-92. It is used by a facility, such as a hospital or skilled nursing facility, for the purpose of billing charges. Due to new changes, both the CMS-1500 and CMS-1450 forms had to be revised. Other types of claim forms are the American Dental Association ADA-94, which is a dental claim form, and the CMS 485, 486, and 487, which are home health care claim forms. Besides submitting a paper claim, charges can be billed electronically. The term for electronic billing is Electronic Data Interchange (EDI). Reimbursement time is a lot quicker with EDI, but the medical office software has to be capable of billing electronically as well as be compliant with the Health Insurance Portability and Accountability Act (HIPAA). This type of software is usually more expensive, but electronic billing is the way to go. We will cover this later in the book.

The upper portion of the claim form covers patient data, which consists of the patient name and address along with the insurance company information and who any charges should be billed to once the insurance company has paid and balance is the patient's responsibility. Information is located in Chapter 2, Patient Data Entry, Step 3 Registration of a Patient.

The lower portion of the claim form covers information related to the charges, which consists of three parts. Information is located in Chapter 3, Charge Entry, Step 4 The Appointment (location where service took place), Step 5 Charge Entry, Step 6 Billing (file date).

Unit II: Introduction to the Top Portion of the Claim Form

The top portion of the CMS-1500 can be broken into four areas of information and each area is located in a specific box (or block):

1. Patient information: Name of the patient, patient date of birth, patient relationship to the policyholder (insured), patient address, status of patient
2. Coverage information: Type of insurance, policyholder (insured) identification (ID) number, policyholder (insured) name, policyholder (insured) address, policyholder (group number), policyholder (insured) date of birth, policyholder (insured) name of employer or school, name of the plan, policyholder (insured) signature

1

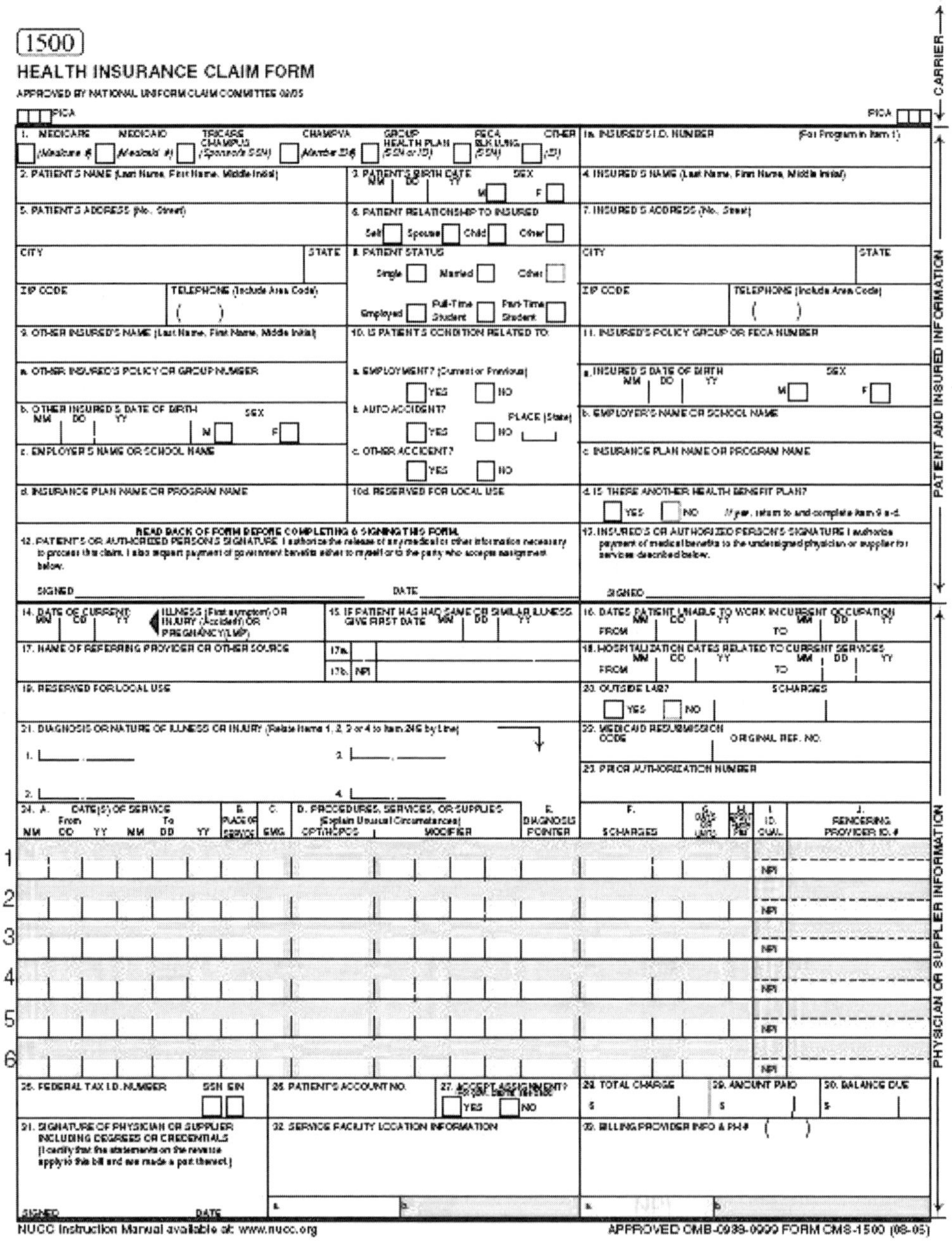
1500
HEALTH INSURANCE CLAIM FORM
APPROVED BY NATIONAL UNIFORM CLAIM COMMITTEE 08/05
PICA
1. MEDICARE MEDICAID TRICARE CHAMPUS CHAMPVA GROUP HEALTH PLAN FECA BLK LUNG OTHER
1a. INSURED'S I.D. NUMBER (For Program in Item 1)
2. PATIENT'S NAME (Last Name, First Name, Middle Initial)
3. PATIENT'S BIRTH DATE SEX
4. INSURED'S NAME (Last Name, First Name, Middle Initial)
5. PATIENT'S ADDRESS (No., Street)
6. PATIENT RELATIONSHIP TO INSURED Self Spouse Child Other
7. INSURED'S ADDRESS (No., Street)
CITY STATE
8. PATIENT STATUS Single Married Other
ZIP CODE TELEPHONE (Include Area Code)
Employed Full-Time Student Part-Time Student
9. OTHER INSURED'S NAME (Last Name, First Name, Middle Initial)
10. IS PATIENT'S CONDITION RELATED TO:
11. INSURED'S POLICY GROUP OR FECA NUMBER
a. OTHER INSURED'S POLICY OR GROUP NUMBER
a. EMPLOYMENT? (Current or Previous) YES NO
a. INSURED'S DATE OF BIRTH SEX M F
b. OTHER INSURED'S DATE OF BIRTH SEX M F
b. AUTO ACCIDENT? PLACE (State) YES NO
b. EMPLOYER'S NAME OR SCHOOL NAME
c. EMPLOYER'S NAME OR SCHOOL NAME
c. OTHER ACCIDENT? YES NO
c. INSURANCE PLAN NAME OR PROGRAM NAME
d. INSURANCE PLAN NAME OR PROGRAM NAME
10d. RESERVED FOR LOCAL USE
d. IS THERE ANOTHER HEALTH BENEFIT PLAN? YES NO
READ BACK OF FORM BEFORE COMPLETING & SIGNING THIS FORM.
12. PATIENT'S OR AUTHORIZED PERSON'S SIGNATURE
13. INSURED'S OR AUTHORIZED PERSON'S SIGNATURE
SIGNED DATE
14. DATE OF CURRENT: ILLNESS (First symptom) OR INJURY (Accident) OR PREGNANCY(LMP)
15. IF PATIENT HAS HAD SAME OR SIMILAR ILLNESS. GIVE FIRST DATE
16. DATES PATIENT UNABLE TO WORK IN CURRENT OCCUPATION FROM TO
17. NAME OF REFERRING PROVIDER OR OTHER SOURCE 17a. 17b. NPI
18. HOSPITALIZATION DATES RELATED TO CURRENT SERVICES FROM TO
19. RESERVED FOR LOCAL USE
20. OUTSIDE LAB? YES NO $ CHARGES
21. DIAGNOSIS OR NATURE OF ILLNESS OR INJURY
22. MEDICAID RESUBMISSION CODE ORIGINAL REF. NO.
23. PRIOR AUTHORIZATION NUMBER
24. A. DATE(S) OF SERVICE From To B. PLACE OF SERVICE C. EMG D. PROCEDURES, SERVICES, OR SUPPLIES CPT/HCPCS MODIFIER E. DIAGNOSIS POINTER F. $ CHARGES G. DAYS OR UNITS H. EPSDT Family Plan I. ID. QUAL. J. RENDERING PROVIDER ID. #
1 2 3 4 5 6 NPI
25. FEDERAL TAX I.D. NUMBER SSN EIN
26. PATIENT'S ACCOUNT NO.
27. ACCEPT ASSIGNMENT? YES NO
28. TOTAL CHARGE
29. AMOUNT PAID
30. BALANCE DUE
31. SIGNATURE OF PHYSICIAN OR SUPPLIER INCLUDING DEGREES OR CREDENTIALS
32. SERVICE FACILITY LOCATION INFORMATION
33. BILLING PROVIDER INFO & PH #
SIGNED DATE
NUCC Instruction Manual available at: www.nucc.org
APPROVED OMB-0938-0999 FORM CMS-1500 (08-05)
CARRIER
PATIENT AND INSURED INFORMATION
PHYSICIAN OR SUPPLIER INFORMATION

Figure 1.1 Paper claim form (CMS-1500).

3. Secondary coverage information: Other coverage, policyholder (insured) name, policyholder (group number), policyholder (insured) date of birth, policyholder (insured) name of employer, name of the plan.
4. Accident detail: Patient condition/illness or injury related to an accident (work, auto, or other).

Box Number on the CMS-1500

Figure 1.2 shows the various boxes on the top portion of the CMS-1500 claim form.

1. Box 2: Name of the patient
2. Box 3: Patient's date of birth
3. Box 5: Patient address
4. Box 6: Patient relationship to the policyholder (insured)
5. Box 8: Status of the patient (single, married, other, employed, student)
6. Box 12: Signature of the patient
7. Box 1: Insurer and type of insurance
8. Box 1a: Policyholder (insured) ID number
9. Box 4: Policyholder (insured) name
10. Box 7: Policyholder (insured) address

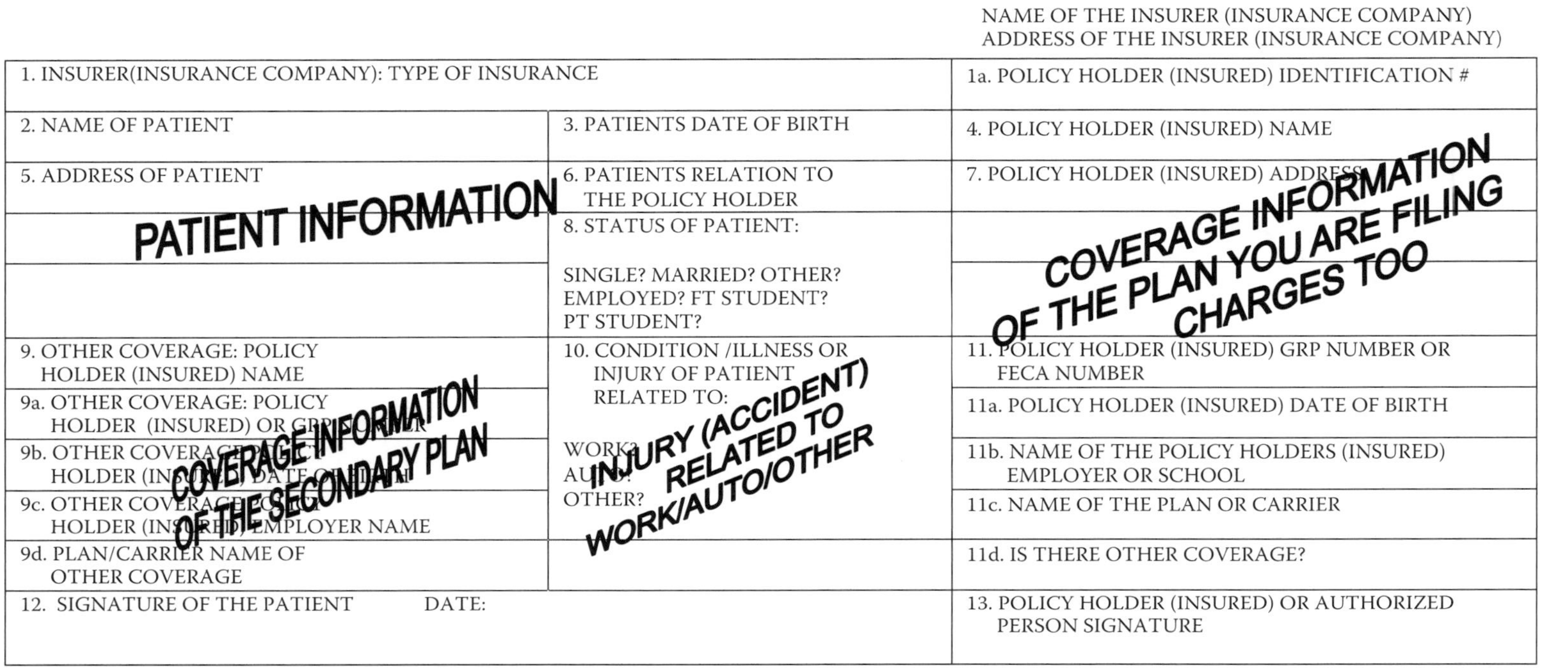

NAME OF THE INSURER (INSURANCE COMPANY)
ADDRESS OF THE INSURER (INSURANCE COMPANY)

1. INSURER(INSURANCE COMPANY): TYPE OF INSURANCE	1a. POLICY HOLDER (INSURED) IDENTIFICATION #
2. NAME OF PATIENT	4. POLICY HOLDER (INSURED) NAME
5. ADDRESS OF PATIENT	7. POLICY HOLDER (INSURED) ADDRESS
3. PATIENTS DATE OF BIRTH	
6. PATIENT'S RELATION TO THE POLICY HOLDER	
8. STATUS OF PATIENT: SINGLE? MARRIED? OTHER? EMPLOYED? FT STUDENT? PT STUDENT?	
10. CONDITION /ILLNESS OR INJURY OF PATIENT RELATED TO: WORK? (ACCIDENT) AUTO? RELATED TO/OTHER OTHER?	11. POLICY HOLDER (INSURED) GRP NUMBER OR FECA NUMBER
9. OTHER COVERAGE: POLICY HOLDER (INSURED) NAME	11a. POLICY HOLDER (INSURED) DATE OF BIRTH
9a. OTHER COVERAGE: POLICY HOLDER (INSURED) OR GRP NUMBER	11b. NAME OF THE POLICY HOLDERS (INSURED) EMPLOYER OR SCHOOL
9b. OTHER COVERAGE: POLICY HOLDER (INSURED) DATE	11c. NAME OF THE PLAN OR CARRIER
9c. OTHER COVERAGE: POLICY HOLDER (INSURED) EMPLOYER NAME	11d. IS THERE OTHER COVERAGE?
9d. PLAN/CARRIER NAME OF OTHER COVERAGE	
12. SIGNATURE OF THE PATIENT DATE:	13. POLICY HOLDER (INSURED) OR AUTHORIZED PERSON SIGNATURE

(Overlaid labels: PATIENT INFORMATION; COVERAGE INFORMATION OF THE SECONDARY PLAN; INJURY RELATED TO AUTO/OTHER WORK; COVERAGE INFORMATION OF THE PLAN YOU ARE FILING CHARGES TOO)

Figure 1.2   The top portion of the CMS-1500 claim form.

11. Box 11: Policyholder (insured) group number
12. Box 11a: Policyholder (insured) date of birth
13. Box 11b: Policyholder (insured) employer
14. Box 11c: Name of the plan
15. Box 13: Policyholder (insured) signature
16. Box 11d, 9, 9a, 9b, 9c, 9d: secondary coverage information
17. Box 10: Patient condition/illness or injury related to an accident (work, auto, or other)

Unit III: Introduction to the Bottom Portion of the Claim Form

The bottom portion of the CMS-1500 can be broken up into eight areas of information and each area is located in a specific box (or block):

1. Type of service, procedure, or supply that was provided to the patient
2. Patient diagnosis (patient complaint)
3. Place where the service was rendered (location)
4. Name of the facility where service was rendered
5. Dates
6. Physician and other provider of service identification
7. Fee amount

8. Paid amount
9. Authorization/referral or case number

Box Number on the CMS-1500

Figure 1.3 shows the various boxes on the bottom portion of the CMS-1500 claim form.

1. Box 24D: Type of service, procedure or supply (*Current Procedural Terminology* [CPT]-4 and Healthcare Common Procedure Coding System [HCPCS] codes)
2. Box 21: Linked to Boxes 24E, patient diagnosis (*International Classification of Diseases, 9th Revision, Clinical Modification* [ICD-9-CM])
3. Box 24B: Place where the service was rendered (point of service [POS] codes)
4. Box 32: Name of the facility
5. Boxes 14, 16, 18, 24A, and 31: Dates of service
6. Boxes 17, 17a, 17b, 24J, 31, 32a, and 33a: Physician or other provider of service
7. Box 24F, 28, 30: Fee amount
8. Box 29: Paid amount
9. Box 23: Authorization/referral or case number; required if service is to be billed to an HMO (health maintenance organization), IHS (Indian Health Services), or WC (workers compensation)

14. DATE CONDITION OR INJURY OCCURRED?	15. HAS CONDITION OR INJURY OCCURRED BEFORE? IF SO, WHEN	16. WHAT ARE THE DATES THE PATIENT IS UNABLE TO WORK?
17. NAME OF REFERRING DOCTOR	17a. PROVIDER UPIN # 17b. PROVIDER NPI #	18. WHAT ARE THE DATES THE PATIENT WAS HOSPITALIZED?
19. THIS SPACE CAN BE USED FOR ADDITIONAL PURPOSE		20. ANY LAB WORK ORDERED OUTSIDE THE OFFICE?
21. LIST OF THE ICD-9 (DIAGNOSIS) CODES GO HERE 1. 562.11 3. 564.0 2. 789.0 4. Link Diagnosis with that procedure		22. USE FOR MEDICAID
		23. AUTHORIZATION NUMBER GOES HERE

24. A DATE SERVICE TOOK PLACE	B LOCATION	C	D CODING / MOD	E LINK DIAGNOSIS	F (CHARGES) $ AMOUNT	G	H	I	J. PROVIDER ID#
LINE 1 FROM 07/08/07 TO 07/08/07	11		99203	1,2,3	$125.00	D A			666555444
LINE 2 FROM 07/08/07 TO 07/08/07	11		74150	1,2,3	$ 55.00	Y S			666555444
LINE 3 FROM _/_/_ TO _/_/_						OR			
LINE 4 FROM _/_/_ TO _/_/_						U			
LINE 5 FROM _/_/_ TO _/_/_						N I			
LINE 6 FROM _/_/_ TO _/_/_						T S			

25. PROVIDER TAX ID# 000112222	26. PATIENT ACCT # 123456	27. DOES PROVIDER ACCEPT ASSIGNMENT? Y	28 TOTAL $ AMT $ 180.00	29. PAID AMT $	30. DUE AMT $

31. PHYSICIAN SIGNATURE GOES HERE OR NAME OF SUPPLIER SIGNATURE DATE	32. NAME OF FACILITY GOES HERE Somewhere In Time Clinic 00100 Future Ln LuckyVille, OK 00111 a. 666555444 b. PROVIDER NPI #	33. PROVIDERS BILLING ADDRESS GOES HERE Somewhere In Time Clinic 00100 Future Ln LuckyVille, OK 00111 a. 666555444 b. PROVIDER NPI #

Figure 1.3 The bottom portion of the CMS-1500 claim form.

Chapter 2

Patient Data Entry (Steps 1, 2, and 3)

Contents

FRONT OFFICE

Patient check-in and patient registration are handled through the front office. The front office or front desk includes several people who specialize in specific areas. These areas consist of:

Front Office Manager: Delegates the work and make sure everything runs smoothly
Front Office Receptionist: Checks patients in and out
Front Office Clerk: Verifies insurance coverage and benefits
Patient Data Entry Clerk: Enters patient information
Scheduler: Schedules patient appointments
Medical Records Clerk: Compiles patient charts
Transcriptionist: Transcribes doctors' notes

Unit I: Steps 1, 2, and 3, Introduction

Purpose

The purpose of Steps 1, 2, and 3 is to help guide you through the first three steps required for handling a medical claim in a doctor's office or clinic. Step 1 involves the schedule, Step 2 covers medical records, and Step 3 concerns registration of a patient. These three steps are always handled in the front office because the front office personnel obtain the patient information. That information is either documented in the medical practice computer or on paper. Later, once the information is keyed into the computer, we will look at how that information is applied to the claim form and its importance.

This chapter is probably the most important because it deals with information that must be the most accurate. If not, a claim will be denied or rejected. Some of the most common reasons for returned or denied claims are the insurance company cannot identify the member (policyholder), the claim was mailed to an incorrect address, or insurance coverage terminated. Because these instances happen quite

frequently, the process is slowed down. That is why it is so important that the information is keyed in correctly. There are ways to avoid incorrect keying and I will cover this later in the book.

Unit II: Step 1, the Schedule

The first step in understanding how charges in a doctor's office are billed on a claim form begins with the schedule, when a patient contacts your office.

Part A: Calendar

JUNE 2010						
S	M	T	W	TH	F	S
1	2	3	4	5	6	7
8	9	10	11	12	13	14
15	16	16	18	19	20	21
22	23	24	25	26	27	28
29	30	31				

The schedule determines the day the patient sees the doctor or the day on which a particular service was or will be provided to the patient. As you will learn, the claim form contains *from* and *to* dates, depending on the doctor's specialty. You will learn that there are treatment plans that consist of more than one day of treatment and will require a date range. We will cover this in more detail in Step 5.

The term that is used for the date on which a patient sees the doctor is called the *date of service*. It is also referred to as the date when a service was rendered.

Part B: Appointment Type

The appointment type (see Figure 2.1) indicates what type of appointment the patient is scheduled for, or the purpose of the visit. Specific times are given for specific types of appointments depending on the needs of the patient. Not every office appointment type is set up in the same way. Appointments are set up according to the particular doctor's specialty. Different types of appointments are new or established patient, follow-up or post-op, surgery or in-office procedure, radiology, and durable medical equipment (DME).

APPOINTMENT TYPE DATE __/__/__						
TIME	EXAM ROOM 1	EXAM ROOM 2	EXAM ROOM 3	EXAM ROOM 4	EXAM ROOM 5	EXAM ROOM 6
8:00 am						
8:15 am						
8:30 am						
8:45 am						
9:00 am						
9:15 am						
9:30 am						
9:45 am						
10:00 am						
10:15 am						
10:30 am						
10:45 am						
11:00 am						
11:15 am						
11:30 am						
11:45 am						
12:00 pm	lunch	lunch	lunch	lunch	lunch	Lunch
12:15 pm	lunch	lunch	lunch	lunch	lunch	Lunch
12:30 pm	lunch	lunch	lunch	lunch	Lunch	lunch
12:45 pm	lunch	lunch	lunch	lunch	lunch	Lunch
1:00 pm						
1:15 pm						
1:30 pm						
1:45 pm						
2:00 pm						
2:15 pm						
2:30 pm						
2:45 pm						
3:00 pm						
3:15 pm						
3:30 pm						
3:45 pm						
4:00 pm						
4:15 pm						
4:30 pm						
4:45 pm						
5:00 pm						
Color Chart	Consult		Surgery		Post Op	
	Est patient		Emergency		Follow Up	
	New patient					

1. Select time slot and type in patient name

Appointment Types are assigned specific codes which identify what the patient was seen for or what type of service was provided. These codes are keyed into the computer then applied to the claim form with its own fee attached. Below I have provided examples of the type of appointments that are used with their specific code number. They are as follows:

In Office: New Patient = time 45 minutes	Code range from 99201 – 99205	Emergencies = 1 hour
In Office: Established patient = time 15 minutes	Code range from 99211 – 99215	In Office Procedure = 1 hour	Code Range from 10000 ^
In Office: Follow Up = time 15 minutes	Code range from 99211 - 99215	In Office Consultation = 45 minutes	Code range from 99241 - 99245
Post Op Care = time 15 minutes	Code 99204	

Policies, Rules and Regulations: There might be specific rules you have to remember; for example, if a patient with Medicare comes to see the doctor, in order for that patient to be reconsidered as a new patient there has to be a 3-year period from the last visit in order to be billed out as a new patient.

When a patient contacts your office, there will be specific questions you will need to ask in order to help determine what type of appointment to schedule the individual's specific needs. Through my experience some of the questions that will need to be asked are as follows, not necessarily in this order:
- Are you a new patient or have you been seen here before? If so, how long ago?
- Did you have any particular day you wish to see the doctor?
- Find out what is wrong with the individual. What is sypmtom? Purpose of the visit?
- Is there a specific time during the day you wish to see the doctor?
- Determine if this person will be a new patient or is he/she an established patient.

High Points to remember when scheduling appointments:
- Make sure name is spelled correctly. If booking a patient who has same name as a patient in the system identify by date of birth.
- Make sure to repeat the date and time back so there is no misunderstanding as to when the appointment is scheduled.
- Allow enough time for each appointment making sure they do not overlap each other
- If the patient is scheduled to return several times make sure you try and schedule that patient on same day and same time to make it easier for that patient to remember his/her appointment. If you are scheduling a patient for an appointment in the office fill out an appointment card.
- Allow extra time for emergencies.

Figure 2.1   Appointment schedule.

Unit III: Step 2, Medical Records

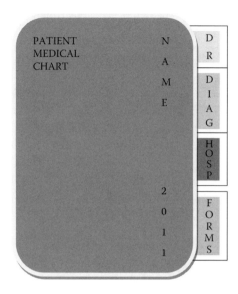

The second step in understanding how charges are billed in a doctor's office involves medical records. Step 2 includes four items: doctors and nurses notes, diagnostic, hospital, and forms and correspondence.

Putting a patient chart together is referred to as *charting*. Charts are color coded to identify each doctor. The patient's full name, with the last name first, and the date of birth are marked on the chart. Date of birth helps to avoid pulling the wrong chart for a patient with the same name. Papers are arranged in chronological order, with the most recent date on the top. When pulling a chart from medical records, it is a good idea to replace the chart with a form that is referred to as an *out guide* or *out folder*. If someone else is looking for the chart you just pulled, they will know who has it.

Policies, rules, and regulations must always be followed. If any information changes, such as the patient's diagnosis, make sure that the medical records are updated in the patient chart. If a service is billed, make sure that service was actually provided by making sure there are dictated notes concerning the service.

Part A: Doctors and Nurses Notes

This item includes the history and physical (H&P) (Figure 2.2), progress notes, orders for physical therapy (PT) or diagnostic tests, and prescriptions (RX). Doctor and nurses notes, may be hand written on a form, but most offices now use a mini-recorder to record notes, which are then transcribed. The patient will fill out a medical history questionnaire.

During the exam, the doctor will go over specific questions in order to assess the patient's situation (Figure 2.3).

Part B: Diagnostic

These are notes, forms, or reports that pertain to results of diagnostic testing such as x-rays, magnetic resonance imaging (MRI), computed tomography (CT), and so on. A laboratory report is another medical record item that may be filed in a patient chart. It could be for blood work or a pathology report for a biopsy (Figure 2.4).

Part C: Hospital Notes

Hospital notes may include several different types of documents, such as an operative report, emergency room (ER) report, inpatient consultation, or discharge report (Figure 2.5).

Part D: Forms and Correspondence

Figure 2.6 lists examples of forms and correspondence that may appear in a patient file.

Unit IV: Step 3, Registration of a Patient

Step 3 is the most crucial step when billing charges in a doctor's office or clinic. If this information is not correct, it can slow down the whole process. It can cause claims to be returned and rejected causing more work, and can be quite costly for any office because it will delay payment.

The patient registration information is located on the top half of the claim form. The necessary information is obtained from the patient on the initial visit. This section of the claim form consists of four parts; patient, guarantor, insured, and the insurance company information (insurer) (Figure 2.7).

Collecting the information and understanding these four parts will help you know who is responsible for the service and to whom you must send the bill. Remember, the patient may be covered under two different policies. You will need to know which policy is primary and which is secondary. This information is located in the top half of the claim form.

Part A: Patient

The patient is the person who is seeing the doctor for some type of care. It is necessary that you get the correct spelling of the patient's name. You must know the patient's age; it can affect the guarantor as well as the insurance information. You also need the patient's mailing address, sex, date of birth, Social Security number, and the name of the patient's employer. The patient name is located in Box 2 on the CMS-1500 claim form.

```
                              PATIENT
                  MEDICAL HISTORY QUESTIONNAIRE


Date:_____
Name:_____ Weight:_____ Height:_____
Age:_____  Gender: (Male)_____ (Female)_____
Name of Primary Care
Physician:_____
Phone #:_____
Are you under a Physician's Care: (Yes)_____ (No) _____  If yes, why?_____
What are you being seen for today? (Chief Complaint) _____
Last Menstrual Period (LMP)? _____
Are you pregnant? (Yes)_____ (No)_____ If yes, date you conceived:_____
Date when condition/illness/injury first occurred?_____
Is this a preexisting condition/illness/injury? (Yes)_____ (No)_____ If yes, give first date_____
Condition/Illness/Injury related to:
Work ?_____ Auto ? _____ Other? _____ If Other, explain_____
_____

Was your condition treated at a hospital or by another physician? (Yes)_____ (No)_____
If yes, give Date_____
and Name of Hospital or Name of Physician _____

List all medical conditions:
_____
_____
List all previous surgeries/hospitalizations (type of procedure and date):
_____
List allergies to drugs/medications:
_____

List of non-prescription drugs, alcohol or recreational drugs used in the last seven days
(aspirin, allergy, cocaine or marijuana, cigarettes):
_____
List any other information about your health which we should know about (HBP, heart disease, ABN
EKG, stroke, seizures, cancer, diabetes, asthma):
_____
Signature:_____ Date:_____
Physician:_____
```

Figure 2.2   Patient medical history questionnaire.

Part B: Guarantor

This is the person who gives a guaranty. He or she assumes responsibility for any debt or obligation due on the patient account. If the guarantor is different than the patient, make sure to include the patient's relationship to the guarantor. This can be spouse, parent, or legal guardian.

Part C: Insured

The *insured* is the person who is covered under the insurance; this person may also be referred to as the *policyholder*, or *member*. Medicare patients are referred to a *beneficiary*. You must also determine whether the patient is the insured or a dependent of the parent or spouse's policy. If the patient is a dependent, make sure to include the patient's relationship to the insured. The insured's name or policyholder's name goes in Box 4 on the CMS-1500 claim form.

Part D: Insurance

What is insurance? Insurance is a contract (referred to as policy) that allows insured individuals to receive financial protection against unpredictable expenses, such as a loss or a claim, which transfers the risk from the patient to the insurance company (referred to as the *insurer*) in exchange for monetary compensation, known as a *premium* in order to guarantee active coverage. This protection comes in several different types such as health insurance (e.g., medical, vision, dental, etc.), homeowners insurance (property and casualty), auto insurance (liability and damages), professional insurance

CHIEF COMPLAINT (CC)
THE MAIN REASON WHY THE PATIENT IS BEING SEEN

HISTORY OF PRESENT ILLNESS (HPI)

MEDICATIONS

ALLERGIES

PAST SURGICAL HISTORY (PSH)

PAST MEDICAL HISTORY (PMH)

FAMILY HISTORY (FH)

SOCIAL HISTORY (SH)

REVIEW OF SYSTEMS

PHYSICAL EXAM

DIAGNOSTIC (XRAY, MRI, CT)

DIAGNOSIS

RECOMMENDATIONS/ASSESSMENT

Figure 2.3   Doctor/nurse notes from the patient assessment interview.

(e.g., malpractice insurance to protect doctors against being sued), life, disability, flood, and so on.

In medical billing the term *third-party payer* (TPP) or *third-party carrier* is used when referring to an insurance company. The term *third-party administrator* (TPA) is a health agency or business organization that is under contract with an insurance company to help process medical claims, handle certain aspects of an employee's benefit plan such as repricing or subrogation service to pursue a recovery of medical benefits that have been paid. Insurance companies are referred to as TPPs in the healthcare payment system because the first party is the patient or insured, the second party is the one who provided the service (physician, clinic, health entity that rendered the care), and the third party is the insurer (the insurance company, administrator, or other payer). The term *carrier* is used because the insurance plan underwrites and carries the financial risk for the healthcare of their enrollees.

At the initial visit a new patient fills out the patient registration form and medical history questionnaire. The

Diagnostic Imaging

Name: Ordering Physician:

Exam: Order Diagnosis:
Xray Wrist 2 views LT   729.5 Pain in Limb

Date:
CC/DX:
Technique:
Findings:
Impression:

Reading Radiologist:
Releasing Radiologist
Released Date and time

Figure 2.4   Diagnostic imaging report.

information provided should include coverage information regarding the primary payer and information on any secondary coverage as well. The patient should provide you with an insurance card, which gives you the information necessary to determine the name of the insured, the insured's identification number, the name of the insurance payer, the plan name, the type of plan, and the plan requirements, such as referral or precertification, patient out-of-pocket (OOP) expense, and where the claim should be sent for payment.

Figures 2.8 through 2.11 are examples of insurance cards.

Section 1: Identification: Insurance Card

The identification number, located in Box 1a on the CMS-1500 claim form, identifies the insured person. This is needed in order to verify eligibility and coverage. A Medicare beneficiary's identification number is referred to as the HIC number, which is the patient's nine-digit Social Security number followed by an alpha character. The alpha character identifies who the wage earner (retiree) is or was. The alpha characters are as follows: A indicates self, B indicates spouse, C indicates a child, D indicates an aged widow, T indicates uninsured (temporary), and W indicates a disabled widow.

Identification numbers and plan numbers help lessen confusion. If there is an A at the end of the identification number, the patient was the wage earner, so if a Medicare card was not provided you can at least verify eligibility and coverage. Another situation that is confusing involves Medicare Advantage (MA) Plans. The identification card gives plan number, which helps identify which MA plan the beneficiary is enrolled in, but the card will also provide you with other important information.

```
┌────────────────────────────────────────────────────────┐
│                    OPERATIVE REPORT                      │
│  Patient:                        Chart #:                │
│  Date of Birth:                                          │
│  Date:                                                   │
│                                                          │
│  PreOperative Diagnosis:                                 │
│  PostOperative Diagnosis:                                │
│                                                          │
│  Procedure:                                              │
│  1.                                                      │
│  2.                                                      │
│                                                          │
│  Surgeon                                                 │
│  First Assistant                                         │
│                                                          │
│  Anesthesia:                                             │
│  Anesthesiologist:                                       │
│                                                          │
│  Operative Indication:                                   │
│                                                          │
│  Operative Findings:                                     │
│                                                          │
│  Description of Procedure:                               │
│                                                          │
│                                                          │
└────────────────────────────────────────────────────────┘
```

Figure 2.5 Operative report.

Section 2: Primary, Secondary, and Tertiary

Who do you bill first? Do you know how to tell the difference between the primary payer and secondary payer? If the patient is the insured and is covered under an employer group health plan (GHP), then that plan is the primary payer. Primary payers are those insurers who have the responsibility of paying the claim first. If the patient is a dependent covered under a spouse's policy, that plan would be the secondary payer. It may pick up the expenses that were not covered by the primary payer.

Section 3: Coordination of Benefits

When an insured is covered by two or more different health insurance plans, the plans must coordinate with each other in order to share the cost of benefits. This term is referred to as *coordination of benefits* (COB) by private health insurance companies. The term used by Medicare is *Medicare secondary payer* (MSP). COB does not apply if the insured is only covered by an individual policy.

When COB is involved, it is important to remember that the primary and secondary payers are two separate policies, so other factors may be involved regarding coverage. For instance, the primary policy may cover an office visit but the secondary policy may not. Therefore, if the primary had a $15 co-pay for an office visit and the secondary doesn't pay for office visits, the responsibility for paying the co-pay lies with the patient/member.

The following outlines the rules that apply when coordination of benefits is involved:

- Nondependent/Dependent rule: Dependent children who are full-time students over the age 18 (and up to age 23 or 25, depending on the policy) must fill out a student status questionnaire form stating that they are full-time students.
- Active/Inactive rule: If an individual has a retiree plan, but then takes a job and has healthcare coverage with the new employer, the retiree plan becomes secondary.
- Birthday rule: When a child is covered under both parents' plans, the parent whose birthday has the earlier month and day is primary. If both parents have the same birthday, then the parent who has had the longest coverage under the same plan becomes the child's primary payer.

FORMS AND CORRESPONDENCE

Medical History Questionnaire/Patient Information Registration form
MVA Verification Form
Workers Compensation Form
Referral and/or Authorization Form
Purchase Order (Indian Health Service)
Letter of Medical Necessity
Letter of Causation
Pre-Certification/Pre-Determination Form
Surgery Order
Financial Payment Agreement Form
Waiver of Liability or ABN
Insurance Non-Covered Release form
Disability Form
Consent Form (Authorization to release information from patient)
Family Medical Leave Act (FMLA)
Doctor's Note (Excusing patient from work or school)
Medical Release Form/Work Comp work Release and Rating
HIPAA Compliance Forms
Letters to Peers (referrals, patient update)
Letter to Insurance Commissioner (Request for Assistance)

Figure 2.6 Types of forms and correspondence that might be included in a patient file.

■ Separation/Divorce rule: The insurance coverage of the parent who is appointed by the court as being financially responsible for the child would be the child's primary payer.

■ Medicare/Medicaid rule: The general rule when a person has employer group health coverage and is also covered by Medicare is that the employer plan would be considered primary to Medicare and Medicaid, depending on number of employees. There are exceptions to this rule (covered later in this section). If a person has Medicare and Medicaid, Medicaid is secondary to Medicare. If a third-party liability is involved, Medicaid is the payer of last resort.

■ Payer of Last Resort: In some cases, there are specific rules that apply to specific entities that will only pay after all other available third-party payers have been billed. The Indian Health Service (IHS) is one of those exceptions; they will only pay after all others have paid. Another example is a situation where a student is injured during a school activity such as football. The school attended by that student will not pay until all services have been paid by other primary payers. Sometimes this can make collection very difficult.

Secondary health insurance can be used to pick up expenses left unpaid by the primary payer. Medigap insurance is a health plan that covers the difference or "gap" between the expenses reimbursed by Medicare and the total amount charged. Medigap plans are offered by several different private payers. Not all Medigap plans pick up Medicare's Part B deductible; only Plans C, F, and J do. Therefore, Medigap plans do not fill in all the gaps between Medicare and the cost of services.

An example of a supplemental policy is Tricare for Life. It acts as a secondary payer to Medicare and benefits include covering Medicare's coinsurance and Part B deductible. Other examples are AARP's supplemental Plan F and Blue 65 offered by Blue Cross/Blue Shield (BCBS).

Medicare secondary payer (MSP) is similar to the coordination of benefits clause in private health insurance. For Medicare to be the secondary payer, certain conditions have to exist. Figure 2.12 provides a list to help determine when Medicare is the secondary payer.

Eligibility and Benefits

Verification of benefits is the first step when determining who to bill as it establishes whether the patient is eligible

PATIENT INFORMATION FORM

Title: (Mr., Mrs., Ms.) First Name:_____ Middle Initial:_____ Last Name:_____

Address:_____

City:_____ State:_____ Zip:_____

Home Phone:_____ Cell Phone:_____

Gender: (M)____ (F)____ Date of Birth:_____ Age:_____ Social Security #:_____

Guarantor: (Person who assumes responsibility for any debt or obligation on Patient Account)

First Name:_____ Middle Initial:_____ Last Name:_____

Address:_____

City:_____ State:_____ Zip:_____

Home Phone:_____ Cell Phone:_____

Patient Relationship to Guarantor: (Self)_____ (Spouse)_____ (Mother)_____ (Father)_____ (Other)_____

Status of Patient:

(Single)____ (Married)____ (Widow)____ (Divorced)____

Employed: (FT)____ (PT)____ (Retired)____ (Not Employed)____ Name of Employer:_____

Address:_____

City:_____ State:_____ Zip:_____

Employer Phone #:_____

Student: (FT)____ (PT)____ Name of School:_____

By Whom were you Referred:_____

PRIMARY COVERAGE

Name of Insurance Plan or Carrier: _____

Please provide Insurance card so our office can make copy

(Another name for the insured)

Policy Holder Name:_____

Policy Holder Identification #:_____

Policy Holder Home Phone # (if different than above) :_____

Policy Holder Date of Birth:_____

Group Number:_____ Group Name:_____

Is this an Employer Health Insurance Plan? (Yes)_____ (No)_____

If Yes name of Employer:_____

Patient relationship to the Policy Holder: (Self)_____ (Spouse)_____ (Child)_____ (Other)_____

SECONDARY OR SUPPLEMENTAL COVERAGE

Name of Insurance Plan or Carrier: _____

Please provide Insurance card so our office can make copy

(Person who the Insurance is covered under)

Policy Holder Name:_____

Policy Holder Identification #:_____

Policy Holder Home Phone # (if different than above) :_____

Policy Holder Date of Birth:_____

Group Number:_____ Group Name:_____

Is this an Employer Health Insurance Plan? (Yes)_____ (No)_____

If Yes name of Employer:_____

Patient relationship to the Policy Holder: (Self)_____ (Spouse)_____ (Child)_____ (Other)_____

AUTHORIZATION AND ACKNOWLEDGMENT

I do state that the above information is to be true and correct to the best of my knowledge. I authorize the above name provider of service to release any information that has gathered during the course of the my treatment to my insurance company, employer, physicians, institutions or third party payers, upon their request on any or all claim(s) that have been filed.

If for any reason a service or charge(s) is not covered by my insurance carrier or no longer have coverage I take full responsibility for any and all fees billed on my account

_____   _____

(Signature of Patient, Parent, Legal Guardian or Policy Holder)   (Date)

Figure 2.7   Patient Information Form.

```
        ┌─────────────────────────────────────────┐
        │░░░░░░░░░░░░░░░░░░░░░░░░░░░░░░░░░░░░░░░░░░░│
        │         MEDICARE HEALTH INSURANCE        │
        │░░░░░░░░░░░░░░░░░░░░░░░░░░░░░░░░░░░░░░░░░░░│
        │                                          │
        │  NAME OF BENEFICIARY                     │
        │  First Middle Last                       │
        │  MEDICARE CLAIM NUMBER        SEX         │
        │  ###-##-####-A                           │
        │  IS ENTITLED TO              EFFECTIVE DATE
        │  HOSPITAL (PART A)                       │
        │  MEDICAL (PART B)                        │
        │  Sign                                    │
        │  Here _____     │
        └─────────────────────────────────────────┘
```

Figure 2.8 Medicare insurance card.

```
        ┌─────────────────────────────────────────┐
        │  BCBS                              PPO   │
        │  ─────────────────────────────────────  │
        │  POLICY ID NUMBER      Office Visit Copay: $15
        │  ############           Specialist: $30  │
        │  GROUP ID NUMBER        Emergency Room: $135
        │  #######                Urgent Care: $25 │
        │  GROUP NAME             RX: $10 / 20/ 40 │
        │  Employer Name                           │
        │  INSURED NAME           Network CoInsurance:
        │  Stewart Little         In Net:  80% / 20%
        │                         Out of Net 60% / 40%
        │  PLAN CODE:             Medical / Prescription
        └─────────────────────────────────────────┘
```

Figure 2.9 Front of an employer insurance card. The insurance company is Blue Cross/Blue Shield (BCBS).

```
┌─────────────────────────────────┐   ┌───────────────────────────────────┐
│ Customer Service: 800-###-####  │   │ AARP / MedicareComplete           │
│                                 │   │        SecureHorizons             │
│ PreCertification: Prior to      │   │ ID: ########        Group #: #####│
│ surgery precertification is     │   │ Member:            PLAN Code: H3749│
│ required.                       │   │                                   │
│                                 │   │                                   │
│ Provider Services:              │   │ PCP Name:                         │
│ Mail claims to: Blue Cross Blue │   │  Copay: Office $10                │
│            Shield of OK         │   │         Spec  $35                 │
│            PO Box 3283          │   │         ER    $50                 │
│            Tulsa, OK  74102     │   │                                   │
│                                 │   │      AARP MedicareComplete HMO    │
└─────────────────────────────────┘   └───────────────────────────────────┘
```

Figure 2.10 Example of the back of an insurance card, which provides the mailing address for claim submission.

Figure 2.11 An insurance card for Medicare Advantage (a plan that supplements Medicare coverage) through a private payer.

MEDICARE IS THE PRIMARY PAYER and GROUP HEALTH PLAN (GHP), RETIREE, COBRA IS SECONDARY PAYER when the following conditions exist:

	Number of Employees:
Working Aged Beneficiary:	
65 and older	
Covered through GHP Employed, No Spouse	Less than 20
Covered under Spouse GHP and unemployed	Less than 20
Disabled Beneficiary:	
Under 65	
Covered through Large GHP Employed, No Spouse	Less than 100 and more than 100
Covered under Spouse LGHP and unemployed	Less than 100
Retiree Beneficiary:	
Employer GHP	
Beneficiary with ESRD:	
Covered under GHP	who is after their 30 months of eligibility & MCR entitlement
Covered under Cobra	who is after their 30 months of eligibility & MCR entitlement

GHP, COBRA, WORKERS COMP, NO-FAULT & LIABILITY IS PRIMARY PAYER and <u>MEDICARE IS SECONDARY PAYER</u> (MSP) when the following conditions exist:

	Number of Employees:
Working Aged Beneficiary:	
65 and older	
Covered through GHP Employed, No Spouse	20 or more
Covered under Spouse GHP and unemployed	20 or more
Disabled Beneficiary:	
Under 65	
Covered through LGHP Employed, No Spouse	100 or more
Covered under Spouse LGHP and unemployed	100 or more
Retiree Beneficiary:	
Employer GHP 65 or older	
Beneficiary with ESRD:	
Covered under GHP	who is their first 30 months of eligibility & MCR entitlement
Covered under Cobra	who is their first 30 months of eligibility & MCR entitlement
Beneficiary:	
Workers Comp	
Beneficiary:	
Accident	
No-Fault or Liability	

Figure 2.12   Determining whether Medicare is primary.

for benefits. Before information can be provided, most insurance companies require an identification (ID) number, but if you don't know the patient's ID number, you can use the patient's Social Security number.

Patient information can be obtained from insurance cards, through interactive voice response (IVR), websites, or by phone.

A certificate of creditable coverage (COCC) is a document that shows proof of prior healthcare coverage. The COCC was created by the Health Insurance Portability and Accountability Act (referred to as HIPAA) and was designed to ensure that individuals who are changing from one health insurance plan to another will have continuous coverage for ongoing medical treatments. As a new enrollee in a health plan, the patient may be subject to a waiting period before coverage is offered for preexisting conditions, but due to the federal law, the certificate of creditable coverage provision in HIPAA provides that if the insured had at least eighteen months of medical coverage, that person does not have to endure another waiting period when changing health insurance.

Jurisdiction and Regions

How do you know who handles Medicare claims? Medicare claims are processed by a TPA. The TPAs are under contract with Medicare and are identified as Medicare administrative contractors (MACs).

To determine which TPA handles the Medicare claims for the state of Oklahoma, for example, you must find out the jurisdiction in which the state falls; there are fifteen different jurisdictions. The state of Oklahoma falls under Jurisdiction 4 (J4) (see Figure 2.13). For J4, the MAC (fiscal intermediary) for Part A and Part B (carrier) expenses is TrailBlazer Health Enterprises, LLC (http://www.trailblazerhealth.com).

Trailblazer health handles claims for patients with Medicare Part B, but charges for medical supplies and durable medical equipment and prosthetics, orthotics, and supplies (DMEPOS) are submitted to Cigna Government Services under Jurisdiction C (durable medical equipment regional carrier, or DMERC) (http://www.cignagovernment.com).

Claims are submitted to Tricare in three regions, North, South, and West. Each region has a contract with a different agency. If you live in Oklahoma, your claims are processed under the South Region and the contractor is Humana Military HealthCare service. The North Region contractor is Health Net Federal Services, and the West Region contractor is TriWest Healthcare Alliance. Claims mailing addresses are located on the back of the insurance card.

Section 3: Different Types of Health Insurance

There are many different insurance companies to select from, but it depends on what type of health insurance coverage you are looking for and if that insurance company offers it. Healthcare coverage is handled either by a private payer (health insurance company) or a government payer (federal health programs such as Medicare, Medicaid, Tricare, Department of Labor, etc.).

■ **Private payers** are regulated by state laws and offer individual and family plans. They offer group health plans for employers or organizations and also offer Medicare Advantage plans (Part C), Medigap (Medicare supplemental plans A–J), and Medicare prescription drug plans (Part D). These companies include United Healthcare, BCBS, Aetna, and Cigna.

■ **Government payers** are regulated by federal laws and are managed by government entities. Federal programs include Medicare, RR Medicare, Medicaid, Tricare, and Department of Labor plans.

Medicare is a federal health insurance program that offers coverage for seniors age 65 and older, people on Social Security disability, and those individuals with end-stage renal disease (ESRD).

Medicare is comprised of four parts, which cover specific services. Medicare Part A covers hospital services such as inpatient care, skilled nursing facilities, hospice, or home health care. Medicare Part B covers medical services such as the doctor's fees. Medicare Part C is referred to as Medicare Advantage Healthcare Plans, and includes coverage under health maintenance organizations (HMOs), preferred provider organizations (PPOs), or point of service (POS) plans. These plans are offered by private insurance companies that are approved by Medicare and have a signed contract with Medicare. The Medicare beneficiary must be enrolled in Medicare itself in order to obtain an MA plan. The Medicare Advantage plans include Part A, Part B, and Part D coverage. Medicare Part D covers some prescription drugs.

Railroad (RR) Medicare is a comprehensive retirement benefit plan for railroad workers and their families under the Railroad Retirement and Railroad Unemployment Insurance Act. Palmetto GBA is the Part B carrier for Railroad Medicare and is contracted by the independent Federal Agency Railroad Retirement Board. There has always been some confusion as to how to identify an original Medicare and a RR Medicare beneficiary. A RR Medicare beneficiary can be identified by their card and identification number. The RR insurance card is almost identical to a Medicare card, but the identification number will be different. Instead of an alpha character at the end of the nine-digit Social Security number, the alpha character appears in front of the Social Security number. There are two alpha characters, A and MA, which help identify those patients who are eligible for Medicare under Railroad Retirees.

Medicaid is a federal program that is administered by the state. It offers coverage for individuals and families with limited income.

The Center of Medicare and Medicaid Services (CMS) is a branch of the US Department of Health and Human Services that administers the Medicare program and monitors the Medicaid program offered by each state. The CMS website is http://www.cms.gov.com.

Fiscal Intermediaries and Carriers

What is the difference between a fiscal intermediary and a carrier? A carrier is a company that has a contract with Medicare to pay claims for Medicare professional services or Medicare Part B (medical) claims for Medicare beneficiaries and providers. They are referred to as Medicare administrative contractors (MACs). A fiscal intermediary (FI) is a company that has a contract with Medicare to pay claims for Medicare institutional services or Medicare Part A (hospital) claims for Medicare beneficiaries and providers.

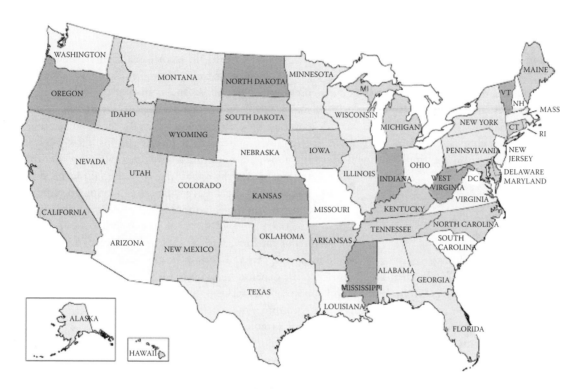

MEDICARE'S A/B MAC JURISDICTIONS
(OKLAHOMA)

JURISDICTION #1: American Samoa, California, Guam, Hawaii, Nevada and Northern Mariana Islands

JURISDICTION #2: Alaska, Idaho, Oregon and Washington

JURISDICTION #3: Arizona, Montana, North Dakota, South Dakota, Utah and Wyoming

JURISDICTION #4: Colorado, New Mexico, Oklahoma and Texas (MAC is Trail Blazer Health Enterprises, LLC)

JURISDICTION #5: Iowa, Kansas, Missouri and Nebraska

JURISDICTION #6: Illinois, Minnesota and Wisconsin

JURISDICTION #7: Arkansas, Louisiana and Mississippi

JURISDICTION #8: Indiana and Michigan

JURISDICTION #9: Florida, Puerto Rico and U.S. Virgin Islands

JURISDICTION #10: Alabama, Georgia and Tennessee

JURISDICTION #11: North Carolina, South Carolina, Virginia and West Virginia

JURISDICTION #12: Delaware, District of Columbia, Maryland, New Jersey and Pennsylvania

JURISDICTION #13: Connecticut and New York

JURISDICTION #14: Maine, Massachusetts, New Hampshire, Rhode Island and Vermont

JURISDICTION #15: Kentucky and Ohio

MEDICARE'S DME MAC JURISDICTIONS
(OKLAHOMA)

JURISDICTION A: Connecticut, Delaware, District of Columbia, Maine, Maryland, Massachusetts, New Hampshire, New Jersey, New York, Pennsylvania, Rhode Island and Vermont

JURISDICTION B: Illinois, Indiana, Kentucky, Michigan, Minnesota, Ohio and Wisconsin

JURISDICTION C: Alabama, Arkansas, Colorado, Florida, Georgia, Louisiana, Mississippi, New Mexico, North Carolina, South Carolina, Oklahoma, Puerto Rico, Tennessee, Texas, U.S. Virgin Islands, Virginia and West Virginia (DME MAC is Cigna Government Services)

JURISDICTION D: Alaska, American Samoa, Arizona, California, Guam, Hawaii, Idaho, Iowa, Kansas, Missouri, Montana, Nebraska, Nevada, North Dakota, South Dakota, Northern Mariana Islands, Oregon, Utah, Washington and Wyoming

Figure 2.13   Medicare TPA jurisdictions.

Tricare is healthcare coverage that is offered to US military personnel who are on active duty or in the reserves, their dependents, and those who are retired. As an example, in Oklahoma, the South Region contractor is Humana Military HealthCare service, the North Region contractor is Health Net Federal Services, and the West Region contractor is TriWest Healthcare Alliance.

The US Department of Labor (DOL) provides workers compensation coverage for government employees who are injured on the job.

Section 4: Different Types of Healthcare Coverage

Depending on your needs, healthcare coverage can be obtained in three different ways: (1) individual and family coverage, (2) federal and state employers (group health), and (3) Medicare (age 65 and older) and retirees. Depending on what type of healthcare coverage you are looking for, there are several different types including the following:

- Medical
- Dental
- Vision
- Prescription drug
- Short-term care
- Long-term care
- Disability
- Life
- COBRA

Things to consider when making a healthcare insurance decision include

- Monthly premiums
- Coverage and benefits
- Out-of-pocket (OOP) expenses such as co-pays, coinsurance, and deductibles
- Choice of doctors, hospitals, and other providers

Section 5: Different Health Insurance Plans

Under individual, group, and Medicare (age 65 and older) and retiree plans, there are five main types of health insurance plans that are offered. They are as follows:

Indemnity or Traditional Fee-for-Service (FFS) Plans

These plans used to only cover expenses relating to illness or injury, but now offer other options that cover preventative care. The TPP pays the provider after a service has been rendered and the provider is reimbursed for each covered service that was provided.

FFS-type health insurance plans often result in higher OOP expenses because covered individuals pay a monthly premium, deductible, and coinsurance. When the insurer shares payment of medical expenses with the insured the coverage is called *coinsurance*. An example is the 80/20 coinsurance rate, which means the insurer covers 80% of the allowed amount of a covered service and the insured is responsible for the remaining 20%. FFS limits how much an insurer pays. They place what is a capitation amount which is a maximum benefit amount that your policy will only cover.

There are two kinds of FFS health coverage, basic and major medical. Basic covers many doctor's services, including surgery, and certain hospital fees. Major medical covers those expenses not covered by basic, including some doctor's visits, office services, and so on. Some policies may combine both into a more comprehensive plan.

Examples of FFS plans are Medicare Part B and Medicaid. Each service, procedure, or test has a set fee allowance, which can be located on a fee schedule. To assure correct reimbursement (allowable), the fee schedule should be accessible on the insurer's website. If the doctor's office bills their fees using the contracted fee schedule, it must be set up the same way for every such fee. If you don't bill off of the contracted fee schedule, then you must determine if you will use the Medicare allowable × 4. If you bill in this fashion, then you must bill the same fees across the board no matter what type of insurance is involved.

Managed Care Plans

Managed care plans involve an insurer that has contracted agreements with healthcare providers to provide their members with quality care at a discounted rate. Such plans form a group of network providers who monitor the needs of patients and control healthcare costs. There are three different types of managed care plans: HMOs, PPOs, and POS plans.

HMO

HMOs are the most restrictive type of health plan because members have the least choice in selecting a healthcare provider, but members are provided with more comprehensive (basic and major medical) health benefits with the lowest OOP expenses. Besides a monthly premium, most HMOs and PPOs require a copayment for certain services. A co-payment is a specific dollar amount that is paid by the insured at the time of the visit. For example, some PPOs require a $15 co-pay at the time of the visit, and if the insured sees a specialist, the co-pay could be higher. Members of an HMO plan are required to select a primary care physician

(PCP) from the network of providers in order to be reimbursed by the HMO. If the member receives care from an out-of-network provider, the HMO will not pay for the care unless it was preauthorized by the member's PCP or deemed an emergency. A PCP monitors and coordinates the plan member's healthcare needs, and if the member needs to see a specialist, a referral is required from the PCP.

Some examples of HMO plans are Tricare Prime, Secure Horizons, BlueLincs, IHS, and SoonerCare. Tricare Prime is a managed care HMO plan for retired military. Members pay a monthly or quarterly premium and pay a $12 co-pay at every doctor's visit. If there is a need to be seen by a specialist, a referral is required.

Secure Horizons is a Medicare Advantage HMO plan that is offered by United Healthcare Insurance Company. A referral is required and Secure Horizons' timely filing period is only 60/90 days, so it is vital to bill a correct claim within the time frame so the claim will not be denied.

Indian Health Services (IHS) and tribal programs provide a wide array of individual health services to Native Americans. Medical care services are purchased from outside the IHS system through a contract health service (CHS) program when medical care is needed but is unavailable at a tribal facility. The CHS program is funded through tribal programs that are administered locally by several area offices that monitor and evaluate healthcare facilities that provide care. CHS payments are issued to healthcare providers from a designated service area where there is no IHS or tribal direct care facility. These service areas are located at federal, tribal health, or urban health facilities and can be located in several different places around the state, depending on the patient's residence. A directory for the Oklahoma City area can be requested from the IHS Central Health Services. By regulation, the IHS is always the payer of last resort. If a healthcare provider is seeing a Native American, a referral is required to receive any reimbursement. Once a referral is received, that referral must be attached to a claim and forwarded to the area office within the designated service area. Once the claim is received, a form called a purchase order (PO) is mailed to the provider of service. A PO is then attached to the claim again and submitted for reimbursement. In order to receive reimbursement from IHS the office or clinic must meet certain requirements. A provider of service must sign up for a Data Universal Numbering System (D-U-N-S) number. A D-U-N-S number is a nine-digit numbering system that identifies an individual business. A provider must also maintain an active registration in the Central Contractor Registry (CCR) database. The CCR home page is http://www.bpn.gov/ccr/.

Soonercare is an HMO plan offered under Medicaid. A referral is required, but there are specific requirements. Also, eligibility must be verified every month.

PPO

Preferred provider organizations are a combination of a traditional FFS and HMO plans. They have a limited number of providers who are referred to as *preferred providers* or *network providers*. If this type of plan is chosen, when a doctor is visited, a small copayment is required for that visit. Like an HMO, a PPO requires a primary care doctor be chosen to monitor the member's healthcare needs, but unlike an HMO, a member can choose a doctor who is not part of the plan. They will still receive some health insurance coverage, but their OOP expenses will be larger than if they saw an in-network provider. Some people do prefer this option. One of the things most people like about this type of plan is the ability to see any doctor or specialist they want, in network or out of network, and no referral is required.

POS

Point of Service plans combine an HMO and a PPO, allowing a member to use a PCP to coordinate their care or have the option to see any doctor of their choice.

COBRA

Employers offer employees Consolidated Omnibus Budget Reconciliation Act of 1985 (COBRA) coverage, according to a federal act that requires most employers with group health plans to allow employees and their covered dependents to temporarily continue group healthcare coverage for a stated period of time due to qualifying events such termination of employment, layoff, death or divorce of a covered employee, or other change in employment status that causes the loss of group health coverage. COBRA is a way to help former employees to continue healthcare coverage until other healthcare coverage becomes available. This coverage can be obtained through the employer. The plan administrator will send COBRA benefits information if the person qualifies for coverage.

Consumer-Directed Health Plans (CDHPs)

Health savings accounts (HSAs), health reimbursement arrangements (HRAs), and flexible savings arrangements (FSAs) are self-insured plans. The payer is an employer or other group that may assume full risk for the payment of healthcare services by taking the premium it would have paid to an insurance mechanism and establishing a fund to provide benefits for its employees or group members. Self-insured employers usually contract with a TPA that acts on behalf of the self-insured plan to process the claims.

HSA

Health savings accounts are medical savings accounts that allow individuals to save money to help pay for any current and future medical expenses on a tax-free basis. To be eligible, an individual must be covered under a high-deductible health plan and cannot be enrolled in any other health insurance. HSAs do have a lower premium than HMOs, PPOs or POS plans, but their OOP expenses are higher. An employee and their employer can contribute funds to the HSA.

HRA

Health reimbursement arrangements are set up by an employer to help pay for employee medical expenses. The employer is the only one who can contribute to its funding. The employer is the one who decides how much to contribute, but the employee can withdraw funds from the HRA to cover his or her medical expenses. HRAs are often established in conjunction with a high-deductible health plan, but they can also be combined with any type of health plan or can stand alone.

FSA

Flexible savings arrangements are set up by an employer to allow employees to set aside pretax dollars to cover medical expenses during a calendar year. The employer may or may not contribute to the account, but there may be a limit to the amount that employers and employees can contribute. A health FSA can be offered in conjunction with any type of health insurance plan or can stand alone.

Figures 2.14 through 2.18 are examples of insurer charts to show the different plan options. The plan names may not exist, but the chart shows the differences among the plans offered.

There are several large health insurance companies offering different plans, for example, BCBS, Aetna, and United Healthcare (UHC). They offer the following types of plans:

- Individual (single) and family (including dependents) coverage
- Group health plans:
  - Small business (2–50 employees)
  - Medium-sized business (51–300 employees)
  - Large business (more than 300 employees)
  - State and federal government employees
- Medicare choice plans:
  - Original Medicare (Part A covers hospital; Part B covers medical); Medicare Advantage plans (Part C); Medicare supplemental (Medigap); and Prescription Drug (Part D)

Please note that it is very important to be sure your doctor participates in your insurance company's network.

What best suits you will depend on your specific needs. Do you want flexibility regarding doctors and hospitals or are you more concerned about OOP expenses? If you are looking for flexibility, an indemnity (FFS) plan would best suit you, but if you want lower costs, a managed care plan would be the one to select.

(M)=Medical (D)=Dental (WC)=Workers Compensation

INSURER Or ADMINISTRATOR	TYPE OF COVERAGE			PLAN NAME	PLAN TYPE				
	INDIVIDUAL & FAMILY	GROUP (EMPLOYER)	MEDICARE/ RETIREES		INDEMNITY (FFS)	HMO	PPO	POS	CDHP
MEDICARE AGE 65 OR SS DISABILITY (MAC: Trailblazer)			(M)	PLAN B	XX				
MEDICARE (MAC: Cigna Government)			(M)	DMEPOS	XX				
MEDICAID LOW INCOME (OKLAHOMA HEALTH CARE AUTH)	(M)			Title 19	XX				
MEDICAID				SOONERCARE		XX			
MEDICAID		(M)		O-EPIC	XX				
TRICARE MILITARY COVERAGE (SOUTH REGION HUMANA)		(M)		STANDARD	XX				
TRICARE			(M)	TRICARE PRIME			XX		
TRICARE for Life (SUPPLEMENTAL PLAN TO MCR)			(M)	TRICARE FOR LIFE					

GOVERNMENT: SOCIAL SECURITY (elderly or disability), LOW INCOME

Figure 2.14 Government plans.

INSURER Or ADMINISTRATOR	TYPE OF COVERAGE			PLAN NAME	PLAN TYPE				
	INDIVIDUAL & FAMILY	GROUP (EMPLOYER) 20-50	MEDICARE/ RETIREES		INDEMNITY (FFS)	MANAGED CARE HMO	MANAGED CARE PPO	MANAGED CARE POS	CDHP
AETNA MEDICARE CHOICES: Medicare Advantage (MA) Plan			(M)	Traditional Choice	XX				
Medicare Advantage (MA) Plan			(M)	MA Plan		XX			
Medicare Advantage (MA) Plan			(M)	MA Plan			XX		
AETNA MEDICARE CHOICES: Medicare Supplemental Plan			(M)	Plans A, B & F					
AETNA OPEN ACCESS MANAGED CHOICE (OAMC)	(M)			OAMC 2500					
	(M)			OAMC 5000					
	(M)			OAMC HSA 3500					XX
	(M)			OAMC HSA 5000					XX
	(M)			Value 5000					
AETNA	(M)	(M)		Traditional Choice	XX				
	(M)	(M)		HMO		XX			
	(M)	(M)		PPO			XX		
AETNA OPEN ACCESS MANAGED CHOICE (OAMC)		(M)		OAMC 500					
		(M)		OAMC 1000					
		(M)		OAMC 1500					
		(M)		OAMC 2000					
		(M)		OAMC 3000					
		(M)		OAMC 5000					
AETNA CHOICE POS OPEN ACCESS (CPOS)		(M)		CPOS 1500				XX	
		(M)		COST ADVANTAGE 2000					
		(M)		COST ADVANTAGE 3000					
AETNA HEALTH SAVINGS ACCOUNT (HSA)		(M)		HIGH DEDUCTIBLE PLAN					XX
AETNA HEALTH REIMBURSEMENT ARRANGMENT (HRA)		(M)		HEALTH FUND					XX
AETNA CAFETERIA PLANS		(M)		FSA, POP TRA					XX
AETNA COBRA		(M)							
AETNA DENTAL	(D)			PPO MAX PLAN			XX		

Figure 2.15 Plans offered by Aetna.

INSURER Or ADMINISTRATOR	TYPE OF COVERAGE			PLAN NAME	PLAN TYPE				
	INDIVIDUAL & FAMILY	GROUP (EMPLOYER)	MEDICARE/ RETIREES		INDEMNITY (FFS)	HMO	PPO	POS	CDHP
						MANAGED CARE			
BCBS Medicare Supplemental Plan			(M)	Blue Plan 65 Plans A, F, N					
BCBS		(M)		Blue Traditional	XX				
BCBS		(M)		Blue Choice			XX		
BCBS		(M)		Blue Preferred			XX		
BCBS		(M)		BlueOption			XX		
BCBS		(M)		BlueLincs		XX			
BLUE CROSS WORK PLACE		(WC)		BlueWorks					
BCBS	(M)			Health Check Basic	XX				
	(M)			Health Check HSA					XX
	(M)			Health Check Select					
	(M)			Blue Transitions					
BCBS DENTAL	(D)			BlueSelect					

Figure 2.16 BCBS of Oklahoma.

INSURER Or ADMINISTRATOR	TYPE OF COVERAGE			PLAN NAME	PLAN TYPE				
	INDIVIDUAL & FAMILY	GROUP (EMPLOYER)	MEDICARE/ RETIREES		INDEMNITY (FFS)	HMO	PPO	POS	CDHP
						MANAGED CARE			
HEALTHCHOICE		(M)		High Option Plan					XX
HEALTHCHOICE		(M)		Basic Plan					
HEALTHCHOICE		(M)		USA Plan			XX		
HEALTHCHOICE		(M)		HSA					XX
COMMUNITYCARE		(M)				XX			
GLOBAL HEALTH		(M)				XX			
PACIFICARE		(M)				XX			
COMPSOURCE		(WC)							

Figure 2.17 Oklahoma State and Education Employers Group (OSEEGIB) plans for members of law enforcement, transportation workers, Department of Rehabilitation, Department of Corrections, and teachers.

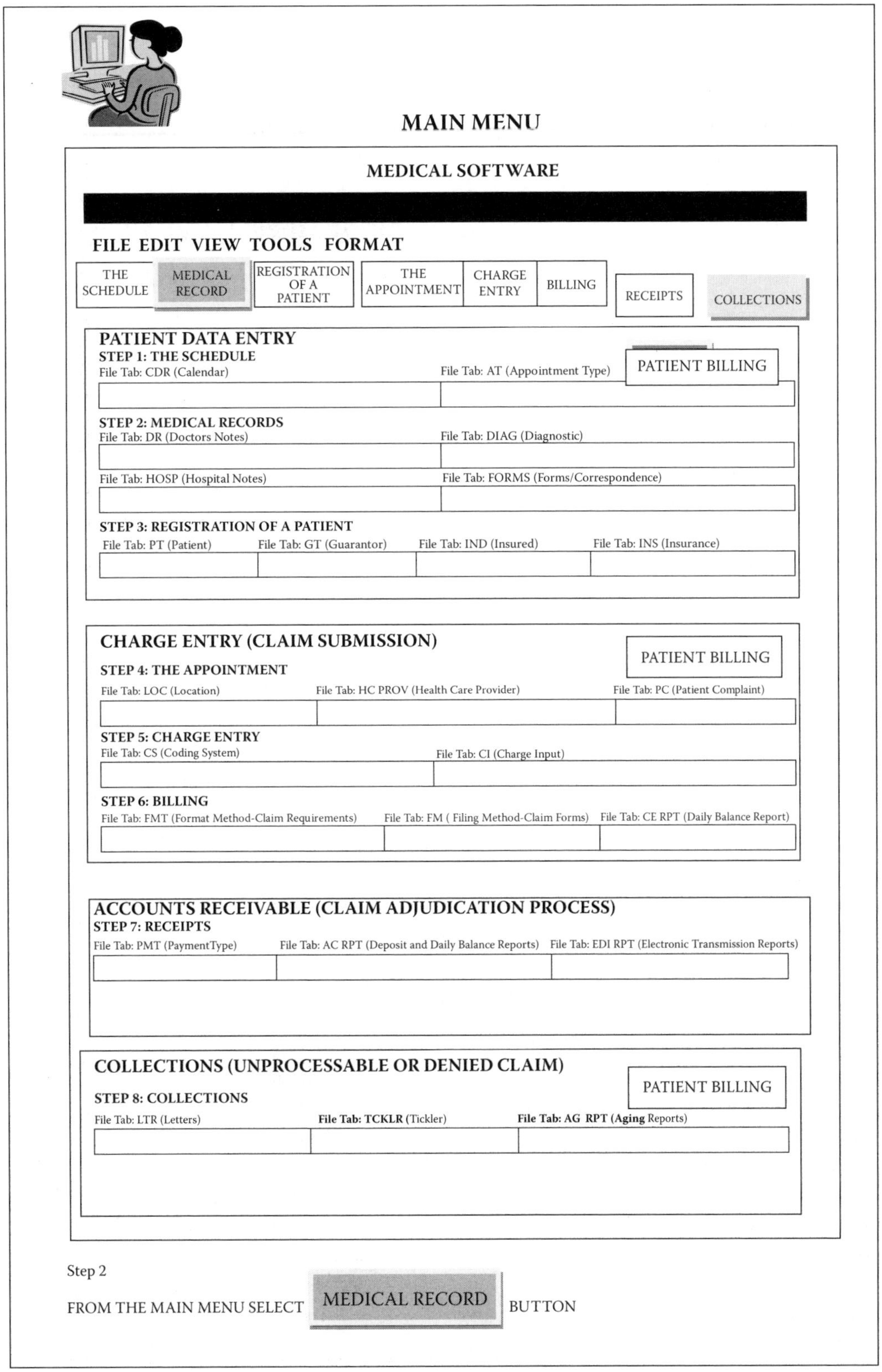

MAIN MENU

MEDICAL SOFTWARE

FILE EDIT VIEW TOOLS FORMAT

| THE SCHEDULE | MEDICAL RECORD | REGISTRATION OF A PATIENT | THE APPOINTMENT | CHARGE ENTRY | BILLING | RECEIPTS | COLLECTIONS |

PATIENT DATA ENTRY

STEP 1: THE SCHEDULE

File Tab: CDR (Calendar)　　　　File Tab: AT (Appointment Type)　　PATIENT BILLING

STEP 2: MEDICAL RECORDS

File Tab: DR (Doctors Notes)　　　File Tab: DIAG (Diagnostic)

File Tab: HOSP (Hospital Notes)　　File Tab: FORMS (Forms/Correspondence)

STEP 3: REGISTRATION OF A PATIENT

File Tab: PT (Patient)　　File Tab: GT (Guarantor)　　File Tab: IND (Insured)　　File Tab: INS (Insurance)

CHARGE ENTRY (CLAIM SUBMISSION)　　PATIENT BILLING

STEP 4: THE APPOINTMENT

File Tab: LOC (Location)　　File Tab: HC PROV (Health Care Provider)　　File Tab: PC (Patient Complaint)

STEP 5: CHARGE ENTRY

File Tab: CS (Coding System)　　File Tab: CI (Charge Input)

STEP 6: BILLING

File Tab: FMT (Format Method-Claim Requirements)　File Tab: FM (Filing Method-Claim Forms)　File Tab: CE RPT (Daily Balance Report)

ACCOUNTS RECEIVABLE (CLAIM ADJUDICATION PROCESS)

STEP 7: RECEIPTS

File Tab: PMT (PaymentType)　　File Tab: AC RPT (Deposit and Daily Balance Reports)　File Tab: EDI RPT (Electronic Transmission Reports)

COLLECTIONS (UNPROCESSABLE OR DENIED CLAIM)　　PATIENT BILLING

STEP 8: COLLECTIONS

File Tab: LTR (Letters)　　**File Tab: TCKLR** (Tickler)　　**File Tab: AG RPT (Aging** Reports)

Step 2

FROM THE MAIN MENU SELECT MEDICAL RECORD BUTTON

Figure 2.18 Federal employees health benefits (FEHB): United States Postal Service, Tinker Air Force Base.

Section 6: Plan Type Requirements: Policy Rules and Regulations

Indemnity versus Managed Care

Indemnity plans are fee for service, and managed care plans include health maintenance organizations (HMOs), preferred provider organizations (PPOs) and point of service (POS) plans.

Certain rules and regulations are required prior to services being rendered; some are as follows:

- HMOs require a referral.
- Medical equipment, services, or procedures may require precertification and/or prior authorization.
- There is a time limit for filing a claim.
- Members' OOP expenses are required, such as premiums, deductibles, copayments, coinsurance.
- Age restriction (under age 26).
- Conservative treatment prior to surgery.

To see what your rules and regulations are, pull up each payor's individual medical policy for specific requirements.

Section 7: Different Types of Financial Class

This will determine how to set up the patient account financial status regarding how to bill or collect on services provided to a patient:

- Health insurance: Indemnity (FFS) or managed care plans (HMO, PPO, POS)
- Third-party liability: Automobile insurance, worker's compensation, other liability (property) insurance
- Self-pay: Patient is not insured or is self-funded (HSA, HRA, FSA)

Part E: Self-Pay

- Self-pay patients are those who do not have any healthcare coverage or who may belong to a group that is self-funded.
- A provider may offer self-pay accounts some type of financial arrangement or may also provide some kind of financial help through organizations such as Care Credit.

It is important to have an understanding of some of the important functions of each department in a medical office, such as appointment scheduling, inputting patient information, and handling medical billing. It is also important to show how that data is transferred and input into medical practice software and how that information is applied to the claim form. To do this, I came up with my own example of a very simple window-based menu to show how to key in data and its importance. Based on several types of software that I have used, I developed the following information to help you understand these functions.

Unit V: Steps 2 and 3 Patient Data Entry

Part A: Medical Records

Step-by-Step Guide: How to Gather Patient Data

Gathering patient data begins when the patient chart is set up. A chart is put together prior to the patient being seen. This unit of the book is divided into two sections: medical records, which consist of four parts: doctor notes (including medications prescribed for the patient), hospital notes, diagnostics, and forms (documentation). The second section consists of patient registration, which also contains four parts: patient, guarantor, insured, and insurance information.

Information is first gathered through the completion of the forms. The forms (documentation) are then filed in the patient chart. Different types of medical documentation can be accessed using the medical software.

To give you an idea, let's pull up a list of the different types of medical documentation that would be scanned into the medical software under both Electronic Health Record (EHR) and Electronic Medical Record (EMR). In order to access that list and visualize how you would pull up that list in the medical software, view Steps 1 and 2 (Figures 2.19 and 2.20).

Step 1. In the medical software, pull up the "Main Menu."
Step 2. From the main menu, select the "Medical Record" button.
  Once the medical record screen is pulled up you can select from one of the following: Doctors Notes, Hospital Notes, Diagnostic (Radiology and Pathology), or Forms.
Step 3. Double click in the "Forms" box; a window will pop up. Mark (x) next to the specific document you want to print, such as Patient Registration Form, and select the "Print" button.

Now that you have reviewed the list of the different types of documents let's see what the steps are for how to apply patient information from the registration form. For the next step, go to Patient Information Input.

INSURER Or ADMINISTRATOR	TYPE OF COVERAGE			PLAN NAME	PLAN TYPE				
	INDIVIDUAL & FAMILY	GROUP (EMPLOYER)	MEDICARE/ RETIREES		INDEMNITY (FFS)	MANAGED CARE			CDHP
						HMO	PPO	POS	
BCBS		(M)			XX	XX	XX		XX
GEHA		(M)							
MAIL HANDLERS		(M)							
APWU		(M)							
DEPARTMENT OF LABOR		(WC)							

Figure 2.19   Federal employees health benefits (FEHB): United States Postal Service, Tinker Air Force Base.

Part B: Patient Information Input

Step-by-Step Guide: How to Apply Patient Data

Step 1. In the medical software, pull up the "Main Menu" (Figure 2.21).

Step 2. From the main menu, select the "Registration of a Patient" Button. Once you are in the patient registration screen, you can transfer information from the patient registration form (Figure 2.22) into the medical software by selecting from one of the following: Patient/Guarantor (Figure 2.23) or Insured/Insurance (Figure 2.24).

Step 3. Double click in the box that is marked "Patient/Guarantor." A window will pop up so you can transfer and key in the information from the patient registration form into the medical software.

Step 3

NOW THAT YOU ARE IN THE MEDICAL RECORD SCREEN "Double click in box" IN A SPECIFIC WINDOW IN ORDER TO PRINT OUT SPECIFIC MEDICAL DOCUMENTATION. SELECT AND PRINT

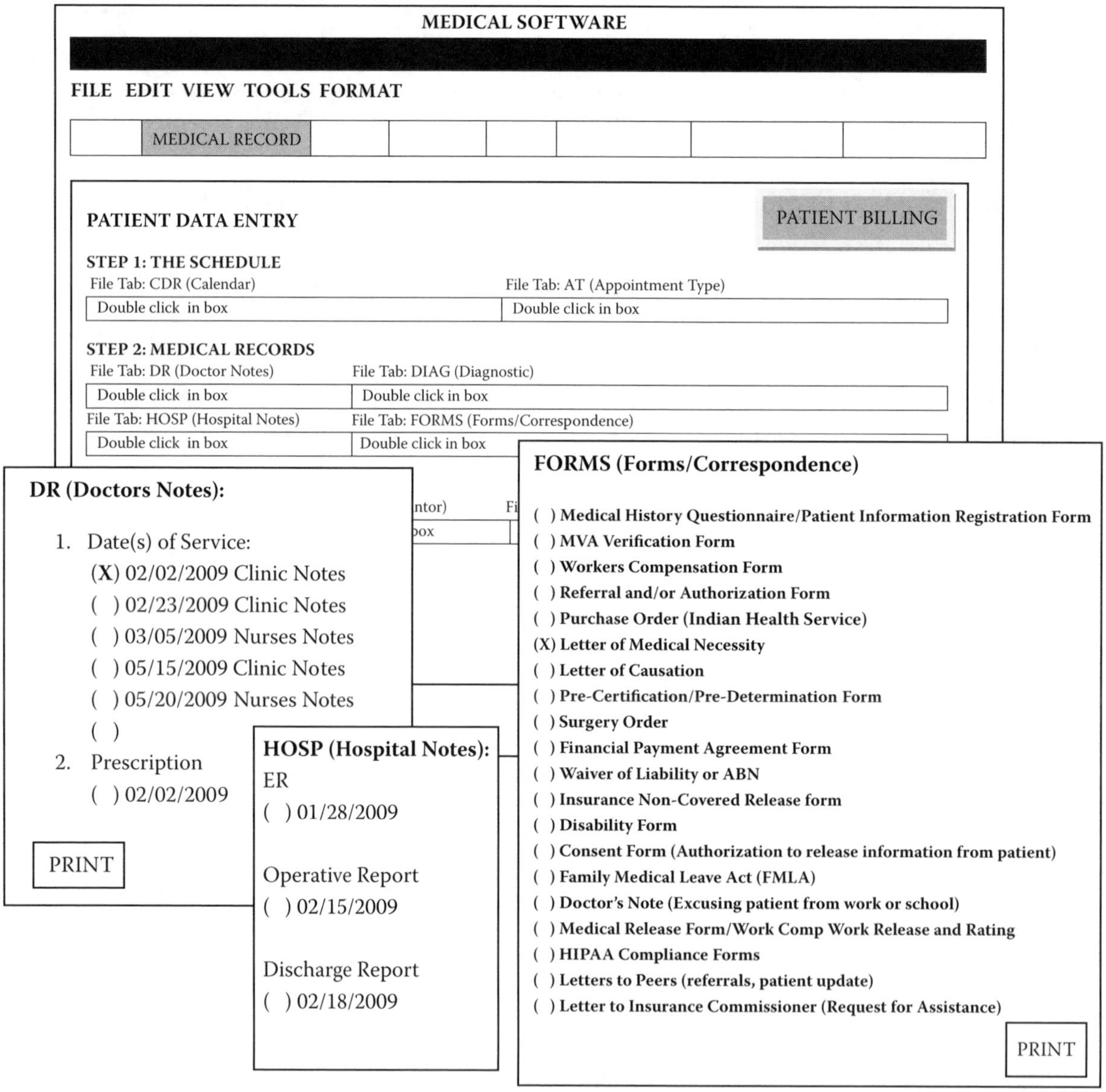

MEDICAL SOFTWARE

FILE EDIT VIEW TOOLS FORMAT

| MEDICAL RECORD | | | | | | |

PATIENT DATA ENTRY   PATIENT BILLING

STEP 1: THE SCHEDULE
File Tab: CDR (Calendar)   File Tab: AT (Appointment Type)
Double click in box   Double click in box

STEP 2: MEDICAL RECORDS
File Tab: DR (Doctor Notes)   File Tab: DIAG (Diagnostic)
Double click in box   Double click in box
File Tab: HOSP (Hospital Notes)   File Tab: FORMS (Forms/Correspondence)
Double click in box   Double click in box

DR (Doctors Notes):

1. Date(s) of Service:
   (**X**) 02/02/2009 Clinic Notes
   ( ) 02/23/2009 Clinic Notes
   ( ) 03/05/2009 Nurses Notes
   ( ) 05/15/2009 Clinic Notes
   ( ) 05/20/2009 Nurses Notes
   ( )
2. Prescription
   ( ) 02/02/2009

PRINT

HOSP (Hospital Notes):
ER
( ) 01/28/2009

Operative Report
( ) 02/15/2009

Discharge Report
( ) 02/18/2009

FORMS (Forms/Correspondence)

( ) **Medical History Questionnaire/Patient Information Registration Form**
( ) **MVA Verification Form**
( ) **Workers Compensation Form**
( ) **Referral and/or Authorization Form**
( ) **Purchase Order (Indian Health Service)**
(X) **Letter of Medical Necessity**
( ) **Letter of Causation**
( ) **Pre-Certification/Pre-Determination Form**
( ) **Surgery Order**
( ) **Financial Payment Agreement Form**
( ) **Waiver of Liability or ABN**
( ) **Insurance Non-Covered Release form**
( ) **Disability Form**
( ) **Consent Form (Authorization to release information from patient)**
( ) **Family Medical Leave Act (FMLA)**
( ) **Doctor's Note (Excusing patient from work or school)**
( ) **Medical Release Form/Work Comp Work Release and Rating**
( ) **HIPAA Compliance Forms**
( ) **Letters to Peers (referrals, patient update)**
( ) **Letter to Insurance Commissioner (Request for Assistance)**

PRINT

Figure 2.20   Select and print the different types of medical documents.

PATIENT INFORMATION FORM

Title: (Mr., Mrs., Ms.) First Name:_____ Middle Initial:_____ Last Name:_____
Address:_____
City:_____ State:_____ Zip:_____
Home Phone:_____ Cell Phone:_____
Gender: (M)_____ (F)_____ Date of Birth:_____ Age:_____ Social Security #:_____

Guarantor: (Person who assumes responsibility for any debt or obligation on Patient Account)
First Name:_____ Middle Initial:_____ Last Name:_____
Address:_____
City:_____ State:_____ Zip:_____
Home Phone:_____ Cell Phone:_____

Patient Relationship to Guarantor: (Self)_____ (Spouse)_____ (Mother)_____ (Father)_____ Other)_____

Status of Patient:
(Single)_____ (Married)_____ (Widow)_____ (Divorced)_____
Employed: (FT)_____ (PT)_____ (Retired)_____ (Not Employed)_____ Name of Employer:_____
Address:_____
City:_____ State:_____ Zip:_____
Employer Phone #:_____
Student: (FT)_____ (PT)_____ Name of School:_____

By Whom were you Referred:_____

PRIMARY COVERAGE
Name of Insurance Plan or Carrier: _____
Please provide Insurance card so our office can make copy
(Another name for the insured)
Policy Holder Name:_____
Policy Holder Identification #:_____
Policy Holder Home Phone # (if different than above) :_____
Policy Holder Date of Birth:_____
Group Number:_____ Group Name:_____
Is this an Employer Health Insurance Plan? (Yes)_____ (No)_____
If Yes name of Employer:_____
Patient relationship to the Policy Holder: (Self)_____ (Spouse)_____ (Child)_____ (Other)_____

SECONDARY OR SUPPLEMENTAL COVERAGE
Name of Insurance Plan or Carrier: _____
Please provide Insurance card so our office can make copy

(Person who the Insurance is covered under)
Policy Holder Name:_____
Policy Holder Identification #:_____
Policy Holder Home Phone # (if different than above) :_____
Policy Holder Date of Birth:_____
Group Number:_____ Group Name:_____
Is this an Employer Health Insurance Plan? (Yes)_____ (No)_____
If Yes name of Employer:_____
Patient relationship to the Policy Holder: (Self)_____ (Spouse)_____ (Child)_____ (Other)_____

AUTHORIZATION AND ACKNOWLEDGMENT
I do state that the above information is to be true and correct to the best of my knowledge. I authorize the above name provider of service to release any information that has gathered during the course of the my treatment to my insurance company, employer, physicians, institutions or third party payers, upon their request on any or all claim (s) that have been filed.
If for any reason a service or charge(s) is not covered by my insurance carrier or no longer have coverage I take full responsibility for any and all fees billed on my account

_____   _____
(Signature of Patient, Parent, Legal Guardian or Policy Holder)   (Date)

Figure 2.21   Example of a patient information form.

Step 1

FROM THE MAIN MENU SELECT

> REGISTRATION
> OF A
> PATIENT

BUTTON

MAIN MENU

MEDICAL SOFTWARE

FILE EDIT VIEW TOOLS FORMAT

| THE SCHEDULE | MEDICAL RECORDS | REGISTRATION OF A PATIENT | THE APPOINTMENT | CHARGE ENTRY | BILLING | RECEIPTS | COLLECTIONS |

PATIENT DATA ENTRY

STEP 1: THE SCHEDULE
File Tab: CDR (Calendar)   File Tab: AT (Appointment Type)

STEP 2: MEDICAL RECORDS
File Tab: DR (Doctors Notes)   File Tab: DIAG (Diagnostic)

File Tab: HOSP (Hospital Notes)   File Tab: FORMS (Forms/Correspondence)

STEP 3: REGISTRATION OF A PATIENT
File Tab: PT (Patient)   File Tab: GT (Guarantor)   File Tab: IND (Insured)   File Tab: INS (Insurance)

CHARGE ENTRY (CLAIM SUBMISSION)

STEP 4: THE APPOINTMENT
File Tab: LOC (Location)   File Tab: HC PROV (Health Care Provider)   File Tab: PC (Patient Complaint)

STEP 5: CHARGE ENTRY
File Tab: CS (Coding System)   File Tab: CI (Charge Input)

STEP 6: BILLING
File Tab: FMT (Format Method-Claim Requirements)   File Tab: FM (Filing Method-Claim Forms)   File Tab: CE RPT (Daily Balance Report)

ACCOUNTS RECEIVABLE (CLAIM ADJUDICATION PROCESS)
STEP 7: RECEIPTS
File Tab: PMT (Payment Type)   File Tab: AC RPT (Deposit and Daily Balance Reports)   File Tab: EDI RPT (Electronic Transmission Reports)

COLLECTIONS (UNPROCESSABLE OR DENIED CLAIM)

STEP 8: COLLECTIONS
File Tab: LTR (Letters)   **File Tab: TCKLR (Tickler)**   **File Tab: AG RPT (Aging Reports)**

Figure 2.22   Pull up patient registration screen.

Step 3

DATA ENTRY: TRANSFER INFORMATION FROM PATIENT REGISTRATION FORM TO THE MEDICAL SOFTWARE. "Double click in box" IN A SPECIFIC WINDOW IN ORDER TO TRANSFER PATIENT AND GUARANTORS INFORMATION THEN MOVE TO THE OTHER TWO PARTS AND ENTER INSURED AND INSURANCE INFORMATION.

MEDICAL PRACTICE SOFTWARE

FILE   EDIT   VIEW   TOOLS   FORMAT

		REGISTRATION OF A PATIENT				

PATIENT DATA ENTRY
STEP 1: THE SCHEDULE
File Tab: CDR (Calendar)   File Tab: AT (Appointment Type)

STEP 2: MEDICAL RECORDS
File Tab: DR (Doctors Notes)   File Tab: DIAG (Diagnostic)

File Tab: HOSP (Hospital Notes)

STEP 3: REGISTRATION OF A PATIENT
File Tab: PT (Patient)   File Tab: GT (Guarantor)

Double click in box	Double click in box

STEP 3: REGISTRATION OF A PATIENT
Patient:

Patient Name: First_____Middle_____Last_____(Mr/Mrs/Ms)
Address_____
City_____State_____Zip code_____
Phone: Home#_____Cell#_____
Date of Birth_____Sex: (M)____(F)_____Social Security #:_____

Status: (Single)____(Married)____(Widow)____(Divorced)____

Employed: (FT)_____(PT)_____(Retired)_____(Not Employed)_____(Self Employed)_____
Name of Employer:_____
Employer Phone#:_____

Student: (FT)_____ (PT)_____
Name of School:_____

Guarantor:

(Guarantor is the one who assumes responsibility for any debt or obligation due on the patient account)
Patient Relationship to the Guarantor: (Self)____(Spouse)____(Mother)____(Father)_____(Other)_____

*Spouse   Name: First_____Middle_____Last_____
*Mother/Father Name: First_____Middle_____Last_____
*Other   Name: First_____Middle_____ Last_____
Home#_____Cell#_____

By Whom were you Referred?_____

Patient Profile ( )   Statement ( )

Figure 2.23   Data entry screen (patient and guarantor information).

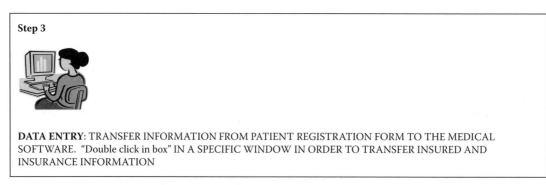

Step 3

DATA ENTRY: TRANSFER INFORMATION FROM PATIENT REGISTRATION FORM TO THE MEDICAL SOFTWARE. "Double click in box" IN A SPECIFIC WINDOW IN ORDER TO TRANSFER INSURED AND INSURANCE INFORMATION

MEDICAL PRACTICE SOFTWARE

FILE EDIT VIEW TOOLS FORMAT

		REGISTRATION OF A PATIENT					

PATIENT DATA ENTRY

STEP 1: THE SCHEDULE

File Tab: CDR (Calendar)   File Tab: AT (Appointment Type)

STEP 2: MEDICAL RECORDS

File Tab: DR (Doctors Notes)   File Tab: DIAG (Diagnostic)

File Tab: HOSP (Hospital Notes)   File Tab: FORMS (Forms/Correspondence)

STEP 3: REGISTRATION OF A PATIENT

File Tab: PT (Patient)	File Tab: GT (Guarantor)	File Tab: IND (Insured)	File Tab: INS (Insurance)
Double click inbox	Double click inbox	Double click inbox	Double click inbox

STEP 3: REGISTRATION OF A PATIENT

Insured:

(Name of the policy holder)

Patient relationship to the policy holder: (Self)____(Spouse)_____(Child)_____(Other)

Name: First_____Middle_____Last_____
Home#_____Date of Birth:_____ Sex: (M)___(F)____Social Security #:_____

Insurance:
Primary:
Secondary:
Tertiary:

(X) PRIMARY COVERAGE:
Plan name: _____
Identification#:_____

Group #:_____ Group Name:_____

Plan Type (Bill Type):_____

Notes: _____

( ) SECONDARY COVERAGE:
( ) TERTIARY COVERAGE:

BCBS   **PPO**

POLICY ID NUMBER   Office Visit Copay: $15
###########   Specialist: $30
GROUP ID NUMBER   Emergency Room: $135
#######   Urgent Care: $25
GROUP NAME   RX: $10 / 20/ 40
Employer Name
INSURED NAME   Network CoInsurance:
Stewart Little   In Net: 80% / 20%
                                            Out of Net 60% / 40%
PLAN CODE: Medical / Prescription

Figure 2.24   Data entry screen (insured and insurance information).

Chapter 3

Chapter 3

Charge Entry (Steps 4, 5, and 6)

Contents

BUSINESS OFFICE

Charge entry takes place in the business office. Charge sheets are filled out. Then information is transferred into the medical software. Surgery notes are received, coded, and keyed in. The business office includes several people who specialize in specific areas:

Charge Entry: Enters services provided by physician and non-physician practitioner (NPP): evaluation and management (E/M) visits, diagnostic, etc.

Coders: Codes procedures such as surgeries, and bills for them

Unit I: Steps 4, 5, and 6, Introduction

Purpose

In Chapter 2 we went over the information that covers the upper portion of the claim form, which consists of the patient name and address along with the insurance information including the address to which claims are sent. Chapter 3 will cover the next 3 steps, which involve the bottom portion of the CMS-1500 claim form (see Figure 3.1).

Chapter 3 is what I consider the body of this guidebook. When it comes to billing for charges, there is so much information you need to know before a claim can even be submitted to the insurance company.

The easiest way to understand medical billing is to break the information into several parts and then show how each part consists of a set of codes and how those code sets are tied together on the bottom portion of the CMS-1500 claim form.

Medical codes are used to help identify things that affect reimbursement and to describe a patient's diagnosis and treatment. If these code sets are not in place correctly, it will delay the processing of a claim.

In Step 4 we will cover one set of codes, called place of service (POS) codes, which represent the location where the service took place. In Step 4 we will also cover the importance of identification numbers for healthcare providers as well as specific dates.

Step 5 will cover five sets of codes: *Current Procedural Terminology* (CPT-4), type of service (TOS), Healthcare Procedure Coding System (HCPCS), modifiers, and *International Classification of Diseases*, 9th edition (ICD-9).

In Unit IV of this chapter, a case example is provided that will take you through how a service or procedure is provided, how that service or procedure is coded, how that service or procedure is applied to the bottom portion of the CMS-1500 claim form, and how that charge is submitted to the insurance company or carrier.

Specific boxes on the claim form are tied together for certain reasons (see Figure 3.2):

1. Place where the service was rendered in Box 24B has to be linked to the information in Box 32. This information helps determine the type of benefits that are to be paid by the insurance carrier for doctor charges for office, inpatient, or outpatient services.
2. Type of service, procedure, or supply in Box 24D has to be linked to the patient diagnosis that is in Box 24E (Box 24E is linked to line 1, 2, 3, or 4 in Box 21) to determine if it is a covered benefit or not. This box contains the information that will determine if the procedure was medically necessary for that particular diagnosis.
3. The physicians name in Box 31 is linked to the identification number in Boxes 24J, 25, 32a, and 33a, and determines who gets paid, the payment amount, and where payment is sent.

Unit II: Step 4, the Appointment

Part A: Location

The description in Box 24b on the CMS-1500 claim form is filled in with the place of service. To record the location where a service or procedure took place on the claim form, two-digit codes were developed and are maintained by the Centers for Medicare and Medicaid Services (CMS) (see Table 3.1).

These code sets are referred to as place of service (POS) codes, and they help determine the reimbursement rate. POS codes identify where the physician's professional service was provided: in a nonfacility (NF) setting, such as a physician's office or patient home; or in a facility (F) setting, such as a hospital, skilled nursing facility (SNF), hospice, ambulatory surgery center (ASC), or inpatient rehabilitation facility. This is known as the site-of-service payment differential. For example, if you were to look in the Medicare physician fee schedule at a surgical procedure that was performed in a physician's office, which is a nonfacility setting, the fee amount may be different than if done in a hospital, which is a facility setting. The reason for this difference is related to practice

14. DATE CONDITION OR INJURY OCCURRED?		15. HAS CONDITION OR INJURY OCCURRED BEFORE? IF SO, WHEN		16. WHAT ARE THE DATES THE PATIENT IS UNABLE TO WORK?				
17. NAME OF REFERRING DOCTOR		17a. PROVIDER UPIN # 17b. PROVIDER NPI #		18. WHAT ARE THE DATES THE PATIENT WAS HOSPITALIZED?				
19. THIS SPACE CAN BE USED FOR ADDITIONAL PURPOSE				20. ANY LAB WORK ORDERED OUTSIDE THE OFFICE?				
21. LIST OF THE ICD-9 (DIAGNOSIS) CODES GO HERE 1. Link Diagnosis with service/procedure 3. Link Diagnosis with service/procedure 2. Link Diagnosis with service/procedure 4. Link Diagnosis with service/procedure				22. MEDICAID/ORIGINAL REFERENCE NUMBER				
				23. AUTHORIZATION OR CASE NUMBER GOES HERE				

24 A. DATE SERVICE TOOK PLACE	B LOCATION	C What kind of service was provided	D CODES C H P or C M T P O C / D	E LINK BOX 24D TO BOX 21 1,2,3 OR 4	F (CHARGES) $ AMT	G	H	I	J. RENDERING PROVIDER ID#
LINE 1 FROM _/_/_ TO _/_/_						D A			
LINE 2 FROM _/_/_ TO _/_/_						Y S			
LINE 3 FROM _/_/_ TO _/_/_						OR			
LINE 4 FROM _/_/_ TO _/_/_						U			
LINE 5 FROM _/_/_ TO _/_/_						N I			
LINE 6 FROM _/_/_ TO _/_/_						T S			

25. PROVIDER TAX ID#	26. PATIENT ACCT #	27. DOES PROVIDER ACCEPT ASSIGNMENT?	28. TOTAL $ AMT $	29. PAID AMT $	30. DUE AMT $
31.PHYSICIAN SIGNATURE GOES HERE OR NAME OF SUPPLIER SIGNATURE DATE	32. NAME OF FACILITY GOES HERE a. PROVIDER NPI #	b.	33.PROVIDERS BILLING ADDRESS GOES HERE a. PROVIDER NPI #	b.	

Figure 3.1 Bottom of the CMS-1500 claim form.

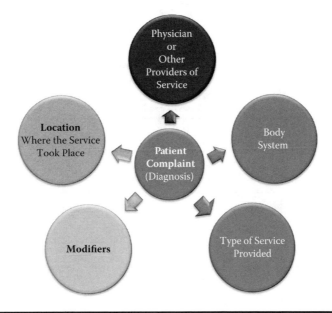

Figure 3.2 This illustration highlights how various parts of the color-coded claim form are connected.

Table 3.1   Place of Service (POS) Code Sets

Place Where the Service Took Place	Description	Two-Digit Code
Indian Health Services		05
Indian Health Services		06
Indian Health Services		07
Office (NF)	Location where the healthcare professional provides health exams, diagnosis, and treatment of illness or injury on an ambulatory basis	11
Home (NF)		12
Assisted living (NF)		13
Group home (NF)		14
Mobile unit (NF)		15
Urgent care facility (NF)		20
Hospital (F)	Patient was seen as an inpatient, which means the patient stayed in the hospital	21
Hospital (F)	Patient was seen as an outpatient	
Service provided but patient went home same day	22	
Emergency room-hospital (F)		23
Ambulatory surgery center (F)	Freestanding surgery center where surgical and diagnostic services are provided on an ambulatory basis	24
Birthing center (NF)		25
Military treatment facility		26
Skilled nursing facility (F)	A facility that provides inpatient skilled nursing care but does not provide the level of care available in a hospital	31
Nursing facility (NF)	A facility that provides skilled nursing care to residents	32
Custodial care facility (NF)		33
Hospice (F)		34
Ambulance: By land (F)		41
Ambulance: By air or water (F)		42
Independent clinic (NF)		49
Federally qualified health center (NF)		50

Table 3.1 (continued)   Place of Service (POS) Code Sets

Place Where the Service Took Place	Description	Two-Digit Code
Inpatient psychiatric facility (F)		51
Psychiatric facility-requires partial hospitalization (F)		52
Community mental health center (F)		53
		54
		55
		56
		57
		60
		61
		62
		65
		71
		72
Independent laboratory (NF)		81

expenses. If a physician's service was provided in nonfacility setting, such as the physician's office, expenses would include such things as rent for the space, supplies, equipment, and staffing, so the rate would be higher. If the physician's service was provided in a facility setting, such as a hospital, the rate would be lower because the physician would not incur the expenses of a full staff, equipment, space, or supplies, for which the hospital would be reimbursed for.

Table 3.1 is a list of place of service (POS) code sets. This list shows whether the service took place in a nonfacility (NF) setting or facility (F) setting.

Section 1: Dates

Specific dates are required to identify when a service was provided (date of service, or DOS); the date when the patient's symptoms, condition or illness, or injury occurred (date of illness or injury, or DOI); if hospitalized, the date when the patient was admitted and/or discharged; and the date when

the claim was billed. The date when the claim was filed and billed is important if there is ever a need to prove timely filing. Some carriers will only allow 90 days to file a claim. If you do not submit the claim within that time, the office will have to write off the charges.

Other sets of numbers that may be required are authorization/referral numbers. These numbers are used when a service has been authorized by the insurance company.

Part B: Healthcare Professional (Physicians, Nonphysician Practitioners, and Other Suppliers)

A healthcare provider is an individual who provides healthcare services to a patient. A healthcare professional is someone who by education, training, certification, or licensure is qualified to and is engaged in providing healthcare. To indentify these individual healthcare professionals, identification numbers are required.

Section 1: Identification Numbers

As of 2007, all healthcare providers who are covered entities under the Health Insurance Portability and Accountability Act of 1996 (HIPAA) were required to obtain what is called a National Provider Identifier (NPI), which is a ten-digit number. The NPI is used to identify a healthcare provider in standard transactions, such as a healthcare claim. Physicians and nonphysician practitioners who provide services to Medicare beneficiaries must enroll and complete the CMS-855I Medicare enrollment form, but must obtain an NPI from the National Plan and Provider Enumeration System (NPPES) prior to enrollment.

A healthcare provider can apply online by logging into the NPPES website or they can request a copy of the paper NPI Application form (CMS-10114) by either downloading it from the CMS website or by contacting the NPI Enumerator at 800-465-3203. Once enrollment is complete, healthcare provider data will be available on the NPI Registry. The NPI Registry enables you to search for a provider's NPPES information. Users may search for an individual or provider employed by an organization either by NPI or by legal business name.

If a healthcare provider belongs to a group of physicians, that group will be assigned a group NPI as well as individual NPIs for each provider. If a provider is part of a group of physicians, he or she must register for an individual NPI as well as be under a Group NPI number for two reasons: for reimbursement to be paid under the Group NPI, and to identify who rendered the services—each provider must have his or her own individual NPI number as well.

Medicare Provider Enrollment

The CMS developed an alternative way for providers, physicians, nonphysician practitioners, and other suppliers to enroll if they choose not to use the paper CMS-855I enrollment process. It is the Internet-based Provider Enrollment, Chain, and Ownership System (PECOS), which allows Medicare healthcare providers and suppliers to manage their information online by either checking status of enrollment or by making any necessary changes.

Physicians and nonphysician practitioners (NPPs) who enroll will be assigned individual provider identification numbers (PIN), which are required on the claim form along with ID qualifier. The ID qualifier is a 2 alpha-numeric character. It is used to help identify a provider's PIN number. The ID qualifier is reported in Box 24I on the CMS-1500 claim form. The two-digit alphanumeric ID qualifier for Blue Shield is 1B, for Medicare it is 1C, and for Medicaid, it is 1D.

Other numbers that providers are required to have are a Tax ID number (TIN) and Unique Physician Identification Number (UPIN). The use of a UPIN number is only required when the provider referred, ordered, or supervised the service(s) or supply(s) on the claim form. These numbers are required in several areas of the claim form.

PTAN

All healthcare providers who wish to bill Medicare for medical services provided to Medicare beneficiaries must obtain a provider transaction access number (PTAN). It is used by Medicare to help identify the healthcare provider as a client. Claims that are submitted without a PTAN will be rejected and returned.

Submitter ID (Electronic Billing):

A healthcare provider who submits claims electronically to Medicare is required to obtain a submitter ID, only if bills are submitted directly rather than going through a clearinghouse. A clearinghouse is used to help manage all electronic claims by making it possible for providers to batch electronic claims and submit them to one central location. A clearinghouse securely transmits the electronic file to each individual payer by meeting the strict standards that are set up by HIPAA. Clearinghouses help reduce rejected claims by scrubbing claims for front-end and billing errors. They also help decrease by half the turnaround time for reimbursement. If an office also wishes to utilize the common working file, you must obtain a submitter ID number. A common working file (CWF) is a Medicare data source that maintains information regarding health insurance benefit and coverage information for Medicare beneficiaries. It provides information such as patient eligibility, claim history, benefits, Medicare Secondary Payer (MSP) and Medicare Advantage enrollment data.

Supplier ID (DME Billing):

Providers who provide, sell, or rent durable medical equipment (DME), prosthetics, orthotics, or supplies (DMEPOS) to Medicare beneficiaries and meet the supplier standards must obtain a supplier ID number. To apply, you must enroll with the National Supplier Clearinghouse (NSC).

If a claim is rejected because the provider was not authorized, it usually means that the proper ID did not appear on the claim. The claim is rejected or denied by the carrier because provider was not eligible at the time of service.

Section 2: Medical Specialists

Table 3.2 is a list of several physician specialties and their areas of expertise.

Table 3.2 Physician Specialties

Specialty	Title	Description
General practice	General Practitioner (GP)	Provides primary care based on an understanding of all illness and does not restrict his/her practice to any particular field of specialty, but may need to initiate a referral to a specialist.
Family practice	Family Practitioner (FP)	Similar to general practice but centers around the family
Internal medicine	Internist	Diagnoses and treating diseases and disorders of the internal organs
Obstetrics	Obstetrician	Care for pregnant females during pregnancy, childbirth, and immediately thereafter
Gynecology	Gynecologist	Diagnoses and treats diseases and disorders of the female reproductive system; strong emphasis on preventative measures
Dermatology	Dermatologist	Diagnoses and treats disorders of the skin
Pediatrics	Pediatrician	Diagnoses and treats diseases and disorders of children; strong emphasis on preventative measures
Geriatrics	Gerontologist	Diagnoses and treats diseases, disorders, and problems associated with aging
Orthopedics	Orthopedist	Diagnoses and treats disorders and diseases of the bones, muscles, ligaments, and tendons as well as treating fractures of the bones
Pulmonology	Pulmonary Specialist	Diagnosing and treating disorders and diseases of the lungs
Cardiology	Cardiologist	Diagnoses and treats disorders and diseases of the heart
Optometry	Optometrist	Measures the accuracy of vision to determine if corrective lenses are required.
Ophthalmology	Ophthalmologist	Diagnoses and treats disorders and diseases of the eye.
Dentistry	Dentist-DDS/DMD	Diagnoses and treats disorders and diseases of the teeth and gums.
Dentistry	Oral & Maxillofacial Surgeon	Treats disorders, diseases, injuries of mouth, jaws, and face
Dentistry	Orthodontist	Study and treatment of malocclusions
Chiropractic	Chiropractor	Manipulative treatment of disorders originating from misalignment of the spinal vertebrae (back)
Anesthesiology	Anesthesiologist	Administers the anesthetic agent before and during surgery
Otorhinolaryngology	Otorhinolaryngologist "ENT Specialist"	Diagnoses and treats disorders and diseases of the ear, nose, and throat
Cosmetic	Plastic Surgeon	Treats patients with deformities and injuries to the skin
Oncology (radiation therapy, chemotherapy	Oncologist	Diagnoses and treats tumors and cancer
Pathology	Pathologist	Analysis of tissue samples to confirm diagnosis
Radiology	Radiologist	Diagnoses and treats disorders and diseases with x-rays and other forms of radiant energy

Continued

Table 3.2 (continued)   Physician Specialties

Specialty	Title	Description
Urology & male genital services	Urologist	Diagnoses and treats disorders and diseases of the urinary system of females and genitourinary system of males
Neurology & neurosurgery	Neurologist	Diagnoses and treats disorders and diseases of the central nervous system
Nephrology	Nephrologist	Diagnoses and treats disorders and diseases of the kidneys
Hematology	Hematologist	Diagnoses and treats disorders and diseases of the blood and blood-forming tissues
Gastroenterology	Gastroenterologist	Diagnoses and treats disorders and diseases of the stomach and intestines
Physical medicine	Physical Medicine Specialist	Diagnoses and treats disorders and diseases with physical agents (physical therapy)
Psychology	Psychologist	Evaluates and treats emotional problems
Psychiatry	Psychiatrist	Diagnoses and treats pronounced manifestations of emotional problems or mental illness that may have an organic causative factor

Part C: Patient Complaint

Why is the patient being seen? Is it for several problems or just one? To have an understanding, we must first understand the medical language.

Section 1: Medical Language

Medical language consists of two major areas: medical terminology and the organization of the human body. Knowledge and understanding of these two subject areas will enable you to interpret the patient's diagnosis and have a better understanding of the area of treatment and plan of treatment prescribed by the physician. These subject areas must be understood before learning how to code.

Medical terms (Table 3.3) are made up of a combination of four different word parts: root word, combining form, prefix, and suffix. The root of the word will either indicate the body part or main term of the word. Combining form is where the root of the word has a vowel added to the end. A suffix is added to the end of the root word and indicates location, time, number, or status. A prefix is added at the beginning of the root word and indicates the procedure, conditions, disorder, or disease.

The organization of the human body (Table 3.4) is very complicated. To better understand the body structure and function of human anatomy, it is separated into several divisions: body planes, body cavities, abdominopelvic regions

Table 3.3   Examples of Medical Terms and Their Construction

Root	Combining Form	Meaning	Prefix	Meaning	Suffix	Meaning
Arthr	Arthr/O	Joint		Pain	Algia	
Term			Description			
Arthralgia			Pain In Joint			

Root	Combining Form	Meaning	Prefix	Meaning	Suffix	Meaning
Cardi	Cardi/0	Heart	Tachy			Rapid
Term			Description			
Tachycardia			Rapid Heart Beat			

Table 3.4 Examples of Human Anatomy Separations

Body Planes	Body Cavities	Abdominopelvic Regions and Quadrants	Divisions of the Back	Anatomical Directions	Body Systems
Frontal (coronal)	Thoracic	Right upper quadrant	Lumbar (lower back)	Anterior	Respiratory system

and quadrants, divisions of the back, anatomical directions, and several body systems.

The human body is broken up into different body systems, which are outlined in Figure 3.3).

Unit III: Step 5, Charges
Part A: Coding System

There are several different sets of medical codes that must be learned to submit bills for medical services. The first set of codes consists of Level I and Level II codes. Level I codes are called Current Procedural Terminology (CPT-4) codes. They identify the type of service (TOS) and the procedure performed by a physician or other healthcare provider. CPT codes are five-digit numbers. Type of service (TOS) codes correspond to the type of service provided to the patient and are identified by a one-digit number. Level II codes are Healthcare Common Procedure Coding System (HCPCS) codes; the acronym is commonly pronounced "Hick Picks." They help identify medical products, supplies, and other types of services and procedures performed by dentists, orthodontists, optometrists, and ambulance services, which are not listed in the CPT coding system. HCPCS codes consist of a five-digit alphanumeric code where the first character is a letter. The second set of codes is called the *International Classification of Diseases, 9th revision, Clinical Modification* (ICD-9-CM) codes; they describe the patient's disease, symptoms, condition, illness, or injury. These codes consist of 3, 4, or 5 digits. The third set of codes is called the modifiers, which may be added to help modify a CPT/HCPCS code to provide additional information to help explain that something unusual has occurred during the service provided or to help identify a certain area of the body. These codes consist of a 2-digit number or a 2-digit alpha designation. The fourth set of codes is called place of service (POS) codes. They help identify where a service was provided. They consist of 2-digit numbers (see Table 3.5).

To have an understanding of the information that is required and where that information is placed on the claim form, sets of specific codes were developed to help identify specific information that is required on the claim form. The code sets are shown in Figures 3.4 through 3.7.

Part B: Charge Sheet

You may be thinking, "In Box 24D, how will I know exactly what type of service, procedure, or supply was provided in order to know what to charge the insurance carrier?" Medical office software is designed to print a form called a *charge sheet*, which can also be referred to as an encounter form, superbill, or ticket) (see Figure 3.8). These charge sheets are set up with specific codes according to the doctor's specialty or practice. For a physician to be reimbursed by the insurance carriers for professional services and supplies, sets of codes were set up and developed to help report and identify the type of service, procedure, or supply that was provided to the patient as well as to help identify patient diagnosis. Sets of 2-digit codes were created to help report and identify the place of service and codes called modifiers (Figure 3.6) help by providing additional information. Once the charge sheet is printed, it is attached to the patient chart and given to the doctor at the time of the appointment. The charge sheet is then marked by the doctor or whoever provided the service and is then turned over to the billing department so the charge entry clerk can key in charges in order to bill the insurance carrier.

The charge sheet is then forwarded to the charge entry clerk so that the charges can be keyed into the system and billed. What happens when the doctor has seen the patient at the hospital before the patient visits the office? In this case, you will wait until you receive an operative report (Figure 3.9) or an emergency room (ER) report from the hospital to know exactly what charges should be billed. The coder will review the notes and enter in the codes based on what the information in these reports. If the patient is seen in the office and scheduled for surgery, a PreCert (precertification) or PreD (predetermination) is completed and a surgery order is written up and both documents are forwarded to the coder, and a claim or ticket is created. After the surgery has taken place, the hospital will send you the operative report (Op report), which will allow you to determine the charges to be submitted.

To bill for a procedure that took place at a hospital, the coders download hospital notes by logging into the hospital's network or the hospital can e-mail or fax them to the doctor's office. Once coders receive the hospital notes, they will use them to key in charges.

Key factors: When coding multiple procedures, there are a couple of factors to keep in mind. Is the procedure being

Body Systems	Codes
Integumentary System	10000–19999
Musculoskeletal System	20000–29999
Respiratory System	30000–32999
Cardiovascular System	33010–38200
Hemic and Lymphatic System	40000–49999
Digestive System	50010–53899
Urinary System	54000–59899
Reproductive System	60001–60699
Endocrine System	61000–64999
Nervous System	65091–69990
Eye & Auditory System	38204–38999

Key Note: Codes will change throughout each year. They can be deleted, revised or added so they will not always stay the same.

Figure 3.3   Body systems and the corresponding CPT code range.

Table 3.5   Examples of the Various Coding Systems

Codes Sets	Codes	Examples	Description
1	CPT-4	99213	
	TOS	1	Office Visit:Est Patient
			Medical Care
2	HCPCS	J3480	Injection of potassium chloride
3	Modifiers	F5	Right hand, thumb
4	ICD-9	719.4	Pain in joint
5	POS (discussed in Step 4 A)	11	Doctor's office

Code set consists of Level I and Level II codes.

1. **Level I, called CPT-4 (Current Procedural Terminology)** identifies what type of service (TOS), procedure or supply was provided: a set of 5 numbers. A CPT code book is broken up into 6 sections.

2. **Level II, called HCPCS (HCFA Common Procedural Coding System)**, pronounced Hick Picks, identifies other types of services, procedures or supply that are not listed in the CPT coding system: a 5-position alphanumeric code with the first digit a letter. HCPCS code book is listed in alphabetical order beginning with A0000 thru V5999. These codes are subject to change.

Level I CPT-4		Examples	5 Digit Numeric Code
Section 1	Evaluation and Management	Office visit/Consultation	99201-99409
Section 2	Anesthesia		00100-01999, 99100-99140
Section 3	Surgery		10040-69979
Section 4	Radiology		70010-79999
Section 5	Pathology and Laboratory		80002-89399
Section 6	Medicine		90701-99199

Type Of Service (TOS) *Not always required*	Numeric/alpha character Codes
Medical Care	1
Surgery	2
Consultation	3
Diagnostic Radiology	4
Diagnostic Laboratory	5
Radiation Therapy	6
Anesthesia	7
Surgical Assistant	8
Other Medical Service	9
Used DME	A
Ambulance	B
Chiropractic Service	C
DME Purchase	D
Ambulatory Surgery Center	F

Level II HCPCS	Examples	5 Digit Alphanumeric
A=Transportation service including ambulance		A0000-A0999
A=Medical Supplies		A4000-A8999
B= Enteral and Parenteral Therapy		B4000-B9999
D=Procedures		D0000-D9999
E=Durable Medical Equipment		E0100-E9999
G=Procedure/Professional Services		G0000-G9999
H=Alcohol and Drug Abuse Treatment Services		H0001-H2037
J=Drug Administered other than Oral Method		J0000-J9999
L=Orthotic Procedures		L0000-L4999
V=Vision Services		V0000-V2999
V=Hearing Services		V5000-V5999
K=Temporary Codes		K0000-K9999
Q=Drug Administered		Q0035-Q9968

Figure 3.4   Level I and Level II codes.

LEVEL I CPT-4 SECTION 1

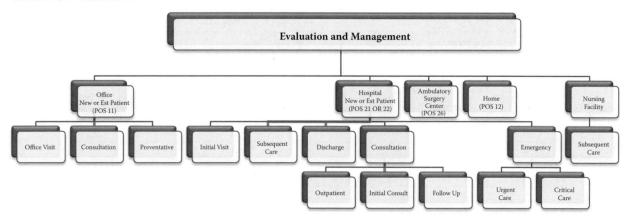

LEVEL I CPT-4 SECTIONS 2, 3, 4, 5 and 6
LEVEL II HCPCS

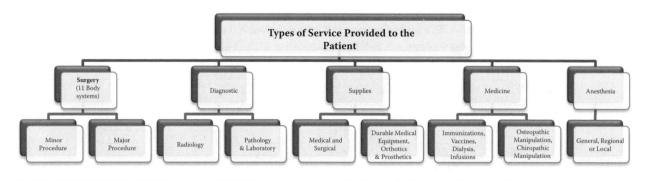

Figure 3.5 Place of service and type of service.

performed on the same anatomical site, and is the approach done through the same incision?

If a procedure is performed through the same incision as another procedure on the same site during the same encounter, it is likely to be denied because the procedure is considered to be an integral part of a more comprehensive service and not separately reportable. As an example, a palmar fasciectomy of the left hand (CPT code 26121) with carpal tunnel release of the left hand (CPT code 64721) are procedures performed on the same hand and using the same approach or incision site. As a result, the carpal tunnel release is denied because it is considered to be bundled with (part of) the palmar fasciectomy. (Refer to the Medicare correct coding initiative edits. In Chapter 5, Unit II, or go to the Centers of Medicare and Medicaid (CMS) website: http://www.cms.gov and pull up the Medicare Physician Fee Schedule database.)

There are some procedures that can be performed on the same anatomical site, such as a knee because the knee has three different compartments. If an arthroscopic surgical procedure was performed in separate compartments on the same knee, all three procedures can be billed.

Unit IV: Steps 4 and 5, Step-by-Step Guide

Part A: Charge Input

Understanding the area of treatment:

- Human body, how it is broken up into systems.
- Systems are broken up by specialty.
- Description of medical terminology is broken up into parts and word structure.

Presenting Problem: Symptoms, how they became ill or injured?

Understanding these four things—patient complaint, service type, location, and the provider the patient is seeing—will make it much easier when billing charges.

Section 1: Data Entry: Medical Software

Case Example A: On the charge sheet (refer to Figure 3.8) under *Office Visits*, an X was marked next to CPT code 99203, which indicates a new patient and detailed services. Under *Diagnostic*, an X was marked next to CPT code 74000. Under *Diagnosis*,

3. Code Set consist of codes called Modifiers.

Modifiers ensure appropriate reimbursement by identifying more detailed information on the claim.

They are used in addition to the CPT and HCPCS codes to provide more information consisting of a 2-digit number or 2-alpha character.

Not always required

Modifiers are applied in Box 24d on the CMS-1500 claim form

**For complete descriptions of Modifiers see the Medicare website: Publications; Manuals, Modifiers

	2-DIGIT CODE
ASC	SG, 73, 74, FB, FC
Anesthesia	AA, AD, G8, G9, P1, P2, P3, P4, P5, P6, QK, QS, QY, QZ
Assistant Surgeon	80, 81, 82
Physician Assistant	AS
Bilateral	50
Evaluation and Management	24, 25, 57
Eye	E1, E2, E3, E4, LS
Foot/toes	TA, T1, T2, T3, T4, T5, T6, T7, T8, T9
Hand/fingers	FA, F1, F2, F3, F4, F5, F6, F7, F8, F9
Hospice	GW or GV
Lab	QW
Locum Tenens	Q5, Q6
NCCI (Anatomical modifiers)	E1, E2, E3, E4, F1, F2, F3, F4, F5, F6, F7, F8, F9, FA, LT, RT, T1, T2, T3, T4, T5, T6, T7, T8, T9, TA
Radiology and Pathology	26, TC, UN, UP, UQ, UR, US
Repeated Procedures	76
Surgical	51, 58, 59, 78, 79
Split or Shared Surgical Service	54, 55, 56
Teaching Physician	GE, GC

Figure 3.6   Modifier codes.

X's are marked for the patient's chief complaints, abdominal pain (ICD-9 789.0) and constipation (ICD-9 564.0).

Now that you know the patient's diagnosis and the charges to bill, let's go ahead and access the medical software (see Figure 3.11 through Figure 3.15).

Section 2: Step-by-Step Guide: Applying Charges (Figure 3.10)

Step 1: In the medical software, pull up the "Main Menu" (Figure 3.11).

Step 2: From the main menu, select the "Charge Entry" (Figure 3.12) button. Once you are in the charge entry screen transfer the information from the charge sheet form (Figure 3.8) into the medical software.

Step 3: Double click in the box that is marked "Charge Input" (Figure 3.13) and do a search for that patient. When you have located the patient, select the claim/ticket regarding the particular date of service.

Step 4. Mark (x) next to the claim/ticket. A screen titled "Charge Entry" will pop up. Then transfer and key in the patient diagnosis and CPT codes from the charge sheet (Figure 3.13).

Key in the patient diagnosis and CPT codes from the charge sheet (Figures 3.12–3.13).

Once everything has been coded and input, the claim form is now ready to be submitted for insurance payment. Figure 3.14 and Figure 3.15 show how everything is tied together on the CMS 1500 claim form. How are the charges billed out to the insurance company? There are three ways: electronic, paper, or online. Details will be covered in Step 6.

Unit V: Step 6, Billing

Part A: Format Method

Information must be set up in a specific format and reported in certain fields. The format of the claim will depend on the organization to which the charges will be billed. The format

4. ICD-9-CM (International Classification of Disease 9ᵗʰ revision, Clinical Modifications)

describes the patient's disease, symptom, condition, illness, or injury and consists of a 3-, 4- or 5-digit code. The ICD-9-CM code book is in 3 volumes.

Description: The official version of ICD-9 is published by the World Health Organization (WHO). It was a coding system set up to clarify diseases and a wide variety of signs, symptoms, abnormal findings, complaints, social circumstances and external causes of injury or disease. It is used by physicians to diagnosis their patients in order to submit for reimbursement.

Coding system consists of a 3-digit numeric code that may require, in addition, either 4 or 5th digit.

There are other codes that are used as a supplementary code to provide addition information and these are described as E codes or V codes. **ICD-9-CM is divided into three volumes. Remember these codes are subject to change**

Volume I	Volume II	Volume III
Tabular list	Alphabetical Index	
Volume I and II contain medical codes that best describe a diagnosis.		Volume II contains medical codes that describe procedures that are performed in a facility setting.

Symptom, Sign, Disease, ill-Defined Condition or Injury of the patient	Term	3, 4 or 5-Digit numeric Codes/E Codes or V Codes
Constipation	Constipation	564.0
Abdominal Pain	Abdominalgia	789.0
Low Back Pain	Lumbago	724.2
Motor Vehicle Traffic Accidents		E810–E819
Personal History of Malignant Neoplasm		V10
Open biopsy of thyroid gland		06.12 (Vol. III)

5. Code set consists of codes called "POS" (place of service). Refer to Step 4 A

Figure 3.7 ICD-9-CM codes.

used for Medicare is different than the format used for a commercial payer (insurance company). Each payer may require specific information in specific boxes.

Section 1: Claim Requirements

When billing a claim to Medicare and there is no secondary payer, Medicare requires that the word "None" be entered in Box 11 on the CMS-1500 claim form. Other claim requirements must be reported on the CMS-1500 claim to ensure reimbursement. An example would be an individual provider number in Box 24J.

Part B: Filing Method (Claims Submission)

Are you billing out charges for a professional service provided by a physician, or are you billing out charges for teeth cleaning by a dentist? It is important to know the difference in order to know exactly which of the following claim forms you should use to bill out the charges, and the method by which it is going to be sent out, either on paper or electronically.

Claim #: 123456

J Nolastname, M.D.
Address

PATIENT NAME: Doe, John _____   APPT DATE: 07/08/2007 _____

INSURANCE: MEDICARE _____   APPT TIME: 09:45 am _____

COPAY: _____   BALANCE: _____

OFFICE VISITS			PROCEDURE			DIAGNOSIS		
	99202	New pt expanded	40490	Excision, Biopsy of lip			455.6	Hemorrhoids
X	99203	New pt detailed	41100	Excision, Biopsy of tongue			530.1	Esophagitis
	99204	New pt comp	41116	Excision, Lesion of flr of mouth			531.9	Ulcer Gastric
	99212	Est pt focused	42800	Excision, Biopsy of oropharynx			535	Gastritis
	99213	Est pt expanded	43600	Excision, Biopsy of stomach			540.9	Appendicitis
	99024	Post Op	43280	Laparoscopic Fundoplasty			555.9	Crohn's Disease
CONSULTATION				(Diagnostic Laparoscopy included)			558.9	Colitis (Gastroenteritis)
	99241	Focused	43300	Esophagoplasty			562.11	Diverticulitis
	99242	Expanded	43500	Gastrostomy	X		564.0	Constipation
	99243	Detailed	44025	Colotomy, biopsy			564.1	Irritable Bowel Syndrome
	99244	Comp Mod level	44126	Enterectomy			569.0	Anal and rectal polyp
	99245	Comp High level	44140	Colectomy			569.3	Rectal Bleeding
PREVENTATIVE			44300	Enterostomy			569.82	Ulceration of intestine
	99383	New pt (age 5-11)	44950	Appendectomy			571.40	Chronic Hepatitis, unspec
	99384	New pt (age 12-17)	45500	Proctoplasty			572.0	Abscess of liver
	99385	New pt (age 18-39)	46050	I&D, perianal abscess			573.1	Hepatitis
	99386	New pt (age 40-64)	46250	Hemorrhoidectomy, external			574.1	Calculus of gallbladder
SCREENING			46700	Anoplasty; adult			575.12	Cholecystitis
	G0104	Sigmoidoscopy	47600	Cholecystectomy			577.0	Pancreatitis
	G0105	Colonoscopy		DIAGNOSTIC PROCEDURE:			578.9	GI Bleeding
PATHOLOGY/LAB			43235	Endoscopy of Upper GI			787.0	Nausea & Vomiting
	80069	Renal panel	45330	Sigmoidoscopy			787.1	Heartburn
	87045	Culture, stool	45378	Colonscopy	X		789.0	Abdominal Pain
			49320	Laparoscopy			787.91	Diarrhea
INJECTION/IMMUNIZATION			DIAGNOSTIC			SUPPLIES		
			X	74000	Abdomen		A6154	Dressing change
				74150	CT Abdomen		A6448	Ace Wrap
				74181	MRI abdomen			
				74210	Pharynx			
				74220	Esophagus			
				74240	GI Upper			
				74250	Small Intestine			

CHIEF COMPLAINT:
Abdominal pain and Constipation _____

DOCTOR NOTES:
_____

MEDICATION:
_____

NURSES NOTES:
_____

DOCTOR SIGNATURE: _____

OTHER: _____

Figure 3.8   Charge sheet for a physician with a specialty in digestive disorders (case example A).

```
┌──────────────────────────────────────────────────────────────┐
│                      OPERATIVE REPORT                          │
│   Patient:                        Chart #:                     │
│   Date of Birth:                                               │
│   Date:                                                        │
│                                                                │
│   PreOperative Diagnosis:                                      │
│   PostOperative Diagnosis:                                     │
│                                                                │
│   Procedure:                                                   │
│   1. Carpal Tunnel Release, Left Hand (CPT Code 64721)         │
│   2. Palmar Fasciectomy, Left Hand (CPT Code 26121)            │
│                                                                │
│   Surgeon                                                      │
│   First Assistant                                              │
│                                                                │
│   Anesthesia:                                                  │
│   Anesthesiologist:                                            │
│                                                                │
│   Operative Indication:                                        │
│                                                                │
│   Operative Findings:                                          │
│                                                                │
│   Description of Procedure:                                    │
│                                                                │
└──────────────────────────────────────────────────────────────┘
```

Figure 3.9   Operative report.

Here are the three different types of claim forms:

CMS-1500: Used for Professional Billing
CMS-1450 (UB-04): Used for Facility Billing
ADA: Used for Dental Billing

Below are three ways to submit a claim:

Hard Copy (Paper): Paper form is submitted to the payer for reimbursement.
Electronic Data Interchange (EDI): CPID is required (refer to CPID, Chapter 4, Step 7, Unit II: Claim cycle).
Direct Data Entry (DDE): Login online via the Internet through a secure website to a particular payer's computer system and manually key in charges.

```
┌─────────────────────────────────────────────┐
│  CHARGE SHEET (See Figure 3.8)              │
│                                             │
│                                             │
│  Services provided by the doctor:           │
│                                             │
│  Office Visit: E/M 99203                    │
│  Diagnostic: 74000                          │
│                                             │
│                                             │
│  Patient Chief Complaint (CC): Abdominal pain and │
│  constipation.                              │
│                                             │
└─────────────────────────────────────────────┘
```

Figure 3.10   Entering the services provided by the doctor.

Part C: Reports

1. Daily balance: Run at the end of the day and includes all charges billed that day

MEDICAL SOFTWARE

FILE   EDIT   VIEW   TOOLS   FORMAT

THE SCHEDULE	MEDICAL RECORD	REGISTRATION OF A PATIENT		THE APPOINTMENT	CHARGE ENTRY	BILLING	RECEIPTS	COLLECTIONS

PATIENT DATA ENTRY

STEP 1: THE SCHEDULE
File Tab: CDR (Calendar)   File Tab: AT (Appointment Type)

STEP 2: MEDICAL RECORDS
File Tab: DR (Doctors Notes)   File Tab: DIAG (Diagnostic)

File Tab: HOSP (Hospital Notes)   File Tab: FORMS (Forms/Correspondence)

STEP 3: REGISTRATION OF A PATIENT
File Tab: PT (Patient)   File Tab: GT (Guarantor)   File Tab: IND (Insured)   File Tab: INS (Insurance)

CHARGE ENTRY (CLAIM SUBMISSION)

STEP 4: THE APPOINTMENT
File Tab: LOC (Location)   File Tab: HC PROV (Health Care Provider)   File Tab: PC (Patient Complaint)

STEP 5: CHARGE ENTRY
File Tab: CS (Coding System)   File Tab: CI (Charge Input)

STEP 6: BILLING
File Tab: FMT (Format Method-Claim Requirements)   File Tab: FM (Filing Method -Claim Forms)   File Tab: CE RPT (Daily Balance Report)

ACCOUNTS RECEIVABLE (CLAIM ADJUDICATION PROCESS)

STEP 7: RECEIPTS
File Tab: PMT (Payment Type)   File Tab: AC RPT (Deposit and Daily Balance Reports)   File Tab: EDI RPT (Electronic Transmission Reports)

COLLECTIONS (UNPROCESSABLE OR DENIED CLAIM)

STEP 8: COLLECTIONS
File Tab: LTR (Letters)   File Tab: TCKLR (Tickler)   File Tab: AG RPT (Aging Reports)

Figure 3.11   Medical software screen example.

CHARGE SHEET

Services provided by the doctor:

Office Visit: E/M 99203

Diagnostic: 74000

Patient Chief Complaint (CC): Abdominal pain and constipation.

CHARGE ENTRY

MEDICAL SOFTWARE

FILE EDIT VIEW TOOLS FORMAT

			THE APPOINTMENT	CHARGE ENTRY	BILLING		

STEP 4: THE APPOINTMENT

FileTab: LOC (Location)	File Tab: HC PROV (Health Care Provider)	File Tab: PC (Patient Complaint)

STEP 5: CHARGE ENTRY

File Tab: CS (Coding System)	File Tab: CI (Charge Input)

STEP 6: BILLING

File Tab: FMT (Format Method-Claim Requirements)	File Tab: FM (Filing Method-Claim Forms)	File Tab: CE RPT (Daily Balance Report)

Figure 3.12 Accessing the Charge Entry screen.

MEDICAL SOFTWARE

STEP 5: CHARGE ENTRY

PART A: Coding System

DIAGNOSIS: _____

(Description:_____)

PART B: Charge Input

Claim#: 123456

Patient Name: Little, S
[ ]   ( )

SEARCH

All Claims   Single

(X) #123456 Date of Service 07/08/07 Claim Status: NEW
(   ) #789101 Date of Service 07/23/07 Claim Status: Paid
(   ) #112131 Date of Service 08/01/07   Claim Status: Collection (60 days old)

Claim # 123456   **CHARGE ENTRY**

Diagnosis: Patient Complaint: Abdominal Pain & Constipation

1 789.0 (Description: Abdominal Pain)   Date of Injury:
2 564.0 (Description: Constipation)   Date of Hospitalization:
3 _____ (Description:_____)   Discharge Date:
4 _____ (Description:_____)
Facility: Office
Rendering Provider: Referring: Supervising/Ordering:

Line #	Date of Service	Code(s)	Modifier	POS	Unit(s)	$ Fee
1	From 07/08/07 To 07/08/07	99203		11		125.00
2	From 07/08/07 To 07/08/07	74000		11		55.00
3	From To					
4	From To					
5	From To					
6	From To					

Date of Entry:

File Date: __/__/__
Filing Method: HCFA
Filing Type: Electronic
Plan Name: Medicare (P)

Figure 3.13   Entering the charges.

	LOCATION 2 digit code	E/M CPT-4 code	PHYSICIAN or PROVIDER ID	BODY SYSTEM	PATIENT COMPLAINT	DIAGNOSIS ICD-9 code	TYPE OF SERVICE CPT/HCPCS	MODIFIER 2 digit code (# or alpha)
CODE	11 In Office (Box 24 B)	99203 New pt (Box 24D)				1,2,3 Diagnosis In Box 24E & 21		
CODE (Tied Together)	Box 32 a,b Box 33 a,b	1,2,3 Diag In Box 24E & 21				99203 In Box 24D		
CODE (Tied Together)								
CODE (Tied Together)								

BOTTOM PORTION OF THE CLAIM FORM

14. DATE CONDITION OR INJURY OCCURRED?	15. HAS CONDITION OR INJURY OCCURRED BEFORE? IF SO, WHEN	16. WHAT ARE THE DATES THE PATIENT IS UNABLE TO WORK?
17. NAME OF REFERRING DOCTOR	17a. PROVIDER UPIN # / 17b. PROVIDER NPI #	18. WHAT ARE THE DATES THE PATIENT WAS HOSPITALIZED?
19. THIS SPACE CAN BE USED FOR ADDITIONAL PURPOSE		20. ANY LAB WORK ORDERED OUTSIDE THE OFFICE?
21. LIST OF THE ICD-9 (DIAGNOSIS) CODES GO HERE 1. 789.0 Abdominal Pain 3. Link Diagnosis with a procedure code 2. 564.0 Constipation 4. Link Diagnosis with a procedure code		22. USE FOR MEDICAID 23. AUTHORIZATION NUMBER GOES HERE

24. A DATE SERVICE TOOK PLACE		B LOCATION	C	D CODES / MOD	E LINK DIAGNOSIS	F (CHARGES) $ AMOUNT	G	H	I	J. PROVIDER ID#
LINE 1 FROM _/_/_	TO _/_/_	11		99203	1,2		D A			666555444
LINE 2 FROM _/_/_	TO _/_/_						Y S			
LINE 3 FROM _/_/_	TO _/_/_						OR			
LINE 4 FROM _/_/_	TO _/_/_						U			
LINE 5 FROM _/_/_	TO _/_/_						N I			
LINE 6 FROM _/_/_	TO _/_/_						T S			

25. PROVIDER TAX ID# 000112222	26. PATIENT ACCT #	27. DOES PROVIDER ACCEPT ASSIGNMENT?	28. TOTAL $ AMT $	29. PAID AMT $	30. DUE AMT $
31. PHYSICIAN SIGNATURE GOES HERE OR NAME OF SUPPLIER	32. NAME OF FACILITY GOES HERE Somewhere In Time Clinic 00100 Future Ln Luckyville, OK 00111		33. PROVIDER'S BILLING ADDRESS GOES HERE Somewhere In Time Clinic 00100 Future Ln Luckyville, OK 00111		
SIGNATURE DATE	a. 666555444 PROVIDER NPI #	b.	a. 666555444 PROVIDER NPI #	b.	

Figure 3.14   Tying it all together on the CMS-1500 claim form.

	LOCATION 2 digit code	E/M CPT-4 code	PHYSICIAN or PROVIDER ID	BODY SYSTEM	PATIENT COMPLAINT	DIAGNOSIS ICD-9 code	TYPE OF SERVICE CPT/HCPCS	MODIFIER 2 digit code (# or alpha)
CODE						1,2, 3 Diagnosis in Box 24E & 21	74000 CT Abdomen (Box 24D)	
CODE (Tied Together)						74000 CT Abdomen in Box 24D	1,2, 3 Diagnosis in Box 24E & 21	
CODE (Tied Together)								
CODE (Tied Together)								

BOTTOM PORTION OF THE CLAIM FORM

14. DATE CONDITION OR INJURY OCCURRED?	15. HAS CONDITION OR INJURY OCCURRED BEFORE? IF SO, WHEN	16. WHAT ARE THE DATES THE PATIENT IS UNABLE TO WORK?
17. NAME OF REFERRING DOCTOR	17a. PROVIDER UPIN # 17b. PROVIDER NPI #	18. WHAT ARE THE DATES THE PATIENT WAS HOSPITALIZED?
19. THIS SPACE CAN BE USED FOR ADDITIONAL PURPOSE		20. ANY LAB WORK ORDERED OUTSIDE THE OFFICE?
21. LIST OF THE ICD-9 (DIAGNOSIS) CODES GO HERE 1. 789.0 Abdominal Pain 3. Link Diagnosis with a procedure code 2. 564.0 Constipation 4. Link Diagnosis with a procedure code		22. USE FOR MEDICAID 23. AUTHORIZATION NUMBER GOES HERE

24. A DATE SERVICE TOOK PLACE		B LOCATION	C	D CODES / MOD	E LINK DIAGNOSIS	F (CHARGES) $ AMOUNT	G	H	I	J. PROVIDER ID#
LINE 1 FROM __/__/__	TO __/__/__	11		99203	1,2		D A			66655544
LINE 2 FROM __/__/__	TO __/__/__	**11**		**74000**	**1,2**		Y S			66655544
LINE 3 FROM __/__/__	TO __/__/__						OR			
LINE 4 FROM __/__/__	TO __/__/__						U			
LINE 5 FROM __/__/__	TO __/__/__						N I			
LINE 6 FROM __/__/__	TO __/__/__						T S			

25. PROVIDER TAX ID# 000112222	26. PATIENT ACCT #	27. DOES PROVIDER ACCEPT ASSIGNMENT?	28. TOTAL $ AMT $	29. PAID AMT $	30. DUE AMT $
31. PHYSICIAN SIGNATURE GOES HERE OR NAME OF SUPPLIER SIGNATURE DATE	32. NAME OF FACILITY GOES HERE a. 666555444 PROVIDER NPI #	b.	33. PROVIDER'S BILLING ADDRESS GOES HERE a. 666555444 PROVIDER NPI #	b.	

Figure 3.15   Tying it all together on the CMS-1500 claim form.

Chapter 4

Accounts Receivable (Step 7)

Contents

BUSINESS OFFICE

ALLOWED CLAIM

All of the business transpires through the business office. This is the core of the medical clinic. The business office consists of several people who specialize in specific areas:

> *Receipt Poster*: Posts Insurance payments and patient payments

Unit I: Step 7, Introduction

Purpose

The purpose of Step 7 is to help you understand how a claim is processed by the carrier, insurer, or payer, what they look at, the steps it takes to receive reimbursement for services provided, and how that payment is posted.

Unit II: Step 7, Claim Adjudication Process

Figure 4.1 is a diagram of a claim cycle showing how a claim is handled throughout the process.

The adjudication of a claim is the process used by a carrier or insurer for a claim that has properly completed/finalized its operational process and decision has been made whether to reject, pay or deny the claim. Once a decision is made that information is then transmitted onto an explanation of benefits (EOB) where specific codes are used to identify the decision made on that particular claim.

Oklahoma Statutes Citationized, Title 36 Chapter 1 Article 12 section 1219 (36 O.S. § 1219) states that the insurer has thirty (30) calendar days from receipt of the claim to notify, in writing, the insured, enrollee or subscriber, assignee of the insured, and health care provider if there is a problem with a submitted claim. If there is a delay in processing of a claim, the written notice needs to state what part of the claim is causing a delay along with an explanation as to any

DIFFERENT TYPES OF CLAIM STATUS

45 days for a claim to be processed

1. Acknowledgment that the claim is received. Always note the date that the claim was received by the payer (claim is scanned into the payer's system and a claim number is been assigned)
2. Claim is being processed
3. Claim is pending and awaiting information for review before the claim can be adjudicated.
4. Claim has been processed, completed or finalized. (Claim has been paid, rejected, or denied)

The following pages will explain the claim cycle process including how a claim is submitted and how it is processed.

additional information or corrections needed. Failure constitutes prima facie evidence that the claim will be paid according to the terms of the policy. Upon receipt of the additional information or corrections, if it is determined that information is accurate, the insurer shall either pay or deny the claim within forty-five (45) calendar days.

Part A: Claim Cycle

Section 1: Submission of a Claim

After professional services are rendered and the charges are recorded, the claim is submitted to the carrier or insurer in one of three ways:

1. Hard copy: A paper claim form (CMS-1500) is submitted.
2. Electronic billing: The claim is submitted via electronic data interchange (EDI).
3. Direct data entry (DDE): The claim is submitted via an online system (via the Internet through a secure website).

The difference among these submission methods is the reimbursement time. When submitting a claim online, the carrier can easily and quickly determine what is being paid or denied, and if a correction is necessary, it can be fixed and resubmitted online. Electronic billing of claims usually results in claim processing within 14 days, compared to hard copy submission, which usually takes 30 to 45 days. One of the biggest problems when submitting a hard copy is that there is a tendency for the paper to get lost along the way. To avoid this problem it is a good idea to

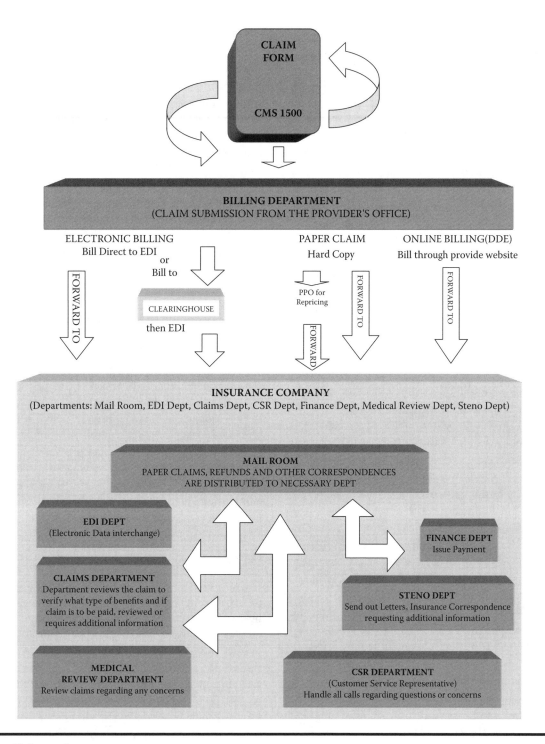

Figure 4.1   Claim cycle.

send paper claims via certified mail, which provides proof of receipt.

CMS-1500 (HCFA)

For directions on how to fill out this type of claim form, please access this website: http://nucc.org

Electronic Data Interchange (EDI)

EDI is a method for electronic transmission of data that is used to transfer business documents electronically from one computer system to another and from one organization to another (such as electronic healthcare claims and supplemental information) using a standard format.

EDI allows entities within the healthcare system to exchange medical, billing, and other information to process transactions in a more expedient and cost-effective manner. The use of EDI reduces handling and processing time and eliminates the risk of lost paper documents, therefore reducing administrative burdens, lowering operating costs, and improving overall data quality.

Setting up electronic billing requires software that is *Health Insurance Portability and Accountability Act* (HIPAA) compliant. Providers must complete a payer agreement with the organizations to which claims are being transmitted. Payer ID and carrier payor identification (CPID) numbers must be entered into the system in order to identify an insurance payer's electronic address. A list of CPID numbers can be located at http://portaltransactions.mckhboc.com. You can also google professional remittance payor connections. This will pull up websites and links to all clearing houses, not just McKesson.

HIPPA Compliance

In August of 1996 the US Congress passed a law called the Health Insurance Portability Accountability Act (HIPAA) to provide security and privacy for all parties involved in the healthcare industry. It mandates the use of certain standard transactions for electronic healthcare data exchanges, such as submission of electronic claims and remittance advice, eligibility, and enrollment information. These transactions must comply with the format requirements of each standard.

HIPAA Title I protects health insurance coverage for workers and families when they change or lose their jobs. HIPAA Title II, Subtitle F, known as the Administrative Simplification (AS) provisions, requires the establishment of national standards for electronic healthcare transactions and national identifiers for providers, health insurance plans, and employers. This is intended to help people keep their information private, though in a medical practice it is normal for providers and health insurance plans to require a waiver of HIPAA rights as a condition of service in order to transfer private information with consent from a patient.

The Administrative Simplification provisions also address the security and privacy of health data. The standards are meant to improve the efficiency and effectiveness of the nation's healthcare system by encouraging the widespread use of electronic data interchange in the US healthcare system.

Direction of Transmission: Outbound versus Inbound

Once charges are entered, the claim is batched and will sit until ready to be submitted electronically; this is done in the software by EDI submission management. Once the transmission is complete, to verify if an electronic claim was accepted or rejected, you will need access to some type of an EDI response management system that will provide a report to let you know at what level the claim was transmitted. The company I work for today uses a clearinghouse to transmit all electronic claims, so we go through three levels of transmission. The first level is the batch level as claims are batched together ready to be transmitted to the clearinghouse. The second level is the clearinghouse level. The clearinghouse then will forward them on to the third level, which is the payer level.

Files can be retrieved to print reports such as rejected claims and for reimbursement such as Electronic Remittance Advice (ERA) reports. Specific reports are identified as RS, F8, CR, or RX. There are other files, but these four reports will let you know if an electronic claim was accepted or not.

The Level II report, identified as RS, is a remittance data report. This report will tell you if the claim was transmitted to the clearinghouse without any problems. The F8 report is the claim print image report. It will provide you with the all the information from that particular claim. The CR is the payer report, which will tell you if the claim was accepted or rejected by the payer. The RX report is the remittance advice report, which will provide you with payment information or will inform you if the claim was denied and why. For more information about these reports, refer to Chapter 5, Step 8, Unit II, Part B, Section 3.

To interpret the transmission of a claim, different transaction EDI standards were developed so that computer programs can translate data to and from internal formats, eliminating the need for users to program their own computer systems to accommodate multiple formats.

What Is a Standard?

A standard is a widely recognizable method of coding data to help bring about electronic data interchange for business transactions. Standards translate the human readable data to a computer readable format in order for businesses to electronically exchange transactions. Standards prescribe the formats, character sets, and data elements used in the exchange of business documents and forms. The EDI standard defines the pieces of information that are mandatory for a particular document, the pieces that are optional, and provides the rules for the structure of the document.

Who Develops and Accredits These Standards?

The American National Standards Institute (ANSI) is a private, nonprofit membership organization that coordinates the development of voluntary national standards in the United States. The institute houses a number of voluntary standards committees that are composed of organizational members, company members, educational members, international members, individual members, as well as governmental members, including the Center for Medicare and Medicaid Services (CMS). ANSI encourages these accredited organizations to develop standards and accredits those developed under a consensus process as American National Standards (ANSs). These accredited organizations are referred to by ANSI as Accredited Standards Developers (ASDs) or Standards Development Organizations (SDOs). One such accredited organization is the Accredited Standard Committee X12 (ASC X12). The ASC X12 is the SDO that is accredited by the ANSI with helping to design national electronic standards for a wide range of administrative and business applications across many industries. The national standards that are developed by the ASC are known as the ASC X12 Standard or the X12 Standard. The electronic data interchange standard that was released by ASC X12 is referred to as the EDI X12 Standard. It is used to select the pieces of information that are mandatory for a particular document and the pieces that are optional. It sets the rules to ensure that the same data format is used on a particular document when electronically transmitting a business transaction. EDI specifications are referred to as the EDI Implementation Guide (IG). The IG is a document that explains the proper use of a standard for a specific business purpose. The IG provides instructions on how to program healthcare software according to HIPAA electronic standard requirements. Health plans, payers, billing services, and software vendors rely on these documents to comply with the electronic transaction and code set requirements of HIPAA. The IG defines the specific activities related to each transaction, lists nonmedical standardized code sets, and provides directions for how data should be moved electronically. The IG explains how information is ordered including loops, segments, description, and language.

The ASC X12 is composed of subcommittees that represent both private and public industries that are responsible for developing standards in their own areas of expertise. They are broken up into groups, one of which is known as the X12N, the insurance subcommittee. A member of the X12N is the Washington Publishing Company (WPC), which manages and distributes EDI information, primarily in the form of documentation and software tools, to healthcare organizations so they can develop, maintain, and implement EDI standards. Included in the EDI information the WPC provides to healthcare organizations is a list of codes that are external to the X12 family of standards. This list of codes provides Claim Adjustment Reason Codes (CARCs), Remittance Advice Remark Codes (RARCs), claim status codes, and more, on how an electronic claim was processed. For a complete code list, refer to Chapter 5, Step 8, Unit II, Part B, Section 5, 5a.

The purpose of the ASC X12N insurance subcommittee is to develop and maintain EDI X12 standards, standards interpretations, and guidelines as they relate to all aspects of

insurance and insurance-related business processes, including healthcare programs such as Medicare.

Within X12N healthcare are Task Groups 2 (TG2) and 4 (TG4). ASC X12N/TG2 oversees the work of multiple work groups (WGs) in developing standards and industry implementation guides. ASC X12N/TG2 assures coordination within the WGs and provides the first level of official voting in approving the standards. Each WG specializes in a particular area:

■ Work group 1 (WG1) specializes in healthcare eligibility
■ Work group 2 (WG2) specializes in healthcare claims
■ Work group 3 (WG3) specializes in claim payments
■ Work group 4 (WG4) specializes in enrollments
■ Work group 5 (WG5) specializes in claim status
■ Work group 9 (WG9) specializes in patient information
■ Work group 10 (WG10) specializes in healthcare services review
■ Work group 12 (WG12) specializes in interactive healthcare claims
■ Work group 15 (WG15) specializes in provider information
■ Work group 20 (WG20) specializes in insurance transaction acknowledgment

ASC X12N/TG4 coordinates and monitors all X12N activities relating to the development, approval, and publication of technical reports Type 3 and X12N implementation guides.

ANSI Accreditation

How Does It Work? — When a subcommittee has developed a draft standard in their area of expertise, the full ASC X12 membership reviews and approves it according to their operating policies and procedures. Anytime a standard is developed or revised it requires the consensus approval of the full ASC X12 membership. The approved standard becomes a draft standard for trial use for a reasonable trial period. After the trail period, the draft standards are submitted to ANSI to become an American National Standard (ANS).

What Are Some of the EDI X12 Standards?
The following is a list of some of the approved EDI (ANSI X12 standards) documents for EDI version 4 Release 1 (004010): Order Series, Materials Handling Series, Tax Service Series, Warehousing Series, Financial Series, Government Series, Manufacturing Series, Delivery Series, Engineering Management & Contract Series, Insurance/Health Series, Miscellaneous ANSI X12 Transaction Series, Mortgage Series, Product Services Series, Student Information Series, and Transportation.

Each release contains a list of several transaction sets. A transaction set is a single business document such as a purchase order, invoice, or healthcare claim. Each set of transaction data is identified by a message type and assigned a specific three-digit number.

There are approximately 28 message types released under the document insurance/health series (see Table 4.1). For the purpose of this book, we are only interested in the ANSI Transaction Sets in Table 4.1.

The most widely used EDI standards document currently in the healthcare industry is the 5010 version (005/010). It is the first release that was Y2K HIPAA compliant. Since I started preparing this book, a new version (5010) is being released.

The healthcare industry recognized the benefits of EDI, which brought about increased usage over the past decade. Healthcare plans were and still are encouraging healthcare providers to move toward electronic transmission of claims. One of the main benefits of EDI is that it eliminates the submission of paper claims, therefore eliminating paperwork and letting the office staff accomplish more in less time. The elimination of paper claims also saves the costs associated with postage and the purchase of claim forms.

EDI reduces errors, so claims are processed more accurately and consistently. Beyond saving time and money, electronic claims submission ensures faster payment. This submission method also provides electronic reports for better business management. One report in particular, the X12N 997 Functional Acknowledgment, confirms that your claim was received. The Batch Processing Report and the MCS Pre-pass Error Report (Medicare Part B only) summarize the claim information that was submitted electronically. Also available is the X12N 835 daily ERA, which provides payment information including check numbers, check dates, and patient control numbers. Support Personnel-EDI services is a department dedicated to supporting your electronic claim submitters.

Example of EDI X12 File

ANSI ASC X12N 837(P) Version /Release 005010, http://www.cms.gov/electronicbillingEDItrans/5010-D.O.

Direct Data Entry (DDE)

Copying or importing data from a source, such as a claim form, and entering that information into the computer software allows you direct online access to Medicare and Medicaid.

Vendors, such as Ivans, Inc., can provide a direct connection to the DDE system through a high-speed Internet connection via a secure and leased line for a monthly fee. As a provider, you have access to the claims you submit including claim entry, eligibility verification (for the Part A common working file or CWF), error correction, claim status inquiry, remittance advice, claims adjustment, precertification or referral, claim submission, and confirmation.

Table 4.1 Insurance/Health Series

ANSI Transaction 3-Digit Number	Message Type	ANSI Transaction 3-Digit Number	Message Type
100	Insurance plan description	276	Healthcare claim status report
112	Property damage report	277	Healthcare claim status notification
148	Report of injury, illness, or incident	278	
186	Insurance underwriting requirement reporting	288	
		362	
252			
255		835	Healthcare claim payment/advice
267		837 (P)	Professional healthcare claim
268		837 (I)	Institutional healthcare claim
270	Eligibility, coverage or benefit inquiry	837 (D)	Dental
271	Eligibility, coverage or benefit Info		
272		997	Acknowledgment
273			
274			
275			

Section 2: Operational Process within Carrier or Insurer Departments

After a submitted claim is received, the next step is to understand how a claim is processed.

Depending on the way the claim is submitted and how that particular carrier or insurer is set up will determine how a claim is edited. The systems of some carriers and insurers are set up to electronically edit claims, but other carriers and insurers are set up to have claims manually edited by a claims examiner. Claims that are electronically submitted to Medicare are edited electronically. In some cases, such as in Oklahoma, a vendor will scan paper claims into their system. For most insurers, a hard copy of a claim is received and scanned into the system, assigned a claim number, then viewed and edited by a claims examiner. As a claims examiner, it was my job to manually edit the claim and determine if claim was to be rejected, paid, or denied. To facilitate access, a unique claim number is assigned to each claim.

Insurance companies are organized into different departments with each department responsible for a specific task or function. These may include the following departments.

Mail Room

All mail is handled by mail clerks who are responsible for making sure that paper claims and correspondence are distributed to the appropriate department.

Claims Department

In this department, claims are edited by a claim examiner who reviews the claim to decide an appropriate course of action. To accomplish this, the examiner:

- Checks to see if the patient is covered under the policy and if the coverage is still effective. If the claim is for a child, is the child covered under the family plan? If the claimant is over 18, is he or she a full-time student?
- Checks the policy to see if the service rendered is a covered service.
- Determines if the claim is a UB or CMS-1500? Does the policy cover inpatient and/or outpatient hospital services?
- Determines if there are any restrictions such as preexisting conditions, riders, or exclusions, such as a waiting period.
- Determines if any state mandates are involved.
- Review the accuracy of the claim codes (does the diagnosis match the procedure).
- Determines if any frequency (number of similar types of service in a specific time period) or dollar limits have been exceeded.
- Forwards the claim to a customer service representative (CSR) if there is a question to be asked, or the Financial, Steno, or Medical Review department.

CSR Department

This department is responsible for answering questions from insured individuals, their dependents, and providers. This service is usually provided via the telephone or written correspondence, but some companies use electronic methods such as e-mail.

EDI Department (IT/Technical Support)

This department handles the electronic claims and is responsible for the accuracy of the electronic processing methods and HIPAA compliance requirements.

Medical Review Department

This department is responsible for reviewing any questions regarding preexisting conditions, or any appeals (medical necessity, redetermination).

Steno Department

This department handles letters that need to be mailed to both the insured and/or the provider's office. In order for a claim to be processed for payment it may be necessary for a letter to be sent regarding a specific question.

Formatted letters are also set up that may consist of a list with several different questions. For example, the claim form in box 10 asks if the patient's condition is related to employment, auto, or other and the box "other" is marked so a letter will be sent out with a question asking how the injury, illness or condition happened? The payer will want to know if it was due to an auto, work, or other type of accident. Another example is when the claim is for an insured's dependent child. The payer may need to know if the patient's child, who is 21 years of age, is a full-time student, because the policy states dependent children will be covered up to age 21 only if enrolled in school as a full-time student.

Financial Department

This department is responsible for accounts receivable (payments from the insurer). This department is also responsible for issuing reimbursement for services provided to clients by physicians or a facility and for refund requests or offsets.

Figure 4.2 is a diagram of the inner departments of an insurance company. In Step 7 we are only concentrating on claims that were allowed (processed) as clean claims.

Section 3: Clean Claim

A clean claim is a claim that was processed, services were allowed, and no errors were found.

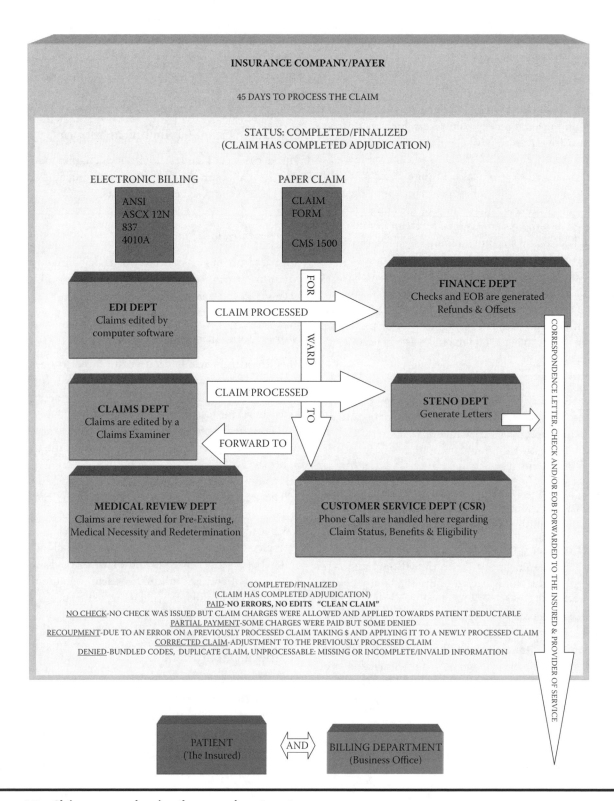

Figure 4.2 Claim process showing the payer departments.

For a step-by-step guide and an example of how a clean claim is posted, refer to Unit III, Part A, Section 2.

In Unit II we went over the claim cycle. In Unit III we will discuss how reimbursement is determined and how payment is applied.

Part B: Third-Party Reimbursement

Section 1: Terms: What Does Third-Party Reimbursement Mean?

Reimbursement

Reimbursement refers to the compensation or receiving of payment by a third-party payer (TPP) for healthcare services provided to the first party, the insured (see Figure 4.3).

Third-Party Payer

A third-party payer (TPP) is a health insurance company or health agency (administrators). The first party is the patient or insured; the second party is the individual or entity that provided the service (physician, clinic, hospital); the third party is the insurer. Third-party reimbursement is the payment received from the insurance company or health agency that pays the second party (provider) for the care or service that was provided to the first party, the patient (see Figure 4.4).

Third-Party Administrators

Third-party administrators (TPAs) are the insurance companies or other business organizations that have contracted with the government or with organizations to provide claim processing services. For Medicare, they are identified as Medicare administrative contractors (MAC).

In Oklahoma, claims processing responsibility it falls under Jurisdiction 4 (see Figure 4.5). For J4 the MAC for Part A Intermediary and Part B the carrier is TrailBlazer Health Enterprises, LLC (http://www.trailblazerhealth.com). Trailblazer Health handles claims for patients with Medicare Part B, but for medical supplies and durable medical equipment and prosthetic, orthotics, and supplies (DMEPOS), claim services are handled by Cigna Government Services under Jurisdiction C or Region C (DMERC, or durable medical equipment regional carrier) (http://www.cignagovernment.com).

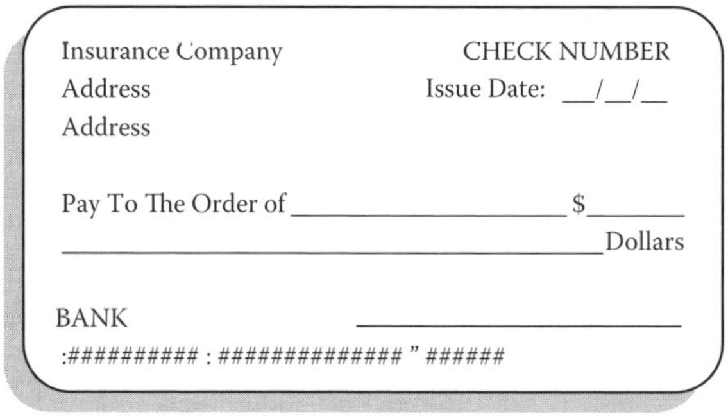

Insurance Company — CHECK NUMBER
Address — Issue Date: __/__/__
Address

Pay To The Order of ____________________ $_______
____ Dollars

BANK ____________________
:########## : ############## " ######

Figure 4.3 Reimbursement check.

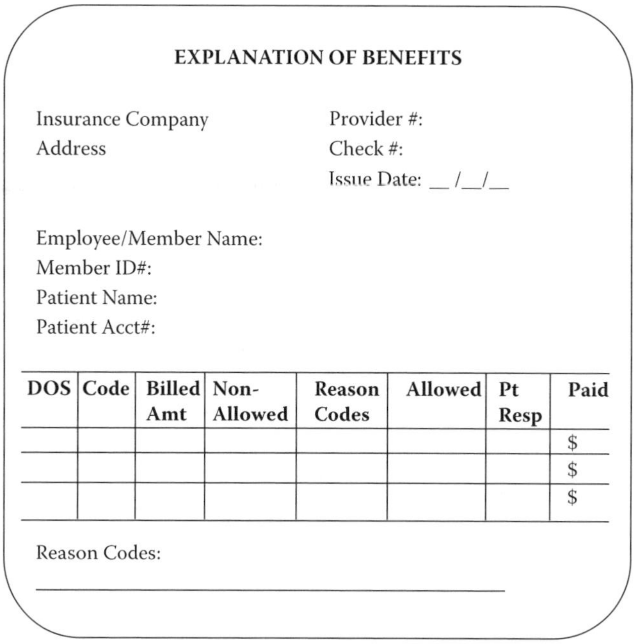

EXPLANATION OF BENEFITS

Insurance Company — Provider #:
Address — Check #:
Issue Date: __/__/__

Employee/Member Name:
Member ID#:
Patient Name:
Patient Acct#:

DOS	Code	Billed Amt	Non-Allowed	Reason Codes	Allowed	Pt Resp	Paid
							$
							$
							$

Reason Codes:
____

Figure 4.4 Explanation of Benefits.

Fiscal Intermediaries and Carriers

Some carriers are contracted by Medicare to pay claims for Medicare professional services or Medicare Part B (medical) claims for Medicare beneficiaries and providers. They are referred to as Medicare administrative contractors (MACs).

A fiscal intermediary (FI) is contracted by Medicare to pay claims for Medicare institutional services or Medicare Part A (hospital) claims for Medicare beneficiaries and providers.

Section 2: Factors That Determine Payment

Different types of health insurance:

- Indemnity plans (traditional fee-for-service plans)
- Government healthcare programs (Medicare, Medicaid)
- Managed care organizations (health maintenance organizations [HMOs], preferred provider organizations [PPOs], exclusive provider organization [EPOs])

When signing any contract with any insurance company, it is the responsibility of each person to be aware of the terms of the policy, know what is covered, and know the expenses for which they are responsible.

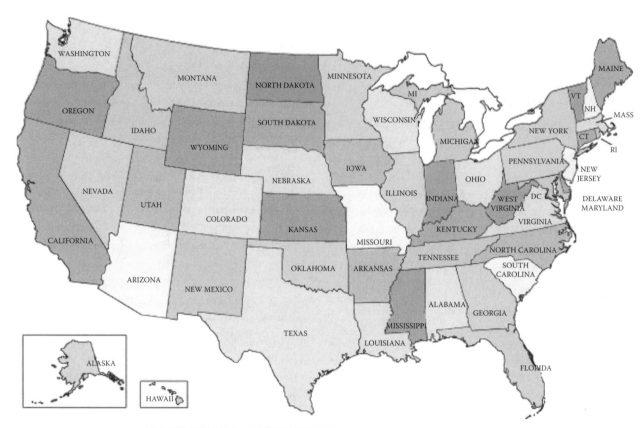

MEDICARE'S A/B MAC JURISDICTIONS

JURISDICTION #1: American Samoa, California, Guam, Hawaii, Nevada and Northern Mariana Islands
JURISDICTION #2: Alaska, Idaho, Oregon and Washington
JURISDICTION #3: Arizona, Montana, North Dakota, South Dakota, Utah and Wyoming
JURISDICTION#4: Colorado, New Mexico, Oklahoma and Texas (MAC is Trail Blazer Health Enterprises, LLC)
JURISDICTION #5: Iowa, Kansas, Missouri and Nebraska
JURISDICTION #6: Illinois, Minnesota and Wisconsin
JURISDICTION #7: Arkansas, Louisiana and Mississippi
JURISDICTION #8: Indiana and Michigan
JURISDICTION #9: Florida, Puerto Rico and U.S. Virgin Islands
JURISDICTION #10: Alabama, Georgia and Tennessee
JURISDICTION #11: North Carolina, South Carolina, Virginia and West Virginia
JURISDICTION #12: Delaware, District of Columbia, Maryland, New Jersey and Pennsylvania
JURISDICTION #13: Connecticut and New York
JURISDICTION #14: Maine, Massachusetts, New Hampshire, Rhode Island and Vermont
JURISDICTION #15: Kentucky and Ohio

MEDICARE'S DME MAC JURISDICTIONS

JURISDICTION A: Connecticut, Delaware, District of Columbia, Maine, Maryland, Massachusetts, New Hampshire,
     New Jersey, New York, Pennsylvania, Rhode Island and Vermont
JURISDICTION B: Illinois, Indiana, Kentucky, Michigan, Minnesota, Ohio and Wisconsin
JURISDICTION C: Alabama, Arkansas, Colorado, Florida, Georgia, Louisiana, Mississippi, New Mexico, North Carolina,
South Carolina, Oklahoma, Puerto Rico, Tennessee, Texas, U.S. Virgin Islands, Virginia and West Virginia
JURISDICTION D: Alaska, American Samoa, Arizona, California, Guam, Hawaii, Idaho, Iowa, Kansas, Missouri,
     Montana , Nebraska, Nevada, North Dakota, South Dakota, Northern Mariana Islands, Oregon,
     Utah, Washington and Wyoming

Figure 4.5   Medicare jurisdictions.

The following factors help determine if the services provided are payable under the plan.

Coverage and Benefits

A verification of benefits needs to be obtained prior to services being rendered to indicate who is responsible for payment, either the insurance company or the patient. Call to check if the policy covers the following:

- Primary and secondary payers: Do they coordinate benefits?
- Eligibility at the time of service: Effective date
- Age limitation
- Physician visits, preventative, screenings and hospital (inpatient, outpatient, ER)
- Diagnostic
- Surgery, basic coverage (acute care)
- Major medical (long-term care)
- Durable medical equipment, prosthetic orthotic and supplies (DMEPOS)
- Exclusions (non-covered)
- Rider in the policy for pre-existing conditions, waivers, or grace period
- Facility in-network

Plan Type Requirements: Indemnity versus Managed Care

Once coverage and benefits have been verified, there are certain requirements that must be met before services or procedure can be provided.

- Office Visit: Require a referral, or copayment
- Surgery: Pre-certification or authorization, documentation (clinical), pre-testing (lab work, medical clearance, or cardiac clearance needed), conservative treatment, procedure medically necessary or considered as cosmetic
- Diagnostic: Written orders from the ordering physician, or require authorization
- DMEPOS: Written order and/or documentation such as a letter or certificate of medical necessity, or require authorization

In-Network versus Out-of-Network

Payment is based on whether or not the provider is contracted (in-network or out-of-network provider) and if the provider has the appropriate credentials. In-network or out-of-network benefit levels can be 70%, 80%, 90%, or 100%. The EOB will indicate the payment and in-network payments are usually higher. Out-of-network claims will be paid to the provider if the member has assigned benefits to that provider, but the policyholder/member will pay more out of pocket.

For example, if a doctor who is not contracted with an HMO plan the claim will be paid as POS (point of service), paying at 50% and the patient would be responsible for a $300 deductible. If that same provider was an in-network provider, the patient would only have a $12 copay.

This will not always be the case, some insurers will not process the claim and it can be denied stating provider was not contracted and patient is responsible.

Always check with the patient's plan to see if they will process the claim if the doctor's office bills for the charges.

Assignment of Benefits

An assignment of benefits is signed by the patient, usually when the registration form is completed, in which the patient agrees to have the payer send the benefit payment directly to the healthcare provider.

Out-of-Pocket Expenses

These expenses include, but are not limited to, premium, deductible, copayment, and coinsurance.

Liability: Who Is Responsible for the Bill?

Is the patient's condition or injury due to an accident? If so, workers compensation insurance may be responsible, or automobile, homeowners, church, retail, or other insurance may have some liability. If billing health insurance, will they subrogate by coordination of benefits?

Section 3: Healthcare Methods of Reimbursement

How is reimbursement determined? Providers are usually reimbursed via three different methods: fee-for-service (discounted FFS), capitation, or by episode of care.

A *fee* is a set amount charged by the healthcare provider (the second party) for services rendered to a patient/insured (the first party). The health insurance company (third party) will reimburse that provider for each fee charged for a covered service.

The *allowable fee* represents the average or maximum amount the third-party payer will reimburse providers for the service.

A *fee schedule* is list of fees that the third-party payer allows in payment for all healthcare services.

Fee-for-Service (FFS)

A fee is charged for a service and that fee can be paid as follows:

- *Self-pay:* The patient pays the provider once service has been provided and files the claim him- or herself.
- *Traditional FFS retrospective payment system:* The third-party payer pays the provider after a service has been rendered. The provider is reimbursed for each service that is provided.
- *Discounted FFS* is TPP reduced fee negotiated for members or insureds. The two common types of discounted FFS payment methods are usual, customary, and reasonable (UCR), for which the insurance company determines the fee, and resource-based relative value scale (RBRVS), which are developed and maintained by the Center for Medicare and Medicaid Services (CMS). CMS assigns a dollar amount for each Current Procedural Terminology [CPT] code by RBRVS. RBRVSs were developed to determine allowable fees for each service provided, adjusted for the provider's geographic location.

Capitation

Capitation is a reimbursement method in which the carrier reimburses the provider a fixed amount per person for a period, usually per month. The per member, per month (PMPM) amount is the amount of money paid each month for each individual enrolled in the health insurance plan. Capitation is a characteristic of HMOs.

Episode of Care

Episode of care is a reimbursement method in which providers receive one lump sum for all of the services provided that are related to a condition or disease.

Surgical Episode of Care: This is what is referred to as the "Global Surgical Package," which means that follow-up care is included in the surgical package that is tied to a service or procedure that was performed.

Example: OB GYN. Procedure and after care are included.

Section 4: Medicare Payment Systems

Physician (Professional) Method of Reimbursement

Pricing and Payment Policy Indicators (Updated Quarterly): The Medicare Physician Fee Schedule provides the allowed fee for services, each of which has three components that are based on relative value units (RVU) for work, practice expense (PE), and malpractice (MP).

The physician work RVU reflects the time, skills, and effort furnished as part of the service that was provided.

The practice expense RVU reflects the overhead expenses incurred based on the physician's rent, staff, supplies, and equipment necessary to provide the service. There are two types of PE RVUs: facility (PE-f), which represents hospital, skilled nursing facility (SNF), or ambulatory surgery center (ASC) expenses, and nonfacility (PE-nf), which include physician office, patient home, or any other noninstitutional facility expenses.

The malpractice RVU reflects the risk or liability associated with providing the service.

The conversion factor (CF) is a national uniform dollar conversion factor for the services that converts the relative values into payment amounts.

Geographical Practice Cost Indexes (GPCIs) reflect the relative costs for each of the units for a specific geographic area in comparison with the national average.

How does Medicare determine reimbursement for multiple (indicated by a 51 modifier) procedures or bilateral (indicated by a 50 modifier) anatomical sites if performed by a physician on the same patient at the same session on the same day? How does Medicare determine reimbursement on services provided by an assistant surgeon (indicated by a 80 modifier), a physician assistant (indicated by an AS modifier), co-surgeon (indicated by a 62 modifier), or team surgeon (indicated by a 66 modifier)? For answers, the Medicare Physician Fee Schedule Database (MPFSDB) provides pricing information and payment policy indicators under the Physician Fee Schedule (PFS) that help determine the Medicare allowable fee and whether payment is allowed. The MPFSDB also helps determine if the services require payment adjustments or other specific adjustments to the Healthcare Common Procedure Coding System or Current Procedural Terminology (HCPCS/CPT) codes.

The payment policy indicator provides procedure code status indicators that show whether the code is listed in the fee schedule, or it's separately payable, and if it's a covered service. Code indicators are as follows: A (Active Code: if covered, paid separately under PFS); B (Bundled code: not paid separately, payment is bundled); C (carrier will determine by the Relative Value Unit (RVU), which is a formula regulated by Medicare to determine reimbursement for services provided by a physician); Exc (Excluded Code: payment made on reasonable charge basis); NV1 (Nonvalid: providers are to use other codes); NV2 (Nonvalid: no longer appear in MPFS); Non (Noncovered: service not covered by Medicare); Inj (Injections).

Global Period (GP) or follow-up days refers to services that are associated with an operative procedure and are considered integral parts of that procedure. An indicator "0" under GP indicates there are no days for follow-up for that particular procedure; "10" indicates there are ten days for a follow-up period for that particular procedure; "60" indicates sixty days for a follow-up period for that particular procedure; "90" indicates ninety days for a follow-up period for that particular procedure.

Medically Unlikely Edits (MUE) indicates the maximum number of units allowed for that service.

Physician Supervision (Suprv) indicates the level of supervision required for a diagnostic test to be performed: general supervision, direct supervision, personal supervision of a physician. They are indicated by "01," "02," or "03," respectively. If the indicator is "04" or "05," the physician supervision policy will not apply if the procedure is furnished by a psychologist, audiologist, or physical therapy specialist. If the indicator is "06," the procedure must be performed by a physician or physical therapist who is certified by the American Board of Electrophysiologic Clinical Specialists under state law. If the indicator is "09," it does not apply. For a complete listing please refer to the NCCI Edits Manual.

Example: Procedure Code 20610

Relative Value Units						
Work	MP	PE-nf	PE-f	TL-nf	TL-f	GP
0.79	0.12	1.14	0.55	2.05	1.46	0
Modifiers						
50	51	62	66	80,82	Suprv	Status
1	4	NPD	NPD	NPD	09	A

To locate the fee schedule, pricing information, and payment policy indicators, go to the TrailBlazer Health website (http://www.trailblazerhealth.com). For information on the MPFSDB, go to the CMS website (http://cms.gov). All of this information is provided in the CCI Edits manual.

National Correct Coding Initiatives (NCCI) or CCI edits were developed by CMS to prevent inappropriate payment of services that should not be billed by the same physician for the same patient on same date of service. NCCI edits are used by Medicare carriers for adjudicating claims and are also utilized by many commercial payers and Medicaid agencies.

Medically Unlikely Edits (MUE) are edits that were established by CMS and developed and maintained by the NCCI contractor to prevent providers of service from billing an excessive number of units on a specific service or procedure.

I have put together a basic outline of how Medicare reimburses a physician who provides services to Medicare Part B beneficiaries. In this step, my focus is to point out key factors necessary to understand Medicare's method of reimbursement for services provided by a physician.

Benefits covered under Medicare Part B: To understand Medicare's policy regarding coverage, I always turn to the Local Coverage Determination (LCD, http://www.trailblazerhealth.com). The LCD and National Coverage Determination (NCD, http://cms.gov) will give you guidelines and limitations on services and procedures.

Medicare Part B is a fee-for-service reimbursement plan based on a fee schedule. Each physician's service corresponds to a CPT or HCPCS code, and each code is assigned an RVU.

Hospital Method of Reimbursement

The Prospective Payment System (PPS) was set up to reimburse hospitals for services provided for outpatient/inpatient healthcare for which a pre-determined rate is set for treatment of a specific illness.

■ Outpatient Prospective Payment System (OPPS) is a payment system for Medicare Part B services that were provided on an outpatient basis in a hospital.
■ Inpatient Prospective Payment System (IPPS) is a payment system for Medicare Part A services that were provided for hospital services based on two ways:
  – Case Rate (DRG)—Diagnostic Related Group: Patients are classified by the type of care they were given and are assigned a "grouped" program that is based on the primary and secondary diagnosis, primary and secondary procedure, age, sex, and length of hospitalization.
  – Per Diem: Third-party payers pay for inpatient services on a per diem (per day) basis, with separate rates for medical and surgical cases (maximum amount allowed per day).

Skilled Nursing Facility Consolidated Billing: When a patient is a resident of a skilled nursing facility (SNF), the SNF is responsible for overseeing and coordinating the patient's entire package of care during his or her course of a covered Part A stay, which will also include any outside suppliers. The SNF is responsible for the billing of all claims to Medicare with the exception of those excluded services not subject to consolidated billing (CB). Services that are furnished to a SNF resident that are excluded are physician's services and certain diagnostic tests that include both a professional component and a technical component. Charges that represent the physician's interpretation are not subject to CB and are billed separately to the Part B MAC, but charges that represent the technical component are subject to CB. For more information, refer to the Skilled Nursing Facility Manual at the Part B MAC website for Oklahoma (http://www.trailblazerhealth.com).

Section 5: Explanation of Benefits

An EOB (Figure 4.6) is a form that the insurer/payer uses to notify the insured and the provider of services of the action has been taken on a claim. It explains what services and procedures are allowed, what they (the insurer) paid, and what, if anything, is owed. Refer to the example of an EOB (top portion, Figure 4.6), locate in bold lettering where it

SEPARATE EXAMPLES OF AN EOB AND RA

EXPLANATION OF BENEFITS

(A Statement of what has been done with member's claim and how it was allowed)

NAME OF INSURANCE CARRIER
ADDRESS CITY STATE ZIP

Employee/Member Name   Provider #
Member ID#/HIC #   Date
Patient Name   (Date when check was issued)

DATE OF SERVICE FROM TO	CPT CODE	BILLED AMT	NON-ALLOWED Or INELIGIBLE	MESSAGE CODE or REASON CODE	PROV DISC or CONT W/O	ALLOWED AMT (WHAT WAS APPROVED)	DEDUCT	COINS	COPAY	PLAN COV %	AMT PAID TO PROV	PATIENT LIABILITY (PT RESP)
		$	$		$	$	$	$	$		$	$
		$	$		$	$	$	$	$		$	$
		$	$		$	$	$	$	$		$	$
		$	$		$	$	$	$	$		$	$
		$	$		$	$	$	$	$		$	$
TOTAL		$	$		$	$	$	$	$		$	$
										NET	$	

MEDICARE PART B   **REMITTANCE ADVICE**

Provider#:
Check/EFT (Electronic Fund Transfer) #:   Issue Date: 00/00/2009

Name: HIC   ACCT (Claim/Ticket #)   ICN (Identifies the claim with the insurance carrier)

PROV #	DOS	POS	NOS	CPT	MOD	BILLED $	ALLOW	DEDUCT	COINS	GRP/RC	AMT	PAID PROV $
	051408	11	1	99213		74.00	0.00	0.00	0.00	CO-45	74.00	24.25
											NET	24.25

Name: HIC   ACCT (Claim/Ticket #)   ICN (Identifies the claim with the insurance carrier)

PROV #	DOS	POS	NOS	CPT	MOD	BILLED $	ALLOW	DEDUCT	COINS	GRP/RC	AMT	PAID PROV $
	051408	11	1	99213		74.00	0.00	0.00	0.00	CO-97	74.00	0.00
				REM: M144								
											NET	0.00

Name: HIC   ACCT (Claim/Ticket #)   ICN (Identifies the claim with the insurance carrier)

PROV #	DOS	POS	NOS	CPT	MOD	BILLED $	ALLOW	DEDUCT	COINS	GRP/RC	AMT	PAID PROV $
	051408	11	1	99213		74.00	0.00	0.00	0.00	CO-109	74.00	0.00
				REM: M101								
											NET	0.00

Message Codes: Group/CARC/RARC
Ex: CO/ 97/M101

Figure 4.6   Examples of an EOB and an RA.

states "Exclusions." This means that services were not allowed or patient was not eligible at the time that services were rendered. Message or Reason codes will indicate why services were excluded. The bold lettering showing "Considered Benefits" indicates the services that were allowed, and how much and what the patient's/insured's out-of-pocket (OOP) expenses are.

I work for a large group clinic where 250 patients can be seen in one day, which makes for a lot of claims. Not all are Medicare patients, but for those patients covered under Medicare Part B, we file all their claims electronically. Doctors are then reimbursed based on the FFS payment method. The Medicare reimbursement check comes in the mail, but to know for whom and where net payment needs to be posted to we print the ERA report (see Figure 4.6). Once the ERA is run and printed, the total amount of the check then gets distributed along with several claims on several different patients. In order to automatically post each net payment to each claim, and so we do not have to manually perform this task, we have to plug in the check number and issue date of the check. Electronic billing makes it much easier to process and bill for a claim and reimbursement time is much faster as well. Reimbursement can also be set up using electronic funds transfer (EFT).

The EOB must contain the member/insured name, patient name, date of birth (DOB), accident detail information, codes (*International Classification of Diseases, 9th Revision* [ICD-9], HCPCS, CPT-4), billing information, provider information, and identification numbers of the insured as well as the provider.

Provider Identification (Provider of Services)

For providers who are contracted with Medicare, in order to know who provided what service to a patient, each provider has their own National Provider Identifier (NPI) number as well as a group NPI if billing within a group. This allows Medicare to know who provided what service to a patient. The following is a list of the different kinds of ID numbers a provider is required to have:

- National Provider Identifier (NPI)
- Provider Transaction Access Number (PTAN)
- Tax Identification Number (TIN)
- National Supplier ID number in order to provide durable medical equipment (DME)

Section 6: Remittance Advice (RA)

Instead of actually receiving a separate EOB for each Medicare beneficiary, a doctor's office or clinic will receive a Remittance Advice report (Figure 4.6). It states the same thing as an EOB, but it provides a list of several claims for different dates of service for several patients. The RA is attached to a check, or in some cases will need to be printed through the Medicare Remit Easy Print (MREP) software. The RA is used to post payments and contractual adjustments to claims. It provides a list of patient names (beneficiaries) and claim numbers (patient accounts) with sets of codes that are used to show how benefits were covered and paid.

There are two types of RAs, the Standard Paper Remittance (SPR) and the ERA. Both contain the same information. The SPR is in paper format, is attached to the check, and is received in the mail. The ERA is in an electronic format and is downloaded from the MREP and printed.

The Electronic Remittance Advice is identified under the EDI Transaction set ANSI ASC x12N 835 Healthcare Payment/Advice. Claims that are electronically filed are identified under ANSI ASC x12N 837 (see more details in Unit II, Claim Cycle).

The MREP software is required to convert an ANSI ERA 835 file into a readable SPR. You can download this software from the website of the Medicare MAC for the state of Oklahoma, which is TrailBlazer Health Enterprises, LLC.

ANSI Code List

In order to understand how the claim was processed, providers use the RA to post payment and review claim adjustments. The RA contains detailed and specific claim decision information. An adjustment may be made for any number of reasons. These reasons are identified on the RA through standardized code sets that include three sets of codes, the Payment Adjustment Group codes, Claim Adjustment Reason Codes (CARCs), and Remittance Advice Remark Codes (RARCs). The American National Standards Institute (ANSI) developed these codes (refer to Unit II, Part A, Section 1, 1b for more details).

Since ANSI Reason Codes were developed for all health payers, only a few are Medicare specific, so CMS developed and maintains Medicare-specific supplemental message codes called Remark Codes. A standard set of numeric or alphabetic codes were developed and approved by ANSI Insurance Subcommittee, ANSI ASC X12N. The code sets are covered in the following paragraphs.

Payment Adjustment Group Codes: These codes point out who the financially responsible party is or indicate the category in which a payment adjustment is needed on a particular claim. Group codes will always be assigned with a CARC. Group codes are PR (patient responsibility), CO (contractual obligation), OA (other adjustment), and CR (correction on a previously processed claim).

Claim Adjustment Reason Codes (CARC): These codes provide financial information about a decision made on a claim.

Remittance Advice Remark Codes (RARC): These codes, in conjunction with CARCs, help explain an adjustment or help indicate if appeal rights apply. There are some RARCs that are used to relay informational messages even when there is not an adjustment. Any RARC may be reported at the service-line level or the claim level on any ERA or SPR.

A list of these codes can be located at the Washington Publishing Company website: http://www.wpc-edi.com/codes.

Part C: Managing the Money

Payment posting is handled by the receipt poster. Receipt posting is basically the receiving and posting of a payment, from the patient, the patient's health insurance company, or another third-party payer (other liability MVA (motor vehicle accident), workers compensation [WC]).

The receipt poster is responsible for making sure that all payments, contractual obligations, late fees, interest, automatic adjustments (CO-54), and offsets (recoupments) are posted for each and every claim. The poster is also responsible for making sure that a balance due on any service is transferred to the patient's responsibility or that any secondary coverage is billed (if applicable).

For services that are denied, the poster will leave the claim as pending and change the status to reflect that it has been sent to collections.

Reviewing EOBs: It is important to make sure the claim was processed correctly. It may have been processed as an out-of-network claim when the provider of service was actually in the network, and therefore paid at a lower rate. Also, in working with workers compensation coverage, it has been my experience that they do what is called *double dipping*. They approve what is allowed and then they take an additional discount.

In Centricity medical practice software, in order for the billing specialist to work with services that were rejected or denied, they work off the collection module under status that identified by collection.

Section 1: Mail: Separating the Mail

As a receipt poster, the concern is with checks and EOBs. The receipt poster is responsible for separating personal checks from insurance checks, and must make sure the insurance check matches with the check number and issue date of the correct EOB.

- Payment Types:
  - Insurance: Payment may be issued in one of three ways: direct deposit, electronic funds transfer (EFT), or check.
  - Personal: Payment may be issued in one of three ways: personal check, money order, or credit Card.
- Explanation of Benefits (EOBs): EOBs can be two types: the SPR (Standard Paper Remittance) attached to a check, or the ERA (Electronic Remittance Advice). A Remittance Advice will show payment in one of three ways, with a check (net payment) or no check, services were allowed but no payment was received because the fee was applied toward patient out-of-pocket (OOP) expenses, or an overpayment was issued in error on some previously processed claim. So instead of requesting a refund, the money is recouped and applied to the current claim.

EOBs

EOBs are of two types: the SPR, or Standard Paper Remittance (attached to a check), and the ERA, or Electronic Remittance Advice. The difference between the two is that a standard paper remittance will be delivered through the mail whereas an electronic remittance is electronically transmitted.

- *Net payment* is the amount paid to the provider by the insurance company.
- *No-Check* is when services were allowed and applied toward the patient deductible or services were rejected or denied.
- *Partial payment* occurs when only a portion of the provided services were allowed.
- *Offset (recoupment)* occurs when an overpayment was previously paid on a claim in error that will need to be adjusted. Once the claim is adjusted, it will then need to be corrected and reprocessed. You will need to find out why the original payment is being recouped in order to reprocess the claim correctly.

Section 2: Receipt Posting

When a payment is made through direct deposit by Electronic Fund Transmission (EFT), you will not receive a physical check; however, it is necessary to make sure that once a check has been deposited into the bank that you run off an Electronic Remittance Advice (ERA) in order to post all payments to each claim and to work those claims that were denied.

- Payment Types:
  - Insurance Payment: Payment issued by primary payer, secondary payer, or tertiary payer.
  - Personal Payment: Check, money order, or credit card payment from the patient.
- Codes of Concern: Seven payment adjustment Group Codes for Use on an RA. Group codes must always be used in conjunction with a Claim Adjustment Reason Code (CARC).
  - Net: The amount payable on the claim.
  - CO (Contractual Obligation): A contracted agreement made between the provider and Medicare. Provider is not permitted to bill the beneficiary for that particular amount.
  - PR (Patient Responsibility): Used if services that were provided are a non-covered benefit and payment is the beneficiary's responsibility.
  - CR (Correction and Reversal): Used for correcting a prior claim. A change was made to the previously processed claim.
  - OA (Other Adjustment): Used when no other Group Code applies on that particular claim.
  - FB (Forwarding Balance): Medicare is forewarning you that this is the amount that has been paid on a previously processed claim and is getting ready to be withheld.
  - WO (Withholding): Indicates funds that have been withheld from the net payment. This is the result of an overpayment that has been reversed

on a previously processed claim (both pertain to Offsets [Recoupment]).

■ Adjustment Types: Receipt poster should be concerned about these.
  – Contractual Write Off (Group Code: CO): Adjust off
  – Other Adjustment (Group Code: OA): Automatically adjust off. An example would be OA-54 (Group Code OA & CARC #54).

Payment Types

Insurance Payment

■ Types of payers: Primary payer, secondary payer or supplemental (Medigap), or tertiary payer
■ Adjustment types: Contractual write off (Group Code: CO), offsets/recoupment (Code FB or WO on Medicare, and automatic adjustment that is manually set up.

Personal Payment

■ Patient received a statement: check, money order or credit card
■ Attorney's office for medical records
■ Family medical leave of absence (FMLA)

Section 3: Reports

At the end of the day once you have completed posting insurance and personal payments, two reports need to be completed and turned in; they are the following:

■ Deposit Report
  – A deposit report will list all your deposits for that day, per claim, per patient's account, by either insurance or personal payment. Make sure to balance out the deposit slip with the deposit report.
  – Attach a deposit slip, and be sure to endorse the back of the checks.
■ Daily Business
  – At the end of the day run this report. It will show everything you have posted for that day, including payments and any adjustments you have made.

We will get into more details in Chapter 5, Step 8, regarding claim denials, but for the purpose of this chapter, let's say that services that were provided and submitted on the CMS-1500 (professional fees) have been determined by the insurance policy to be a covered benefit. The provider who rendered the service is in-network and Box 27 is

marked yes (accept assignment), so payment will be issued to the provider.

Unit III: Step 7, Step-by-Step Guide
Part A: Receipt Posting
Section 1: Data Entry: Medical Software
How to Apply Payment

When posting a payment, there are two types, an insurance payment or personal payment.

Once a claim has been processed, service was allowed and applied toward patient Out-of-Pocket expenses three ways: Deductible, Co-pay or Coinsurance.

Posting the Explanation of Benefits (EOB) or Remittance Advice (RA): there are six steps for posting an insurance payment.

From the Remittance Advice (Figure 4.7a), you want to transfer the net payment into the medical software. In order to do that, follow the next six steps:

Step 1: In the medical software, pull up the "Main Menu" (Figure 4.7b), then select the "Receipts" button.
Step 2: Pull up the claim or ticket # off the EOB or RA. It will be listed as the account number. Select the box under Step 7 and double click to get to your patient in order to pull up his or her claims (Figure 4.8).
Step 3: Select Type of Payment, Insurance or Personal. In this case you will select Insurance (x).
Step 4: Method of Payment. You will select "Check." Payment was issued by a check.
Step 5: Enter the check number and the issue date from the check.
Step 6. Post your payment under the Payment Column, select Payment type "Insurance," post the contractual writeoff under the Disallow/Adj (adjustment) Column, select under the Disallow/Adj Type "Contractual w/o (write off)," and under coins/copay (patients OOP expenses) post patient responsibility and if no secondary coverage, then transfer over to Patient responsibility.

Posting of a personal payment from a check for $25.00 was determined by the patient responsibility from the Remittance Advice (Figure 4.10). In order to post the payment into the medical software, follow the next six steps:

Step 1: In the medical software, pull up the "Main Menu" and select the "Receipts" button (Figure 4.9).
Step 2: Pull up claim or ticket # from the EOB or RA. It will be listed as the account number. Select the box

MEDICARE PART B   **(ERA) REMITTANCE ADVICE**

Provider#:

Check/EFT (Electronic Fund Transfer) #:   Issue Date: 00/00/2009

Name: HIC   ACCT (Claim/Ticket #) 778889   ICN (Identifies the claim with the insurance carrier)

PROV #	DOS	POS	NOS	CPT	MOD	BILLED $	ALLOW	DEDUCT	COINS/ COPAY	GRP/RC	AMT	PAID PROV $
#######	070809	11	1	99203		125.00	80.00	0.00	16.00	CO-45	45.00	64.00
#######	070809	11	1	74150		55.00	20.00	0.00	4.00	CO-45	35.00	16.00
PT RESP	20.00			CLAIM TOTAL		180.00	100.00	0.00	20.00		80.00	80.00
											NET	80.00

Name: HIC   ACCT (Claim/Ticket #) 766881   ICN (Identifies the claim with the insurance carrier)

PROV # (Ind NPI#)	DOS	POS	NOS	CPT	MOD	BILLED $	ALLOW	DEDUCT	COINS/ COPAY	GRP/RC	AMT	PAID PROV $
								ASG Y		MOA MA01 MA18		
##########	060109	11	1	99213		74.00	54.50	54.50	0.00	CO-45	19.50	0.00
											NET	0.00

CLAIM INFORMATION FORWARDED TO: AARP

Name: HIC   ACCT (Claim/Ticket #) 779101   ICN (Identifies the claim with the insurance carrier)

PROV # (Ind NPI#)	DOS	POS	NOS	CPT	MOD	BILLED $	ALLOW	DEDUCT	COINS/ COPAY	GRP/RC	AMT	PAID PROV $
								ASG Y	MA02			
##########	072209	22	1	28285	AS T7	532.00	0.00	0.00	0.00	CO-54	532.00	0.00
											NET	0.00

Name: HIC   ACCT (Claim/Ticket #) 766995   ICN (Identifies the claim with the insurance carrier)

PROV # (Ind NPI#)	DOS	POS	NOS	CPT	MOD	BILLED $	ALLOW	DEDUCT	COINS/ COPAY	GRP/RC	AMT	PAID PROV $
										MOA MA01		
##########	061109	11	1	99213		74.00	54.50	0.00	25.00	CO-45	19.50	29.50
											NET	29.50

TOTALS: #OF CLAIMS/BILLED AMT/ALLOWED AMT/DEDUCT AMT/COINS COPAY AMT/TOTAL RC-AMT/PROV PD AMT/PROV ADJ AMT/CHECK AMT

     4   860.00   209.00   54.50   45.00   0.00   109.50   651.00   109.50

MESSAGE CODES: GROUP/CARC/RARC

          CO /45 54/ MA18

Step 1   Pull up Main Menu Select   [RECEIPTS]   Button

Figure 4.7(a)   Posting an insurance payment, Step 1.

under Step 7 and double click to pull up your patient in order to get to his or her claims (Figure 4.10).

Step 3: Select Type of Payment, Insurance or Personal. In this case you will select Personal (x).

Step 4: Method of Payment, you will select "Check." Payment was issued by a check.

Step 5: Enter the check number and the issue date from the check.

Step 6: Post your payment under the Payment Column, select Payment type "Patient," post patient responsibility (Copay). There is no Disallow/Adj or Disallow/Adj Type to enter. If you were going to adjust the $25.00 Copay, then under the Disallow/Adj Column you would enter $25.00 and select Disallow/Adj Type "Courtesy."

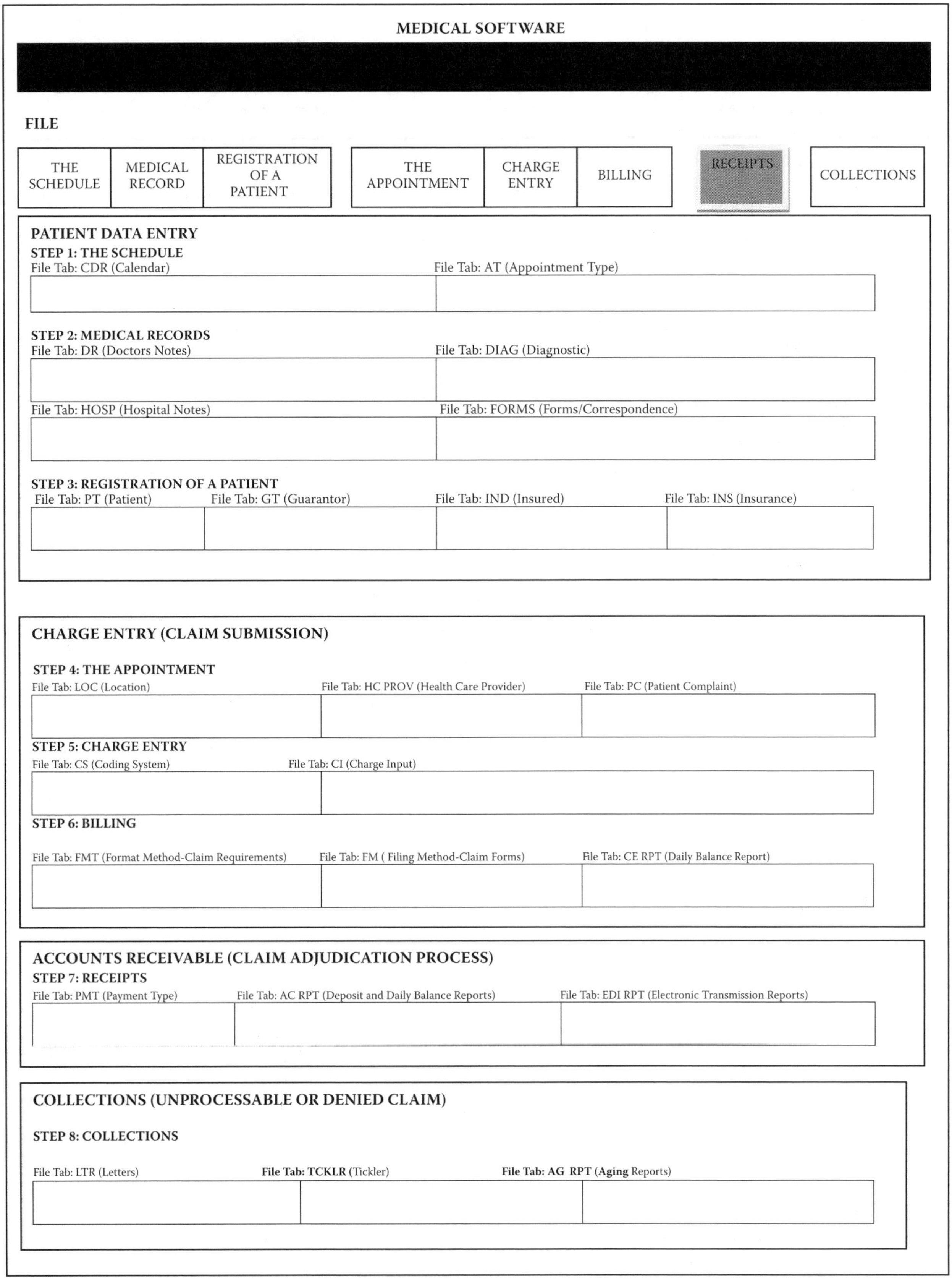

MEDICAL SOFTWARE

FILE

THE SCHEDULE	MEDICAL RECORD	REGISTRATION OF A PATIENT		THE APPOINTMENT	CHARGE ENTRY	BILLING	RECEIPTS	COLLECTIONS

PATIENT DATA ENTRY

STEP 1: THE SCHEDULE

File Tab: CDR (Calendar)   File Tab: AT (Appointment Type)

STEP 2: MEDICAL RECORDS

File Tab: DR (Doctors Notes)   File Tab: DIAG (Diagnostic)

File Tab: HOSP (Hospital Notes)   File Tab: FORMS (Forms/Correspondence)

STEP 3: REGISTRATION OF A PATIENT

File Tab: PT (Patient)   File Tab: GT (Guarantor)   File Tab: IND (Insured)   File Tab: INS (Insurance)

CHARGE ENTRY (CLAIM SUBMISSION)

STEP 4: THE APPOINTMENT

File Tab: LOC (Location)   File Tab: HC PROV (Health Care Provider)   File Tab: PC (Patient Complaint)

STEP 5: CHARGE ENTRY

File Tab: CS (Coding System)   File Tab: CI (Charge Input)

STEP 6: BILLING

File Tab: FMT (Format Method-Claim Requirements)   File Tab: FM (Filing Method-Claim Forms)   File Tab: CE RPT (Daily Balance Report)

ACCOUNTS RECEIVABLE (CLAIM ADJUDICATION PROCESS)

STEP 7: RECEIPTS

File Tab: PMT (Payment Type)   File Tab: AC RPT (Deposit and Daily Balance Reports)   File Tab: EDI RPT (Electronic Transmission Reports)

COLLECTIONS (UNPROCESSABLE OR DENIED CLAIM)

STEP 8: COLLECTIONS

File Tab: LTR (Letters)   **File Tab: TCKLR** (Tickler)   **File Tab: AG RPT (Aging** Reports)

Figure 4.7(b)   Main menu, select button marked receipts.

Step 2: Pull up Claim or Ticket # of the EOB or RA. It will be listed as the Account#. Select the box under Step 7 Receipts and double click to pull up his or her claims.

Step 3. Select Type of Payment, Insurance or Personal. In this case, you will select Insurance (X).

Step 4. Method of Payment, you will select "Check." Payment was issued by a check.

Step 5. Enter in the Check number and the issue date on the check.

Step 6. Post your payment under Payment Column, Select Payment Type "Insurance," Post patient responsibility (Coinsurance), and if no secondary transfer to Patient Responsibility, Post Contractual Write Off under Disallow/Adj column and select under Disallow/Adj Type "Contractual w/o."

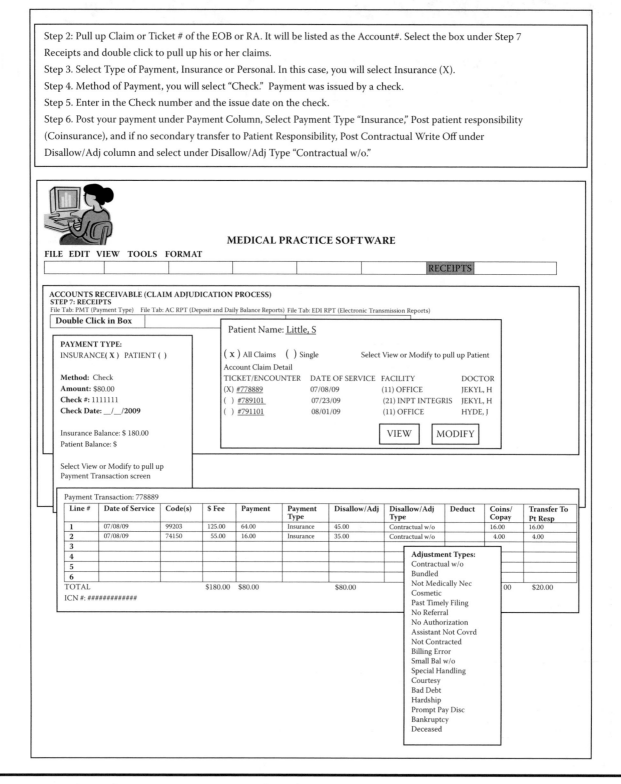

Figure 4.8   Posting an insurance payment, Steps 2 through 6.

Ms Doubtfire
Address
Address

CHECK NUMBER 0000
Issue Date: __ / __ /2009

Pay To The Order of _Somewhere In Time Clinic_ $____25.00__
_____Twenty Five and 00/100_____Dollars

BANK   _Ms Doubtfire_____

: ######### :##############"######

Patient responsibility from the RA is $25.00

MEDICARE PART B   **REMITTANCE ADVICE**

Provider NPI# (Large Clinic with several doctors will have their own group NPI# as well as Individual NPI#s)

Check/EFT (Electronic Fund Transfer) #:   Issue Date: 00/00/2009

Name: HIC   ACCT (Claim/Ticket #) 766995   ICN (Identifies the claim with the insurance carrier)

PROV # (Ind NPI#)	DOS	POS	NOS	CPT	MOD	BILLED $	ALLOW	DEDUCT	COINS/ COPAY	GRP/RC	AMT	PAID PROV $
										MOA MA01		
#########	061109	11	1	99213		74.00	54.50	0.00	25.00	CO-45	19.50	29.50
											NET	29.50

TOTALS: #OF CLAIMS/BILLED AMT/ALLOWED AMT/DEDUCT AMT/COINS COPAY AMT/TOTAL RC-AMT/PROV PD AMT/PROV ADJ AMT/CHECK AMT

          4   860.00   209.00   54.50   45.00   0.00   109.50   651.00   109.50

MESSAGE CODES: GROUP/CARC/RARC

          CO /45 54/ MA18

Step 1: Pull up Main Menu, Select Button

Step 2: Pull up Claim or Ticket # from the EOB or RA. It will be listed as the Account #. Select the box under Step 7 Receipts and double click to pull up his or her claims.

Step 3. Select Type of Payment, Insurance or Personal. In this case, you will select Patient (X).

Step 4. Method of Payment, you will select "Check." Payment was issued by a check.

Step 5. Enter in the Check number and the issue date on the check.

Step 6. Post your payment under Payment Column, Select Payment Type "Patient," Post patient responsibility (Copay). There is no Disallow/Adj or Disallow/Adj Type to enter. If we were going to adjust the $25.00 Copay then under the Disallow/Adj Column you would enter in $25.00 and select Disallow/Adj Type "Courtesy."

Figure 4.9   Posting a personal payment, Steps 1 through 6.

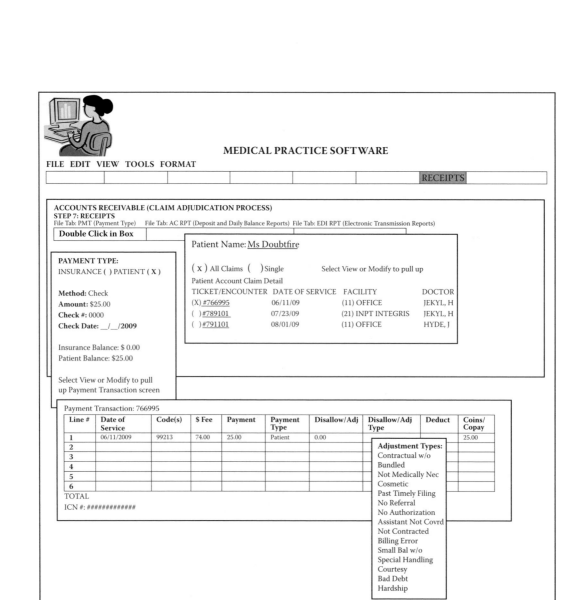

Figure 4.10   Posting of a personal payment.

Chapter 5

Collections (Step 8)

Contents

Unit I: Step 8, Introduction

Purpose

The purpose of this step is to help you understand how a claim is processed by the carrier or insurer, what they look at, different types of claim status, how to work on claims, how to be organized, how to communicate, and the importance of documenting everything so you can be the best at your job. I want you to be able to look at an explanation of benefits (EOB), understand it, and know exactly what steps to take so the doctor can be reimbursed for his or her service.

Unit II: Step 8, Collections

This step is handled by a billing collector (also called a medical billing specialist, billing clerk, accounts receivable [AR] rep).

The main function of medical billing specialist is to make sure that all claims have reached their destination and have been processed correctly. Their responsibilities include calling and checking on claim status, working on claims that were rejected, denied, or are outstanding as well as correspondence from the carrier or insurer. It is also important to inform the office manager of any new updates, changes, and any issues that come up. This can be an extremely important duty, especially in a group medical practice, but with the proper tools and proper information, the job can be done successfully.

The most difficult claims to work on are for patients enrolled in federal and state government plans such as Medicare (Social Security and Railroad), Medicaid, Indian Health Services, and Tricare (military). As a medical billing specialist, I have worked with many different types of carriers and insurers, such as BCBS, United Healthcare, United American, and IHS, but I have the most experience working with Medicare and Medicaid. The reason I wrote this book is to pass my knowledge and experience on to readers. If you can work on Medicare claims, then you can work on all others because Medicare is the most difficult because of the many requirements and guidelines. I want to provide you with the necessary tools needed to do your job and to do it well.

The key to making the billing collector's job easier and more effective is to manage the claims, set up your work area efficiently, and knowing the information that is essential to completing your task successfully. I will cover some of this information under helpful tips.

Part A: Helpful Tips

In medical billing, there are so many things one must remember. There are those things you have to learn by experience and those are the things I want to pass on to you.

Tip 1: Managing Your Time

Each day should be set up to help you accomplish your tasks. I have found the following schedule to be helpful:

Monday: Work on Medicare (current and outstanding claims)
Tuesday: Work on Medicaid (current and outstanding claims)
Wednesday: Work on mail (correspondence)
Thursday: Work with the claims transmission reports (rejected claims)
Friday: Work on your tickler (follow-ups) and patient balances

See Part B, Figure 5.1 regarding your Daily Work Sheet.

When contacting a carrier or insurer, always have a status call sheet, which should contain all pertinent information regarding each particular claim along with all patient information (notes, insurance card, print screen) so when you make your call you have everything you need in front of you.

Tip 2: Managing Claims

It is the responsibility of the medical billing specialist to manage claims. In order to do that, you have to understand and teach yourself four things: organize, prioritize, prepare, and follow up. Once you are comfortable with these, how do you know what claims to work on? The size of the practice will determine how things are divided. In a single-physician office, tasks are usually handled by one or two people, but in a large group practice or clinic, work is usually divided into departments. Claims are all handled in the business office where the office manager will decide who works on which claims. Billing collectors are sometimes assigned claim responsibility based on a dollar amount or by plan. At one point in time,

S	M	T	W	TH	F	S
JUNE						
1	2	3	4	5	6	7
8	9	10	11	12	13	14
15	16	16	18	19	20	21
22	23	24	25	26	27	28
29	30	31	1	2	3	4

Figure 5.1 Daily schedule.

claims were assigned by dollar amount, but after time it was determined that splitting up claims by dollar amounts did not work out very well because too many hands would work the same account, which became very confusing. It is more efficient to have incoming mail handled by one person. The correspondence should be worked on, noted in the patient account, and then filed, which can be very time consuming. In my opinion, it is more vital to work on trying to collect money. Claims should be delegated by plan type: HMOs, PPOs, WC, MVA (all liability cases), Medicare, Medicaid, BCBS, commercial, and self-pay. By having one person work on claims from a particular group plan or carrier, that person will become an expert on those claims.

The four key things to learn and understand:

- **Organize:** The key to being organized is prioritizing, knowing what to work on first, and having the right tools available and accessible. It is crucial to have everything you need to do the job including a fax machine, books, websites, and the proper tools (see "Tip 3: Setting Up Your Desk" in this chapter). You must have a good filing system for Local Coverage Determination (LCD), letters, fax coversheets, forms, and problems that have been worked. A phone should be within reach along with an address and telephone number file. Maintain a special place within sight for call–backs, and make notes or keep information in plain sight as a reminder. Working at a cluttered desk is difficult, so organization is very important.
- **Prioritize:** What do you work on first? Work on those items you know have a time limit for filing. Know which carriers/insurers have filing period limits such as Secure Horizons with a 90-day period and Aetna and UnitedHealthcare (UHC), which have 90- or 120-day filing periods. Next, work on front-end errors such as claims that were rejected on Electronic Data Interchange (EDI) transmission or claims that were denied under specific American National Standards Institute (ANSI) reason and remark codes on the EOB. When reviewing the EOBs, highlight those to work on first, such as those with ANSI denial codes like PR-31, MA127 (carrier/payer cannot identify member/beneficiary or insured). Also, work on claims that were denied because the patient/insured had no coverage at the time of service,

and claims denied with a B7 code (provider is either not contracted with that insurance company or their ID information is not loaded on the carrier/insurers system). These types of claims affect the whole account, so it is always a good thing to update or correct so you can either rebill the claim or collect from the patient or member. The next task is to work on the aging report because this report represents the oldest claims. It is important to work the oldest as well as the current claims. The last task is to work on the high-dollar claims. Remember to group all these types of claims together when calling the insurance carrier so you can check the status on all claims from the same carrier/insurer at the same time.

- **Follow Up:** Another key task is to follow up on the outstanding claims. A simple way to do this is to set up what is called a tickler file. This file is used to help you follow up on pending claims and the process will be more successful if you purchase an expandable file folder index 1–31 (covering all possible days in a month). Some medical office software packages have a tickler, but if your software does not, you can also use the calendar in Microsoft Outlook email. Set up a reminder to follow up on claims on specific dates.

Tip 3: Setting Up Your Desk

Having the right tools handy will make your job a lot easier and make things go a lot more smoothly. Here are some of the necessary tools you will need to help you do your job more efficiently and effectively.

- Tools
  - Resources: Where to go to find answers
  - Websites: Save under favorites on your web browser
  - Forms: Can be located on carrier websites, or your business office may have created their own forms, such as a letter of medical necessity.
    - Status Call Sheet
    - Redetermination (Inquiry)
    - Precert or Preauth
    - Surgery Order
  - Letters:
    - Patient collection letters
    - Insurance requesting information

- Tickler: Follow up on claims that you have worked on or need to set up for follow up
- Equipment
  - Medical software
  - Fax machine
  - Copier
  - Calculator
- Books: *Current Procedural Terminology* (CPT), *International Classification of Diseases, 9ʰ Revision, Clinical Modification* (ICD-9-CM)

Tip 4: Information You Need to Know

There is so much information you need to know and I feel the more information I can supply you with the better job you will be capable of doing.

- **Importance of keeping up with incoming mail:** By keeping up with mail you will be able to see if there is any current issues that need your attention. If you received a remittance advice/EOB containing several denials regarding the same denial code or the same CPT code, you will be alerted to a potential problem, which will need to be addressed by the coders and office manager. Also, if you have a claim that is returned due to a new address update, this might be a new carrier address and will also need to be addressed. If this information is not addressed as soon as you are aware of it, it will turn into a major problem which will slow down the processing of claims.
- **The importance of documenting everything:**
  - Doctor's notes: These should refer to what was done for the patient at each visit. This is important if the office is ever audited.
  - Billing notes: Make sure when taking notes that anyone could understand them. If someone reads your notes, they should know exactly what you have done with that account. If a different person takes over that account, they should be able to know what needs to be done next. If you ever have a need to build a case to resolve and insurance issue with the state insurance commissioner, you should have everything documented from A to Z.
- **Preview the claim before submission**
  - Make sure it is going to the correct carrier/insurer.
  - Make sure the dollar amounts are correct.
  - Make sure that any corrections you have made were properly done.

Part B: Daily Work

As a medical billing specialist, there are several duties that must be performed on a daily basis. Managing your claims and having the proper tools will help you will perform these duties successfully (Figure 5.2).

Section 1: Incoming Calls

Requesting Information: Find out what the caller needs. If the call is from the patient, do whatever you can to help resolve the call. If you do not know the answer to their question, place the patient on hold and try to find the answer. If the patient has been bounced around from person to person, do not transfer them again. If they are calling to pay a bill, ask them if they received a bill; if the answer is yes, ask the caller what the balance is on the bill. Always have the caller provide that information. If someone other than the patient is calling, they must verify their relationship to the patient and verify the fact that the patient has authorized the doctor's office to provide the information to that person. With Health Insurance Portability and Accountability Act (HIPAA) laws, it is vital that patient information be protected.

Attorney's Office

Other calls might include a request for information, an itemized statement, or a copy of medical records. This information should only be provided if the patient has signed an Authorization to Release Information . If you do not have the authorization, you can have the caller fax that information to you. It is important to verify the signature and date and put the release form in the patient chart.

Section 2: Incoming Mail

Keeping up with correspondence, including returned statements, requests for refunds, and so on, is crucial to performing your job responsibilities effectively. Correspondence should be sorted by priority, such as a claim returned by an insurance company because it is not for one of their insureds or an insurance company requesting information.

B: DAILY WORK SHEET

			JUNE			
S	M	T	W	TH	F	S
1	2	3	4	5	6	7
8	9	10	11	12	13	14
15	16	17	18	19	20	21
22	23	24	25	26	27	28
29	30	31				

YOUR DUTIES ARE AS FOLLOWS:

#1 INCOMING CALLS
#2 INCOMING MAIL
#3 CLAIMS TRANSMISSION REPORT
#4 TICKLER: FOLLOW UPS
#5 WORKING CURRENT & OUTSTANDING CLAIMS
#6 PATIENT BALANCES: ACTION TO TAKE
#7 INNER OFFICE REPLY
#8 REPORTS: RUN AT THE END OF DAY

Figure 5.2 Daily duties.

Correspondence

Patient Correspondence

Patient correspondence primarily consists of returned statements. You may also receive a letter from a patient regarding their bill or a concern. It's just as important to handle patient correspondence as it is to work on insurance company correspondence. If a patient has concerns about their bill, it is best to review the account and then contact the patient. Inform the patient that you received their letter and what you found out as a result of your review. If the patient feels they have already paid charges on their account, ask them to provide you with a receipt or a copy of the canceled check so you have some proof of payment. Tell the patient that once that information is received, you will review their account again.

Do not ignore a patient's concern. If you were in their shoes, how would you feel if someone ignored you? Do whatever you can to help the patient.

Patient correspondence can also consist of bankruptcy notifications, death certificates, or returned checks. All of these are vital documentation that can affect the office's ability to collect on patient accounts.

Insurance Correspondence

Correspondence will also come from insurance companies requesting additional information such as detailed accident reports or student status. To process these kinds of requests, check to see if the patient is coming into the office soon or contact the patient to see if they received a letter of request from the insurance company. If the patient will be coming into the office soon, have the patient bring in a copy so you can take the initiative to fax it to the insurance company directly, if needed. In most cases, the patient has sent the information, but when you contact them, they will often inform you that they never received the requested information.

Correspondence regarding claims returned by the insurance company usually involves claims submitted a wrong address. Check the address on the patient's insurance card. If the address was not correct, update it and resubmit the claim to the correct claims mailing address. If correspondence states that the carrier cannot identify the member/insured, check the ID number on the copy of the patient's insurance card and take the necessary steps to correct the error.

Attorney's Office

When something is received from an attorney's office it is usually a request for medical records. Make sure the office has received a signed authorization to release information from the patient before anything is mailed out.

Section 3: Claim Transmission Reports

EDI Submission: Transmitted

This report identifies those claims that were billed and batched for electronic transmission to a clearinghouse. (See Table 5.1.)

EDI Response: Accepted and/or Rejected

This report identifies remittance data report and remittance advice report (ERA 835 file) of claims that were processed and paid or denied by the carrier or payer. It also reports those claims that were accepted or rejected by the clearinghouse or by the carrier or payer.

In order to convert an American National Standards Institute (ANSI) ERA 835 file into a readable Standard Paper Remittance (SPR), you must download the Medicare Remit Easy Print (MREP) software. You can download this from the website of a Medicare administrative contractor (MAC) in your jurisdiction. (See Table 5.2.)

Table 5.1

File Name	Clearinghouse	# of Items	Total Charges	Transmission Status	Submission #	Created By	Date Created
McKsn12	McKesson	5	224.00	Transmitted	99911	Crc	00/00/0000
McKsn34	McKesson	8	532.00	Transmitted	99912	Crc	00/00/0000
McKsn56	McKesson	15	753.00	Transmitted	99913	Crc	00/00/0000
McKsn88	McKesson	35	3400.50	Ready to Transmit	99998	Crc	00/00/0000
McKsn99	McKesson	12	658.00	Ready to Transmit	99999	Crc	00/00/0000

| SEND | DELETE |

Table 5.2

File Name	Clearinghouse	Date and Time Received	Status	Description of the Report
CR_04012010	McKesson	00/00/0000 14:18:39	Not processed	
CR_04012011	McKesson	00/00/0000 14:18:40	Not processed	
F8_04012012	McKesson	00/00/0000 14:18:41	Not processed	
F8_04012013	McKesson	00/00/0000 14:18:42	Not processed	
RS_04012014	McKesson	00/00/0000 14:18:43	Not processed	
RX-Remit_04012015	McKesson	00/00/0000 14:18:44	Not processed	
RS_Remit_04012016	McKesson	00/00/0000 14:18:45	Not processed	

Note: CR = Accepted and/or Rejected claims; F8 = Claim Images; RS = Remittance Data Report; RX = Remittance Advice Report

Table 5.3

Claim Form Box #	Claim Form Description	Loop	Segment	Electronic Data Interchange Description
1	Type of Insurance	2000B	SBR09	Primary Payer Responsibility
			SBR01	Primary Payer
1a	Policy Holder ID #	2010BA	NM101	Insured or Subscriber
			NM102	Person
			NM108	Member Identification Number
			NM109	Subscriber Primary Identifier
2	Name of Patient	2010BA	NM103	Last Name
			NM104	First Name
			NM105	Middle Name
			NM107	Suffix (e.g.., Jr., Sr.)
3	Patient Date of Birth	2010BA	DMG02	Birth Date
			DMG03	Gender
24j	Rendering Provider ID#	2310B or 2420A	NM101	Rendering Identifier Code
			NM108	Identification Code Qualifier
			NM109	Identification Code

Crosswalk to the CMS-1500 Claim Form

For data to transmit from each box of the CMS-1500 (in one format) to the electronic data interchange standards, that information is identified by specific segments and loops.

To understand how to read a payer report (CR) and claim print image (F8). (See Table 5.3.)

Section 4: Tickler File

Reviewing and Checking the Status of a Claim:

Work on the tickler first since it covers those claims that you have already worked on and where you must checking back to see if the claim has been processed or paid.

Some medical office software allows you to set a follow-up date for review. Once payment is posted, the software will clear the charges out of collection status. An expandable file folder is also a good idea, so that once claim is paid or processed it can be filed in your daily business.

There will be times when you call to check the status of a claim and find that the claim was never processed, so you will have to start over again. At other times you may find that a claim was never resubmitted for processing, and you will also have to start over.

Section 5: Processing and Handling of a Claim

Before you can understand how to work a claim, there are a couple of areas that I want to go over. First, I want to go over how a claim is handled by the insurance carrier to show how reimbursement determined. The reasons a claim is denied or paid are printed on the EOB, a copy of which is forwarded to the provider's office as well as the member.

I also want to review how a claim is handled by the provider's office to show how to determine if payment was correct, why a claim was denied, and how to correct it.

INSURANCE CARRIER
Processing of a Claim

Editing Process: Correct Coding Initiative and Mue Edits

When a claim is received by a payer it will go through some type of editing process, either by a computerized system or manually by a claims examiner. If the information submitted is questioned by the examiner, he or she can deny the claim outright, send a letter, or contact the provider of service for correct information. The following are a few claim situations that could pose problems:

1. Is the patient covered under the policy? If a child, is he or she covered under a family plan? If the patient is over 18, is he/she covered as a full-time student?

2. Does the policy cover the type of service provided? For example, are office visits, injections, durable medical equipment (DME) covered under the policy?
3. Does the policy cover the patient's diagnosis? If the patient's diagnosis is cancer, does the policy cover cancer? Or, for example, treatment for a diagnosis of flat foot is not covered under Medicare.
4. Does the policy cover hospital services (outpatient, inpatient)?
5. Does the service or procedure provided require precertification or prior authorization?
6. Are there any limitations and specific requirements that must be met prior to the service or procedure that is being provided?
7. Medication: Does the policy cover the drug and the doctor bills for administration only.
8. Are there any restrictions such as preexisting conditions, a rider, or exclusions in the policy for the service provided? Is there a waiting period?
9. Are there state mandates regarding the service that require payment?
10. Is the service or procedure coded correctly (does the diagnosis match the procedure)?
11. Has the patient reached a frequency limit for the medical service provided?
12. Have benefit maximums been reached for the particular condition?

Plan of action: From my experience at the company I worked for, a claim was forwarded to the financial department where it will either be denied or allowed, to the CSR department where a phone call will be made, the steno department where a letter will be sent with the claim to provider's office, or to the medical director for medical review.

The medical director is responsible for a clinical review of the claim for medical necessity or any preexisting condition or to review any appeal that is submitted.

If a claim is pending information, it is placed into "pending" status. This is usually done for one of two reasons: more information is needed for the claim to be adjudicated or a question exists as to the necessity for the type of procedure that was performed. Also, claims are reviewed for potential preexisting conditions.

Medicare Part B claims are processed through a computerized coding edit system. These edits are known as the National Correct Coding Initiative (NCCI) edits and Medically Unlikely Edits (MUEs). The CCI edits are used to help control and eliminate improper coding of code pairs and code combinations by preventing unbundling of a service that is not separately payable. *Unbundling* is the inappropriate billing of individual codes that are components of

a more comprehensive code. To unbundle a code is proper only when that particular service or procedure is not essential to completing the other procedure. Certain procedures are necessary in order to accomplish the primary procedure, are therefore incidental to the primary procedure, and cannot be reported separately.

MUE edits are used to help control the maximum number of units of service (UOS) allowed for a single Current Procedural Terminology (CPT) or Healthcare Common Procedure Coding System (HCPCS) code on the same day. Not all CPT/HCPCS codes have MUE edits in place. Mue edits only apply to certain services or procedures. These CCI and MUE edits were designed to detect coding errors to help eliminate inappropriate payments.

Within the CCI edits are two types of CCI tables: the Column 1/Column 2 edit table and the Mutually Exclusive edit table. The Column 1/Column 2 edit table contains comprehensive edits that are applied to a code combination where one of the codes in Column 2 is considered a component of a more comprehensive code in Column 1. Payment will be issued on the code (procedure) in Column 1 while the code (procedure) in Column 2 is not payable because it is considered to be bundled with the code (procedure) in Column 1. The Mutually Exclusive edit table consists of two code pairs for services that should not, or would not, be performed on the same patient at the same encounter. This table also has two columns. Payment is issued on the code (procedure) in Column 1 while the code (procedure) in Column 2 is denied. If you can justify that the code (procedure) was billed correctly, you may need to submit medical documentation in order for the procedure to be reviewed. If you can append a modifier to the code (procedure) in Column 2 to bypass the edit, payment on code pairs and code combinations may be allowed.

A helpful tool that I use for Medicare Physician Fee Schedule (MPFS) indicators (resource-based relative value scale [RBRVS], global period, physician supervision, status, modifiers), CCI edits, and MUE edits is the Medicare Correct Coding Guide manual. It is a tool I refer to all the time. (See Table 5.4.)

Payment indicators are used to determine the level of payment for a particular service or procedure. Each indicator can be identified in the Medicare Physician Fee Schedule Database (MPFSDB), which is available at the Medicare website (http:// www.cms.gov).

Even though a code combination may be listed as a CCI edit, The Centers for Medicare and Medicaid Services (CMS) does allow payment of two codes that are identified in a code pair edit under certain circumstances, when submitted with the appropriate modifier. CCI identifies each code combination edit with a modifier indicator to identify which procedure code combination may be billed together with

Table 5.4 28104

Relative Value Units								
WORK	*MP*	*PE-nf*	*PE-f*	*TL-nf*	*TL-f*	*GP*	*MUE*	
5.26	0.54	9.20	4.39	15.00	10.19	90	—	
Modifiers Payment Indicator								
50	*51*	*62*	*66*	*80,82*	*Phys Supervision*		*Status*	
0	4	DOC	NPD	8	09		A	
CCI Edits								
01470	0213T	0216T	0228T*	0230T*	10060*	10140*	10160*	11011 √
11012 v	20552*	20615*	28020*	28072*	28113^	28288*		
28307	28308	28309	29130	29131	29540			

Note: A symbol key, such as an asterisk (*) or check mark (√) are used to help identify and direct you to the section in the General Correct Coding Policies in the Medicare Correct Coding Guide to identify the problem and how to correct it if necessary.

Table 5.5 Download: CPT Code 20000–29999 Col 1/Col 2

COLUMN 1	*COLUMN 2*	*= In Existence Prior To 1996*	*Effective Date*	*Deletion Date*	*Modifier 0 = not allowed 1= allowed 9 = not applicable*
28104	28288		19960101		"1"

the use of a modifier. CMS utilizes three types of modifier indicators: 0, 1, and 9.

To locate these codes, access the Medicare website (http://www.cms.gov), click **Medicare**, then select **Coding National Correct Coding Initiative Edits**. On the left side of the screen, select **NCCI Edits – Physician**. We want to identify CPT codes 28104/28288. Under Service Type, select **Surgery: Musculoskeletal System**. Under Code Range, select CPT Codes 20000–29999 Col 1/Col 2 (see Table 5.5).

Once you have downloaded the Text Document under code Range CPT Codes 20000–29999, scroll down column 1 of the table until you come to CPT Code 28104 and under column 2 CPT Code 28288 is listed.

The CPT Code in column 1 indicates the one that is payable, whereas the code in column 2 indicates the one that is not payable when billed with the code in column 1. The third column indicates if the edit existed prior to 1996. The fourth column indicates the effective date of the edit. The fifth column indicates the deletion date of the edit. The sixth column indicates if a modifier is allowed with the edit.

The adjudication of a claim during the editing process can result in one of the four different claim status types, depending on whether there is an error or issue with that claim. The error can be a front-end error, a coding error, or other issue.

Assigning Claim Status Types

Unprocessable versus processed claim (See Table 5.6: Different Claim Status Types):

1. Rejected or denied (front-end errors)
2. In processing
3. Pending: In review, waiting for additional information, or placed on hold
4. Finalized: Denied (billing or coding errors and other claim issues) or allowed

I have provided a list of front-end errors (See Table 5.7), a list of billing or coding errors (See Table 5.8), and a list of other claim issues (See Table 5.9) that can result in a claim rejection or be denial.

Table 5.6 Different Claim Status Types

No claim on file, rejected or denied, accepted and is in processing, pending, or finalized (denied or allowed)	
Status Type	*Description*
1. No claim on file (NCOF)	Claim was never received; system not able to locate by date of service
2. Claim was never accepted into the adjudication system (considered unprocessable)	
Rejected or Denied	Claim contained front-end errors (see examples in Table 5.2)
3. Claim has been accepted into the adjudication system	
In Processing	Claim is being processed
4. Claim in pending status	
In Review	Claim is suspended and is being reviewed for further action
Additional Information	Carrier/insurer has requested information from either the provider or from the member (patient)
System HOLD	Claims examiner or medical reviewers have placed a HOLD on the claim
5. Claim completed adjudication (processed) and has been finalized	
Denied	No payment forthcoming
	Claim contained billing or coding errors or claim contained other issues (see examples in s 5.3 or 5.4)
Allowed	Payment will be issued or services were allowed on the claim

Table 5.7 Examples: Claim Rejected or Denied for Front-End Errors

Format
Noncompliant: Certain information has to comply with carrier requirements for the claim form (e.g., Medicare requires that if they are primary, the word *None* must appear in Box 11)
Missing Numbers: NDC #, Provider ID #
Invalid provider (doctor's credentials are not in the system)
Typographical Errors: Incorrect Information Keyed
Incorrect member or policyholder ID number
Incorrect insurance information
Billed under incorrect financial class: Other liability such as MVA or workers compensation
Patient date of birth or gender is wrong: Procedure has an age requirement or is only provided to a male or female patient
Other Front-End Issues
No referral (must have a referral at time of the office visit)
No authorization or precertification (some types of service and procedures require authorization before the service can be provided)
Timely filing: Claim was not filed within the time limitation for that specific payer

Note: Be aware that a carrier/insurer will occasionally deny claims due to a technical glitch in their system.

Note: To avoid front-end errors, it is always a good idea to scrub the claim; this means double-check patient registration (front-end of the claim form) to verify that the information has been input correctly. This review includes such items as correct insurance carrier and ID.

Table 5.8   Examples: Claim Denied for Billing or Coding Errors

NCCI and MUE Edit Errors
Incidental to, Bundled, or Mutually Exclusive
Incidental to: For a service or supply to be classified as *incidental to* other care, the following must occur: 1. Service or procedure is considered an integral part of the patient's course of treatment. An example would be a situation where the patient had surgery and came back for post-op care. In order to evaluate the patient, a surgical incision removal and replacement of a wound pouch (A6154) were performed but considered incidental to the patient's course of treatment. 2. Service should be rendered without charge (the expense is included in the physician's surgery bill (post-op care: E/M Code 99213 follow up). 3. Charge was for supplies that are commonly furnished in a physician's office. Examples are gauze, ointments, and bandages. Charges are *not* classified as *incidental to* other services when a supply is clearly of a type that a physician is not expected to have on hand or when a service is of a type not considered medically appropriate to be provided in a physician's office. Bundled: When code pairs are considered to be the same component of a more comprehensive procedure. Mutually exclusive: When code pairs cannot reasonably be performed during the same session by the same surgeon because one or the other can provide the same type of treatment, which would exclude the possibility of doing the other procedure. Only one method would be necessary.
MUE: Maximum number of units of service (UOS) allowed for a single code (procedure) were exceeded. Example: For code J0704, Medicare will only allow 1 unit per injection.
Term Global Period (GP) Global surgical package: Global period for a minor procedure has a 10-day post-operative care limit. Global period for a major procedure has a 90-day post-operative care limit. Description: Services that have been provided that are related to an operative procedure are considered an integral part of that procedure. The global period refers to the time frame during which all services related to the surgical procedure are included in the fee schedule amount. When a patient comes in for follow-up care from surgery, the appropriate E/M code to bill for post-op is CPT Code 99024. Carriers may determine their own GP. The Blue Cross Blue Shield (BCBS) GP for a major procedure can be 42 or 60 days.
Highest level of specificity: Diagnosis was not coded to include either a 4th or 5th digit Example: ICD-9-CM code 715 requires a 4th digit, 715.9 or 715.9 requires a 5th digit, 715.96
Add-on code is missing: The code billed is considered an additional code, which requires a primary code. Examples: The primary procedure CPT code 11200 is for the removal of a skin tag; the add-on code 11201 is for each additional skin tag. The primary procedure CPT Code 96410 is for the first hour of IV chemotherapy administration; the add-on code 96412 is for up to 8 hours. Note: If the primary procedure has an add-on code, the CPT manual will identify the additional code with a plus (+) symbol.
Family of codes: A group of codes that are related to each other that may be performed in various combinations. Some codes may describe limited component services whereas other codes may describe various combinations of component services. If a single more comprehensive code can best describe the service performed, then the physician should not report multiple codes.
Invalid modifier and code combination: The procedure code is inconsistent with the modifier used.

Table 5.8 (continued)   Examples: Claim Denied for Billing or Coding Errors

Diagnosis inconsistent with the procedure: The diagnosis states "fracture of ankle" but the procedure was on the shoulder.
Not a primary diagnosis: The diagnosis that was used cannot be reported alone or as a primary diagnosis.
Separate procedure: If the CPT code book states in parenthesis "Separate Procedure," it means if that procedure is performed by itself during an encounter it can be billed separately. However, if that procedure is performed in a session during which another procedure is performed, and that procedure is performed in a totally different anatomical site, it can be billed as long as the 59 modifier is appended.
Other Errors
Invalid dates such as: date of service (DOS), date of injury/illness (DOI), hospitalization date and discharge Date range is incorrect (number of units shows 6 days but date range only shows 5 days: ex: 2/3/2008–2/7/2008 @ 6 units)
Wrong place of service (location where the service took place) was selected
Billed wrong code: Example: billed 99203 when it should have been 99213
Procedure code invalid at time of service. Example: Billed for code A4590; new code is Q____

Table 5.9   Examples: Claim Denied for Other Claim Issues

Timely Filing: Each carrier/payer allows a specified number of days to submit a claim.
Preexisting Condition: Patient may be treated for asthma Wavier: certificate of creditable coverage (COCC) letter Policy Rider: Waiting period of at least 6 months.
Frequency Limit: Number of units allowed per service.
Capitation Limit $: Maximum benefit amount is capped at $10,000.
Insufficient Documentation: Documents submitted do not support the need for a particular procedure that was provided, and therefore the claim was denied.
Utilization Review: It was determined that the facility where the service was provided was not the appropriate place for care.
Unnecessary Procedure: The procedure performed was not medically necessary. Are the services/procedures and patient condition covered under the patient's policy? If the answer is yes, can the service be considered medically necessary? Is the patient's condition causing health issues?
Reconstructive versus Cosmetic: Surgery required for medical or health reasons or for improvement in physical appearance.
Not a Covered Procedure: The charge is not covered due to the fact the service is not covered for the particular condition according to the patient/member's policy.
No Coverage at Time of Service: Patient was not covered under the policy at the time the service or procedure was rendered.
Limitations and Requirements were not met.
Primary Insurer Paid More than the Secondary Insurer Allowed: Primary paid 45; secondary allows only 35.

Insurance carriers may use many different coding edits, but it is difficult to verify if the edits they use are the same as the NCCI edits developed by CMS.

The following is a list of editing errors that are identified through the editing process as well as other reasons why a claim might be denied, and how those edits are identified by ANSI reason and remark codes.

Assigning ANSI Group, CARC, and RARC CODES (Refer to: Chapter 4, Unit II, Part B, Step 7)

1. ANSI Group, Claim Adjustment Reason Code (CARC), and Remittance Advice Remark Code (RARC) codes that identify front-end errors are as follows:
   - Group and CARC: PR-31, CO-140, OA-109, CO-22, B7
   - RARC: MA127

2. ANSI Group, CARC, and RARC codes that identify unbundling coding errors are as follows:
   - Group and CARC: CO-16 and M51 Invalid Code A4590
   - CCI Edits: Bundled codes CO-97 and M144
   - CO-125 and M15
   - CO-B15 and M80
   - RARC: M80

3. ANSI Group, CARC, and RARC codes that identify other claim issues are as follows:
   - Group and CARC:
   - RARC:
   - CO-50 Medically Necessity

For a list of the ANSI codes and descriptions, go to the Washington Publishing Company (WPC) website: http://www.wpc-edi.com.

The WPC is an active member of the Accredited Standard Committee (ASC) X12 and publishes the output of X12's subcommittees. They also assist several organizations with the maintenance and distribution of code lists external to the X12 family of standards. The code lists are maintained by the CMS.

The code lists are as follows:

- Healthcare
  - Claim Adjustment Reason Codes
  - Remittance Advice Remark Codes
  - Claim Status Codes
  - Claim Status Category Codes
  - Healthcare Service Type Codes
  - Healthcare Provider Taxonomy Code Set
  - Provider Characteristics Codes
  - Healthcare Services Decision Reason Codes
  - Insurance Business Process Application Error Codes
- Property and casualty
  - Several EDI-related P&C Code Lists

> **PROVIDER'S OFFICE**
> Handling of a Claim

Working Current Claims

Current claims are those that have not gone past the 45-day processing period. These types of claims usually contain front-end errors:

1. EDI Claim Response Report: claims that have been either accepted and/or rejected through transmission
2. Claim that has been returned
3. EOB: Claim that has been denied or rejected as unprocessable

Working Outstanding Claims

Outstanding claims are claims that are past the 45-day processing limit and are referred to as *aged claims*. Handling of an aged claim can be worked two ways:

1. Tickler: Claim you already worked on that you have placed in follow-up status.
2. Aged Report: 45/60/90/120 Day Bucket

Working aged claims: Most medical billing software is set up to track claims, but if your software is not capable of this, it will be necessary to run an aging report at the beginning of each week. Claims are placed in the 45/60/90/120 day bucket.

Managing your claims: Know what needs to be worked on first (Refer to Step 8, Collections, Unit II, Part A (Helpful Tips), Section 2).

If a claim was allowed, pending, denied, or in some cases returned, and an explanation of benefits or remittance advice was received, what is next? The next steps are to determine where the error (claim form and medical software) was made and then determine some of the ways to fix a denied claim.

Claim Detail: Area of Error—You need to know where the issue is and how to correct it. There are two areas where a front-end error and billing or coding error may exist.

1. Patient Data Entry: Data is keyed into the top portion of the claim form.
   - Registration of a patient: Refer to Chapter 2, Unit IV, Step 3, Part A
   - Insurance company: Refer to Chapter 2, Unit IV, Step 3, Part D
2. Charge Entry: Data is keyed into the bottom portion of the claim form.
   - Format method: Refer to Chapter 3, Unit V, Step 6
   - Filing methods: Refer to Chapter 3, Unit V, Step 6
   - Charge Input: Refer to Chapter 3, Step 4 and Step 5.
   - The Appointment: Refer to Chapter 3, Step 4 (Date of Service, Location)

For examples of front-end errors, billing or coding errors, refer to Chapter 5, Unit III, Step 8, Part A, Case Example, Sections 1 and 2.

When there is a request for documentation, this information must be obtained from the patient chart. In today's world of technology, medical practices are going paperless, which means turning to electronic medical records (EMR) software. EMR is a record of a patient's medical history, such as operative reports, clinic notes, correspondence (insurance and patient), and other office forms stored in the software system that have been scanned into each patient account. It can be viewed or printed without having to go to medical records department and physically pull the patient chart. Everything is accessible to print from the import list in the patient demographics.

What to Work First

Knowing what to work first and doing it on a daily basis will keep you from being overwhelmed and falling behind. Working the following will help guide what you need to do:

1. Claims Transmission Response Report (refer to Chapter 5, Unit II, Step 8, Part B, Section 3 under Daily Worksheet)

   Work the Accepted and/or Rejected claims
2. Insurance Correspondence (refer to Chapter 5, Unit II, Step 8, Part B, Section 2 under Daily Worksheet)

   Work the requests for additional information from the insurance company

   Work the claims that were returned: Claim was submitted to wrong address or insurance unable to identify member/insured
3. Remittance Advice or Explanation of Benefits (refer to Chapter 4, Unit II, Step 7, Part B, Section 4 or 5)

   Determine ANSI reason and remark codes so you know which ones to work first
4. Outstanding/Delinquent Accounts (refer to Chapter 5, Unit III, Step 8)

   Work pending claims that are over 45 days old. Pull them up from the Collection Module or print out and work off an Aging Report (Buckets 30/60/90/120+)

How to Correct and Resolve Claim Issues

Knowing what is collectable and what is not collectable and how to handle each situation will help eliminate claim issues.

What are some of the ways to resolve an issue with a claim? It really depends on what is wrong with the claim. By understanding the ANSI codes you can determine the area of error, but in order to find the best way to resolve the claim issue, there are some questions that will have to be answered.

What Is Collectable and What Is Not Collectable?

You must understand the following four items in order to know if a service to be provided is payable by the insurance company or if it can be billed to the patient. Knowing what to bill and what not to bill will help you to know from whom to collect payment.

1. "Unbundled" and "Bundled" codes: Knowing what codes are bundled will eliminate several problems, such as keeping accounts receivable (AR) down and eliminating extra work. It is important to know the National Correct Coding Initiative (CCI) edits regarding what codes are "Incidental to" a physician's service and which procedure is considered to have the same components as another procedure.
2. Modifiers: Appending the appropriate modifier helps provide additional information that is very useful to bypass CCI edits. Modifiers need to be added on a claim prior to submission; that way you don't have to resubmit a corrected claim.
3. Service or procedure a covered benefit: Knowing what an insurance company will pay for and what they don't pay for will help eliminate the question of from whom to collect. For example, Medicare will not cover a patient who is diagnosed with flat foot or an orthrotripsy for a patient who is diagnosed with plantar fasciitis. Both are not covered benefits so in both situations you would collect payment from the patient, unless they have a secondary payer that will cover what Medicare does not.
4. Service or a procedure requires a pre-authorization: It is vital to always verify coverage of benefits prior to any surgery. It may be necessary to get a written authorization or verbal authorization in order for the doctor to be paid. If not and if a particular service comes back denied due to no authorization, the doctor will have to take the loss because we did not do our job prior to the date the service was provided. Depending on the insurance company, there are some cases of a provided service being denied due to no authorization when the

insurance company would allow you to request one after you received the denial. In such cases they would do a retro-authorization.

Knowing these four things will eliminate claim issues and will help eliminate the number of corrected claims being billed out. Too many corrected claims send out flags to the payer that a particular doctor's office does not know what they are doing, which can lead to more medical billing audits. Once you find out a particular service or procedure will require a modifier or does not need to be billed out because it's a bundled code, the best way to handle this is to inform the person who does charge entry or coding to make sure when billing out for that particular code to append a particular modifier or not bill out that particular code. This will stop the problem from happening again.

Contacting the Insurance Company for Claim Status

Important contacts within the carrier or insurance company can provide you with specific information that will be necessary in order for a claim to be covered under the policy. Prior to a service or a procedure being provided some of those contacts will be the Benefit Department, which will give you information about whether the patient has coverage, what type of coverage and if they subrogate. The Pre-Certification Department will tell you if prior authorization will be required on a service or procedure. Other important contacts regarding information about a claim are the Review Department, which has people who can inform you of the outcome of an appeal, and the Customer Service Department, which has people to help answer questions regarding the status of a claim or any other question you may have about a claim.

Before contacting the carrier or insurer some of the questions you may ask yourself are

1. Was the claim ever filed?
2. If a claim was filed, was it accepted or rejected?
3. Did the claim go to the correct carrier/insurer and correct address?
4. Have 45 days passed since you filed the claim?
5. If it is over 45 days, why hasn't the carrier or insurer processed the claim?
6. Do we have the EOB or was the claim returned?
7. Is it collectable?
8. Can it be corrected?
9. If the claim is not correctable, can it be appealed?
10. Are we still within the time limit for filing a claim?
11. Do we need to adjust or write off the charges?
12. Is it a covered benefit?
13. Is the patient responsible for balance due?
14. Is there anything else that can be done to get the claim processed more quickly?

The purpose for contacting the Customer Service Department for claim status is to find out what the status is on a claim that you have submitted for payment. When a claim is accepted by a carrier or insurer, it is entered into the adjudication system for processing. If there is a front-end error, that claim will not be accepted, and it will be rejected or denied. Understanding the different status types will help determine what steps need to be taken in order to have the claim processed and paid.

When you contact the carrier or insurer, you will be informed by the interactive voice response (IVR), automated voice response unit (AVRU), or by a customer service representative (CSR) that the claim has been assigned to one of the following status types:

1. No Claim on File (NCOF):
   a. Claim was never received.
2. In Processing:
   a. Claim was accepted and is being processed
3. Pending:
   a. The claim has been placed on a system hold because a request for additional information has been sent or the claim is in review. Once the requested information is received and the review is completed, the claim can be adjudicated.
4. Finalized (denied or allowed):
   a. Claim has been finalized and is to be paid/allowed. The claim has completed the adjudication cycle and was processed as a clean claim with no errors.
   b. Claim has finalized. The claim completed the adjudication cycle but was denied and no payment is forthcoming.
   c. Claim has been denied. The claim did not complete the adjudication cycle and was rejected and considered an unprocessable claim.

Below are examples of questions and answers on how to resolve an issue on each claim status type.

Example #1: NCOF (No Claim on File)

If the carrier tells you there is no claim in the system for the date of service:

Question: Was the claim ever filed? (electronically or on paper).

Question: If electronically, was it accepted or rejected (review electronic claim transmission report)?

Question: If filed on paper, did it go to the correct carrier/insurer and correct address?

Question: Claims for this carrier/insurer are filed online. Did you ever receive that particular claim in order to bill it out online?

Answer: Fax the claim to the carrier/insurer and follow up to make sure the claim was received.

Answer: Send the claim via certified mail to receive a receipt of confirmation.

Example #2: Pending

If the carrier tells you that the claim is pending because they are waiting for additional information from the patient:

Question: What information is the carrier requesting?
Question: Do we need to do anything?
Question: Did we ever receive notification?
Question: What can I do to help get the requested information to the carrier to speed up processing?
Answer: Contact the patient and have him or her provide you with the information and fax it to the insurance company yourself. Remember, insurance companies have a tendency to lose things.

Example #3: In Processing

If the carrier informs you that the claim is still in processing and it has been more than 45 days since the claim was filed:

Question: When was the claim received (exact date)?
Question: Why is the claim still in processing?
Answer: Explain that you need an answer. If the person you are speaking to on the phone cannot provide you with an answer, ask to be transferred to that person's supervisor. DO NOT accept, "I don't know why." They have to provide you with an answer.

Note: Always get a reference number for your call.

Ways to Fix a Denied Claim

When confronted with a denied claim, you must determine if it can be corrected and resubmitted, if it should be adjusted or written off, if it is appealable, or if it should be reprocessed by the insurance company.

Once the type of error has been determined and your questions have been answered, the next step is to determine the best way to fix the claim.

There are four ways to fix a claim:

1. **Correct** the claim, then either refile or resubmit it. When correcting a claim, depending on the area of error, it may be necessary to make corrections to information in the patient demographics or the charge tab. It may also be necessary to contact the patient by telephone or letter in order to correct a problem with the claim.
   a. Patient Demographics, Step 3: This information is obtained when the patient checks in and completes paper work.
   b. Charge Entry, Step 5: To correct a code or add a code you must correct the charge input.

2. **Appeal** the denied claim with the insurer, TPA, or carrier. Medicare has five Levels of appeals as follows:
   a. Level I: Redetermination
   b. Level II: Reconsideration
   c. Level III: Administrative Law Judge (ALJ) hearing
   d. Level IV: Medicare Appeals Council (MAC) review
   e. Level V: Judicial review in U.S. District Court

There are several different kinds of appeal letters:

- Letter of Medical Necessity (LMN). The biller will provide this letter initially, but an LMN and a Letter of Rationale for treatment may also be necessary from the doctor. Example: Cosmetic and Reconstructive Surgery
- Letter of Causation. Example: CTS (carpal tunnel syndrome)
- Letter for timely filing.
- Letter for Unlisted procedure code.
- Letter for separate procedure (usage of the modifier 59)

For information on constructing appeal letters, I suggest that you access the TrailBlazer Health Enterprises website at http://www.trailblazerhealth.com. You will also find helpful information in publications and manuals such as the Medicare Part B Appeal Manual. For information on how to set up an appeal letter, see the example provided in Figure 5.3.

If you are appealing the claim, you must reprint the claim. If you are correcting an unprocessable claim, then you must refile it as a New claim. This will reset or update the filing date on the claim. This date is the date that shows when the claim was filed and can be used for proof of timely filing. Date is located in Box #31 on the claim form.

3. **Adjustment** of the claim by either writing off the charge(s) or transferring over to patient responsibility. Is the adjustment under the insurance or the patient?

Below is a list of the different types of adjustments that you would post under insurance:

Bundled
Contractual write-off
Timely filing
No referral
No authorization
Not medically necessary
Assistant not covered

Here is a list of the different types of adjustments that you would post and transfer over to Patient Responsibility or to Other Payer (secondary/supplemental insurance):

Letter head Stationary

Date: January __ , 20??

Address: Who & Where you are submitting the Appeal

Patient Information:
Patient Name
Date of Birth
Identification #
Internal Control Number (ICN)
(This is the number that is assigned by the insurance company, carrier or payer to identify a particular submission of a claim)

To Whom It May Concern:

Introduction Paragraph (Opening Paragraph)
    1) Identify who you are
    2) State what you are appealing (Identify the service or procedure that is under appeal)

Second Paragraph
    1) Make your opening case as to why you are appealing the decision

    Provide them with sufficient reason for the decision for this particular service procedure to be reviewed for reimbursement. Provide them with specific facts. Provide documentation supporting your facts.

Closing Paragraph
    1) What remedy are you seeking?

    Simply summarize why you urge the recipient of the letter to take all the facts presented into consideration as a basis for reversing the current decision.

Signature

CC:

Enclosure(s):

Figure 5.3 **"How to" set up an appeal letter.**

Not a covered benefit
No coverage at time of service
Applied towards patient out-of-pocket expenses (deductible, co-pay, co-insurance)

4. **Request reprocessing** of the claim by the insurance company, TPA, or carrier/fiscal intermediary. Contact the insurance company if the claim was denied in error, and request that the claim be reprocessed. There have been several occasions when the carrier or insurer denied a claim in error due to a problem on its part because of an error in its system or because it did not update patient coverage information.

Section 6: Working Patient Balances

Working on Current Balances

Current balances are those that have not gone past the 45-day processing period. These accounts include (1) uninsured (self-pay) accounts, (2) those accounts on which payment was received from the insurance company and the balance remaining is the patient's out-of-pocket (OOP) expense, or (3) claims for services that were denied because they were a noncovered benefit or where coverage was not in effect at the time of service and therefore have become the patient's responsibility.

Uninsured (Self-Pay) Accounts: These accounts should be collected at the time of the appointment. Collection is done when the patient checks out. If a surgery is to be scheduled it is important to go over the costs with the patient. Inform the patient that he or she will be responsible for at least three types of bills: doctor's fee, anesthesiologist's fees, and the hospital fees. Always collect fees up front.

Working EOB/RA

Services were allowed but the remaining balance is the patient's out-of-pocket expense. Services were denied, no coverage at time of service, or no covered benefits.

When working on an EOB or remittance advice (RA), it is important to know which item to work on first. My experience has shown that the claims to work on first are those that Medicare denied, especially those denied because the patient did not have coverage at the time of service. Check to see if the patient may be covered under a different payer. If not, it's important to update the whole account and set it to self-pay. If the patient returns, we will have identified that the patient does not have coverage and is responsible for the bills every time he or she comes into the office. This is why insurance verification should be done before a patient's first appointment in the office. It is usually difficult to collect after the service has been performed and insurance has denied payment. Once the account has been updated, always send out a new statement informing the patient that the doctor's office is aware he or she has no medical coverage and is responsible for the balance due on the account. If a service is denied because it's not a covered benefit, the patient has been notified via the EOB, but may not understand or even be aware of the situation. The office should try to determine if a service will require authorization or if a service will be covered, but it is impossible to be correct every time.

Working on Outstanding Balances

Outstanding claims are those claims that are past the 45-day processing limit and are referred to as *aged claims*. Some reasons why a claim may have become aged can include (1) information requested was never received, (2) the balance was transferred to the patient's responsibility, or (3) statements have gone out but no payment or response has been received.

Collection Module or Aged Report (30/60/90/120-day bucket): Accounts that are pending patient balance. Whether working from the collection module or from the aging report

it's best to juggle and work on the oldest accounts receivable, but also work on the high-dollar claims.

To effectively manage the claims for which you are responsible, it is crucial that you know what needs to be worked on first. (Refer to Step 8, Collections, Unit II, Part A, (Helpful Tips) Section 2.)

"How To" Collect On Current and Delinquent Accounts

What is next? The next two things are to determine where the problem is by being able to answer certain questions in order to know where the Area of Error is and then to determine what are some of the ways to resolve a claim issue.

The key to collecting is to be persistent. The more persistent you are the more likely they will pay to get you off their backs.

Questions to Ask

Here are some questions you will need to ask yourself first before you will know how to resolve an issue with a claim:

1. Have we received any type of notification, such as patient has filed bankruptcy or patient is deceased, which will affect the patient balance?
2. Is it collectable?
3. Do we need to adjust off charges?
4. Is it a covered benefit?
5. Does the patient have secondary insurance? If yes, will the secondary coordinate benefits and pick up the patient's OOP expenses?
6. Was the claim/ticket worked correctly?
7. Did we miss something?
8. Are statements going out correctly?

If you know the service, procedure, or item is not billable to the insurance and you know it is the patient's responsibility, collect at the time the service is provided. It is always harder to collect once that patient leaves the clinic.

Always check to see if the balance is actually patient responsibility. It may have been put to patient responsibility in error. Other than patient out-of-pocket expenses, what are some other reasons why charges would be turned over to patient responsibility?

1. Requested information from the insurance company to the patient was never received, so the insurance company closed the case. Patient is responsible for making sure requested information is submitted in a timely manner. If the patient is not responding to the insurance company's request or if we've tried to get a response from the patient with no luck as well, because

the case is closed we turn over charges to patient responsibility hoping he or she will then respond. In some cases this works, but for others it does not.

2. If the patient did not have coverage at the time of the service, set up the account as self-pay.
3. Services that were provided are not a covered benefit and are therefore the patient's responsibility.

What is the policy when collecting balances on a patient account? What about the patient's inability to pay due to financial hardship, such as loss of income, bankruptcy, death, or disability? Every office should have a collection policy and procedures in place, and they must be consistently applied to everyone. Having a set policy will provide you with the information you need in order to know exactly the steps you should take. A policy is a document that is intended to establish criteria to determine the appropriate course of action when making any present or future decision, and in this case, will assist in developing billing policies in order to run a successful billing office within a clinic setting.

What is legal and what is not legal? Is it okay to waive Medicare deductible? Is it a breach of contract having a billing policy in place that will waive patient responsibilities for his or her contractual duties? Waiving Medicare and Medicaid OOP expenses is not allowed, except under limited circumstances for documented lack of ability to pay. The intent of the policy is to waive a patient's OOP fee only when that patient falls under financial hardship. As a medical billing collector in a medical clinic it is my responsibility to make every effort to collect co-pays, co-insurance and deductibles, but there are those individual cases to whom we can offer help if they are having a financial hardship as long as they fall under certain criteria and conditions that are listed in the policy. It is so important to document indigent accounts by setting up specific adjustment types. There is no required method of documenting financial hardship; however, consistency is suggested.

Knowing what is and isn't collectable and having policies in place will provide the information you need to handle each situation and will help eliminate claim issues such as patients not responding or who are unable to pay.

Ways to Resolve a Claim Issue

What are some of the ways to resolve an issue with a claim? It really depends on what is wrong with the claim. By understanding the ANSI reason and remark codes and once you are able to answer the prior questions, the next step is to determine what the best way is to resolve the claim issue.

There are five ways to resolve a claim issue regarding patient balance: (1) billing policies and procedures, (2) patient involvement, (3) adjustment, (4) other resources (helpful websites and other contacts), and (5) third-party collection agency (outside source).

1. *Billing policies and procedures*: I have provided three examples of different types of policies (examples only):
   a. Collection Policy (Figure 5.4),
   b. Financial Hardship Policy (Figure 5.5),
   c. Prompt Pay Discount Policy (Figure 5.6).
   It is always a good idea to have such a document drawn up by an attorney, if at all possible.
2. Patient involvement:
   a. Contact the patient. If there is no answer, leave a message to call you back. Tell the patient it is important but don't indicate you want to discuss a bill because it is likely that the patient will not return your call.
   b. When the patient answers the phone, explain that you are calling regarding an account balance. If the patient tells you he or she is having difficulty making a payment, then offer help. Tell the patient that you can offer financial assistance by setting up monthly payments, but that a financial payment agreement form must be completed. If asked about any type of discount you may offer, explain that you can offer a 25% discount if payment can be made within 15 business days.
   c. Appointments: At every appointment, always request updates and provide the patient with a form that he or she must review and sign asking if anything has changed (employer, insurance, and address).
   d. Letters: Send the patient the appropriate letters regarding his or her balance due (collection letter) or requesting their help to resolve an issue (letter of request).
3. Adjustment Types
   Do you need to make a necessary adjustment, and if so, what kind of adjustment do you need to make? When making adjustments, even if you are not going to charge the patient, the charges must still be input and then the balance written off using one of the following adjustment types:
   a. Transfer to patient responsibility: No coverage at the time of service, not a covered benefit, no referral, allowed amount applied toward patient out-of-pocket expenses.
   b. Balance written off: Special Handling is used only at the doctor's request. Small Balance is used when a balance of $50 or less is uncollectable (Collection Policy Rule #5f). Bad Debt is used when a balance of $50 to $200 is uncollectable (Collection Policy Rule #5g). Courtesy Adjustment is used for employees, family members. Loss of Income (Financial Hardship Policy). Bankruptcy (Financial Hardship Policy). Deceased (Financial Hardship Policy). Prompt Pay (Prompt Pay Discount Policy).
   c. Financial Monthly Payment Arrangements

LETTERHEAD

TITLE: Patient Account Collection Policy within the clinic	
Document No.	Effective Date:
	Revision Date:
Approval By:	

(Depending how the doctor(s) or Business Office manager wants to set the dollar amount(s) will determine how the rules are set up)

Purpose: The intent of this policy is to provide an effective inner office collection procedure for patient's out-of-pocket expenses such as co-pay, co-insurance or deductible as well as other patient responsibilities

Policy: It provides a set of six rules for certain procedures that must be followed when collecting the balance on all patient accounts under each area within the clinic.

Procedure: 5 Rules

Front Office:

Rule #1: Collect Patient Co-payment at the time of the visit

Rule #2: Request payments on patient balances that are $100 or less

Rule #3: Patient wishes to speak with someone regarding the balance front office will notify Financial Counselor

Rule #4: Not able to locate Financial Counselor, contact the Business Office

Business Office:

Rule #5: Collect Patient Out-Of-Pocket expenses and other patient responsibilities. Steps to collect:

a. Two Statements have been mailed out

b. No response, send out Collection Letter 1 and set 30 day follow up (Tickler/Calendar).

c. No response, send out Collection Letter 2 and set 15 day follow up (Tickler/Calendar).

d. No response, Send out Final Demand Letter and set another 15 day follow up (Tickler/Calendar).
*Final Demand Letter: If possible have an Attorney write a demand letter. The terminology they use can be more successful getting the point across.

e. Call the patient, if no answer leave a message to call back. It is important but do not say you want to discuss the bill because it is more likely they will not return your call. Set a 2 day follow up.

f. No response and balance is less than $50 make adjustment to "Small Balance" write off.

g. No response and balance is between $50 and $200 make adjustment to "Bad Debt" and place an alert on patient account that if patient is to return he or she will need to pay bad debt before being seen.

h. No response and balance if over $200 turn account over to outside source, a Third Party Collection Agency (Outsource patient balance).
*f. g. h. are those patient accounts that are Uncollectable

Financial Counselor:

Rule #6: Provide financial counseling on patient accounts that require help regarding payment issues. That person will determine how to handle each patient situation based on a case-by-case basis. See *Financial Hardship* policy.

Figure 5.4   Patient account collection policy.

4. Other Resources (helpful websites, other contacts)
    a. Websites:
       The White Pages website (http://www.whitepages.com) can help locate a patient's address.
       The Availity website (http://www.availity.com) can help verify eligibility and benefit information on a patient or to find a patient's address.
    b. Other outside contacts:
       Use specific hospital websites to access a patient's Face Sheet (administration records) and to help find a patient's address.
       You can also contact the patient's primary care provider to obtain assistance finding the patient's address.

5. Third-Party Collection Agency (Outside Source)
   Why would any office want to pay for a third-party collection agency? Don't they add additional costs and won't you be losing money? Collection agencies can be used to assist in collecting those accounts that cannot be collected by your office and have a balance of $250 or more, and for those accounts you are unable to locate because the patient has moved and left no forwarding address. Some collection agencies are customers of "Skip Tracing," a fee-based website that will locate people.
   When setting up accounts for outside collection, set up only accounts with a specific dollar amount, such as $200 or more (according to your collection policy), and that are uncollectable. It must be worth it financially

---

LETTERHEAD

TITLE: Financial Hardship	
Document No.	Effective Date:
	Revision Date:
Approval By:	

Purpose: The intent of this policy is not to waive patient responsibility as a breach of contract but to offer help for those financially indigent accounts when a patient is unable to pay due to conditions listed under this policy. This policy also applies to those uninsured (self-pay) accounts that fall under the same conditions listed in this policy as well.

Policy: Our practice will not waive or discount any patients Out-Of-Pocket expenses, such as co-pay, co-insurance, or deductible unless authorized by this policy.

Guidelines:

1. Conditions for assessing Financial Hardship are based under the following proof:
   - a. Loss of Primary Income   d. Disability
   - b. Bankruptcy   e. Chronic Illness
   - c. Death   f. Divorce
2. Criteria to establish Financial Hardship
   - a. Patient or Family income in relation to the National/State Poverty Level
   - b. Patient or Family Discretionary Income (Debt Ratio)
   - c. Other Documentation: Bankruptcy Notification, Death Certificate, etc....

Procedure:

Financial Counselor

Provide financial counseling on patient accounts that require help regarding payment issues. That person will determine how to handle each patient situation based on a case-by-case basis. Confidentiality of the patient or family member requesting financial assistance will be protected under HIPAA compliance or *Patient Confidentiality* policy.

1. Patient completion of a Financial Hardship Application. Once completed will determine if that patient meets one of the criteria he or she falls under
   - a. Waiver of Patient Liability
   - b. Financial Monthly Payment Agreement

Figure 5.5   Financial hardship policy.

because the agency is paid a certain percentage of the collected payment.

Collection agencies have the ability to collect in ways that a doctor's office doesn't. Their employees are trained in ways to collect from a patient, while in a medical office the main focus is collecting from the insurance company. A third-party collection agency can also help collect from the insurance company, but they are not usually set up to report a patient's bad debt to a credit bureau. The companies that do this are referred to as debt collection agencies.

Examples: RA/EOB, Patient Correspondence and Delinquent Accounts (Figure 5.7)

Example #1: Per the RA/EOB the service was denied because the patient was not covered at the time of the service (Account # 556677).

Question to ask:
Q: Why was this missed when insurance was verified?
A: Services were provided after the insurance was canceled, and the insurance was canceled after the verification occurred.

```
                          LETTERHEAD

                   TITLE: Prompt Pay Discount
  Document No.                        Effective Date:
                                      Revision Date:
  Approval By:
```

Purpose: The intent of this policy is to write off a partial amount that is owed for services that were rendered in the clinic for those patients who are uninsured and do not have a third-party payer to help cover expenses. This prompt payment discount can only be offered at the request of the patient. If patient can provide payment within 15 business days then we will honor the 25% prompt payment discount.

Policy: It provides a set of seven rules for certain procedures that must be followed when collecting the balance on all patient accounts under each area within the clinic.

Policy: A 25% prompt payment discount will be offered by the clinic for services or procedures that have been provided in clinic, outpatient or inpatient. Any other financial hardship will need to be addressed to the Financial Counselor. This policy does not apply to those accounts who are under contract with either a private or government payer.

Procedure: 7 Rules
  Business Office:
    Rule #2-5e: Follow the rules and procedure under ***Patient Account Collection*** policy.
    Rule #6: Patient calls back or calls in and asks if we offer any type of discount. At this time, you explain that we offer a 25% prompt pay discount only if payment received within 15 business days.
  Financial Counselor:
    Rule #7: Provide financial counseling on patient accounts that require help regarding payment issues. That person will determine how to handle each patient's situation based on a case-by-case basis. See ***Financial Hardship*** policy.

Figure 5.6   Prompt-pay discount policy.

Ways to resolve a claim issue:
(Refer to Item #2 Patient Involvement)
Request updates from the patient. Every time a patient comes in for an appointment, have him or her sign a form asking if anything has changed, such as employment, insurance or address.

Example #2: Per the RA/EOB the service was denied because it is not a covered benefit (Account #778899).

Question to ask:
Q: Is the service or item collectable?
A: Yes, the RA/EOB states that it is the patient's responsibility

Ways to resolve a claim issue:
(Refer to Item #3 Adjustment Type)
Transfer the charge over to the patient responsibility and mail out a statement.

It is a good idea to verify what is covered under the patient's plan and what is not. Check the patient's insurance card for important information. If you are aware that a service is not a covered benefit, collection for that service should be handled at the time of the visit, or a waiver should be provided and signed by the patient acknowledging responsibility for non-covered charges.

Example #3: Per the RA/EOB did not pay anything but what they allowed was applied towards the patient deductible (Account # 789101).

Questions to ask:
Q #1: Does the patient have secondary coverage?
A: Yes
Q #2: Is the secondary a supplemental plan?
A: No
Q#2: Will secondary coverage pick up the deductible?
A: Not necessarily. Some insurance companies will only cover what they allow and if the balance is over the usual, customary, and reasonable (UCR) fee, nothing will be paid, making the balance the patient's responsibility.
Q #3: Was the claim automatically sent to the secondary carrier or should a paper claim be submitted along with the primary carrier's EOB?
A: If the remittance doesn't indicate that the claim was automatically sent to the secondary carrier, you will need to forward a paper claim.

REMITTANCE ADVICE

Provider NPI# (Large Clinic with several doctors will have their own group NPI# as well as Individual NPI#s)

Check/EFT (Electronic Fund Transfer) #:   Issue Date: 00/00/2009

Name: HIC   ACCT (Claim/Ticket #) 123456   ICN (Identifies the claim with the insurance carrier)

PROV # (Ind NPI#)	DOS	POS	NOS	CPT	MOD	BILLED $	ALLOW	DEDUCT	COINS/ COPAY	GRP/RC	AMT	PAID PROV $
									ASG Y	MOA MA01		
#########	051409	11	1	99203		125.00	85.00	0.00	17.00	C0-45	40.00	68.00
										NET		68.00

Name: HIC   ACCT (Claim/Ticket #) 789101   ICN (Identifies the claim with the insurance carrier)

PROV # (Ind NPI#)	DOS	POS	NOS	CPT	MOD	BILLED $	ALLOW	DEDUCT	COINS/ COPAY	GRP/RC	AMT	PAID PROV $
									ASG Y	MOA MA01	MA18	
#########	040109	11	1	99213		74.00	54.50	54.50	0.00	C0-45	19.50	0.00
										NET		0.00

Name: HIC   ACCT (Claim/Ticket #) 112233   ICN (Identifies the claim with the insurance carrier)

PROV # (Ind NPI#)	DOS	POS	NOS	CPT	MOD	BILLED $	ALLOW	DEDUCT	COINS/ COPAY	GRP/RC	AMT	PAID PROV $
										MOA MA01		
#########	031109	11	1	99213		74.00	54.50	0.00	10.90	C0-45	19.50	43.60
										NET		43.60

Name: HIC   ACCT (Claim/Ticket #) 445566   ICN (Identifies the claim with the insurance carrier)

PROV # (Ind NPI#)	DOS	POS	NOS	CPT	MOD	BILLED $	ALLOW	DEDUCT	COINS/ COPAY	GRP/RC	AMT	PAID PROV $
									ASG Y	MOA MA01		
#########	061509	11	1	99203		125.00	85.00	0.00	25.00	C0-45	40.00	60.00
										NET		60.00

Name: HIC   ACCT (Claim/Ticket #) 556677   ICN (Identifies the claim with the insurance carrier)

PROV # (Ind NPI#)	DOS	POS	NOS	CPT	MOD	BILLED $	ALLOW	DEDUCT	COINS/ COPAY	GRP/RC	AMT	PAID PROV $
									ASG Y	MOA MA01		
#########	062509	11	1	99213		74.00	0.00	0.00	0.00	PR-27	74.00	0.00
										NET		0.00

Name: HIC   ACCT (Claim/Ticket #) 778899   ICN (Identifies the claim with the insurance carrier)

PROV # (Ind NPI#)	DOS	POS	NOS	CPT	MOD	BILLED $	ALLOW	DEDUCT	COINS/ COPAY	GRP/RC	AMT	PAID PROV $
									ASG Y	MOA MA01		
#########	061009	11	1	99203		125.00	0.00	0.00	0.00	PR-96	125.00	0.00
										NET		0.00

TOTALS: #OF CLAIMS/BILLED AMT/ALLOWED AMT/DEDUCT AMT/COINS AMT/COPAY/TOTAL RC-AMT/PROV PD AMT/PROV ADJ AMT/ CK AMT

            6   597.00   279.00   54.50   27.90 25.00   171.60   171.60   318.00   171.60

Message Codes: GRP/CARC/RARC

CO: Contractual Obligation

PR: Patient Responsibility

27: Expenses incurred after coverage termed

96: Non-covered charges

Figure 5.7   Remittance advice.

Ways to resolve a claim issue:

(Refer to Item #4 Other Resources)

You may have to contact the patient's secondary insurance to see if it will pick up the deductible (Refer to Item #3 Adjustment Type).

If the patient's secondary insurance will not pick up the deductible, transfer the balance to the patient's responsibility.

Only a few Medigap plans (Medicare supplemental plans for Medicare beneficiaries) cover the deductible.

Patient Correspondence Examples

Patient correspondence is documentation that may have been returned or received in the mail: (1) a statement, (2) a bankruptcy notification, (3) death certificate, or (4) a returned check marked "Insufficient funds."

Example #1: You've received a "Returned Statement."

Questions to ask:

Q #1: Why did the post office return the statement?

A: Possible reasons are the patient moved and left no forwarding address, the item was not deliverable, the item had an insufficient address, the item was returned to sender no mail receptacle, or no such address exists and the post office attempted but could not forward the mail.

Q #2: Was address keyed in wrong?
A: Yes

Ways to resolve a claim issue:
(Refer to Item #3 Adjustment Type)
Review the patient registration information and see if something was input incorrectly. If the answer is yes, make the correction and resubmit a new statement. Make sure to write a note that you updated the patient's address so that if a statement is returned again you will know when the address was updated and what the old address was.
Q #2: Was address keyed in wrong?
A: No
(Refer to Item #3 Adjustment Type)

Check to see if patient is scheduled for an upcoming appointment. If he or she is scheduled, place an alert note on the patient's account advising that the correct mailing address is needed.
(Refer to Item #2 Patient Involvement)
Call the patient and explain that the mail is being returned and that you need a correct mailing address.
(Refer to Item #4 Other Resources)
"Skip Tracing" websites are available and can help provide up-to-date addresses. A couple of free websites are also available:
White pages: http://www.whitepages.com
US Postal Service: http://www.usps.com
Superpages.com: http://www.superpages.com/555-1212.com: http://www.bigbook.com

A couple of fee-based websites are LexisNexis Accurint: http://www.accurint.com and http://www.searchamerica.com

(Refer to Item #4 Other Resources)
Hospital website: These sites can be used to access a patient's face sheet to see if patient has had surgery, or if the hospital has a more current address on file.

(Refer to Item #4 Other Resources)
Contact insurance company: Do you have access to a website that is used to verify coverage and benefits? If so, check to see if it lists that patient's address.

(Refer to Item #5 Third-Party Collection Agency)
If you outsource your patient balances to a third-party collection agency, determine if they use skip tracing. This feature may be able to provide a current address for the patient or responsibility for collection can be turned over to the agency.

Example #2: Bankruptcy Notification

Questions to ask:
Q #1: What type of bankruptcy was filed?
A: Chapter 7 or Chapter 13
Q#2: What is the difference?
A: In a Chapter 7 bankruptcy, all debts are discharged. In a Chapter 13 bankruptcy, debts must still be paid and can be spread out over 3 to 5 years with payment arrangements made with the creditors.

Ways to resolve a claim issue:
Depending on how the doctor or business office wants to handle the situation, the remaining balance can be written off regardless of the type of bankruptcy filed. Make sure to check to see if the person filing bankruptcy is a guarantor on another account. If the answer is yes, you will need to make the same adjustments.

(Refer to Item #3 Adjustment Type)
Write off the remaining balance under the adjustment type "Bankruptcy" and place an alert note on the patient's account stating that if the patient calls for another appointment, he or she must pay out-of-pocket expenses at the time of the visit.

Example #3: Death Certification

Questions to ask:
Q #1: Did our doctor perform surgery on the patient?
A: Yes
Q #2: When did the doctor perform surgery and when did the patient pass away?
A: Recently, within a day or two.

Ways to resolve a claim issue:
(Refer to Item # 4 Other Resources)
If a letter is received from a family member stating that the patient is deceased, death can be verified by checking the Social Security Death Index (www.ssdi.rootsweb.ancestry.com) and inform the doctor of the situation.

(Refer to Item #3 Adjustment Type)
Make a note on the patient account and adjust off remaining balance.

Example #4: Returned Check

Questions to ask:
Q #1: Why was the check returned?
A: Because patient has insufficient funds to cover the check.

Q #2: How can someone write a check when they know they don't have the funds?

A: Most people realize this by the time the check gets to the bank and have already gotten away with not having to pay.

Q #3: Is writing a check without having sufficient funds in the bank against the law?

A: Yes. It is a crime and is punishable by law.

Q #4: Who do we go to for help?

A: For Oklahoma County, contact Oklahoma County District Attorney's office and the Bogus Check Division.

In Oklahoma a program called the Bogus Check Restitution Program was established and designed to assist in the recovery of money. A merchant representative from the district attorney's (DA's) office will visit your office, provide a packet of information, and review information with you. The information explains the requirements or qualifications for this program and also covers those checks that do not qualify under this program. The felony amount for a bogus check is $500 or more. If the check is for $500 to $1000, the individual who wrote the check can serve a one-year sentence in the county jail. If the check is for more than $1000, the jail time is 10 years. The DA's office will pursue someone who has written a bogus check for $25 or for $500; it is up to the doctor's office to make the decision to do so.

Prior to having the DA's office to pursue any bogus checks, there are a few things to check:

1. Make sure the check has a current date and not a past or future date.
2. Confirm the identity of the person who has written the check using a valid driver's license or some other form of identification. Compare the picture on the driver's license with the person who wrote the check. If the appropriate ID can't be provided, notify the appropriate individual in your office. Quite possibly the person is not who he or she says.
3. On the front of the check, write the driver's license number, sex, race, and date of birth of the person writing the check. Place your initials above that information to identify that you were the person who was in contact with the person writing the check and the one who took the information.
4. Do not accept a starter check, which is a check from a new bank account. They do not provide the individual's name and address. If address is a post office box, you must obtain a street address.
5. Make sure the picture on the driver's license can be seen. The DA's office will need a picture ID in order to go after that person.

This program is free, but it is vital to review the information provided in order to determine if the process is worth your time.

Ways to resolve a claim issue:

There are several ways to resolve a bad check issue. The office's decision will usually be based on the amount of the check.

(Refer to Item #3 Adjustment Type)

Check amount under $250: Reverse the payment that was posted, add it to the patient responsibility, and charge the patient an NSF (No Sufficient Funds) fee. The bank will charge the office a fee for returned checks. Make a note on the account that the patient cannot be seen until he or she pays the amount owed. Place an alert note on the patient account stating that checks should not be accepted.

Patient Involvement: Call the person who wrote the check. State that he or she has three days to provide payment by cash, money order, or credit card. If you are not able to contact the person who wrote the check, send a new statement with a cover letter explaining the situation regarding bad checks, including the law for bogus checks. (Example provided)

(Refer to Item #3 Adjustment Type)

Check amount over $250: Adjust to bad debt and make a note on the account that the patient cannot be seen until he or she pays the amount owed. Place an alert note on the patient account stating that checks should not be accepted.

(Refer to Item #4 Other Resources)

Turn the check writer over to DA's office. If the check writer has been turned over to DA's office and contacts your office, refer him or her to the DA's office. Do not accept any personal checks from the check writer.

Delinquent Accounts Examples

Example #1: Patient not responding

Question to ask:

Q #1: Why is patient not responded?

A: No statements have gone out.

Ways to resolve a claim issue:

(Refer to Item #1 Billing Policies and Procedures)

Collection Policy: Send a statement and follow up after 30 days. If there is no response, send a second statement and then follow up. If there is still no response, send out a collection letter. If the patient doesn't respond to this, turn the case over to a collection agency.

Questions to ask:
Q #2: Why isn't the patient responding?
A: The patient doesn't want to pay.

Ways to resolve a claim issue:
(Refer to Item #3 Adjustment Type)
Make adjustment: If you do not have a third-party collection agency, adjust to bad debt and place an alert note stating that the patient must pay all owed money before he or she can be seen.

Example #2: Patient is not able to pay

Questions to ask:
Q #1: You have contacted the patient and the patient informs you he or she is not able to pay.
A: Find out why the patient is unable to pay.
Q #2: The patient informs you he or she lost their job, has no income, and asks you if you can help.
A: Check to see what your office policy is.

There are other reasons for financial hardship including bankruptcy or patient is deceased.

Ways to resolve a claim issue:
(Refer to Item #3 Adjustments)
Monthly Payment Agreement: Even if the patient can only afford to pay $5.00 per month, it is better than nothing. Once that patient is better off financially, you can set up new payment arrangements.

(Refer to Item #1 Billing Policies and Procedures and Item #3 Adjustment Type)
For a financial hardship case, offer the patient these options:
For uninsured (self-pay) accounts for which the patient has no income, write the amount off to financial hardship, providing the patient submits proof of loss of income.
Waiving patient out-of-pocket expenses: Before you adjust any remaining balance, verify the financial hardship policy guidelines as you do not want to be involved with a breach of contract.

Example #3: Patient is not able to pay full amount that is owed.

Questions to ask:
Q #1: The patient contacts you after receiving a bill and asks if there is any way to receive a discount?
A: Yes, but check to see what the policy is.

Ways to resolve a claim issue:
(Refer to Item #3 Adjustment Type and #1 Billing Policies and Procedures)
Offer Prompt Pay Discount: The policy states that the patient will be eligible for a 25% discount if payment in full is received within 15 business days. Once the payment is received, adjust using the prompt-pay adjustment type.

For a step-by-step guide for working patient balances, see Step 8, Unit III, Section A, 1d.

Section 7: Intra-Office Reply

Waiting for a reply from another department within the office: Other departments handle different situations and you may need information from one in order to process your claim. Examples include medical documentation such as doctor's notes, clinic or operative reports, referrals, or the office may want to set up the account for special handling. It is always important to follow up on these replies so the claim can be completed.

You may also be waiting a reply from a patient, and it is usually best to set reminders in the tickler file or on your calendar. It may be necessary to send a second request because people have a tendency to forget.

Section 8: Reports to Run at the End of the Day

At the end of the day, run the Daily Business Report, which shows every account on which you posted a payment, an adjustment, or billed charges.

Unit III, Step 8

Part A: Step-by-Step Guide on How to Correct and Resolve Claim Issues

Collecting from the insurance company or the patient can be a very difficult job. It takes time and may take several different methods before receiving any response. It seems that today it is a very difficult to get insurance companies and patients to pay their bills. Insurance companies come up with stall tactics so they can make more money and people either don't care or figure it's not their responsibility to pay their bill. If a service is provided to you, don't you feel that person deserves to be paid? What if you provided a service to someone and that person was not willing to pay you—wouldn't you be upset? Doctor's offices are more than willing to help if the patient asks. Do not ignore a situation because it makes it worse.

In a medical office the medical software is set up to provide tools to make collecting easier. Figures 5.8, 5.9, and 5.10 are examples of what a screen may look like in the medical software.

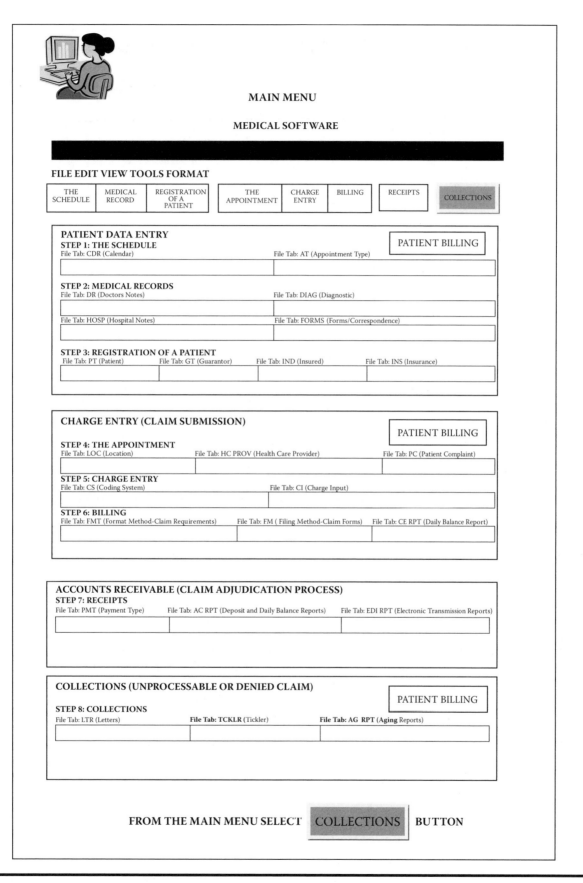

Figure 5.8   Accessing the Collections screen.

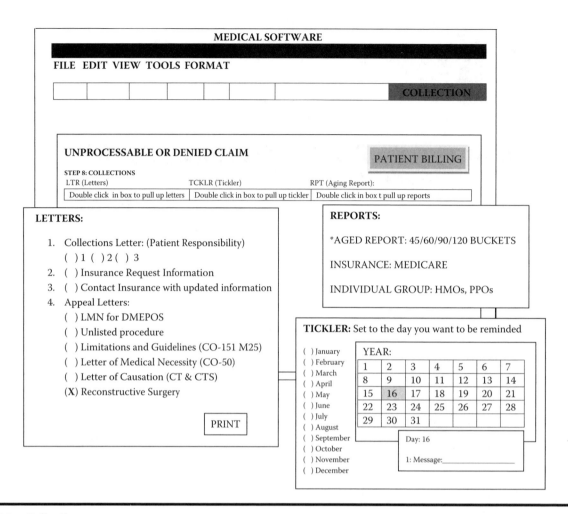

Figure 5.9 Collections screen.

Medical Software

In this section, there are four parts: Letters, Tickler, Aging Report, and Patient Billing (Patient Account Claim Details); see Figure 5.8.

Letters can be used to communicate with your patients. You can format different types of letters including reminder letters, collection letters, a final notification letter, a letter of request to contact the insurance company or to contact your office (see Figure 5.9).

A tickler is used to help follow up on claims or when you are waiting for a reply (see Figure 5.9).

An Aging Report is used to work claims that are over 45 days old (Figure 5.9). Some medical practice software provides some sort of a collection module that will allow you to pull up claims that are over 45 days old, but if your medical software does not provide such a thing, you can work off an aging report.

Patient billing (patient account claim detail) is used to pull up all claims and claim details on a patient account for each date of service for that patient (see Figure 5.10).

The claim form can be reviewed in Chapter 1. Unit I pertains to the top portion and Unit II pertains to the bottom portion of the form.

Where to Go for Help

When working a claim, current or outstanding (45 days past due), there are four (A1–A4) areas that will help answer your questions, direct you to the area of error or concern, and show you the best way to correct or resolve a claim issue. The following four areas (see Figure 5.11) are as follows:

- Area 1 (A1) = Guidebook: When it comes to medical billing one way to guide you on how to work your claims is to refer to the information provided to you in each chapter of this book, especially in this chapter.
  - Key Points: Chapter 2 provides you with patient data information such as patient demographics and insurance information. Chapter 3 goes over charges for services provided by a physician. This chapter provides you with a step-by-step guide on how to resolve a claim issue.

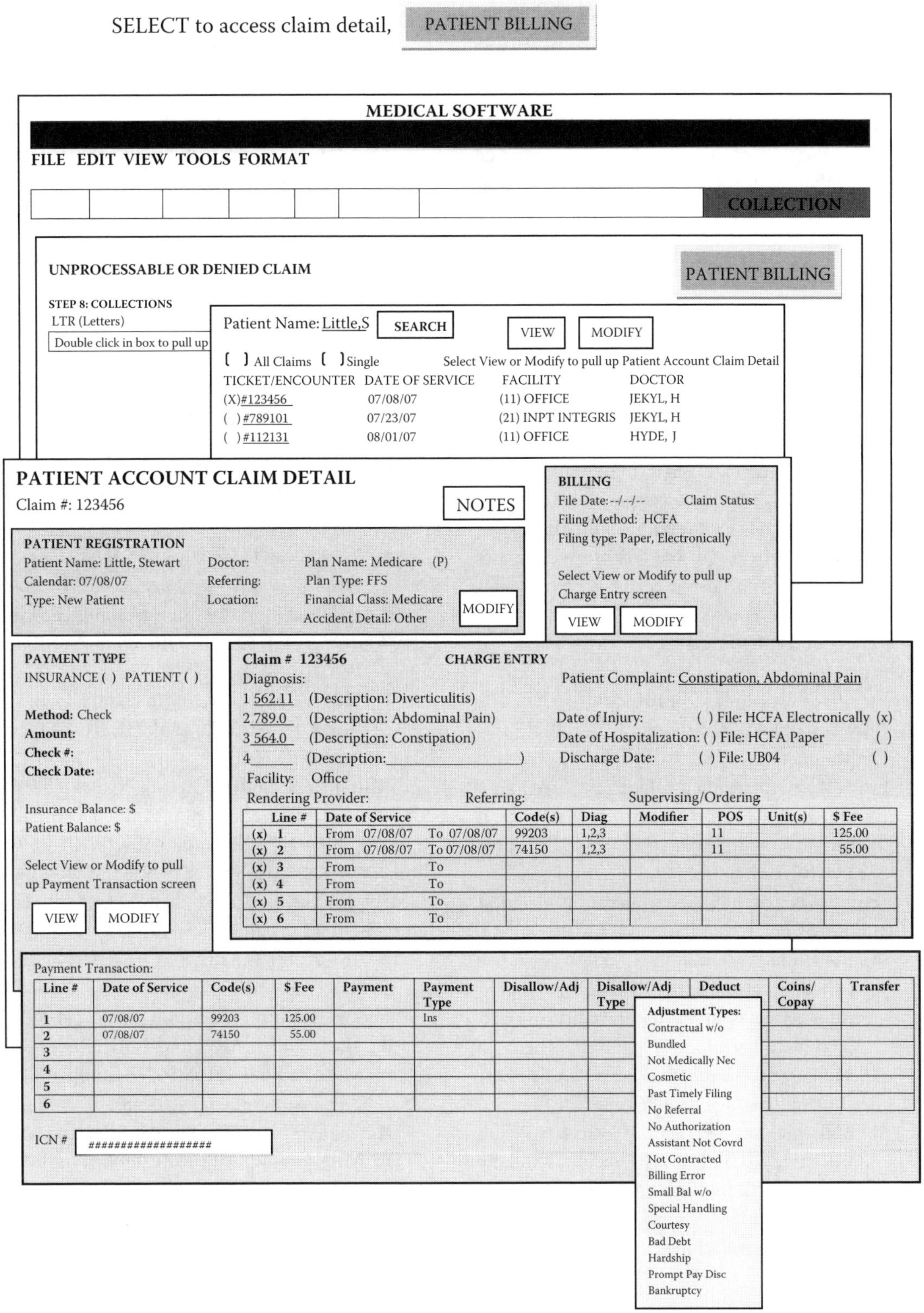

SELECT to access claim detail, | PATIENT BILLING |

MEDICAL SOFTWARE

FILE EDIT VIEW TOOLS FORMAT

| | | | | | | COLLECTION |

UNPROCESSABLE OR DENIED CLAIM

| PATIENT BILLING |

STEP 8: COLLECTIONS
LTR (Letters)
Double click in box to pull up

Patient Name: Little,S | SEARCH | | VIEW | MODIFY |

[ ] All Claims [ ] Single   Select View or Modify to pull up Patient Account Claim Detail

TICKET/ENCOUNTER	DATE OF SERVICE	FACILITY	DOCTOR
(X)#123456	07/08/07	(11) OFFICE	JEKYL, H
( )#789101	07/23/07	(21) INPT INTEGRIS	JEKYL, H
( )#112131	08/01/07	(11) OFFICE	HYDE, J

PATIENT ACCOUNT CLAIM DETAIL

Claim #: 123456 | NOTES |

BILLING
File Date: --/--/--   Claim Status:
Filing Method: HCFA
Filing type: Paper, Electronically

Select View or Modify to pull up
Charge Entry screen

| VIEW | MODIFY |

PATIENT REGISTRATION

Patient Name: Little, Stewart	Doctor:	Plan Name: Medicare (P)
Calendar: 07/08/07	Referring:	Plan Type: FFS
Type: New Patient	Location:	Financial Class: Medicare
		Accident Detail: Other	MODIFY

PAYMENT TYPE
INSURANCE ( ) PATIENT ( )

Method: Check
Amount:
Check #:
Check Date:

Insurance Balance: $
Patient Balance: $

Select View or Modify to pull
up Payment Transaction screen

| VIEW | MODIFY |

Claim # 123456   **CHARGE ENTRY**

Diagnosis: Patient Complaint: Constipation, Abdominal Pain
1 562.11   (Description: Diverticulitis)
2 789.0   (Description: Abdominal Pain)   Date of Injury: ( ) File: HCFA Electronically (x)
3 564.0   (Description: Constipation)   Date of Hospitalization: ( ) File: HCFA Paper   ( )
4 _____   (Description: _____)   Discharge Date: ( ) File: UB04   ( )
Facility: Office
Rendering Provider: Referring: Supervising/Ordering

Line #	Date of Service		Code(s)	Diag	Modifier	POS	Unit(s)	$ Fee
(x) 1	From 07/08/07	To 07/08/07	99203	1,2,3		11		125.00
(x) 2	From 07/08/07	To 07/08/07	74150	1,2,3		11		55.00
(x) 3	From	To						
(x) 4	From	To						
(x) 5	From	To						
(x) 6	From	To						

Payment Transaction:

Line #	Date of Service	Code(s)	$ Fee	Payment	Payment Type	Disallow/Adj	Disallow/Adj Type	Deduct	Coins/Copay	Transfer
1	07/08/07	99203	125.00		Ins					
2	07/08/07	74150	55.00							
3										
4										
5										
6										

Adjustment Types:
Contractual w/o
Bundled
Not Medically Nec
Cosmetic
Past Timely Filing
No Referral
No Authorization
Assistant Not Covrd
Not Contracted
Billing Error
Small Bal w/o
Special Handling
Courtesy
Bad Debt
Hardship
Prompt Pay Disc
Bankruptcy

ICN # | ################## |

Figure 5.10   Accessing the Patient Billing screen.

■ Area 2 (A2) = Patient Involvement : Getting the patient involved! Patients are a vital tool you need to utilize. It is their responsibility to provide you with accurate information. They are the ones paying for the policy. The patient should know what the policy covers. Ultimately, if the patient or insured does not provide the medical office with the correct information, they are responsible for their bill.

– Key Point: A doctor's office does not have to submit a bill to the insurance company; it files charges only as a courtesy.

■ Area 3 (A3) = Insurance company: An insurance company can provide help in two ways, either by phone or by website.

– To check a claim status, verify eligibility and benefits, fee schedule, medical policies (limitations and guidelines), manuals (claim requirements), go to that insurance company's website or use an automated system such as an Interoffice Voice Response (IVR). For more help, call the insurance company and speak to either a customer service representative or a provider representative.

■ Area 4 (A4) = Other Resources
– Websites:
  • http://www.trailblazerhealth.com—Medicare Administrative Contractor (MAC) for Oklahoma
  • http://www.google.com—Utilize for research to help provide information such as medical definitions and different types of medical procedures (surgeries)
  • http://www.cms.gov—Available information and tools are
    ■ Medicare >> Medicare Physician Fee Schedule Data Base (MPFSDB). Pricing information and Payment Indicators can be located here
    ■ Medicare >>Medicare Fee-For-Service Part B Drugs Average Sale Price (ASP)
    ■ Medicare >> National Correct Coding Initiative (CCI) Edits, Medically Unlikely Edits (MUE) for both Practitioner Services MUE and DME Supplier Services MUE
    ■ Medicare >> National Drug Code (NDC) crosswalk
– Books:
  • Medicare Correct Coding Guide Manual: CCI and MUE Edits
  • Coding Books: CPT-4, ICD-9-CM and HCPCS

• Redbook: National Drug Code (NDC) directory for drug approval and data base. Drug products are identified and assigned a unique, three-segment numeric identifier. The first segment identifies the labeler code, the second segment identifies the product code, and the third segment identifies the package code.

What Is the Area of Error or Concern on the Claim Form?

Knowing the ANSI CARC and/or RARC edit codes can help determine where the area of error or concern is on the CMS-1500 claim form. The following are examples of reason and remark codes on an Explanation of Benefits.

1. **Front-End Errors:** PR-31, CO-16 MA27, CO-140, CO-22, CO-16 MA04 N155, CO-109 MA101, CO-109, OA-109, CO-21 and CO-B7.
   ■ The ANSI CARC and/or RARC edit codes that relate to *front-end errors* pertain to Box 1, Box 1a, and Box 7 on the top portion of the CMS-1500.
   ■ The ANSI CARC edit code CO-21 pertains to Box 10 on the CMS-1500.
   ■ The ANSI CARC edit code CO-B7 pertains to Boxes 17, 17a, 17b, 24J, 31, 31a, 32a, and 33a on the CMS-1500.

2. **Billing and Coding Errors:** CO-97 M144, CO-125 M80, CO-B15 M80, B15 M15, CO-16 MA63, CO-16 M51, CO-125 M15, CO-107 N122, CO-A1 M15, CO-97 M86, CO-50 N25 N115, CO-4, CO-151 M25, CO-11 M81, CO-151 N362, CO-B9, OA-58 M77, CO-181 M56.
   ■ The ANSI CARC and/or RARC edit codes that relate to billing and coding errors pertain to Box 24D on the bottom portion of the CMS-1500.
   ■ The ANSI CARC and RARC edit codes CO-97 M86 and C0-151 N362 pertain to Box 24D and Box 24G on the CMS-1500.
   ■ The ANSI CARC and RARC edit codes CO-16 MA63 and CO-11 M81 pertain to Box 21 and 24E on the CMS-1500 .
   ■ The ANSI CARC and RARC edit codes OA-58 and M77 pertain to Box 24B on the CMS-1500.

3. **Other Issues:** CO-29, PR-96, and PR-204.
   ■ The ANSI CARC and/or RARC edit codes that relate to other claim issues pertain to Box 24D and Box 21 on the bottom portion of the CMS-1500.
   ■ The ANSI CARC edit code CO-29 pertains to Box 31 on the CMS-1500.

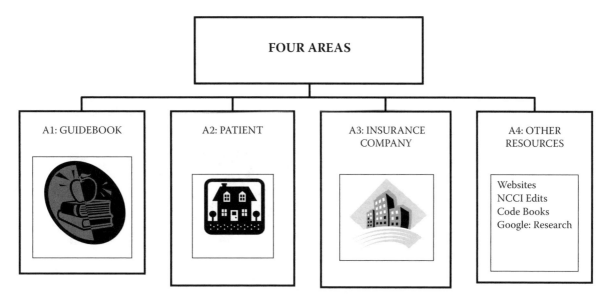

How does each area help resolve or correct a claim issue?

Figure 5.11   Four resources.

There are specific questions you will need to ask yourself in order to arrive at the answer. These questions may include: What does it mean? What do they want? What do we need to do? Do we need to send something? Do we need to correct something?

How Do You Correct a Claim?

There are four different ways to correct a claim and they are as follows:

1. Correct and refile or resubmit a *corrected claim*, by either correcting a code or adding a code.
2. Make an adjustment by adjusting off or voiding the charge, or transfer the charge to patient responsibility.
3. Send an appeal.
4. Contact the insurance company (have them reprocess the claim).

When correcting a claim that was never adjudicated because it was rejected or denied due to front-end errors, you will resubmit it as a new claim. But if the claim was adjudicated and you had to correct a line item by adding a modifier or had to correct the diagnosis or HCPCS/CPT code somewhere on the claim, the claim must state "Corrected Claim," whether it is listed above the code on the same line,

in Box 19, or at the top of the claim form. It will depend on how you resubmit the claim, electronically or via hard copy. Some insurance companies require that you attach an Adjustment Form when resubmitting a corrected claim. The insurance company will provide this form when resubmitting in a corrected claim.

Make sure the claim includes the original submission number, which is the number that is assigned by the payer that identifies the claim. This number can provide proof of when the claim was submitted and received. Medicare assigns claims an Internal Control Number (ICN).

An important factor to remember if you are refiling a corrected claim, such as a Medicare claim, is whether you still within the time limit for filing a claim. I always refile Medicare claims because they are billed out electronically and you have a whole year to file. Refiling a claim electronically will automatically change the date when the claim is batched and filed. If you resubmit a hard copy, you have a choice to either update that particular claim by changing the file date or leaving the original filing date on the claim. If you resubmit a corrected claim, you may wish to set up a follow-up date in your tickler.

I put together a quick reference of eight resolutions on the steps it takes when making an adjustment on a claim and how to apply it to the medical software.

RESOLUTION 1

CASE EXAMPLE A: FRONT-END ERROR

Make adjustment on ticket/claim by pulling up the ticket/claim and transferring charges to patient responsibility.

RESOLUTION: Four steps to correct and resolve the claim issue

Step 1. Main Menu (Figure 5.8), select COLLECTIONS, pull up PATIENT BILLING (Figure 5.9), then pull up the ticket. From the PATIENT ACCOUNT CLAIM DETAIL (Figure 5.10) under "Payment Type," select VIEW. Under the transfer column, key in charges on each line then select OK to save transaction (Figure 5.12). This will transfer charges to patient responsibility (Figure 5.13).

Step 2. Main Menu, select REGISTRATION OF A PATIENT (Figure 5.13), pull up the INS (Insurance) tab, select MODIFY and set the account from Insurance to Self Pay.

Step 3. Send out a new statement. Pull up the GT (Guarantor) tab and under STATEMENT, select PRINT and mail out a new statement.

Step 4. Add notes on how you resolved the claim issue. Pull up PATIENT BILLING under the PATIENT ACCOUNT CLAIM DETAIL, select NOTES, and type in what the problem was and what you did to resolve the claim issue. (**In every medical software there is a place to key in notes on what you did, either on that particular ticket or somewhere on that patient's account.**) An example of how you would type in your notes is as follows:

NOTE: Per the Medicare remittance dated 5/14/2008 denied the service because patient was not eligible for Medicare Part B benefits at the time of service. I transferred charges over to the patient responsibility, set the account to self pay, and mailed out a new statement.

** Key Point: Keeping good notes is another key factor in doing a great job. Putting in good notes will provide information as to what has been done or is being done to resolve the issue with that particular date of service. If someone decides to go into that particular claim, they will see your notes and will know exactly what is being done.

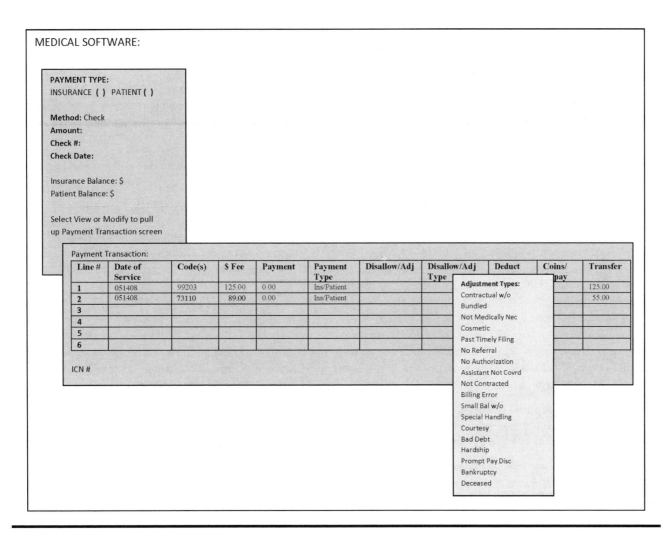

MEDICAL SOFTWARE:

PAYMENT TYPE:
INSURANCE ( ) PATIENT ( )

Method: Check
Amount:
Check #:
Check Date:

Insurance Balance: $
Patient Balance: $

Select View or Modify to pull
up Payment Transaction screen

Payment Transaction:

Line #	Date of Service	Code(s)	$ Fee	Payment	Payment Type	Disallow/Adj	Disallow/Adj Type	Deduct	Coins/pay	Transfer
1	051408	99203	125.00	0.00	Ins/Patient					125.00
2	051408	73110	89.00	0.00	Ins/Patient					55.00
3										
4										
5										
6										

Adjustment Types:
Contractual w/o
Bundled
Not Medically Nec
Cosmetic
Past Timely Filing
No Referral
No Authorization
Assistant Not Covrd
Not Contracted
Billing Error
Small Bal w/o
Special Handling
Courtesy
Bad Debt
Hardship
Prompt Pay Disc
Bankruptcy
Deceased

ICN #

Figure 5.12   Accessing the Payment/Adjustment Transaction screen from the Patient Account Claim detail (Figure 5.10).

RESOLUTION 2

CASE EXAMPLE B: FRONT-END ERROR

Correct the claim by correcting the Insured ID number in Patient Registration. Once corrected, go back and pull up that particular ticket/claim and refile or resubmit a corrected claim to the insurance company.

RESOLUTION: Three steps to correct and resolve the claim issue

Step 1. Main Menu, select REGISTRATION OF A PATIENT (Figure 5.13), pull up the IND (Insured) tab, select MODIFY, and update the ID (verify the Medicare ID number on the patient's Medicare card).

Step 2. Main Menu, select COLLECTIONS (Figure 5.8), pull up PATIENT BILLING (Figure 5.9), and then pull up the ticket. From the PATIENT ACCOUNT CLAIM DETAIL (Figure 5.10) under "Billing," select MODIFY, then in the Charge Entry screen (Figure 5.14) mark (x) next to File: HCFA Electronically so the claim can be batched and then billed out to Medicare. Mark (X) File: HCFA Electronically.

Step 3. Now that you have resolved the claim issue you will need to add your notes. Add notes on how you resolved the claim issue. Pull up PATIENT BILLING (Figure 5.9) under the PATIENT ACCOUNT CLAIM DETAIL (Figure 5.10) and select NOTES. Type in what the problem was and what you did to resolve the claim issue. (**In every medical software there is a place to key in notes on what you did, either on that particular ticket or somewhere on that patient's account.**) An example of how you would type in your notes is as follows:

NOTE: Per the Medicare remittance dated 5/14/2008 denied the service because the wrong patient name pulled up when the claim was being processed because the Medicare ID number was entered incorrectly. I have corrected the ID number from #########A to #########A and resubmitted the claim electronically to Medicare.

** Key Point: Keeping good notes is another key factor in doing a great job. Putting in good notes will provide information as to what has been done or is being done to resolve the issue with that particular date of service. If someone decides to go into that particular claim, they will see your notes and will know exactly what is being done.

MEDICAL SOFTWARE: Correct Insured ID number in Patient Registration

PATIENT DATA ENTRY
STEP 1: THE SCHEDULE
File Tab: CDR (Calendar)   File Tab: AT (Appointment Type)

STEP 2: MEDICAL RECORDS
File Tab: DR (Doctors Notes)   File Tab: DIAG (Diagnostic)

File Tab: HOSP (Hospital Notes)   File Tab: F/ORMS (Forms/Correspondence)

STEP 3: REGISTRATION OF A PATIENT

File Tab: PT (Patient)	File Tab: GT (Guarantor)	File Tab: IND (Insured)	File Tab: INS (Insurance)
	Double Click to open	**Double Click to open**	**Double Click to open**

VIEW TAB

STEP 3: REGISTRATION OF A PATIENT

Insured:

(Name of the policy holder)

Patient relationship to the policy holder: (Self)____(Spouse)_____(Child)_____(Other)

Name: First_____Middle_____Last_____
Home#_____Date of Birth:_____ Sex: (M)___(F)_____ Social Security #:_____

Insurance:
> Primary:
> Secondary:
> Tertiary:

(X) PRIMARY COVERAGE:
Plan name: _____

Identification#:__#########A_____

Group #:_____ Group Name:_____

Plan Type (Bill Type):_____

Notes: _____

( ) SECONDARY COVERAGE:
( ) TERTIARY COVERAGE:
(x) SELF PAY:

Guarantor:

(Person responsible for the bill)

Statement: PRINT

Figure 5.13   Accessing the Patient Registration from the Patient Account Claim Detail (Figure 5.10).

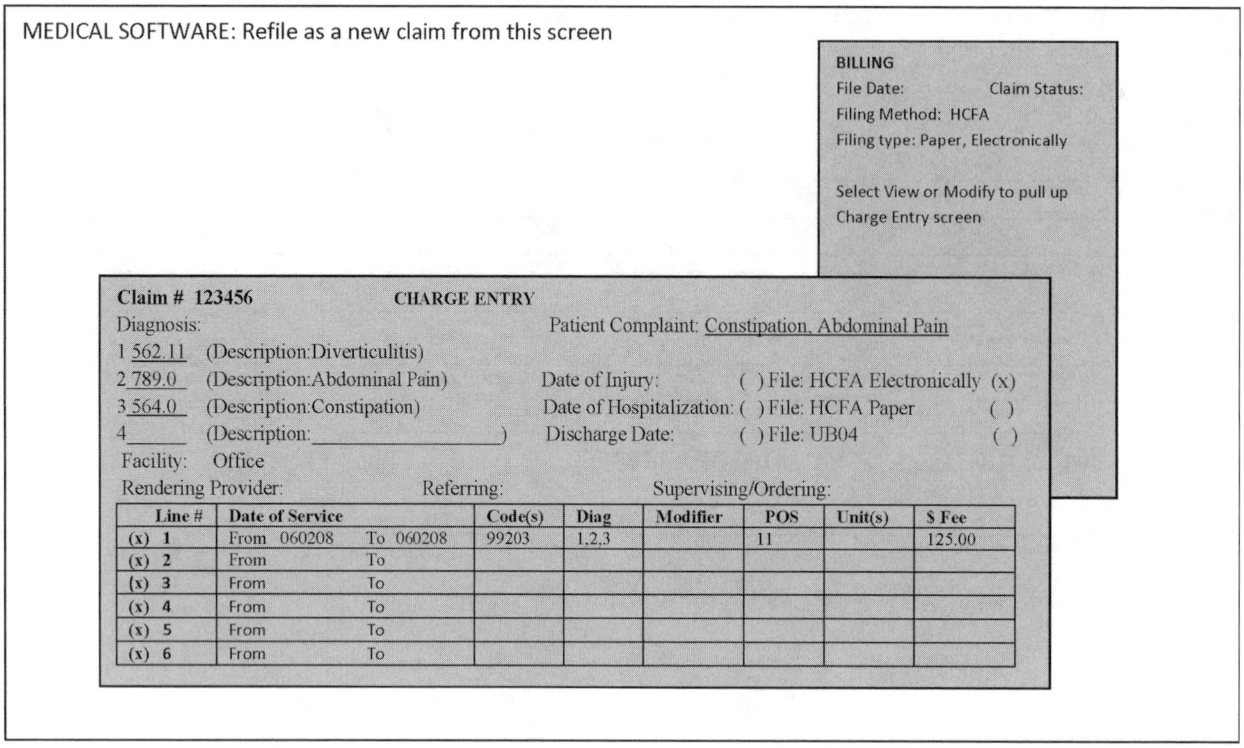

MEDICAL SOFTWARE: Refile as a new claim from this screen

BILLING
File Date: Claim Status:
Filing Method: HCFA
Filing type: Paper, Electronically

Select View or Modify to pull up
Charge Entry screen

Claim # 123456   **CHARGE ENTRY**
Diagnosis: Patient Complaint: <u>Constipation, Abdominal Pain</u>
1 <u>562.11</u>   (Description:Diverticulitis)
2 <u>789.0</u>   (Description:Abdominal Pain)   Date of Injury: ( ) File: HCFA Electronically (x)
3 <u>564.0</u>   (Description:Constipation)   Date of Hospitalization: ( ) File: HCFA Paper   ( )
4_____   (Description:_____)   Discharge Date: ( ) File: UB04   ( )
Facility: Office
Rendering Provider: Referring: Supervising/Ordering:

Line #	Date of Service		Code(s)	Diag	Modifier	POS	Unit(s)	$ Fee
(x) 1	From 060208	To 060208	99203	1,2,3		11		125.00
(x) 2	From	To						
(x) 3	From	To						
(x) 4	From	To						
(x) 5	From	To						
(x) 6	From	To						

Figure 5.14   Accessing the Charge Entry screen from the Patient Account Claim Detail (Figure 5.10).

RESOLUTION 3

CASE EXAMPLE ZZ: BILLING AND CODING ERROR

Correct the claim by voiding out the invalid code and then add in the correct code and refile or resubmit the corrected claim.

RESOLUTION: Three steps to correct the claim.

Step 1. Pull up the original ticket/claim, and pull up the charge entry so you can make the correction. Main Menu (Figure 5.9), select COLLECTIONS, pull up PATIENT BILLING and pull up the ticket. From the PATIENT ACCOUNT CLAIM DETAIL (Figure 5.10) under "Billing," select MODIFY, and then in the Charge Entry screen (Figure 5.14) on line 2, which lists CPT Code J0170, void out the charge (Figure 5.15) and key in the correct HCPCS code J0171.

Step 2. Now that you have made the correction on the ticket/claim, you will need to refile or resubmit the claim electronically to Medicare. In the Charge Entry screen, mark (x) next to File: HCFA Electronically so the claim can be batched and then billed to Medicare.

Step 3. Now that you have resolved the claim issue, the next step is to add your notes on how you resolved the claim issue. Pull up PATIENT BILLING (Figure 5.9) under the PATIENT ACCOUNT CLAIM DETAIL (Figure 5.10) and select NOTES. Type in what the problem was and what you did to resolve the claim issue.
(**In every medical software there is a place to key in notes on what you did, either on that particular ticket or somewhere on that patient's account.**) An example of how you would type in your notes is as follows:

NOTE: Per the Medicare remittance dated 5/14/2008 denied the service because J0170 is an invalid code. The HCPCS code book states to report J0171 in place of J0170. Made correction voiding J0170 and keying in correct code J0171, then rebilled the corrected claim to Medicare.

** Key Point: Keeping good notes is another key factor in doing a great job. Putting in good notes will provide information as to what has been done or is being done to resolve the issue with that particular date of service. If someone decides to go into that particular claim, they will see your notes and will know exactly what is being done.

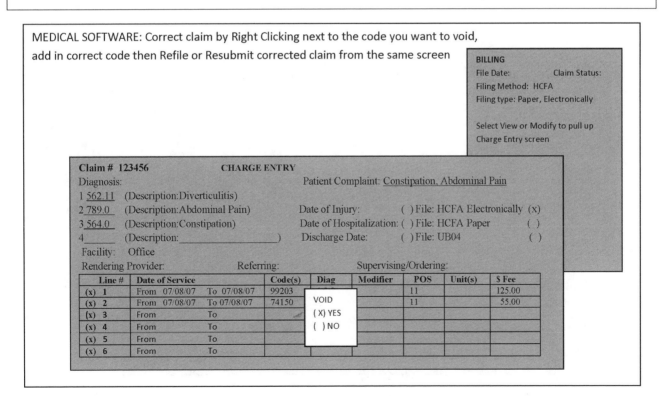

Figure 5.15   **Void an invalid code from the charge entry screen (Figure 5.14).**

RESOLUTION 4

CASE EXAMPLE L: BILLING AND CODING ERROR

Correct the claim by adding a modifier and refile or resubmit the corrected claim.

RESOLUTION: Three steps to correct the claim

Step 1. Now that you know that the second surgery was staged and related to the first surgery, you need to correct the claim by adding a "58" modifier on the ticket/claim. In the Main Menu, select COLLECTIONS (Figure 5.8), pull up PATIENT BILLING (Figure 5.9), then pull up the ticket. From the PATIENT ACCOUNT CLAIM DETAIL under "Billing," select MODIFY, then in the charge entry screen (Figure 5.14) under Charge Entry on line 1, which lists CPT Code 20694, add 58 in the Modifier Column.

Step 2. Refile or resubmit corrected claim. Under Charge Entry, mark (X) File: HCFA Electronically so the claim can be batched and billed to Medicare.

Step 3. Now that you have resolved the claim issue, the next step is to add your notes on how you resolved the claim issue. Pull up PATIENT BILLING (Figure 5.9) under the PATIENT ACCOUNT CLAIM DETAIL (Figure 5.10) and select NOTES. Type in what the problem was and what you did to resolve the claim issue.
(**In every medical software there is a place to key in notes on what you did, either on that particular ticket or somewhere on that patient's account.**) An example of how you would type in your notes is as follows:

NOTE: Per the Medicare remittance dated 5/14/2008 denied the procedure because it was billed within the global period of the previous surgery. Both surgeries are related and because the surgeon went back and removed the pins that he placed, I added a 58 modifier and rebilled the corrected claim to Medicare.

** Key Point: Keeping good notes is another key factor in doing a great job. Putting in good notes will provide information as to what has been done or is being done to resolve the issue with that particular date of service. If someone decides to go into that particular claim, they will see your notes and will know exactly what is being done.

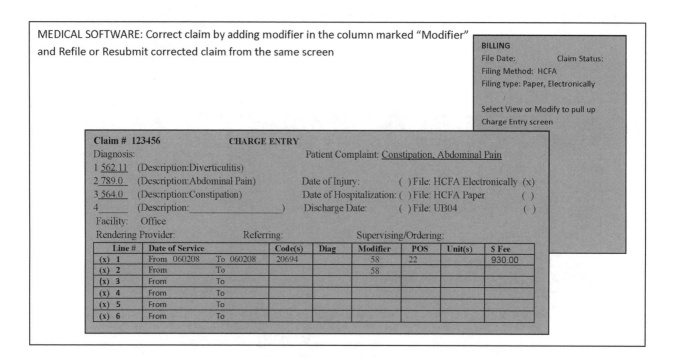

Figure 5.16 Correct the claim (adding a modifier), refile corrected claim from charge entry screen (Figure 5.14).

RESOLUTION 5

CASE EXAMPLE O: BILLING AND CODING ERROR

Correct the claim by adding the diagnosis as the primary diagnosis, listing original diagnosis as secondary, and refile or resubmit the corrected claim.

RESOLUTION: Three steps to correct the claim

Step 1. Correct the claim by changing and adding diagnosis. In the Main Menu, select COLLECTIONS (Figure 5.8), pull up PATIENT BILLING (Figure 5.9), and then pull up the ticket. From the PATIENT ACCOUNT CLAIM DETAIL (Figure 5.10) under "Billing," select MODIFY. Then in the charge entry screen (Figure 5.14) under Charge Entry, locate the diagnosis section, change E code from primary to secondary, add in Diagnosis 719.54 as the primary diagnosis, then on line 1, which lists CPT Code 73140, in the Diagnosis Column, link diagnosis 1 & 2 to line 1.

Step 2. Refile or resubmit corrected claim (Figure 5.17). Under Charge Entry, mark (X) File: HCFA Electronically so the claim can be batched and then billed to Medicare.

Step 3. Now that you have resolved the claim issue, the next step is to add your notes on how you resolved the claim issue. Pull up PATIENT BILLING (Figure 5.9) under the PATIENT ACCOUNT CLAIM DETAIL (Figure 5.10) and select NOTES. Type in what the problem was and what you did to resolve the claim issue.
(**In every medical software there is a place to key in notes on what you did, either on that particular ticket or somewhere on that patient's account.**) An example of how you would type in your notes is as follows:

NOTE: Per the Medicare remittance dated 5/14/2008 denied CPT Code 73140 because the primary diagnosis is missing. Made correction by changing diagnosis E906.0 to the secondary diagnosis, then I added in 719.54 as the primary diagnosis linking both to line 1 and refiled the corrected claim to Medicare.

" Key Point: Keeping good notes is another key factor in doing a great job. Putting in good notes will provide information as to what has been done or is being done to resolve the issue with that particular date of service. If someone decides to go into that particular claim, they will see your notes and will know exactly what is being done.

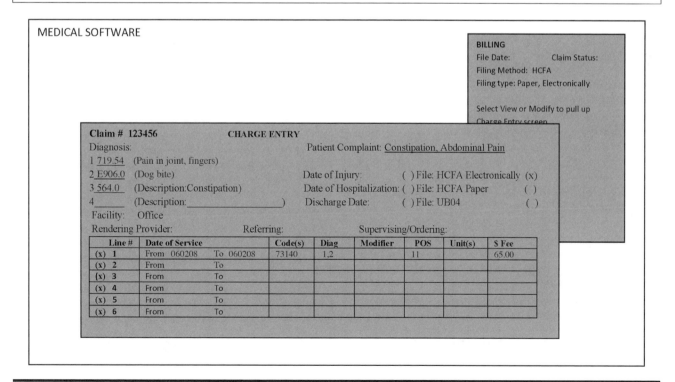

Figure 5.17   Correct the claim (adding diagnosis), refile corrected claim from charge entry screen (Figure 5.14).

RESOLUTION 6

CASE EXAMPLE M: BILLING AND CODING ERROR

Make an adjustment on the claim by adjusting off the charge.

RESOLUTION: Two steps to correct the claim

Step 1. Verify that both procedures were performed on the same anatomical site (LT wrist) during the same session. The one code that was denied will need to be adjusted off as a bundled code. In the Main Menu, select COLLECTIONS, pull up PATIENT BILLING , then pull up the ticket. From the PATIENT ACCOUNT CLAIM DETAIL under "Payment Type," select MODIFY (Figure 5.18). Under Payment Transaction, post charges on each line in the Disallow/Adj Column, and in the Disallow/Adj Type Column drop-down window, select "Bundled." By posting your adjustment it will adjust off the charge.

Step 2. Now that you have resolved the claim issue, the next step is to add your notes on how you resolved the claim issue. Pull up PATIENT BILLING under PATIENT ACCOUNT CLAIM DETAIL and select NOTES. Type in what the problem was and what you did to resolve the claim issue.
(**In every medical software there is a place to key in notes on what you did, either on that particular ticket or somewhere on that patient's account.**) An example of how you would type in your notes is as follows:

NOTE: Per the Medicare remittance dated 5/14/2008 denied the procedure because per CCI Edits it is mutually excluded with the other procedure. Op Notes state that both procedures were performed on the LT Wrist, so I made an adjustment on the claim by adjusting off the charge as a bundled code.

** Key Point: Keeping good notes is another key factor in doing a great job. Putting in good notes will provide information as to what has been done or is being done to resolve the issue with that particular date of service. If someone decides to go into that particular claim, they will see your notes and will know exactly what is being done.

** Key point: Medicare will reimburse only for the lesser-valued of the two procedures.

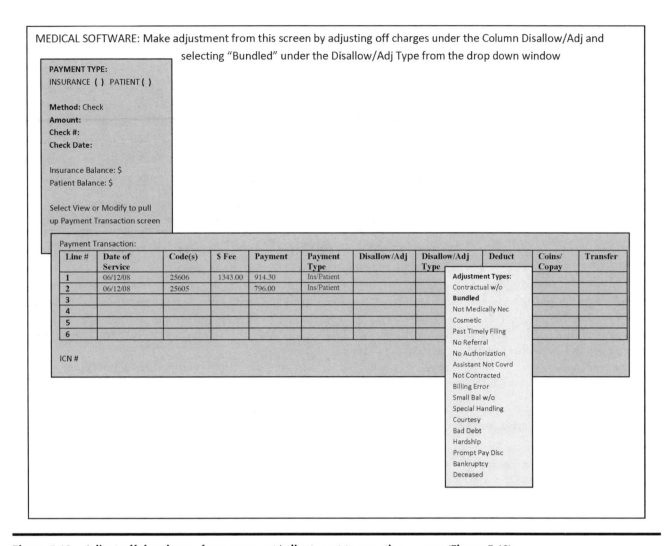

Figure 5.18 Adjust off the charge from payment/adjustment transaction screen (Figure 5.12).

RESOLUTION 7

CASE EXAMPLE DEF: OTHER CLAIM ISSUES

Make an adjustment on the claim by transferring charges to patient responsibility.

RESOLUTION: Three steps to correct the claim

Step 1. In the Main Menu, select COLLECTIONS, pull up PATIENT BILLING, then pull up the ticket. From the PATIENT ACCOUNT CLAIM DETAIL under "Payment Type," select VIEW. Under the Transfer column, key in charges on each line (Figure 5.19), then select OK to save transaction. This will transfer charges to the patient responsibility.

Step 2. In the Main Menu, select REGISTRATION OF A PATIENT, pull up the GT (Guarantor) tab, and under STATEMENT, select PRINT and mail out a new statement.

Step 3. Now that you have resolved the claim issue, the next step is to add your notes on how you resolved the claim issue.

Pull up PATIENT BILLING under the PATIENT ACCOUNT CLAIM DETAIL and select NOTES. Type in what the problem was and what you did to resolve the claim issue.
(**In every medical software there is a place to key in notes on what you did, either on that particular ticket or somewhere on that patient's account.**) An example of how you would type in your notes is as follows:

NOTE: Per the Medicare remittance dated 5/14/2008 denied the service because service or item is not a covered benefit under his or her Part B Medicare plan. I transferred charges over to patient responsibility and mailed out a new statement.

** Key Point: Keeping good notes is another key factor in doing a great job. Putting in good notes will provide information as to what has been done or is being done to resolve the issue with that particular date of service. If someone decides to go into that particular claim, they will see your notes and will know exactly what is being done.

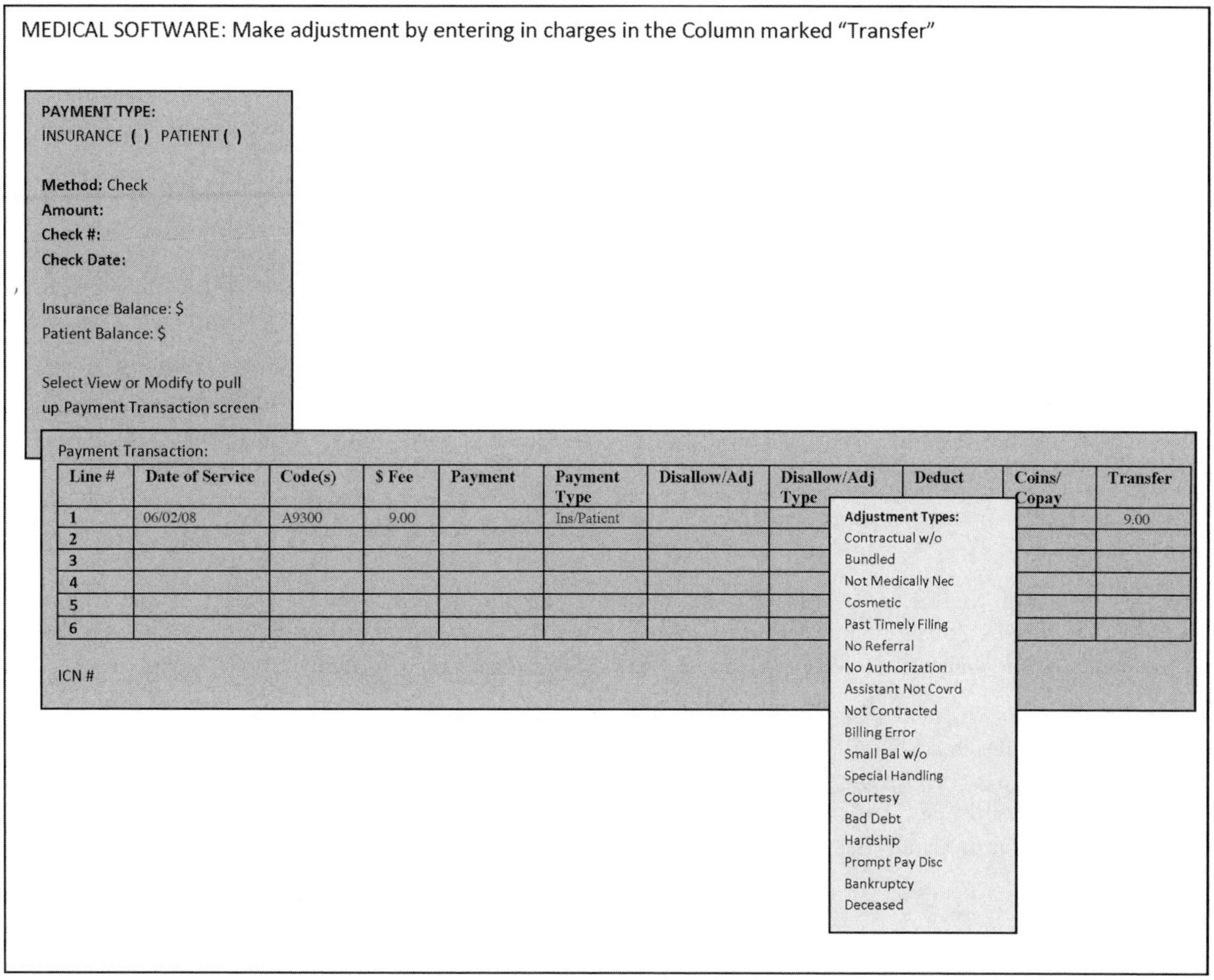

MEDICAL SOFTWARE: Make adjustment by entering in charges in the Column marked "Transfer"

PAYMENT TYPE:
INSURANCE ( )   PATIENT ( )

Method: Check
Amount:
Check #:
Check Date:

Insurance Balance: $
Patient Balance: $

Select View or Modify to pull
up Payment Transaction screen

Payment Transaction:

Line #	Date of Service	Code(s)	$ Fee	Payment	Payment Type	Disallow/Adj	Disallow/Adj Type	Deduct	Coins/Copay	Transfer
1	06/02/08	A9300	9.00		Ins/Patient					9.00
2										
3										
4										
5										
6										

ICN #

Adjustment Types:
Contractual w/o
Bundled
Not Medically Nec
Cosmetic
Past Timely Filing
No Referral
No Authorization
Assistant Not Covrd
Not Contracted
Billing Error
Small Bal w/o
Special Handling
Courtesy
Bad Debt
Hardship
Prompt Pay Disc
Bankruptcy
Deceased

Figure 5.19   Transfer charge amount to patient responsibility from payment/adjustment transaction screen (Figure 5.12).

RESOLUTION 8

CASE EXAMPLE GHI: OTHER CLAIM ISSUES

Submit an appeal.

RESOLUTION: Five steps to correct the claim

Step 1. Print out the Letter of Appeal. In the Main Menu, select the COLLECTIONS (Chapter 5, Step 8) button, double-click in the box under LTR (Letters) (Figure 5.20), mark (x) next to your Letter of Appeal, then select PRINT.

Step 2. Print out Clinic Notes, Op Notes, and Letter of Medical Necessity (LMN). In the Main Menu, select the MEDICAL RECORD (Figure 5.20) (Chapter 2, Step 2) button, double-click in the box under DR (Doctors Notes), mark (x) next to the date of service on which the first visit took place, then select PRINT. Double-click in the box under HOSP (Hospital Notes), mark (x) next to the date of service in question, then select PRINT. Double-click in the box under FORMS (Forms/Correspondence), mark (x) next to "Letter of Medical Necessity," then select PRINT.

Step 3. Send the documentation via Certified Mail to the address on the form. Make a copy, have it scanned in (if software is equipped) or place a copy in the patient's chart.

Step 4. Follow up on your Ticket/Claim. In the Main Menu, select the COLLECTIONS (Chapter 5, Step 8) button, double-click in the box under TCKLR (Tickler) (Figure 5.9), mark (x) next to the month in which you want to follow up on your ticket/claim, double-click on the day, and add the message "Follow up on Appeal Ticket 123456."

Step 5. Now that you have resolved the claim issue, the next step is to add your notes on how you resolved the claim issue (Figure 5.21). Pull up PATIENT BILLING under the PATIENT ACCOUNT CLAIM DETAIL (Figure 5.10) and select NOTES. Type in what the problem was and what you did to resolve the claim issue.
(**In every medical software there is a place to key in notes on what you did, either on that particular ticket or somewhere on that patient's account.**) An example of how you would type in your notes is as follows:

NOTE: Per Medicare Remit dated _/_/_ denied procedures because they were considered to be non-covered charges. This type of procedure is referred to as a "Tummy Tuck," which is considered cosmetic. Patient had undergone several surgeries for recurrent incisional hernia repair due to a hysterectomy for removal of a tumor. Patient also has lost an abnormal amount of weight which has caused an excessive amount of skin that hangs below pubis causing irritation. With these factors in place doctor dictated a Letter of Medical Necessity stating the need for reconstructive surgery, not cosmetic. Mailed out medical documentation certified to Trailblazer (address is listed on the redetermination request form) for redetermination. Placed a copy in the patient chart and set a follow-up for at least 65 days.

NOTE: Tickler: 65-day Follow-up Ticket/Claim # 123456

We received Medicare's Appeal Decision letter and per their decision states "Unfavorable because procedure is cosmetic and patient is responsible for payment for these services." We are appealing their decision and leaving everything still pending insurance. We have been in contact with the patient, who has provided us with medical documentation from her primary care physician. We are attaching original documentation from our first appeal and additional documentation and mailing everything via Certified Mail to Q2 Administrator (address is listed on the reconsideration request form) for a second level of appeal. Placed a copy in the patient chart and set a follow-up for at least another 65 days.

NOTE: Notification was received from Q2 Administrators informing us that our reconsideration (2nd Level of Appeal) was received, assigning it an appeal number. Contact information was also provided if we had any questions or concerns. Medicare Appeal Number ######. Letter is in patient chart.

NOTE: After several weeks of reconsideration, the claim was reprocessed and an additional payment was received. The claim issue was resolved.

** Key Point: Keeping good notes is another key factor in doing a great job. Putting in good notes will provide information as to what has been done or is being done to resolve the issue with that particular date of service. If someone decides to go into that particular claim, they will see your notes and will know exactly what is being done.

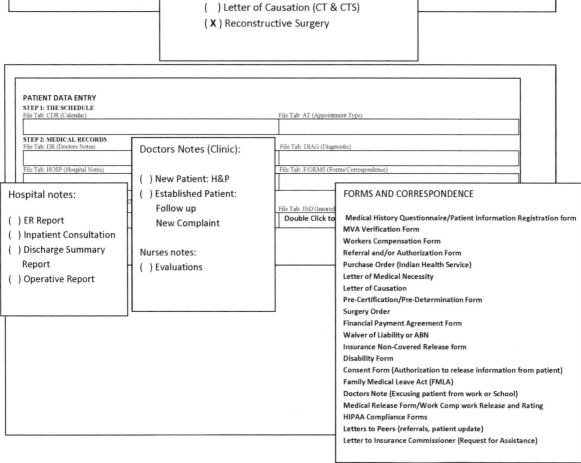

Figure 5.20 Access letters (LTR) from the collection screen (Figure 5.9). Access doctor's (DR) notes in the medical records screen, select from the main menu (Figure 5.8).

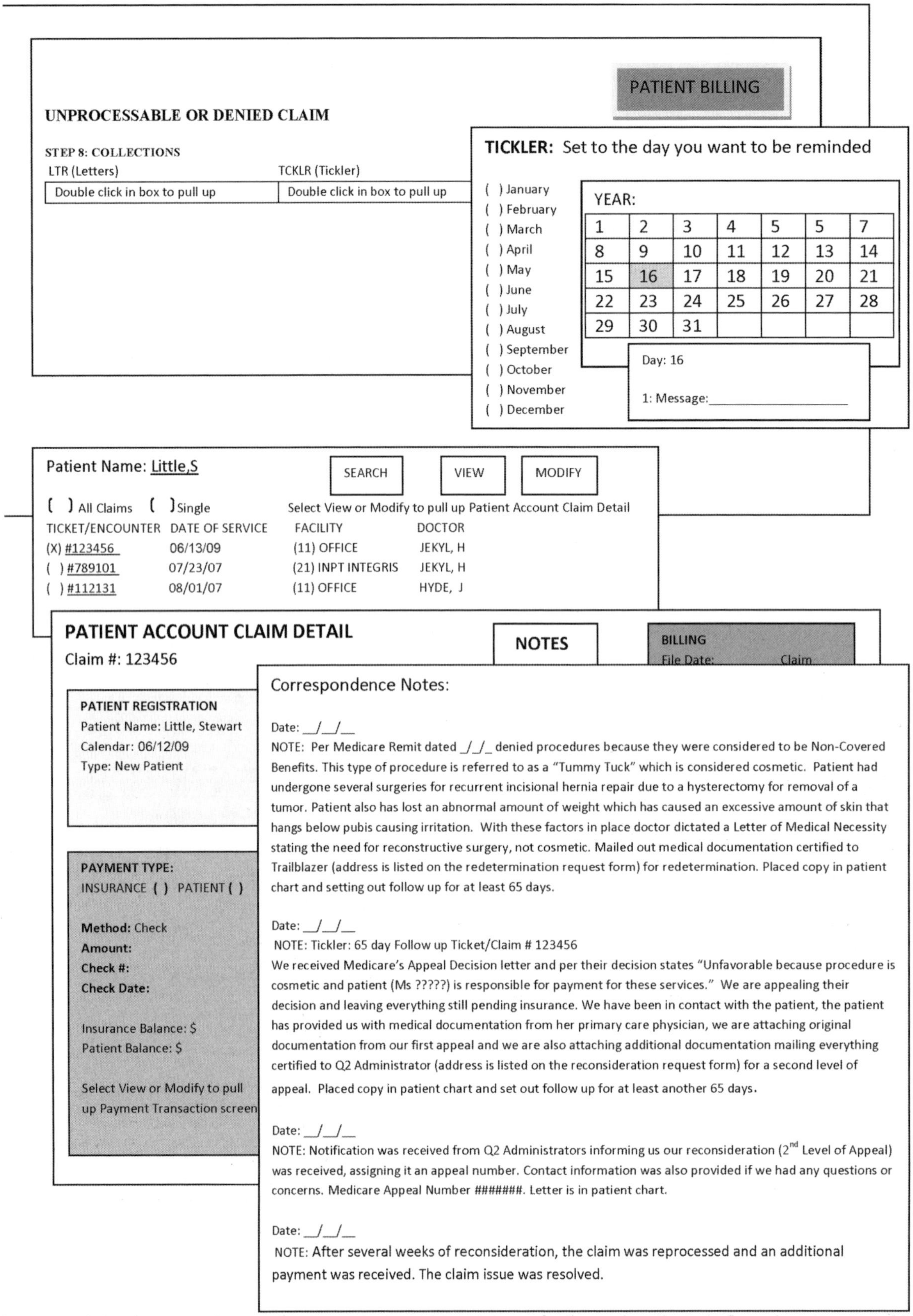

UNPROCESSABLE OR DENIED CLAIM

STEP 8: COLLECTIONS

LTR (Letters)	TCKLR (Tickler)
Double click in box to pull up	Double click in box to pull up

PATIENT BILLING

TICKLER: Set to the day you want to be reminded

( ) January
( ) February
( ) March
( ) April
( ) May
( ) June
( ) July
( ) August
( ) September
( ) October
( ) November
( ) December

YEAR:

1	2	3	4	5	5	7
8	9	10	11	12	13	14
15	16	17	18	19	20	21
22	23	24	25	26	27	28
29	30	31				

Day: 16

1: Message:_____

Patient Name: <u>Little,S</u>

SEARCH   VIEW   MODIFY

( ) All Claims   ( ) Single   Select View or Modify to pull up Patient Account Claim Detail

TICKET/ENCOUNTER	DATE OF SERVICE	FACILITY	DOCTOR
(X) <u>#123456</u>	06/13/09	(11) OFFICE	JEKYL, H
( ) <u>#789101</u>	07/23/07	(21) INPT INTEGRIS	JEKYL, H
( ) <u>#112131</u>	08/01/07	(11) OFFICE	HYDE, J

PATIENT ACCOUNT CLAIM DETAIL

Claim #: 123456

NOTES

BILLING
File Date: Claim

PATIENT REGISTRATION
Patient Name: Little, Stewart
Calendar: 06/12/09
Type: New Patient

Correspondence Notes:

Date: __/__/__
NOTE: Per Medicare Remit dated __/__/_ denied procedures because they were considered to be Non-Covered Benefits. This type of procedure is referred to as a "Tummy Tuck" which is considered cosmetic. Patient had undergone several surgeries for recurrent incisional hernia repair due to a hysterectomy for removal of a tumor. Patient also has lost an abnormal amount of weight which has caused an excessive amount of skin that hangs below pubis causing irritation. With these factors in place doctor dictated a Letter of Medical Necessity stating the need for reconstructive surgery, not cosmetic. Mailed out medical documentation certified to Trailblazer (address is listed on the redetermination request form) for redetermination. Placed copy in patient chart and setting out follow up for at least 65 days.

Date: __/__/__
NOTE: Tickler: 65 day Follow up Ticket/Claim # 123456
We received Medicare's Appeal Decision letter and per their decision states "Unfavorable because procedure is cosmetic and patient (Ms ?????) is responsible for payment for these services." We are appealing their decision and leaving everything still pending insurance. We have been in contact with the patient, the patient has provided us with medical documentation from her primary care physician, we are attaching original documentation from our first appeal and we are also attaching additional documentation mailing everything certified to Q2 Administrator (address is listed on the reconsideration request form) for a second level of appeal. Placed copy in patient chart and set out follow up for at least another 65 days.

Date: __/__/__
NOTE: Notification was received from Q2 Administrators informing us our reconsideration (2nd Level of Appeal) was received, assigning it an appeal number. Contact information was also provided if we had any questions or concerns. Medicare Appeal Number #######. Letter is in patient chart.

Date: __/__/__
NOTE: After several weeks of reconsideration, the claim was reprocessed and an additional payment was received. The claim issue was resolved.

PAYMENT TYPE:
INSURANCE ( ) PATIENT ( )

Method: Check
Amount:
Check #:
Check Date:

Insurance Balance: $
Patient Balance: $

Select View or Modify to pull up Payment Transaction screen

Figure 5.21   Add your notes, access patient account claim detail from the patient billing screen (Figure 5.10).

Case Examples

In the next several pages I will give you a step-by-step guide on how to correct a claim by working an EOB, using insurance correspondence, following up on a claim, and working off an aging report (outstanding claims 45 days old).

The steps include answering questions and showing the area of error or concern and the correct way to resolve a claim issue, which will help you in getting the job done.

Section 1: Front-End Errors

I have provided you with ten case examples (Cases A, B, C, D, E, F, G, H, I and J), with one or two different situations regarding front-end errors. Some may have more than two. Questions and answers are included, along with instructions on how to resolve that particular issue.

Case A: An example Remittance Advice (RA) is provided. The RA shows ANSI CARC and RARC denial codes and what those denial codes mean.

CASE A: SITUATION 1

MEDICARE PART B (ERA) REMITTANCE ADVICE
Provider#:
Check/EFT (Electronic Fund Transfer) #: Issue Date: 00/00/2008

Name: HIC #########A ACCT ICN **CASE A**

PROV #	DOS	POS	NOS	CPT	MOD	BILLED $	ALLOW	DEDUCT	COINS	GRP/RC	AMT	PAID PROV $
######	051408	11	1	99203		125.00	0.00	0.00	0.00	PR-31	125.00	0.00
				73110		89.00	0.00	0.00	0.00	PR-31	89.00	0.00
PT RESP	0.00			CLAIM TOTAL		214.00	0.00	0.00	0.00		214.00	0.00
											NET	0.00

Name: HIC #########A ACCT ICN

PROV #	DOS	POS	NOS	CPT	MOD	BILLED $	ALLOW	DEDUCT	COINS	GRP/RC	AMT	PAID PROV $
######	060208	11	1	99203		125.00	0.00	0.00	0.00	CO-16	125.00	0.00
				REM: MA27								
PT RESP	0.00			CLAIM TOTAL		125.00	0.00	0.00	0.00		125.00	0.00
											NET	0.00

Name: HIC #########A ACCT ICN

PROV	DOS	POS	NOS	CPT	MOD	BILLED $	ALLOW	DEDUCT	COINS	GRP/RC	AMT	PAID PROV $
######	061208	11	1	99203		125.00	0.00	0.00	0.00	CO-140	125.00	0.00
######	061208	11	1	73560	LT	20.00	0.00	0.00	0.00	CO-140	20.00	0.00
######	061208	11	1	73610		78.00	0.00	0.00	0.00	CO-140	78.00	0.00
PT RESP	1.20			CLAIM TOTAL		223.00	0.00	0.00	0.00		223.00	0.00
											NET	0.00

MESSAGE CODES: GROUP/CARC/RARC

Description:

PR Patient Responsibility

31 Patient cannot be identified as insured

CASE A: SITUATION 1

CODING ERROR: ANSI CARC/RARC CODES PR-31

QUESTION: We show that the patient has a Medicare card, so why would this be the patient responsibility?

ANSWER: If you look at the patient insurance (MEDICARE) card, it states that the patient is entitled to Part A Hospital coverage only. If Part B Medical is not stated on the insurance card, this means patient is not enrolled. Part B covers doctor's fees.

For help, go to: Area A1 Guidebook. Refer to: Chapter 2 , Step 3 , Unit Iv , Part D , Section 1

MEDICARE HEALTH INSURANCE	
NAME OF BENEFICIARY	
First Middle Last	
MEDICARE CLAIM NUMBER	SEX
###-##-####-A	
IS ENTITLED TO	EFFECTIVE DATE
HOSPITAL (PART A) ONLY	
Sign	
Here _____	

RESOLUTION: Four steps to correct the claim
Make an adjustment on the ticket/claim by transferring the balance from insurance to the patient responsibility and set the patient account to self-pay.

Step 1. Make an adjustment on the claim by transferring charges to patient responsibility. In the Main Menu, select COLLECTIONS, pull up PATIENT BILLING, then pull up the ticket. From the PATIENT ACCOUNT CLAIM DETAIL under "Payment Type," select VIEW. Under the Transfer column, key in charges on each line and select OK to save transaction. This will transfer charges to patient responsibility.

Step 2. Make another adjustment on the patient account by updating from Insurance to Self-Pay. In the Main Menu, select REGISTRATION OF A PATIENT, pull up the INS (Insurance) tab, select MODIFY, and set the account from Insurance to Self-Pay.

Step 3. Send out a new statement. Pull up the GT (Guarantor) tab. Under STATEMENT, select PRINT and mail out a new statement.

Step 4. Now that you have resolved the claim issue, the next step is to add your notes on how you resolved the claim issue. Pull up PATIENT BILLING under the PATIENT ACCOUNT CLAIM DETAIL and select NOTES. Type in what the problem was, and what you did to resolve the claim issue.

(**In every medical software there is a place to key in notes on what you did, either on that particular ticket or somewhere on that patient's account.**) An example of how you would type in your notes is as follows:

NOTE: Per the Medicare remittance dated 5/14/2008 denied the service because patient was not eligible for Medicare Part B benefits at the time of service. I transferred charges over to the patient responsibility, set the account to self-pay, and mailed out a new statement.

** Key Point: Keeping good notes is another key factor in doing a great job. Putting in good notes will provide information as to what has been done or is being done to resolve the issue with that particular date of service. If someone decides to go into that particular claim, they will see your notes and will know exactly what is being done.

CASE B: SITUATION 1

MEDICARE PART B   (ERA) REMITTANCE ADVICE

Provider#:

Check/EFT (Electronic Fund Transfer) #:   Issue Date: 00/00/2008

Name: HIC #########A   ACCT   ICN   **CASE B**

PROV #	DOS	POS	NOS	CPT	MOD	BILLED $	ALLOW	DEDUCT	COINS	GRP/RC	AMT	PAID PROV $
######	051408	11	1	99203		125.00	0.00	0.00	0.00	PR-31	125.00	0.00
				73110		89.00	0.00	0.00	0.00	PR-31	89.00	0.00
PT RESP	0.00			CLAIM TOTAL		214.00	0.00	0.00	0.00		214.00	0.00
											NET	0.00

Name: HIC #########A   ACCT   ICN

PROV #	DOS	POS	NOS	CPT	MOD	BILLED $	ALLOW	DEDUCT	COINS	GRP/RC	AMT	PAID PROV $
######	060208	11	1	99203		125.00	0.00	0.00	0.00	CO-16	125.00	0.00
				REM: MA27								
PT RESP	0.00			CLAIM TOTAL		125.00	0.00	0.00	0.00		125.00	0.00
											NET	0.00

Name: HIC #########A   ACCT   ICN

PROV	DOS	POS	NOS	CPT	MOD	BILLED $	ALLOW	DEDUCT	COINS	GRP/RC	AMT	PAID PROV $
######	061208	11	1	99203		125.00	0.00	0.00	0.00	CO-140	125.00	0.00
######	061208	11	1	73560	LT	20.00	0.00	0.00	0.00	C0-140	20.00	0.00
######	061208	11	1	73610		78.00	0.00	0.00	0.00	C0-140	78.00	0.00
PT RESP	1.20			CLAIM TOTAL		223.00	0.00	0.00	0.00		223.00	0.00
											NET	0.00

MESSAGE CODES: GROUP/CARC/RARC

Description:

CO   **Contractual Obligation**

16   **Claim lacks information for adjudication**

MA27   **Missing/Incomplete/Invalid entitlement number or name shown on the claim**

CASE B: SITUATION 1

CODING ERROR: ANSI CARC/RARC CODES CO-16 and MA27

QUESTION: Is the patient ID number incorrect or is the patient name spelled wrong?

ANSWER: The ID number was entered incorrectly, so the name on the remittance is not our patient.

For help, go to: Area A1 Guidebook. Refer to: Chapter 2, Unit IV, Step 3, Part D, Section 1

MEDICARE HEALTH INSURANCE

NAME OF BENEFICIARY

First Middle Last

MEDICARE CLAIM NUMBER   SEX

###-##-####-A

IS ENTITLED TO   EFFECTIVE DATE

HOSPITAL (PART A)

MEDICAL (PART B)

Sign

Here _____

RESOLUTION: Three steps to correct the claim

Correct the ID number and refile to Medicare as a new claim so it can be processed under the correct patient.

Step 1. Correct the information in patient registration. In the Main Menu, select REGISTRATION OF A PATIENT, pull up the IND (Insured) tab, select MODIFY, and update the ID (verify the Medicare ID number on the patient's Medicare card).

Step 2. Refile or resubmit corrected claim. In the Main Menu, select COLLECTIONS, pull up PATIENT BILLING, and then pull up the ticket. From the PATIENT ACCOUNT CLAIM DETAIL under "Billing," select MODIFY. In the Charge Entry screen mark (x) next to File: HCFA Electronically so the claim can be batched and then billed to Medicare

Step 3. Now that you have resolved the claim issue, the next step is to add your notes on how you resolved the claim issue. Pull up PATIENT BILLING under the PATIENT ACCOUNT CLAIM DETAIL and select NOTES. Type in what the problem was and what you did to resolve the claim issue.

(**In every medical software there is a place to key in notes on what you did, either on that particular ticket or somewhere on that patient's account.**) An example of how you would type in your notes is as follows:

NOTE: Per the Medicare remittance dated 5/14/2008 denied the service because the wrong patient name pulled up when the claim was being processed because the Medicare ID number was entered incorrectly. I have corrected the ID number from #########A to #########A and resubmitted the claim electronically to Medicare.

** Key Point: Keeping good notes is another key factor in doing a great job. Putting in good notes will provide information as to what has been done or is being done to resolve the issue with that particular date of service. If someone decides to go into that particular claim, they will see your notes and will know exactly what is being done.

CASE C: SITUATION 1

MEDICARE PART B   **(ERA) REMITTANCE ADVICE**

Provider#:

Check/EFT (Electronic Fund Transfer) #:   Issue Date: 00/00/2008

Name: HIC #########A   ACCT   ICN   **CASE C**

PROV #	DOS	POS	NOS	CPT	MOD	BILLED $	ALLOW	DEDUCT	COINS	GRP/RC	AMT	PAID PROV $
#######	051408	11	1	99203		125.00	0.00	0.00	0.00	PR-31	125.00	0.00
				73110		89.00	0.00	0.00	0.00	PR-31	89.00	0.00
PT RESP	0.00			CLAIM TOTAL		214.00	0.00	0.00	0.00		214.00	0.00
											NET	0.00

Name: HIC #########A   ACCT   ICN

PROV #	DOS	POS	NOS	CPT	MOD	BILLED $	ALLOW	DEDUCT	COINS	GRP/RC	AMT	PAID PROV $
#######	060208	11	1	99203		125.00	0.00	0.00	0.00	CO-16	125.00	0.00
				REM: MA27								
PT RESP	0.00			CLAIM TOTAL		125.00	0.00	0.00	0.00		125.00	0.00
											NET	0.00

Name: HIC #########A   ACCT   ICN

PROV	DOS	POS	NOS	CPT	MOD	BILLED $	ALLOW	DEDUCT	COINS	GRP/RC	AMT	PAID PROV $
######	061208	11	1	99203		125.00	0.00	0.00	0.00	CO-140	125.00	0.00
######	061208	11	1	73560	LT	20.00	0.00	0.00	0.00	C0-140	20.00	0.00
######	061208	11	1	73610		78.00	0.00	0.00	0.00	C0-140	78.00	0.00
PT RESP	1.20			CLAIM TOTAL		223.00	0.00	0.00	0.00		223.00	0.00
											NET	0.00

MESSAGE CODES: GROUP/CARC/RARC

Description:

CO   Contractual Obligation

140   Patient/Insured health identification number and name do not match

CASE C: SITUATION 1

CODING ERROR: ANSI CARC/RARC CODES CO-140

QUESTION: Is the patient ID number incorrect or is the patient name spelled wrong?

ANSWER: The ID number was entered incorrectly because the patient name on the remittance is our patient.

ANSWER: For help, go to: Area A1 Guidebook. Refer to: Chapter 2, Unit IV, Step 3, Part D, Section 1

> **MEDICARE HEALTH INSURANCE**
>
> NAME OF BENEFICIARY
>
> First Middle Last
> MEDICARE CLAIM NUMBER   SEX
> ###-##-####-A
> IS ENTITLED TO   EFFECTIVE DATE
> HOSPITAL (PART A)
> MEDICAL (PART B)
>
> Sign
> Here _____

RESOLUTION: Three steps to correct the claim
Correct the claim by correcting the ID number and refile the claim to Medicare as a new claim.

Step 1. In the Main Menu, select REGISTRATION OF A PATIENT, pull up the IND (Insured) tab, select MODIFY, and update the ID number (verify the Medicare ID number on the patient's Medicare card).

Step 2. In the Main Menu, select COLLECTIONS, pull up PATIENT BILLING, and then pull up the ticket. From the PATIENT ACCOUNT CLAIM DETAIL under "Billing," select MODIFY. Under Charge Entry mark (X) File: HCFA Electronically so the claim can be batched and billed to Medicare.

Step 3. Now that you have resolved the claim issue, the next step is to add in your notes on how you resolved the claim issue. Pull up PATIENT BILLING under the PATIENT ACCOUNT CLAIM DETAIL and select NOTES. Type in what the problem was and what you did to resolve the claim issue.

(**In every medical software there is a place to key in notes on what you did, either on that particular ticket or somewhere on that patient's account.**) An example of how you would type in your notes is as follows:

NOTE: Per the Medicare remittance dated 5/14/2008 denied the service because the wrong Medicare ID number was entered. I have corrected the ID number from #########A to #########A and resubmitted the claim electronically to Medicare.

** Key Point: Keeping good notes is another key factor in doing a great job. Putting in good notes will provide information as to what has been done or is being done to resolve the issue with that particular date of service. If someone decides to go into that particular claim, they will see your notes and will know exactly what is being done.

CASE D: SITUATIONS 1 AND 2

MEDICARE PART B   **(ERA) REMITTANCE ADVICE**

Provider#:

Check/EFT (Electronic Fund Transfer) #:   Issue Date: 00/00/2008

Name: HIC #########A   ACCT   ICN   **CASE D**

PROV #	DOS	POS	NOS	CPT	MOD	BILLED $	ALLOW	DEDUCT	COINS	GRP/RC	AMT	PAID PROV $
######	051408	11	1	99203		125.00	0.00	0.00	0.00	CO-22	125.00	0.00
				73110		89.00	0.00	0.00	0.00	CO-22	89.00	0.00
PT RESP	0.00			CLAIM TOTAL		214.00	0.00	0.00	0.00		214.00	0.00
											NET	0.00

Name: HIC #########A   ACCT   ICN

PROV #	DOS	POS	NOS	CPT	MOD	BILLED $	ALLOW	DEDUCT	COINS	GRP/RC	AMT	PAID PROV $
######	060208	11	1	99203		125.00	0.00	0.00	0.00	CO-16	125.00	0.00
######	061208	11	1	73560	LT	20.00	0.00	0.00	0.00	CO-16	20.00	0.00
				REM: MA04 N155								
PT RESP	0.00			CLAIM TOTAL		125.00	0.00	0.00	0.00		125.00	0.00
											NET	0.00

Name: HIC #########A   ACCT   ICN

PROV	DOS	POS	NOS	CPT	MOD	BILLED $	ALLOW	DEDUCT	COINS	GRP/RC	AMT	PAID PROV $
######	061208	11	1	99203		125.00	55.00	0.00	11.00	CO-45	70.00	44.00
######	061208	11	1	73520	LT	20.00	0.00	0.00	0.00	C0-109	20.00	0.00
				REM: MA101								
PT RESP	11.00			CLAIM TOTAL		145.00	55.00	0.00	11.00		90.00	44.00
											NET	44.00

PROV	DOS	POS	NOS	CPT	MOD	BILLED $	ALLOW	DEDUCT	COINS	GRP/RC	AMT	PAID PROV $
######	061208	11	1	99203		125.00	55 .00	0.00	11.00	CO-45	70.00	44.00
######	061208	11	1	73560	LT	20.00	9.00	9.00	0.00	CO-45	11.00	0.00
######	061208	11	1	L4360		78.00	0.00	0.00	0.00	CO-109	78.00	0.00
PT RESP	20.00			CLAIM TOTAL		223.00	59.00	9.00	11.00		159.00	44.00
											NET	44.00

PROV	DOS	POS	NOS	CPT	MOD	BILLED $	ALLOW	DEDUCT	COINS	GRP/RC	AMT	PAID PROV $
######	061208	11	1	99203		125.00	0.00	0.00	0.00	OA-109	125.00	0.00
######	061208	11	1	73560	LT	20.00	0.00	0.00	0.00	OA-109	20.00	0.00
######	061208	11	1	73610		78.00	0.00	0.00	0.00	OA-109	78.00	0.00
PT RESP	1.20			CLAIM TOTAL		223.00	0.00	0.00	0.00		223.00	0.00
											NET	0.00

MESSAGE CODES: GROUP/CARC/RARC

Description:

CO   Contractual Obligation

22   Care maybe covered by another payer per Coordination of Benefits (COB)

CASE D: SITUATION 1

CODING ERROR: ANSI CARC/RARC CODES CO-22
We billed Medicare as the primary payer, but according to Medicare they show the patient having other primary coverage.

QUESTION: Is there a copy of another insurance card in the patient's chart?
ANSWER: Yes.
QUESTION: Does the insurance card indicate group coverage (it will list name of an employer and will have a Group ID number)?
ANSWER: Yes.
QUESTION: Is the patient age 65 or under the age of 65?
ANSWER: Verified in Patient Registration under Patient information that patient is under age 65.
QUESTION: Is the patient disabled or ESRD?
ANSWER: Patient is disabled.
QUESTION: Is the insured the patient or the spouse?
ANSWER: Verified in Patient Registration under Insured information that the insured is the patient's spouse.
For help, go to: Area A1. Refer to: Chapter 2, Unit IV, Step 3, Part A (patient age under Date of Birth)
                Area A1. Refer to: Chapter 2, Unit IV, Step 3, Part D, Section 1 (example of Insurance card: Group Health Plan)

In this case, the patient is under age 65, disabled, and the card indicates Group Coverage under the patient's spouse. The next step is to verify this information.

For help, go to: Area A3. Insurance Company: Call CSR/IVR and verify eligibility and benefits over the phone.
                Area A4. Other Resources: Website; Availity to verify eligibility and benefits (see the following example)

Availity Eligibility & Benefits Results

Patient Information:	Subscriber Information:
Patient Name:	Name:
Payer: Medicare/CMS	ID:
Member ID:	Address:
Date of Birth	Eligibility Date:
Gender:	

Plan Information:
Status: Active Coverage
Coverage Level: Individual

Insurance Type: Medicare Part A/B
Eligibility Date:

Other or Additional Payer:
Coverage Level:
Insurance Type: Medicare Secondary Disabled Beneficiary Under Age 65 with LGHP
Insurance Policy Number:
Coordination of Benefits:
Primary Payer: Blue Cross Blue Shield of OK
Address: PO Box 3283
                Tulsa, OK 74102

** If the patient was of age 65, retired, and covered under the spouse, additional payer information would look like this:

Other or Additional Payer:
Coverage Level:
Insurance Type: **Medicare Secondary Working Aged Beneficiary or Spouse with Employer Group Health Plan (GHP)**
Insurance Policy Number:
Coordination of Benefits:
Primary Payer: Blue Cross Blue Shield of OK
Address: PO Box 3283
                Tulsa, OK 74102

RESOLUTION: Four steps to correct the claim
We verified that the patient Primary Payer is other insurance and that the insurance we have listed as primary is actually the secondary payer. We need to correct by updating Patient Registration and each ticket/claim and then bill the service to the correct primary payer as a new claim.

Step 1. In the Main Menu, select REGISTRATION OF A PATIENT, pull up the INS (Insurance) tab, select MODIFYm and update the primary payer by switching Medicare as the primary insurance to Medicare Secondary Payer (MSP) and BCBS from secondary to Primary insurance.

Step 2. In the Main menu, select COLLECTIONS, pull up PATIENT BILLING, and pull up the ticket/claim. From the PATIENT ACCOUNT CLAIM DETAIL under "Patient Registration," select MODIFY and update the Primary Payer from TrailBlazer (MAC for Original Medicare Part B) to BCBS (LGHP).

Step 3. In the Main Menu, select COLLECTIONS, pull up PATIENT BILLING, and then pull up the ticket. From the PATIENT ACCOUNT CLAIM DETAIL under "Billing," select MODIFY. In the Charge Entry screen mark (x) next to File: HCFA Electronically so the claim can be batched and then billed to Medicare.

Step 4. Now that you have resolved the claim issue, the next step is to add in your notes on how you resolved the claim issue. Pull up PATIENT BILLING under the PATIENT ACCOUNT CLAIM DETAIL and select NOTES. Type in what the problem was and what you did to resolve the claim issue.

(**In every medical software there is a place to key in notes on what you did, either on that particular ticket or somewhere on that patient's account.**) An example of how you would type in your notes is as follows:

NOTE: Per the Medicare remittance dated 5/14/2008 denied the service because Medicare states care is covered by another payer. I viewed a copy of the patient insurance cards which indicates group coverage under the spouse. I also verified Eligibility and Benefits on Availity's website and it shows Medicare as secondary payer because the patient has coverage under a group health plan. I updated the patient registration as well as the visit and billed the claim to the correct primary payer, BCBS.

** Key Point: Keeping good notes is another key factor in doing a great job. Putting in good notes will provide information as to what has been done or is being done to resolve the issue with that particular date of service. If someone decides to go into that particular claim, they will see your notes and will know exactly what is being done.

CASE D: SITUATION 2

CODING ERROR: ANSI CARC/RARC CODES CO-22
We billed Medicare as the Primary Payer, but according to Medicare, they show the patient having other primary coverage.

QUESTION: Is there a copy of another Insurance card in the patient chart?

ANSWER: No.

QUESTION: Is the patient age 65 or under the age of 65?

ANSWER: Verified in Patient Registration under Patient information, patient just turned age 65.

For Help, Go To: Area A1 Refer to: Chapter 2, Step 3, Unit IV, Section A (patient age under Date of Birth)

QUESTION: Do we still have patient set under "Medicare Secondary Disabled Beneficiary Under Age 65 with LGHP"?

ANSWER: Yes. We have not updated our system because it is still set under "Medicare Secondary Disabled Beneficiary Under Age 65 with LGHP" as well. Patient is no longer under age 65.

RESOLUTION: Four steps to correct the claim

Medicare does not always update their system. If something has changed, it is up to the beneficiary to contact Coordination of Benefits (COB) and have them update the Medicare system.

Step 1. In the Main Menu, select REGISTRATION OF A PATIENT, pull up the INS (Insurance) tab, select MODIFY, and update the primary payer by switching Medicare as the primary insurance to Medicare Secondary Payer (MSP) and LGHP from secondary to Primary insurance.

Step 2. In the Main Menu, select COLLECTIONS, pull up PATIENT BILLING, and pull up the ticket/claim. From the PATIENT ACCOUNT CLAIM DETAIL under "Patient Registration," select MODIFY and update Primary Payer from TrailBlazer (MAC for Original Medicare Part B) to patient LGHP and ADD TrailBlazer as the Secondary Payer.

Step 3. In the Main Menu, select COLLECTIONS, pull up PATIENT BILLING, and then pull up the ticket. From the PATIENT ACCOUNT CLAIM DETAIL under "Billing," select MODIFY. In the Charge Entry screen mark (x) next to File: HCFA Electronically so the claim can be batched and then billed to Medicare.

Step 4. Now that you have resolved the claim issue, the next step is to add your notes on how you resolved the claim issue. Pull up PATIENT BILLING under the PATIENT ACCOUNT CLAIM DETAIL and select NOTES. Type in what the problem was and what you did to resolve the claim issue.

(**In every medical software there is a place to key in notes on what you did, either on that particular ticket or somewhere on that patient's account.**) An example of how you would type in your notes is as follows:

NOTE: Per the Medicare remittance dated 5/14/2008 denied the service because Medicare states care is covered by another payer. I viewed a copy of the patient insurance cards which indicate group coverage under the spouse. I also verified Eligibility and Benefits on Availity's website and it shows Medicare as secondary payer because patient has coverage under a group health plan. I updated the patient registration as well as the visit and billed the claim to the correct primary payer, which is GHP.

** Key Point: Keeping good notes is another key factor in doing a great job. Putting in good notes will provide information as to what has been done or is being done to resolve the issue with that particular date of service. If someone decides to go into that particular claim, they will see your notes and will know exactly what is being done.

CASE E: SITUATIONS 1 AND 2

MEDICARE PART B   **(ERA) REMITTANCE ADVICE**

Provider#:

Check/EFT (Electronic Fund Transfer) #:   Issue Date: 00/00/2008

Name: HIC #########A   ACCT   ICN   **CASE E**

PROV #	DOS	POS	NOS	CPT	MOD	BILLED $	ALLOW	DEDUCT	COINS	GRP/RC	AMT	PAID PROV $
######	051408	11	1	99203		125.00	0.00	0.00	0.00	CO-22	125.00	0.00
				73110		89.00	0.00	0.00	0.00	CO-22	89.00	0.00
PT RESP	0.00			CLAIM TOTAL		214.00	0.00	0.00	0.00		214.00	0.00
											NET	0.00

Name: HIC #########A   ACCT   ICN

PROV #	DOS	POS	NOS	CPT	MOD	BILLED $	ALLOW	DEDUCT	COINS	GRP/RC	AMT	PAID PROV $
######	060208	11	1	99203		125.00	0.00	0.00	0.00	CO-16	125.00	0.00
######	061208	11	1	73560	RT	20.00	0.00	0.00	0.00	CO-16	20.00	0.00
				REM: MA04 N155								
PT RESP	0.00			CLAIM TOTAL		125.00	0.00	0.00	0.00		125.00	0.00
											NET	0.00

Name: HIC #########A   ACCT   ICN

PROV	DOS	POS	NOS	CPT	MOD	BILLED $	ALLOW	DEDUCT	COINS	GRP/RC	AMT	PAID PROV $
######	061208	11	1	99203		125.00	55.00	0.00	11.00	CO-45	70.00	44.00
######	061208	11	1	73520	LT	20.00	0.00	0.00	0.00	C0-109	20.00	0.00
				REM: MA101								
PT RESP	11.00			CLAIM TOTAL		145.00	55.00	0.00	11.00		90.00	44.00
											NET	44.00

PROV	DOS	POS	NOS	CPT	MOD	BILLED $	ALLOW	DEDUCT	COINS	GRP/RC	AMT	PAID PROV $
######	061208	11	1	99203		125.00	55 .00	0.00	11.00	CO-45	70.00	44.00
######	061208	11	1	73560	LT	20.00	9.00	9.00	0.00	CO-45	11.00	0.00
######	061208	11	1	L4360		78.00	0.00	0.00	0.00	CO-109	78.00	0.00
PT RESP	20.00			CLAIM TOTAL		223.00	59.00	9.00	11.00		159.00	44.00
											NET	44.00

PROV	DOS	POS	NOS	CPT	MOD	BILLED $	ALLOW	DEDUCT	COINS	GRP/RC	AMT	PAID PROV $
######	061208	11	1	99203		125.00	0.00	0.00	0.00	OA-109	125.00	0.00
######	061208	11	1	73560	LT	20.00	0.00	0.00	0.00	OA-109	20.00	0.00
######	061208	11	1	73610		78.00	0.00	0.00	0.00	OA-109	78.00	0.00
PT RESP	1.20			CLAIM TOTAL		223.00	0.00	0.00	0.00		223.00	0.00
											NET	0.00

MESSAGE CODES: GROUP/CARC/RARC

Description:

CO   Contractual Obligation

16   Claim lacks information for adjudication

MA04   Secondary payment cannot be considered without the identity of or payment information from the primary payer.

N155   Our records do not indicate that other insurance is on file. Please submit other insurance information for our records.

CASE E: SITUATIONS 1 AND 2

CODING ERROR: ANSI CARC/RARC CODES CO-16, MAO4, N155
We billed Medicare as the secondary payer, listing BCBS as Primary, but according to Medicare they show the patient as having other primary coverage.

QUESTION: Who do we have listed as the patient's primary payer?
ANSWER: BCBS
QUESTION: Is the patient's illness/injury caused by an accident?
ANSWER: Yes.
QUESTION: What type of accident was involved? Employment, motor vehicle, or other?
ANSWER: On the Patient Registration form, the patient marked as accident but did not mark what type of accident.

In this case, the next step is to verify this information.

For help, go to: Area A4 Other Resources: Website; Availity to verify Eligibility and Benefits (see example to follow)

Availity Eligibility & Benefits Results

Patient Information:
Patient Name:
Payer: Medicare/CMS
Member ID:
Date of Birth
Gender:

Subscriber Information:
Name:
ID:
Address:
Eligibility Date:

Plan Information:
Status: Active Coverage
Coverage Level: Individual
Insurance Type: Medicare Part A/B
Eligibility Date:

LGHP

Other or Additional Payer:
Coverage Level:
Insurance Type: Medicare Secondary Workers Compensation
Insurance Policy Number:
Coordination of Benefits: 8/1/2010
Primary Payer: Gallagher Bassett (handles employer workers compensation)
Address:

Coverage Level:
Insurance Type: Medicare Secondary Disabled Beneficiary Under Age 65 with

Insurance Policy Number:
Coordination of Benefits: 8/1/2010
Primary Payer: Blue Cross Blue Shield of OK

CASE E: SITUATION 1

RESOLUTION: Three steps to correct the claim
We verified that the patient is covered under BCBS, but Workers Compensation is also listed as the patient's primary payer. To correct this, we need to contact the patient.

Step 1. Contact the patient and find out if we need to bill Workers Compensation for illness/injury. If the answer is yes, the patient will need to provide us with that information so we can correct our information and bill the correct payer. If the answer is no, ask why. The reason is because the accident complaint was settled out of court. The patient's attorney will need to contact Medicare to straighten this out. Because the case was settled out of court, Medicare will be the primary payer. You should follow up on this ticket/claim because once it is straightened out and Medicare has updated their system, you will need to rebill the claim to Medicare.

Step 2. In the Main Menu, select COLLECTIONS, pull up the TCKLR (Tickler) tab, select Month and click on the Day on which you want to set your follow up. Select ADD so you can enter your note as to the patient name and ticket/claim number on which you will be following up.

(The day you selected will pop up on your calendar as a reminder: You will pull up that ticket/claim number and read your last date of entry under Notes so you know exactly what you did and why you are following up on this particular ticket/claim.) Step 3. Now that you have resolved the claim issue, the next step is to add your notes on how you resolved the claim issue.

Pull up PATIENT BILLING under the PATIENT ACCOUNT CLAIM DETAIL and select NOTES. Type in what the problem was and what you did to resolve the claim issue.

(**In every medical software there is a place to key in notes on what you did, either on that particular ticket or somewhere on that patient's account.**) An example of how you would type in your notes is as follows:

NOTE: Per the Medicare remittance dated 5/14/2008 denied the service because they show the patient as having other primary coverage. Verified Eligibility and Benefits on Availity's website and they list Medicare as Secondary Payer but show that the patient has Workers Compensation and BCBS as primary payers. I have been in contact with the patient who has informed me that this is not workers comp because it was settled out of court. Patient is going to contact attorney and have the attorney contact Medicare to get this straightened out. I have follow up set for 00/00/2012.

CASE E: SITUATION 2

RESOLUTION: Four steps to correct the claim

We verified that the patient is covered under BCBS, but Workers Compensation is also listed as the patient's primary payer. To correct this, we need to contact the patient.

Step 1. Contact the patient and find out if we need to bill Workers Compensation for illness/injury. If the answer is no, ask why. The reason is because the patient's Workers Compensation case was for the right knee and patient is being seen for the left knee.

Step 2. Make sure that Box 10 on the claim form is marked correctly. Because the patient condition is not related to an accident, all boxes must be marked "No." In the Main Menu, select COLLECTIONS, pull up PATIENT BILLING, and pull up the ticket/claim. From the PATIENT ACCOUNT CLAIM DETAIL under "Patient Registration," select MODIFY and update Accident Detail making sure that Box 10, 10a, 10b, 10c all are marked "No."

Step 3. Make sure that the patient condition all points to the left knee and not the right. In this case, the wrong modifier was entered. In the Main Menu, select COLLECTIONS, pull up PATIENT BILLING, and then pull up the ticket. From the PATIENT ACCOUNT CLAIM DETAIL under "Billing," select MODIFY. In the Charge Entry screen under the column titled "Modifier," correct the modifier from RT to LT. Mark it as a corrected claim. Next, in the Charge Entry screen, mark (x) next to File: HCFA electronically so the claim can be batched and then rebilled.

Step 4. Now that you have resolved the claim issue, the next step is to add your notes on how you resolved the claim issue. Pull up PATIENT BILLING under the PATIENT ACCOUNT CLAIM DETAIL and select NOTES. Type in what the problem was and what you did to resolve the claim issue.

(**In every medical software there is a place to key in notes on what you did, either on that particular ticket or somewhere on that patient's account.**) An example of how you would type in your notes is as follows:

NOTE: Per the Medicare remittance dated 5/14/2008 denied the service because they show the patient as having other primary coverage. Verified Eligibility and Benefits on Availity's website and they list Medicare as Secondary Payer but show the patient as having Workers Compensation and BCBS, both as primary payers. I have been in contact with the patient who has informed me that this is not Workers Compensation and it has been closed for quite some time. His Workers Compensation case was for the right knee and he was seen regarding his left knee. I pulled up the Accident Detail and it was marked as employment related, so I made a correction marking all boxes "No." Also, an incorrect modifier was used, so I made a correction changing the modifier from RT to LT and resubmitted a corrected claim to Medicare.

** Key Point: Keeping good notes is another key factor in doing a great job. Putting in good notes will provide information as to what has been done or is being done to resolve the issue with that particular date of service. If someone decides to go into that particular claim, they will see your notes and will know exactly what is being done.

CASE F: SITUATION 1

MEDICARE PART B   (ERA) REMITTANCE ADVICE

Provider#:

Check/EFT (Electronic Fund Transfer) #:   Issue Date: 00/00/2008

Name: HIC #########A   ACCT   ICN   **CASE F**

PROV #	DOS	POS	NOS	CPT	MOD	BILLED $	ALLOW	DEDUCT	COINS	GRP/RC	AMT	PAID PROV $
######	051408	11	1	99203		125.00	0.00	0.00	0.00	CO-22	125.00	0.00
				73110		89.00	0.00	0.00	0.00	CO-22	89.00	0.00
PT RESP	0.00			CLAIM TOTAL		214.00	0.00	0.00	0.00		214.00	0.00
											NET	0.00

Name: HIC #########A   ACCT   ICN

PROV #	DOS	POS	NOS	CPT	MOD	BILLED $	ALLOW	DEDUCT	COINS	GRP/RC	AMT	PAID PROV $
######	060208	11	1	99203		125.00	0.00	0.00	0.00	CO-16	125.00	0.00
######	061208	11	1	73560	LT	20.00	0.00	0.00	0.00	CO-16	20.00	0.00
				REM: MA04 N155								
PT RESP	0.00			CLAIM TOTAL		145.00	0.00	0.00	0.00		145.00	0.00
											NET	0.00

Name: HIC #########A   ACCT   ICN

PROV	DOS	POS	NOS	CPT	MOD	BILLED $	ALLOW	DEDUCT	COINS	GRP/RC	AMT	PAID PROV $
######	061208	11	1	99203		125.00	55.00	0.00	11.00	CO-45	70.00	44.00
######	061208	11	1	73520	LT	20.00	0.00	0.00	0.00	C0-109	20.00	0.00
				REM: MA101								
PT RESP	11.00			CLAIM TOTAL		145.00	55.00	0.00	11.00		90.00	44.00
											NET	44.00

PROV	DOS	POS	NOS	CPT	MOD	BILLED $	ALLOW	DEDUCT	COINS	GRP/RC	AMT	PAID PROV $
######	061208	11	1	99203		125.00	55 .00	0.00	11.00	CO-45	70.00	44.00
######	061208	11	1	73560	LT	20.00	9.00	9.00	0.00	CO-45	11.00	0.00
######	061208	11	1	L4360		78.00	0.00	0.00	0.00	CO-109	78.00	0.00
PT RESP	20.00			CLAIM TOTAL		223.00	59.00	9.00	11.00		159.00	44.00
											NET	44.00

PROV	DOS	POS	NOS	CPT	MOD	BILLED $	ALLOW	DEDUCT	COINS	GRP/RC	AMT	PAID PROV $
######	061208	11	1	99203		125.00	0.00	0.00	0.00	OA-109	125.00	0.00
######	061208	11	1	73560	LT	20.00	0.00	0.00	0.00	OA-109	20.00	0.00
######	061208	11	1	73610		78.00	0.00	0.00	0.00	OA-109	78.00	0.00
PT RESP	1.20			CLAIM TOTAL		223.00	0.00	0.00	0.00		223.00	0.00
											NET	0.00

MESSAGE CODES: GROUP/CARC/RARC

Description:

CO   Contractual Obligation

109   Claim not covered by this payer/contractor

MA101   A Skilled Nursing Facility (SNF) is responsible for payment of outside providers who furnish these services/supplies to residents

CASE F: SITUATION 1

CODING ERROR: ANSI CARC/RARC CODES CO-109, MA101

QUESTION: Why is Medicare denying the x-ray but paying on the office visit when care is covered by another payer?

ANSWER: The reason is because the physician saw a patient who is a resident in a Skilled Nursing Facility (SNF). Beneficiaries in a Medicare-covered SNF will be included in a Bundled Prospective Payment that is made through the Fiscal Intermediary (FI). It falls under SNF Consolidated Billing (CB), whereas all services provided to that resident (except for specifically excluded services) would be submitted by the SNF to Medicare under Part A. Therefore, any provider who treated that resident would submit the bill to the SNF. The SNF would then submit the claim to Medicare and the SNF would reimburse the outside provider for his/her services. But, under the "Excluded services" when a physician furnishes a service to SNF resident it may not be subject to CB, and can therefore be billed separately to the Part B MAC. Diagnostic tests fall under such exclusions; they can have both a professional and technical component. The technical component would fall under CB whereas the professional component would fall under Part B. To distinguish the difference between the two, a modifier TC identifies it as a technical component and a modifier 26 identifies it as the professional component.

For help, go to: Area A3. Insurance Company: Website: http://www.trailblazerhealth.com (MAC for Part B in Oklahoma).

Pull up "Publications, Manuals" and locate the manual titled *Skilled Nursing Facility Consolidated Billing*.

QUESTION: How do you know if a particular CPT Code is either a Professional or Technical component?

ANSWER: Check the Fee Schedule under Payment Indicator for Professional/Technical component. CPT Code 73520 is identified with Indicator "1" which for this code will generally have both a professional and technical component. Modifiers will need to be used to identify.

FOR HELP, GO TO: AREA <u>A3</u> Insurance Company: Website: www.trailblazerhealth.com (MAC for Part B in Oklahoma)

Pull up Fee Schedule, then do a search by year and state then by CPT Code.

AREA <u>A4</u> Other Resources: Website: www.cms.gov

Pull up Medicare Physician Fee Schedule (MPFSDB), then do a search by payment indicators, CPT Code.

QUESTION: How will you know if that particular patient is a resident in a Skilled Nursing Facility?

ANSWER: You won't know not unless you ask. In most cases, in a large clinic when they can see 100 to 150 patients in a day they don't have the time to stop and ask every elderly patient that comes in the door.

QUESTION: What happens if you bill diagnostic charges to Part B Medicare and Medicare pays, when and how will Medicare inform you that our patient was in a SNF at time of service?

ANSWER: Medicare will forewarn you by sending out two letters, one requesting a refund and the second letter is informing you that they are going to be recouping their money and on that letter they will provide you the name of the patient and date of service. Medicare will also post adjustment an a remittance before they recoup their money. By the time you receive the letter and the remittance advice (RA) notification, Medicare will have already recouped/Offset their money. Examples are provided below.

Remittance Advice forewarning regarding adjustment: Adjustment will be among the RA

PROV	DOS	POS	NOS	CPT	MOD	BILLED $	ALLOW	DEDUCT	COINS	GRP/RC	AMT	PAID PROV $
######	061208	11	1	99203		-125.00	-55.00	0.00	-11.00	CR-45	-70.00	-44.00
######	061208	11	1	73520	LT	-20.00	-12.00	0.00	-2.40	CR-45	-8.00	-9.60
PT RESP 13.40				CLAIM TOTAL		-145.00	-67.00	0.00	-13.40		-78.00	-53.60
										NET		-53.60
PROV	DOS	POS	NOS	CPT	MOD	BILLED $	ALLOW	DEDUCT	COINS	GRP/RC	AMT	PAID PROV $
######	061208	11	1	99203		125.00	55.00	0.00	11.00	CO-45	70.00	44.00
######	061208	11	1	73520	LT	20.00	0.00	0.00	0.00	C0-109	20.00	0.00
PT RESP 11.00				REM: MA101								
				CLAIM TOTAL		145.00	55.00	0.00	11.00		90.00	44.00
										NET		44.00

MESSAGE CODES: GROUP/CARC/RARC	PLB Reason Code	FCN	HIC	AMOUNT
	FB	#############	#########A	-9.60

Description:

CR   Correction and Reversals

FB   Forwarding Balance

CO   Contractual Obligation

109   Claim not covered by this payer/contractor

MA101 A Skilled Nursing Facility (SNF) is responsible for payment of outside providers who furnish these services/supplies to residents

Remittance Advice with the recoupment: Recoupment will be on the very last page at the end of RA

Name: HIC #########A   ACCT   ICN

PROV #	DOS	POS	NOS	CPT	MOD	BILLED $	ALLOW	DEDUCT	COINS	GRP/RC	AMT	PAID PROV $
######	051408	11	1	99203		125.00	0.00	0.00	0.00	CO-22	125.00	0.00
				73110		89.00	0.00	0.00	0.00	CO-22	89.00	0.00
PT RESP 0.00				CLAIM TOTAL		214.00	0.00	0.00	0.00		214.00	0.00
										NET		0.00

Name: HIC #########A   ACCT   ICN

PROV #	DOS	POS	NOS	CPT	MOD	BILLED $	ALLOW	DEDUCT	COINS	GRP/RC	AMT	PAID PROV $
#######	060208	11	1	99203		125.00	0.00	0.00	0.00	CO-16	125.00	0.00
######	061208	11	1	73560	LT	20.00	0.00	0.00	0.00	CO-16	20.00	0.00
PT RESP 0.00				REM: MA04 N155								
				CLAIM TOTAL		145.00	0.00	0.00	0.00		145.00	0.00
										NET		0.00

Name: HIC #########A   ACCT   ICN

PROV	DOS	POS	NOS	CPT	MOD	BILLED $	ALLOW	DEDUCT	COINS	GRP/RC	AMT	PAID PROV $
######	061208	11	1	99203		125.00	55.00	0.00	11.00	CO-45	70.00	44.00
######	061208	11	1	73520	LT	20.00	0.00	0.00	0.00	C0-109	20.00	0.00
PT RESP 11.00				REM: MA101								
				CLAIM TOTAL		145.00	55.00	0.00	11.00		90.00	44.00
										NET		44.00

MESSAGE CODES: GROUP/CARC/RARC	PLB Reason Code	FCN	HIC	AMOUNT
	WO	#############	#########A	-9.60

Description:

WO   Withholding

QUESTION: How do you know what patient and what ticket/claim the recoupment is for?

ANSWER: The Remittance Advice will indicate the recoupment or offset by listing "WO" under the PLB Reason Code. Under "HIC" this will provide you with the patient MCR Identification number and under "FCN" is the number used to identify that particular ticket/claim for the patient from whom Medicare is recouping the money.

As I stated before, Medicare sends out two letters. The second letter will provide you with the FCN number. You may want to file these letters away so you have some way to identify where the recoupment/offset needs to be adjusted. You can always contact Medicare and give them the FCN and they can provide you with the name of the patient and date of service as well.

QUESTION: How is a recoupment posted?

ANSWER: As a receipt poster, I pull up the ticket/claim on which the offset needs to be posted by going in and reversing the original payment and contractual write-off, then on one of the other tickets listed on the remittance where the recoupment was withheld and apply the –$9.60 credit. If you don't do it this way, your remittance does not balance.

RESOLUTION: Three steps to correct the claim

Once the offset has been applied, you will need to rebill the diagnostic test as a new claim.

For a physician to be reimbursed, add a "26" modifier to CPT code 73520 and file as a new claim.

RESOLUTION: Three steps to correct the claim

Step 1. In the Main Menu, select COLLECTIONS, pull up PATIENT BILLING , then pull up the ticket. From the PATIENT ACCOUNT CLAIM DETAIL under "Billing," select MODIFY. Under Charge Entry on Line 2, which lists CPT code 73520, add "26" in the Modifier column, then unmark Line 1 so the 99203 is not billed again.

Step 2. Under Charge Entry mark (X) File: HCFA Electronically so the claim can be batched and billed.

Step 3. Now that you have resolved the claim issue, the next step is to add your notes on how you resolved the claim issue. Pull up PATIENT BILLING under the PATIENT ACCOUNT CLAIM DETAIL and select NOTES. Type in what the problem was and what you did to resolve the claim issue.

(**In every medical software there is a place to key in notes on what you did, either on that particular ticket or somewhere on that patient's account.**) An example of how you would type in your notes is as follows:

NOTE: Per the Medicare remittance dated 5/14/2008 denied the service because care is not covered by this payer/contractor because patient is a resident in a SNF. X-ray was provided by a physician in clinic and it is considered a professional component, so I added the 26 modifier and billed as just CPT code 73520 to Medicare.

** Key Point: Keeping good notes is another key factor in doing a great job. Putting in good notes will provide information as to what has been done or is being done to resolve the issue with that particular date of service. If someone decides to go into that particular claim, they will see your notes and will know exactly what is being done.

CASE G: SITUATION 1

MEDICARE PART B   (ERA) REMITTANCE ADVICE

Provider#:

Check/EFT (Electronic Fund Transfer) #:   Issue Date: 00/00/2008

Name: HIC ########A   ACCT   ICN   **CASE G**

PROV #	DOS	POS	NOS	CPT	MOD	BILLED $	ALLOW	DEDUCT	COINS	GRP/RC	AMT	PAID PROV $
######	051408	11	1	99203		125.00	0.00	0.00	0.00	CO-22	125.00	0.00
				73110		89.00	0.00	0.00	0.00	CO-22	89.00	0.00
PT RESP	0.00			CLAIM TOTAL		214.00	0.00	0.00	0.00		214.00	0.00
											NET	0.00

Name: HIC ########A   ACCT   ICN

PROV #	DOS	POS	NOS	CPT	MOD	BILLED $	ALLOW	DEDUCT	COINS	GRP/RC	AMT	PAID PROV $
######	060208	11	1	99203		125.00	0.00	0.00	0.00	CO-16	125.00	0.00
######	061208	11	1	73560	LT	20.00	0.00	0.00	0.00	CO-16	20.00	0.00
				REM: MA04 N155								
PT RESP	0.00			CLAIM TOTAL		145.00	0.00	0.00	0.00		145.00	0.00
											NET	0.00

Name: HIC ########A   ACCT   ICN

PROV	DOS	POS	NOS	CPT	MOD	BILLED $	ALLOW	DEDUCT	COINS	GRP/RC	AMT	PAID PROV $
######	061208	11	1	99203		125.00	55.00	0.00	11.00	CO-45	70.00	44.00
######	061208	11	1	73520	LT	20.00	0.00	0.00	0.00	C0-109	20.00	0.00
				REM: MA101								
PT RESP	11.00			CLAIM TOTAL		145.00	55.00	0.00	11.00		90.00	44.00
											NET	44.00

PROV	DOS	POS	NOS	CPT	MOD	BILLED $	ALLOW	DEDUCT	COINS	GRP/RC	AMT	PAID PROV $
######	061208	11	1	99203		125.00	55.00	0.00	11.00	CO-45	70.00	44.00
######	061208	11	1	73560	LT	20.00	9.00	9.00	0.00	CO-45	11.00	0.00
######	061208	11	1	L4360		78.00	0.00	0.00	0.00	CO-109	78.00	0.00
PT RESP	20.00			CLAIM TOTAL		223.00	59.00	9.00	11.00		159.00	44.00
											NET	44.00

PROV	DOS	POS	NOS	CPT	MOD	BILLED $	ALLOW	DEDUCT	COINS	GRP/RC	AMT	PAID PROV $
######	061208	11	1	99203		125.00	0.00	0.00	0.00	OA-109	125.00	0.00
######	061208	11	1	73560	LT	20.00	0.00	0.00	0.00	OA-109	20.00	0.00
######	061208	11	1	73610		78.00	0.00	0.00	0.00	OA-109	78.00	0.00
PT RESP	1.20			CLAIM TOTAL		223.00	0.00	0.00	0.00		223.00	0.00
											NET	0.00

MESSAGE CODES: GROUP/CARC/RARC

Description:

CO   Contractual Obligation

109   Claim not covered by this payer/contractor

CASE G: SITUATION 1

CODING ERROR: ANSI CARC/RARC CODES CO-109

QUESTION: Why did Medicare pay on the E/M, X-ray but not the L code?

ANSWER: The L code is Durable Medical Equipment (DME), which is handled under a different MAC and different Jurisdiction (Region).

For help, go to: Area A1. Guidebook: Refer to: Chapter 2, Unit IV, Step 3, Part D, Section 2

RESOLUTION: Three steps to correct the claim

Once you have located the MAC under Jurisdiction C, you need to correct the claim by updating the Patient Registration and the ticket/claim by adding in Cigna Government Services in order to refile the claim to the correct payer.

RESOLUTION: Four steps to correct the claim

Step 1. In the Main Menu, select REGISTRATION OF A PATIENT, pull up INS (Insurance) tab, select MODIFY, and update by adding Cigna Government Services.

Step 2. In the Main Menu, select COLLECTIONS, pull up PATIENT BILLING, and pull up the ticket/claim. From the PATIENT ACCOUNT CLAIM DETAIL under "Patient Registration," select MODIFY and update Primary Payer from TrailBlazer (MAC for Original Medicare Part B) to Cigna Government Services (MAC for DME).

Step 3. Now that Cigna Government Services have been added to the ticket/claim, from the PATIENT ACCOUNT CLAIM DETAIL under "Billing," select MODIFY. Under Charge Entry mark (X) File: HCFA Electronically so the claim can be billed to correct payer.

Step 4. Now that you have resolved the claim issue, the next step is to add your notes on how you resolved the claim issue. Pull up PATIENT BILLING under the PATIENT ACCOUNT CLAIM DETAIL and select NOTES. Type in what the problem was and what you did to resolve the claim issue.

(**In every medical software there is a place to key in notes on what you did, either on that particular ticket or somewhere on that patient's account.**) An example of how you would type in your notes is as follows:

NOTE: Per the Medicare remittance dated 5/14/2008 denied the service because care is not covered by this payer/contractor. DME is to be billed to Cigna Government, so I updated the Patient Registration as well as the ticket/claim and billed the charges to correct payer.

** Key Point: Keeping good notes is another key factor in doing a great job. Putting in good notes will provide information as to what has been done or is being done to resolve the issue with that particular date of service. If someone decides to go into that particular claim, they will see your notes and will know exactly what is being done.

CASE H: SITUATIONS 1 AND 2

MEDICARE PART B (ERA) REMITTANCE ADVICE

Provider#:

Check/EFT (Electronic Fund Transfer) #: Issue Date: 00/00/2008

Name: HIC #########A ACCT ICN **CASE H**

PROV #	DOS	POS	NOS	CPT	MOD	BILLED $	ALLOW	DEDUCT	COINS	GRP/RC	AMT	PAID PROV $
######	051408	11	1	99203		125.00	0.00	0.00	0.00	CO-22	125.00	0.00
				73110		89.00	0.00	0.00	0.00	CO-22	89.00	0.00
PT RESP	0.00			CLAIM TOTAL		214.00	0.00	0.00	0.00		214.00	0.00
											NET	0.00

Name: HIC #########A ACCT ICN

PROV #	DOS	POS	NOS	CPT	MOD	BILLED $	ALLOW	DEDUCT	COINS	GRP/RC	AMT	PAID PROV $
######	060208	11	1	99203		125.00	0.00	0.00	0.00	CO-16	125.00	0.00
######	061208	11	1	73560	LT	20.00	0.00	0.00	0.00	CO-16	20.00	0.00
				REM: MA04 N155								
PT RESP	0.00			CLAIM TOTAL		125.00	0.00	0.00	0.00		125.00	0.00
											NET	0.00

Name: HIC #########A ACCT ICN

PROV	DOS	POS	NOS	CPT	MOD	BILLED $	ALLOW	DEDUCT	COINS	GRP/RC	AMT	PAID PROV $
######	061208	11	1	99203		125.00	55.00	0.00	11.00	CO-45	70.00	44.00
######	061208	11	1	73520	LT	20.00	0.00	0.00	0.00	C0-109	20.00	0.00
				REM: MA101								
PT RESP	11.00			CLAIM TOTAL		145.00	55.00	0.00	11.00		90.00	44.00
											NET	44.00

PROV	DOS	POS	NOS	CPT	MOD	BILLED $	ALLOW	DEDUCT	COINS	GRP/RC	AMT	PAID PROV $
######	061208	11	1	99203		125.00	55 .00	0.00	11.00	CO-45	70.00	44.00
######	061208	11	1	73560	LT	20.00	9.00	9.00	0.00	CO-45	11.00	0.00
######	061208	11	1	L4360		78.00	0.00	0.00	0.00	CO-109	78.00	0.00
PT RESP	20.00			CLAIM TOTAL		223.00	59.00	9.00	11.00		159.00	44.00
											NET	44.00

PROV	DOS	POS	NOS	CPT	MOD	BILLED $	ALLOW	DEDUCT	COINS	GRP/RC	AMT	PAID PROV $
######	061208	11	1	99203		125.00	0.00	0.00	0.00	OA-109	125.00	0.00
######	061208	11	1	73560	LT	20.00	0.00	0.00	0.00	OA-109	20.00	0.00
######	061208	11	1	73610		78.00	0.00	0.00	0.00	OA-109	78.00	0.00
PT RESP	1.20			CLAIM TOTAL		223.00	0.00	0.00	0.00		223.00	0.00
											NET	0.00

MESSAGE CODES: GROUP/CARC/RARC

Description:

OA

109 Claim not covered by this payer/contractor

CASE H: SITUATION 1

CODING ERROR: ANSI CARC/RARC CODES OA-109

QUESTION: Is there other insurance listed in Patient Registration or another insurance card?

ANSWER: No.

QUESTION: Since no other insurance is listed, what is the next step? Do I call the patient or where else can I go for help?

ANSWER: You can call Medicare's Interactive Voice Response (IVR) system to verify eligibility and benefits. The IVR will tell you if the patient has a Medicare Part A, Medicare Part B, and if Medicare is Primary or Secondary Payer. The IVR will also inform you if the beneficiary has a Medicare Advantage Plan. The IVR will provide you with the plan type, the name of the plan, and the Plan Code.

Another tool that providers can utilize to verify eligibility and benefits is a Health Information network called Availity. Availity offers a multiple health plan transaction that enables a provider to verify eligibility and benefits, authorization and referrals, and claim management such as claim status on several different insurance companies. Those insurance companies include National MCR/CMS, Aetna, BCBS of OK, Cigna, Great West Life, Humana, Other Blue Plans of OK, and Tricare.

For help, go to: Area A4. Other resources: Website: http://www.availity.com.

Another company that offers Health Information via the Internet is called NaviNet. Their website is http://www.navinet.net.

QUESTION: What is a Medicare Advantage (MA) Plan?

ANSWER: Medicare **Part C** is referred to as "Medicare Advantage Healthcare Plans," such as HMO, PPO, or POS that are offered by Private insurance company that are approved by Medicare and have a signed contract with Medicare. Medicare Beneficiary must be enrolled in original Medicare in order to obtain a MA plan. Medicare Advantage Plans include Part A (Hospital), Part B (Medical) and Part D (Prescription Drug). Patient has to be enrolled in Original Medicare but if they select a MA plan, when entering the insurance in Patient Registration you will only key in the MA plan, not original Medicare. It replaces original Medicare, which is why sometimes they will be referred to as a Medicare Replacement plan.

FOR HELP, GO TO: AREA A1 Guidebook REFER TO: CHAPTER 2, STEP 3, UNIT IV, PART D, SECTION 3

QUESTION: If the patient has a MA plan, how do I know which one?

ANSWER: The IVR will give you the plan name and plan code. I rather utilize Availity website to verify Eligibility & Benefits because they will also provide you with the plan name and plan code.

QUESTION: What is a plan code? What is it used for?

ANSWER: Plan code is a contract number that is assigned to each plan type under each payer. It is used to help identify which plan it is under which payer in order to know where to submit the claim.

QUESTION: Where do I go to locate the information?

ANSWER: Locate Centers of Medicare and Medicaid (CMS) website

FOR HELP, GO TO: AREA <u>A4</u> Other Resources: Website; www.cms.gov

Once you have pulled up CMS's website, Select Medicare on the Left Hand side of the page, then select "Research, Statistics, Data & Systems, then under Statistics, Trends & Reports select Medicare Advantage/Part D Contracts & Enrollment. On the Left hand side of the page select "**MA Claims Processing Contacts.**" Open up the file by searching the Plan Code that is on the insurance card or that was provided to you by the IVR.

Example: Search for Plan Code **H3706**

Contract Number:	H3706		
Entity Name:	Global Health, INC		
Organization Market Name:	Generations Healthcare	Contact Title:	Member Services Rep
Plan Type:	HMO/POS	Phone:	

Plan Code H3706: Claim is to be billed to Global Health under an HMO plan.

You can also access the link for "MA Claims Processing Contacts" to CMS website through TrailBlazers website. As soon as you pull up www.trailblazerhealth.com the very first front screen locate where it says "CMS Medicare Advantage Claims Processing Center." It will take you directly to the site.

RESOLUTION: Four steps to correct the claim
Now that you know the patient has an MA plan and who the correct payer is, the next step is to correct the claim by updating the Patient Registration along with the visit and refile the claim with the correct payer.

RESOLUTION: Four steps to correct the claim

Step 1. In the Main Menu, select REGISTRATION OF A PATIENT, pull up the INS (Insurance) tab, select MODIFY, and update by adding the Medicare Advantage Plan.

Step 2. In the Main menu, select COLLECTIONS, pull up PATIENT BILLING, and pull up the ticket/claim. From the PATIENT ACCOUNT CLAIM DETAIL under "Patient Registration," select MODIFY and update the Primary Payer from TrailBlazer (MAC for Original Medicare Part B) to the MA Plan.

Step 3. Now that the MA plan has been added to the ticket/claim, from the PATIENT ACCOUNT CLAIM DETAIL under "Billing," select MODIFY. Under Charge Entry mark (X) File: HCFA Electronically so the claim can be billed to correct payer.

Step 4. Now that you have resolved the claim issue, the next step is to add in your notes on how you resolved the claim issue. Pull up PATIENT BILLING under the PATIENT ACCOUNT CLAIM DETAIL and select NOTES. Type in what the problem was and what you did to resolve the claim issue.

(**In every medical software there is a place to key in notes on what you did, either on that particular ticket or somewhere on that patient's account.**) An example of how you would type in your notes is as follows:

NOTE: Per the Medicare remittance dated 5/14/2008 denied the service because care is not covered by this payer/contractor. I pulled up Eligibility & Benefits under Availity's website and it shows patient having an MA Plan. I updated Patient Registration as well as the ticket/claim and billed the charges to the correct payer.

** Key Point: Keeping good notes is another key factor in doing a great job. Putting in good notes will provide information as to what has been done or is being done to resolve the issue with that particular date of service. If someone decides to go into that particular claim, they will see your notes and will know exactly what is being done.

CASE H: SITUATION 2

CODING ERROR: ANSI CARC/RARC CODES OA-109

QUESTION: Is there another insurance card besides the patient's Medicare card?

ANSWER: Yes.

QUESTION: Does it state "Medicare" anywhere on the card?

ANSWER: Yes.

If the insurance card is not a Medicare card but states "Medicare" on the card, it is a giveaway that the patient may have coverage under a Medicare Advantage (MA) plan.

For help, go to: Area A1 Guidebook. Refer to: Chapter 2, Step 3, Unit IV, Section D1

RESOLUTION: Four steps to correct the claim
Follow the same steps as under CASE H: Situation 1 RESOLUTION with one exception in Step 4. The notes are as follows:

NOTE: Per the Medicare remittance dated 5/14/2008 denied the service because care is not covered by this payer/contractor. I pulled up the Patient Registration and there was another insurance card besides the patient Medicare card. The patient is covered under an MA plan, the Global Health HMO plan. I updated the Patient Registration as well as the ticket/claim by deleting Medicare as the primary payer and listing Global Health, and then filed the claim with the correct payer.

** Key point: Whenever you see the ANSI CARC/RARC code OA in front of the 109, 99% of the time the patient has an MA plan. That is how I determine the difference between CO-109 and OA-109.

CASE I: SITUATION 1

MEDICARE PART B   (ERA) REMITTANCE ADVICE
Provider#:
Check/EFT (Electronic Fund Transfer) #:   Issue Date: 00/00/2008

Name: HIC ########A   ACCT   ICN   **CASE I**

PROV #	DOS	POS	NOS	CPT	MOD	BILLED $	ALLOW	DEDUCT	COINS	GRP/RC	AMT	PAID PROV $
######	051408	11	1	99203		125.00	0.00	0.00	0.00	CO-21	125.00	0.00
				73110		89.00	0.00	0.00	0.00	CO-21	89.00	0.00
PT RESP	0.00			CLAIM TOTAL		214.00	0.00	0.00	0.00		214.00	0.00
											NET	0.00

Name: HIC ########A   ACCT   ICN

PROV	DOS	POS	NOS	CPT	MOD	BILLED $	ALLOW	DEDUCT	COINS	GRP/RC	AMT	PAID PROV $
######	061208	11	1	99203		125.00	0.00	0.00	0.00	CO-B7	125.00	0.00
######	061208	11	1	73560	LT	20.00	0.00	0.00	0.00	CO-B7	20.00	0.00
######	061208	11	1	73610		78.00	0.00	0.00	0.00	C0-B7	78.00	0.00
PT RESP	1.20			CLAIM TOTAL		223.00	0.00	0.00	0.00		223.00	0.00
											NET	0.00

MESSAGE CODES: GROUP/CARC/RARC

Description:

CO   Contractual Obligation
21   Injury/illness is the liability of the no-fault carrier

CASE I: SITUATION 1

CODING ERROR: ANSI CARC/RARC CODES CO-21

QUESTION: How did Medicare know that the patient's injury was due to an accident?
ANSWER: Under PATIENT ACCOUNT CLAIM DETAIL, the Accident Detail states "Other." This information is marked on the Top Portion of the CMS-1500 in Box 10.
For help, go to: Area A1 Guidebook. Refer to: Chapter 2, Step 2, Unit III, Part A

QUESTION: Is the patient's condition due to an accident?
ANSWER: Yes.
QUESTION: What type of accident?
ANSWER: On the Patient Registration form, the patient marked "Other." Patient states she fell at church.

QUESTION: Who is liable for the bill?
ANSWER: Since no one is at fault, it would be reflected under "No-Fault" insurance of the church where the patient fell. The type of coverage in this situation falls under "Medical payment coverage," "Personal injury protection," or "Medical expense coverage." In short, "Med-Pay." It is when an insurer, such as the church, pays for medical expenses of the injured party without regard to who is at fault.
For help, go to: Area A1. Refer to: Chapter 2, Step 3, Unit IV, Part D, Section 2

QUESTION: Can we bill Medicare as the secondary payer?
ANSWER: Yes.
QUESTION: Did the patient provide us with the insurance information for the church?
ANSWER: Yes.
QUESTION: Then why did we bill Medicare as the primary?
ANSWER: Insurance card looks as if it was the patient secondary coverage because the patient is over age 65.

** Key Point: It is important to always check to see if patient condition was due to accident, because then the next question would be to find out who is liable for the bill.

RESOLUTION: Four steps to correct the claim
Now that you know the patient has No-Fault Liability insurance, the next step is to correct the claim by updating the Patient Registration and the visit and refile the claim with the correct payer.

RESOLUTION: Four steps to correct the claim

Step 1. In the Main Menu, select REGISTRATION OF A PATIENT, pull up the INS (Insurance) tab, select MODIFY, and update by adding the church's insurance information.

Step 2. In the Main Menu, select COLLECTIONS, pull up PATIENT BILLING, and pull up the ticket/claim. From the PATIENT ACCOUNT CLAIM DETAIL under "Patient Registration," select MODIFY and update the Primary Payer from Medicare to Secondary Payer and list the church's insurance as the Primary Payer.

Step 3. Now that we've updated the ticket/claim, from the PATIENT ACCOUNT CLAIM DETAIL under "Billing," select MODIFY. Mark (X) File: HCFA Paper so a hard copy of the claim can be sent to the correct payer.

Step 4. Now that you have resolved the claim issue, the next step is to add your notes on how you resolved the claim issue. Pull up PATIENT BILLING under the PATIENT ACCOUNT CLAIM DETAIL and select NOTES. Type in what the problem was and what you did to resolve the claim issue.

(**In every medical software there is a place to key in notes on what you did, either on that particular ticket or somewhere on that patient's account.**) An example of how you would type in your notes is as follows:

NOTE: Per the Medicare remittance dated 5/14/2008 denied the service because patient illness/injury is a Third Part Liability (TPL) case of a no-fault payer. I located the No-Fault payer information in the Patient Registration and I updated the Patient Registration as well as the ticket/claim, changing the primary payer from Medicare to the church's insurance information and billed the charges to the correct payer.

" Key Point: Keeping good notes is another key factor in doing a great job. Putting in good notes will provide information as to what has been done or is being done to resolve the issue with that particular date of service. If someone decides to go into that particular claim, they will see your notes and will know exactly what is being done.

CASE J: SITUATION 1

MEDICARE PART B   (ERA) REMITTANCE ADVICE
Provider#:
Check/EFT (Electronic Fund Transfer) #:   Issue Date: 00/00/2008

Name: HIC ########A   ACCT   ICN   **CASE J**

PROV #	DOS	POS	NOS	CPT	MOD	BILLED $	ALLOW	DEDUCT	COINS	GRP/RC	AMT	PAID PROV $
#######	051408	11	1	99203		125.00	0.00	0.00	0.00	CO-21	125.00	0.00
				73110		89.00	0.00	0.00	0.00	CO-21	89.00	0.00
PT RESP	0.00			CLAIM TOTAL		214.00	0.00	0.00	0.00		214.00	0.00
											NET	0.00

Name: HIC ########A   ACCT   ICN

PROV #	DOS	POS	NOS	CPT	MOD	BILLED $	ALLOW	DEDUCT	COINS	GRP/RC	AMT	PAID PROV $
######	061208	11	1	99203		125.00	0.00	0.00	0.00	CO-B7	125.00	0.00
######	061208	11	1	73560	LT	20.00	0.00	0.00	0.00	C0-B7	20.00	0.00
######	061208	11	1	73610		78.00	0.00	0.00	0.00	C0-B7	78.00	0.00
PT RESP	1.20			CLAIM TOTAL		223.00	0.00	0.00	0.00		223.00	0.00
											NET	0.00

MESSAGE CODES: GROUP/CARC/RARC

Description:
CO   Contractual Obligation
B7   Provider was not certified or eligible to be paid for this procedure/service on this date of service

---

CASE J: SITUATION 1

CODING ERROR: ANSI CARC/RARC CODES CO-B7

QUESTION: Which provider, doctor, or PA provided the service?
ANSWER: By viewing the Rendering Provider ID on the left-hand side column, under PROV # of the RA, is the new doctor's ID, Doctor Jones.

QUESTION: Why would Medicare state that Doctor Jones is not eligible?
ANSWER: It is because the doctor's enrollment with Medicare has not been completed or the effective date of Doctor Jones contract is after the date when services were rendered.

For help, go to: Area A1 Guidebook. Refer to: Chapter 3, Unit II, Step 4, Part B, Section 1

RESOLUTION: 2 STEPS ON HOW TO CORRECT THE CLAIM
Check with the person who does the credentialing for the doctors to find out if doctor Jones is contracted with Medicare, if so, find out what the effective date is. If you were informed that Doctor Jones is contracted with Medicare but the effective date was after the date when he seen his patient, charges will need to be adjusted off because the physician was not contracted at time of service. If you were informed that Doctor Jones is still not contracted with Medicare you will need to place ticket/claim on HOLD until you can resubmit the claim to Medicare. In this case, we are going to adjust off the charges.

Step 1. Main Menu, select **COLLECTIONS,** pull up **PATIENT BILLING** , then pull up the ticket. From the PATIENT ACCOUNT CLAIM DETAIL under "Payment Type" select MODIFY then under Payment Transaction on each line in the Disallow/Adj Column post charges and under the Disallow/Adj Type Column drop down window and select "Non Contracted." By posting your adjustment it will adjust off the charges and will show Claim Status under Billing as Paid.

Now that you have resolved the claim issue, the next step is to add in your notes on how you resolved the claim issue.
Step 2: Pull up **PATIENT BILLING** under the PATIENT ACCOUNT CLAIM DETAIL select NOTES. Type in what the problem was, how and what you did to resolve the claim issue.
(**Every Medical Software there is a place to key in notes on what you did either on that particular ticket or somewhere on that patients account as to what you did**) Example as to how you would type in your notes are as follows:

NOTE: Per the Medicare remittance dated 5/14/2008 denied the service because rendering provider was not eligible at time of service. I have been informed that Doctor Jones was not contracted at the time of service so I adjusted off the charges.

**Key Point: Keeping good notes is another key factor in doing a great job. By putting in good notes will provide information as to what has been done or is being done to resolve the issue with that particular date of service. If someone decides to go into that particular claim they will see your notes and will know exactly what is being done.

Section 2: Billing and Coding Errors

I have provided you with eighteen case examples (Cases K, L, M, N, O, P, Q, R, S, T, U, V, W, X, Y, Z, YY, and ZZ), with one or two different situations regarding Billing and Coding errors. Some may have more than two. A step-by-step guide is provided for each case. I will provide you with questions

and answers, and will then show you how to resolve that particular issue on that claim.

Case K: Example Remittance Advice is provided. The RA shows ANSI CARC and RARC denial codes and what those denial codes mean. I have provided questions with answers. I will also show you how to resolve a particular issue on a claim.

CASE K: SITUATIONS 1 AND 2

MEDICARE PART B   **(ERA) REMITTANCE ADVICE**

Provider#:

Check/EFT (Electronic Fund Transfer) #:   Issue Date: 00/00/2008

Name: HIC   ACCT   ICN   **CASE K**

PROV #	DOS	POS	NOS	CPT	MOD	BILLED $	ALLOW	DEDUCT	COINS	GRP/RC	AMT	PAID PROV $
######	051408	11	1	99213		74.00	0.00	0.00	0.00	CO-97	74.00	0.00
				REM: M144								
PT RESP 0.00				CLAIM TOTAL		74.00	0.00	0.00	0.00		74.00	0.00
											NET	0.00

Name: HIC   ACCT   ICN

PROV #	DOS	POS	NOS	CPT	MOD	BILLED $	ALLOW	DEDUCT	COINS	GRP/RC	AMT	PAID PROV $
######	060208	22	1	20694		930.00	0.00	0.00	0.00	CO-97	930.00	0.00
				REM: M144								
PT RESP 0.00				CLAIM TOTAL		930.00	0.00	0.00	0.00		930.00	0.00
											NET	0.00

Name: HIC   ACCT   ICN

PROV	DOS	POS	NOS	CPT	MOD	BILLED $	ALLOW	DEDUCT	COINS	GRP/RC	AMT	PAID PROV $
######	061208	21	1	25606		1343.00	428.70	0.00	85.74	CO-45	914.30	342.96
######	061208	21	1	25605	51	796.00	0.00	0.00	0.00	CO-125	796.00	0.00
				REM:M80								
PT RESP 85.74				CLAIM TOTAL		2139.00	428.70	0.00	85.74		1710.30	342.96
											NET	342.96

Name: HIC   ACCT   ICN

PROV	DOS	POS	NOS	CPT	MOD	BILLED $	ALLOW	DEDUCT	COINS	GRP/RC	AMT	PAID PROV $
######	052808	22	1	28104		1087.00	310.12	0.00	62.02	CO-58	776.88	248.10
######	052808	22	1	28288	51	808.00	0.00	0.00	0.00	CO-B15	808.00	0.00
				REM: M80								
######	052808	22	1	28126	51	549.00	111.21	0.00	22.24	CO-45	437.79	88.97
PT RESP 84.26				CLAIM TOTAL		2444.00	421.33	0.00	84.26		2022.67	337.07
											NET	337.07

MESSAGE CODES: GROUP/CARC/RARC

CO   Contractual Obligation

97   Payment is adjusted because the benefit for this service is included in the payment/allowance for another service/procedure that has been adjudicated

M144   Pre-/Post Op care payment is included in the allowance for the surgery/procedure

---

CASE K: SITUATION #1 AND SITUATION #2

CODING ERROR: ANSI CARC/RARC CODES CO-97 AND M144

QUESTION: What do they mean, "Pre-/Post Op Care?"
ANSWER: Patients follow-up care relating to prior surgery is all included in with the payment received for the surgery. This time frame is defined as Post-Op care because it is **after** the procedure was performed.
For help, go to: Area A4 Other resources. http//www.trailblazerhealth.com

QUESTION: For Post-Op care, is there a specific time frame?
ANSWER: Yes, it can be 10, 42, 60 or 90 days. This is referred to as Global Period (GP).

QUESTION: What does Global Period (GP) mean?
ANSWER: GP is the time frame which is given to every surgical procedure performed, either in the office or at a hospital.

QUESTION: How do you know what that GP is for a particular procedure?
ANSWER: Minor procedure basically has a 10 day GP, Major procedure basically has a 90 GP.
Keep in mind; the 90 day GP for major procedure may not apply to all insurance companies. They may have a 42 or 60 day GP.
For help, go to: Area A4 Other resources: Book or manual title
"Medicare Correct Coding Guide Mnaual: CCI Edits."

SITUATION 1

QUESTION: If Medicare is stating that the visit is included in with the payment for a surgery because the patient was in post-op care, is the visit related to the surgery and when was that surgery?

ANSWER: Yes, they are related because we pulled up all the billing on this particular patient and located the ticket that stated the service took place at a hospital (INPT/OPT) and compared the patient's condition (diagnosis), body part, and physician at the time of the visit with the surgery. The patient's condition, body part, and physician are the same. Per the MCR Fee Schedule, the surgery, CPT code ??????, which was performed has a 90-day GP and the date of service for the post-op care falls within that 90-day period.

RESOLUTION: Three steps to correct the claim

Correct the claim by voiding the charge; then key in the correct CPT Code. No Need to refile or resubmit the claim.

Step 1. In the Main Menu, select COLLECTIONS, pull up PATIENT BILLING, then pull up the ticket. From the PATIENT ACCOUNT CLAIM DETAIL under "Billing," select MODIFY. Under Charge Entry on line 1, which lists CPT Code 99213, void out the code by right-clicking, then key in the correct CPT Code 99024 (Post-op visit).

Step 2. No need to refile the claim because it's a no charge. Now that you have resolved the claim issue, the next step is to add in your notes on how you resolved the claim issue.

Step 3: Now that you have resolved the claim issue, the next step is to add your notes on how you resolved the claim issue. Pull up PATIENT BILLING under the PATIENT ACCOUNT CLAIM DETAIL and select NOTES. Type in what the problem was and what you did to resolve the claim issue.

(**In every medical software there is a place to key in notes on what you did, either on that particular ticket or somewhere on that patient's account.**) An example of how you would type in your notes is as follows:

NOTE: Per the Medicare remittance dated 5/14/2008 denied the service because payment is included in payment for surgery/procedure. Surgery that was dated 3/05/2008 is related to this visit and is within the 90-day GP, so I am voiding 99213 and keying in the correct CPT code 99024 (post-op).

** Key Point: Keeping good notes is another key factor in doing a great job. Putting in good notes will provide information as to what has been done or is being done to resolve the issue with that particular date of service. If someone decides to go into that particular claim, they will see your notes and will know exactly what is being done.

SITUATION 2

QUESTION: If Medicare is stating that the visit is included in the payment for a surgery because the patient was in post-op care, is the visit related to a surgery and when was that surgery?

ANSWER: No, they are not related because we pulled up all the billing on this particular patient and located the ticket that stated the service took place at a hospital (INPT/OPT) and compared the patient's condition (diagnosis), body part, and physician at the time of the visit with the surgery. The patient condition (diagnosis) and body part is not the same as the surgery. In this case, the appropriate modifier would be reported to provide more information so that the physician can be paid.

For help, go to: Area A4 Other Resources. http://www.trailblazerhealth.com

RESOLUTION: Three steps to correct the claim

Correct the claim by adding a modifier and refile or resubmit as a corrected claim.

Step 1. In the Main Menu, select COLLECTIONS, pull up PATIENT BILLING, then pull up the ticket. From the PATIENT ACCOUNT CLAIM DETAIL under "Billing," select MODIFY. Under Charge Entry on line 1, which lists CPT Code 99213, in the Modifier Column add the 24 modifier.

Step 2. Under Charge Entry, mark (X) File: HCFA Electronically so the claim can be resubmitted as a corrected claim.
** Key Points: You may have to submit an appeal with medical documentation because the insurance company may come back and deny the claim again.

Step 3: Now that you have resolved the claim issue, the next step is to add your notes on how you resolved the claim issue. Pull up PATIENT BILLING under the PATIENT ACCOUNT CLAIM DETAIL and select NOTES. Type in what the problem was and what you did to resolve the claim issue.

(**In every medical software there is a place to key in notes on what you did, either on that particular ticket or somewhere on that patient's account.**) An example of how you would type in your notes is as follows:

NOTE: Per the Medicare remittance dated 5/14/2008 denied the service because payment is included in payment for surgery/procedure. Patient condition (diagnosis) for surgery dated 3/05/2008 and the visit dated 5/14/2008 are not related, so I added the modifier 24 and rebilled the corrected claim to Medicare. Your Initials and Date

** Key Point: When you are resubmitting a corrected claim, make sure to state that it is a corrected claim and to also include the ICN number. This is the number that identifies the original claim.

CASE L: SITUATION 1

MEDICARE PART B (ERA) REMITTANCE ADVICE

Provider#:

Check/EFT (Electronic Fund Transfer) #:   Issue Date: 00/00/2008

Name: HIC   ACCT   ICN   **CASE L**

PROV #	DOS	POS	NOS	CPT	MOD	BILLED $	ALLOW	DEDUCT	COINS	GRP/RC	AMT	PAID PROV $
######	051408	11	1	99213		74.00	0.00	0.00	0.00	CO-97	74.00	0.00
				REM: M144								
PT RESP	0.00			CLAIM TOTAL		74.00	0.00	0.00	0.00		74.00	0.00
											NET	0.00

Name: HIC   ACCT   ICN

PROV #	DOS	POS	NOS	CPT	MOD	BILLED $	ALLOW	DEDUCT	COINS	GRP/RC	AMT	PAID PROV $
#######	060208	22	1	20694		930.00	0.00	0.00	0.00	CO-97	930.00	0.00
				REM: M144								
PT RESP	0.00			CLAIM TOTAL		930.00	0.00	0.00	0.00		930.00	0.00
											NET	0.00

Name: HIC   ACCT   ICN

PROV	DOS	POS	NOS	CPT	MOD	BILLED $	ALLOW	DEDUCT	COINS	GRP/RC	AMT	PAID PROV $
######	061208	21	1	25606		1343.00	428.70	0.00	85.74	CO-45	914.30	342.96
######	061208	21	1	25605	51	796.00	0.00	0.00	0.00	CO-125	796.00	0.00
				REM: M80								
PT RESP	85.74			CLAIM TOTAL		2139.00	428.70	0.00	85.74		1710.30	342.96
											NET	342.96

Name: HIC   ACCT   ICN

PROV	DOS	POS	NOS	CPT	MOD	BILLED $	ALLOW	DEDUCT	COINS	GRP/RC	AMT	PAID PROV $
######	052808	22	1	28104		1087.00	310.12	0.00	62.02	CO-58	776.88	248.10
######	052808	22	1	28288	51	808.00	0.00	0.00	0.00	CO-B15	808.00	0.00
				REM: M80								
######	052808	22	1	28126	51	549.00	111.21	0.00	22.24	CO-45	437.79	88.97
PT RESP	84.26			CLAIM TOTAL		2444.00	421.33	0.00	84.26		2022.67	337.07
											NET	337.07

MESSAGE CODES: GROUP/CARC/RARC

CO   Contractual Obligation

97   Payment is adjusted because the benefit for this service is included in the payment/allowance for another service/procedure that has been adjudicated

M144   Pre-/Post Op care payment is included in the allowance for the surgery/procedure

---

CASE L: SITUATION 1

CODING ERROR: ANSI CARC/RARC CODES CO-97 AND M144

QUESTION: The service that was provided is a surgical procedure, not an office visit. It took place in a hospital as an outpatient, not in an office, so why would it be denied?

ANSWER: It doesn't matter that the service took place in a hospital versus the office. The CCI edit only recognizes that the surgical procedure that was performed falls within the surgical global period of a prior surgery and is being included in the surgical global package.

When a patient has a surgical procedure, there are surgical package guidelines a surgeon must follow within that global period time frame. A surgeon who is providing his or her patient follow-up care should not be billing for any additional services that would be considered part of the surgical care. There are certain aftercare services that are included in the global surgical package and there are other services that are not included in the global surgical package. For a listing of services that are included or not included, go to Medicare's website in your jurisdiction and refer to the Surgery Manual. It will provide you with everything you need to know about Global Surgical Packages.

For help, go to: Area A4 Resources: Website: http://www.trailblazerhealth.com Publications: Medicare Surgery Manual

Claim # 123456   **CHARGE ENTRY**

Diagnosis: Patient Complaint: <u>Pain in the right wrist</u>

1 <u>813.42</u> (Description:Closed Fracture of distal end of Radius)

2_____ (Description:)   Date of Injury: ( ) File: HCFA Electronically

3_____ (Description:)   Date of Hospitalization: ( ) File: HCFA Paper

4_____ (Description:_____) Discharge Date: ( )File: UB04

Facility: Office

Rendering Provider: Jones   Referring: Supervising/Ordering:

Line #	Date of Service	Code(s)	Diag	Modifier	POS	Unit(s)	$ Fee
(x) 1	From 03/15/08 To 03/15/08	20690	1		22		995.00
(x) 2	From To						
(x) 3	From To						
(x) 4	From To						
(x) 5	From To						
(x) 6	From To						

Description: CPT Code 20690 "Application of a Uniplane, external fixation device"

Figure 1: First Procedure

Claim # 234567   **CHARGE ENTRY**

Diagnosis: Patient Complaint: <u>Pain in the right wrist</u>

1 <u>813.42</u> (Description:Closed Fracture of distal end of Radius)

2_____ (Description:)   Date of Injury: ( ) File: HCFA Electronically

3_____ (Description:)   Date of Hospitalization: ( ) File: HCFA Paper

4_____ (Description:_____) Discharge Date: ( )File: UB04

Facility: Office

Rendering Provider: Jones   Referring: Supervising/Ordering:

Line #	Date of Service	Code(s)	Diag	Modifier	POS	Unit(s)	$ Fee
(x) 1	From 06/02/08 To 06/02/08	20694	1		22		930.00
(x) 2	From To						
(x) 3	From To						
(x) 4	From To						
(x) 5	From To						
(x) 6	From To						

Description: CPT Code 20694 "Removal of an external fixation device"

Figure 2: Second Procedure

QUESTION: Even though the procedure is being denied, can the surgeon get paid?

ANSWER: Yes, as long as the service that was provided falls under those services listed in the Surgery Manual that are not included in the surgical global package.

In order to view if a patient had a prior procedure, pull up all the billing on the patient's account. Locate the ticket/claim that states that the service took place at a hospital as either inpatient (INPT) or outpatient (OUTPT), then compare the patient's condition (diagnosis), body part, and surgeon who performed the prior surgery with the surgery that is being denied and ask the following questions (includes answers):

For help, go to: Area A4 Resources: Website: http://www.trailblazerhealth.com Publications: Medicare Surgery Manual.

QUESTION: Is the patient's condition, body part and surgeon are the same for both surgeries?

ANSWER: Yes.

QUESTION: Both surgeries, are they related?

ANSWER: Yes.

QUESTION: The prior surgery, CPT Code 20690, what is the GP?

ANSWER: Per MCR Fee Schedule CPT Code 20690 has a 90 day GP and the date of service for the second surgery did fall within that 90 day global period.

For help, go to: AREA A4 www.trailblazerhealth.com Medicare Fee Schedule, Search by CPT Code, Global Period

QUESTION: Because both surgeries are related and the second surgery is within the GP of the first surgery, in order for the surgeon to get paid, what do we need to do?

ANSWER: In order to bill out another surgical procedure that is payable and should not be included in the surgical global package, a Global Surgery modifier will be required. Global Surgery Modifiers provide additional information in order to separately bill out services and other procedures to help bypass edits so services can be adjudicated for reimbursement and not be denied.

In this case, the first surgery (See Figure 1) that was provided was "Application of a Uniplane, external fixation device" (CPT Code 20690). Patient condition is a "Closed Fracture of distal end of radius" of RT wrist. The second procedure (See Figure 2) that was performed was "Removal of an external fixation device" (CPT Code 20694), which clearly tells me this is a staged or distinct surgical procedure because it was provided in two parts. The decision for the removal would have been made around the same time when the first procedure was performed; therefore, the second procedure is separately billable and payable.

QUESTION: What is the appropriate modifier?

ANSWER: Since the service or procedure was staged by the same surgeon within the surgical post-op period, the Global Surgery Modifier to use is "58."

For help, go to: Area A4. Resources: Website: hyyp://www.trailblazerhealth.com, Publications: Medicare Surgery Manual

Another example, but different modifier required: If a procedure was provided in the office, such as an injection, during the surgical global period, which turned out not to be related because the patient presented a new complaint or new symptom, separate billing is appropriate but would require a Global Surgical Modifier "79" (Unrelated Procedure by same physician during surgical global period).

RESOLUTION: Three steps to correct the claim

Now that you know that the second surgery was staged and related to the first surgery, you need to correct the claim by adding a "58" modifier on the ticket/claim and refiling or resubmitting it as a corrected claim to Medicare.

Step 1. In the Main Menu, select COLLECTIONS, pull up PATIENT BILLING, then pull up the ticket. From the PATIENT ACCOUNT CLAIM DETAIL under "Billing," select MODIFY. Under Charge Entry on line 1, which lists CPT Code 20694, in the Modifier Column add the 58 modifier.

Step 2. Under Charge Entry, mark (X) File: HCFA Electronically so the claim can be billed.

Step 3: Now that you have resolved the claim issue, the next step is to add your notes on how you resolved the claim issue.

Pull up PATIENT BILLING under the PATIENT ACCOUNT CLAIM DETAIL and select NOTES. Type in what the problem was and what you did to resolve the claim issue.

(**In every medical software there is a place to key in notes on what you did, either on that particular ticket or somewhere on that patient's account.**) An example of how you would type in your notes is as follows:

NOTE: Per the Medicare remittance dated 5/14/2008 denied the procedure because it was billed within the global period of a previous surgery. Both surgeries are related and because the surgeon went back and removed the pins that he placed, I added a 58 modifier and rebilled the corrected claim to Medicare.

** Key Point: Keeping good notes is another key factor in doing a great job. Putting in good notes will provide information as to what has been done or is being done to resolve the issue with that particular date of service. If someone decides to go into that particular claim, they will see your notes and will know exactly what is being done.

CASE M: SITUATIONS 1 AND 2

MEDICARE PART B (ERA) REMITTANCE ADVICE

Provider#:

Check/EFT (Electronic Fund Transfer) #: Issue Date: 00/00/2008

Name: HIC ACCT ICN **CASE M**

PROV #	DOS	POS	NOS	CPT	MOD	BILLED $	ALLOW	DEDUCT	COINS	GRP/RC	AMT	PAID PROV $
######	051408	11	1	99213		74.00	0.00	0.00	0.00	CO-97	74.00	0.00
				REM: M144								
PT RESP	0.00			CLAIM TOTAL		74.00	0.00	0.00	0.00		74.00	0.00
											NET	0.00

Name: HIC ACCT ICN

PROV #	DOS	POS	NOS	CPT	MOD	BILLED $	ALLOW	DEDUCT	COINS	GRP/RC	AMT	PAID PROV $
######	060208	22	1	20694		930.00	0.00	0.00	0.00	CO-97	930.00	0.00
				REM: M144								
PT RESP	0.00			CLAIM TOTAL		930.00	0.00	0.00	0.00		930.00	0.00
											NET	0.00

Name: HIC ACCT ICN

PROV	DOS	POS	NOS	CPT	MOD	BILLED $	ALLOW	DEDUCT	COINS	GRP/RC	AMT	PAID PROV $
######	061208	21		25606		1343.00	428.70	0.00	85.74	CO-45	914.30	342.96
######	061208	21		25605	51	796.00	0.00	0.00	0.00	CO-125	796.00	0.00
				REM:M80								
PT RESP	85.74			CLAIM TOTAL		2139.00	428.70	0.00	85.74		1710.30	342.96
											NET	342.96

Name: HIC ACCT ICN

PROV	DOS	POS	NOS	CPT	MOD	BILLED $	ALLOW	DEDUCT	COINS	GRP/RC	AMT	PAID PROV $
######	052808	22	1	28104		1087.00	310.12	0.00	62.02	CO-58	776.88	248.10
######	052808	22	1	28288	51	808.00	0.00	0.00	0.00	CO-B15	808.00	0.00
				REM: M80								
######	052808	22	1	28126	51	549.00	111.21	0.00	22.24	CO-45	437.79	88.97
PT RESP	84.26			CLAIM TOTAL		2444.00	421.33	0.00	84.26		2022.67	337.07
											NET	337.07

MESSAGE CODES: GROUP/CARC/RARC

CO   Contractual Obligation

125   Submission/Billing Error

M80   Not covered when performed during the same session/date as a previously processed service for the patient

CASE M: SITUATIONS 1 AND 2

CODING ERROR: ANSI CARC/RARC CODES CO-125, M80

QUESTION: Why is the denial is stating that the procedure that was performed cannot be covered during the same session as the other procedure that was performed on the same day?

ANSWER: Per the CCI Edit in the Medicare Correct Coding Guide manual, the check mark (√) symbol means that the Code Pairs are mutually exclusive (CPT Code 25605 is mutually exclusive when performed with CPT Code 25606). Both procedures cannot be performed during the same session on the same day because basically one or the other can provide the same type of treatment, which would exclude the possibility of doing the other procedure. Only one method would be necessary unless they were performed on a different anatomical site or in a different patient encounter.

For help, go to: Area A1 Guidebook: Refer to: Chapter 5 , Unit II, Step 8, Part B, Section 5
Area A4 Other Resources: http://www.cms.gov Publications>>Manual Correct Coding Guide.

SITUATION 1

QUESTION: If CPT Code 25605 was performed along with CPT Code 25606 and they were done on the same anatomical site, LT Wrist, how is the claim corrected?

ANSWER: CPT Code 25605 will need to be adjusted off as being "Bundled."

RESOLUTION: Two steps to correct the claim

Because we verified that both procedures were performed on the same anatomical site (LT wrist) during the same session, the one code that was denied will need to be adjusted off as a bundled code.

Step 1. In the Main Menu, select COLLECTIONS, pull up PATIENT BILLING, then pull up the ticket. From the PATIENT ACCOUNT CLAIM DETAIL under "Payment Type," select MODIFY. Under Payment Transaction post charges on each line in the Disallow/Adj Column and under the Disallow/Adj Type Column drop-down window, select "Bundled." Your adjustment it will adjust off the charge.

Step 2: Now that you have resolved the claim issue, the next step is to add your notes on how you resolved the claim issue. Pull up PATIENT BILLING under the PATIENT ACCOUNT CLAIM DETAIL and select NOTES. Type in what the problem was and what you did to resolve the claim issue.

(**In every medical software there is a place to key in notes on what you did, either on that particular ticket or somewhere on that patient's account.**) An example of how you would type in your notes is as follows:

NOTE: Per the Medicare remittance dated 5/14/2008 denied the procedure because per CCI Edits it is mutually excluded with the other procedure. Op Notes state that both procedures were performed on the LT Wrist, so I adjusted off the charge as a bundled code.

** Key Point. Keeping good notes is another key factor in doing a great job. Putting in good notes will provide information as to what has been done or is being done to resolve the issue with that particular date of service. If someone decides to go into that particular claim, they will see your notes and will know exactly what is being done.

** Key point: Medicare will reimburse only for the lesser-valued of the two procedures.

SITUATION 2

QUESTION: If CPT Code 25605 was performed on a different anatomical site, the RT Wrist, how is the claim corrected? ANSWER: Per the CMS modifier indicator for Code pair Col 1/Col 2, CPT Code 25606/25605 has an indicator of "1." The indicator 1 states that the code pairs may be submitted separately for reimbursement as long as the two procedures were performed either in different anatomical sites, through separate incision/excision, or at a different session or patient encounter by the same physician on the same day. A modifier 59 may be attached (separate procedure) and medical documentation must support the use of this modifier.

Even though a code combination may be listed as a CCI Edit, CMS does allow for billing and payment of both codes identified in a Code pair edit under certain circumstances when submitted with the appropriate modifier. CCI identifies each code combination edit with a modifier indicator to identify which procedure code combination may be billed together with the use of a modifier. CMS utilizes three types of modifier indicators: 0, 1, and 9.

For help, go to: Area A1, Guidebook. Refer to: Chapter 5, Unit II, Step 8, Part B: Daily Work 5

RESOLUTION: Three steps to correct the claim
The Op Report states "The fracture was stabilized with a percutaneous bone fixation device." CPT Code 25605 was performed on the RT wrist, not the LT Wrist. After identifying the code pair modifier indicator we need to correct the claim by adding the "59" modifier on the ticket/claim and refile or resubmit as a corrected claim.

Step 1. In the Main Menu, select COLLECTIONS, pull up PATIENT BILLING, then pull up the ticket. From the PATIENT ACCOUNT CLAIM DETAIL under "Billing," select MODIFY. Under Charge Entry on line 1, which lists CPT Code 25605, add 59 in the Modifier Column.

Step 2. Under Charge Entry, mark (X) File: HCFA Electronically so the claim can be billed.

Step 3: Now that you have resolved the claim issue, the next step is to add in your notes on how you resolved the claim issue. Pull up PATIENT BILLING under the PATIENT ACCOUNT CLAIM DETAIL and select NOTES. Type in what the problem was and what you did to resolve the claim issue.

(**In every medical software there is a place to key in notes on what you did, either on that particular ticket or somewhere on that patient's account.**) An example of how you would type in your notes is as follows:

NOTE: Per the Medicare remittance dated 5/14/2008 denied the procedure because, per CCI Edits, it is mutually excluded with the other procedure. Op Notes state that CPT Code 25605 was performed on the RT wrist, not the LT wrist, so I added a 59 modifier and rebilled the corrected claim to Medicare.

** Key Point: Keeping good notes is another key factor in doing a great job. Putting in good notes will provide information as to what has been done or is being done to resolve the issue with that particular date of service. If someone decides to go into that particular claim, they will see your notes and will know exactly what is being done.

** Key point: Medicare will reimburse only for the lesser-valued of the two procedures.**

CASE N: SITUATIONS 1 AND 2

MEDICARE PART B (ERA) REMITTANCE ADVICE
Provider#:
Check/EFT (Electronic Fund Transfer) #: Issue Date: 00/00/2008

CASE N

Name: HIC ACCT ICN

PROV #	DOS	POS	NOS	CPT	MOD	BILLED $	ALLOW	DEDUCT	COINS	GRP/RC	AMT	PAID PROV $
######	051408	11	1	99213		74.00	0.00	0.00	0.00	CO-97	74.00	0.00
				REM: M144								
PT RESP 0.00				CLAIM TOTAL		74.00	0.00	0.00	0.00		74.00	0.00
											NET	0.00

Name: HIC ACCT ICN

PROV #	DOS	POS	NOS	CPT	MOD	BILLED $	ALLOW	DEDUCT	COINS	GRP/RC	AMT	PAID PROV $
######	060208	22	1	20694		930.00	0.00	0.00	0.00	CO-97	930.00	0.00
				REM: M144								
PT RESP 0.00				CLAIM TOTAL		930.00	0.00	0.00	0.00		930.00	0.00
											NET	0.00

Name: HIC ACCT ICN

PROV	DOS	POS	NOS	CPT	MOD	BILLED $	ALLOW	DEDUCT	COINS	GRP/RC	AMT	PAID PROV $
######	061208	21	1	25606		1343.00	428.70	0.00	85.74	CO-45	914.30	342.96
######	061208	21	1	25605	51	796.00	0.00	0.00	0.00	CO-125	796.00	0.00
				REM:M80								
PT RESP 85.74				CLAIM TOTAL		2139.00	428.70	0.00	85.74		1710.30	342.96
											NET	342.96

Name: HIC ACCT ICN

PROV	DOS	POS	NOS	CPT	MOD	BILLED $	ALLOW	DEDUCT	COINS	GRP/RC	AMT	PAID PROV $
######	052808	22	1	28104		1087.00	310.12	0.00	62.02	CO-58	776.88	248.10
######	052808	22	1	28288	51	808.00	0.00	0.00	0.00	CO-B15	808.00	0.00
				REM: M80								
######	052808	22	1	28126	51	549.00	111.21	0.00	22.24	CO-45	437.79	88.97
PT RESP 84.26				CLAIM TOTAL		2444.00	421.33	0.00	84.26		2022.67	337.07
											NET	337.07

MESSAGE CODES: GROUP/CARC/RARC

CO Contractual Obligation

B15 service/procedure requires that a qualifying service/procedure be received and covered. The qualifying other service/procedure has not been received/adjudicated

M80 Not covered when performed during the same session/date as a previously processed service for the patient

CASE N: SITUATIONS 1 AND 2

CODING ERROR: ANSI CARC/RARC CODES CO-B15, M80

QUESTION: What is CPT Code 28288, which code is it being bundled with, and are the codes actually bundled?

ANSWER: Per the CCI Edit in the Medicare Correct Coding Guide Manual, CPT Code 28288 is being bundled with CPT Code 28104 (Column 1). CPT Code 28288 (Column 2) is identified by an asterisk (*) symbol, which indicates "Coding Based on Standards of Medical/Surgical Practice." Procedures that are integral to another procedure are component parts of the more comprehensive procedure, and the CCI edit table places the more comprehensive procedure in Column 1 and the component procedure is then placed in Column 2. When a component procedure is integral to the more comprehensive procedure, it cannot be billed separately. In this case, the component procedure, CPT Code 28288, is necessary in order to complete the more comprehensive service, CPT Code 28104. A better way to describe it is, "In order to do that, you have to do this." CPT Code 28288 is a partial excision of a metatarsal head and CPT Code 28104 is the excision of a bone cyst of a metatarsal. Both consist of the excision of bone from a metatarsal.

SITUATION 1

QUESTION: If CPT Code 28288 was performed along with CPT Code 28104 and they were done on the same anatomical site, the 4th metatarsal, how is the claim corrected?

ANSWER: CPT Code 28288 will need to be adjusted off as being "Bundled."

RESOLUTION: Two steps to correct the claim

Because we verified that both procedures were performed on the same hand, the one code that was denied will need to be adjusted off as a bundled code.

Step 1. In the Main Menu, select COLLECTIONS, pull up PATIENT BILLING, then pull up the ticket. From the PATIENT ACCOUNT CLAIM DETAIL under "Payment Type," select MODIFY. Under Payment Transaction post charges on each line in the Disallow/Adj Column charges and under the Disallow/Adj Type Column drop-down window, select "Bundled." By posting your adjustment it will adjust off the charge.

Step 2: Now that you have resolved the claim issue, the next step is to add your notes on how you resolved the claim issue.

Pull up PATIENT BILLING under the PATIENT ACCOUNT CLAIM DETAIL and select NOTES. Type in what the problem was and what you did to resolve the claim issue.

(**In every medical software there is a place to key in notes on what you did, either on that particular ticket or somewhere on that patient's account.**) An example of how you would type in your notes is as follows:

NOTE: Per the Medicare remittance dated 5/14/2008 denied the procedure because per CCI Edits it is an integral component of a more comprehensive procedure. Op Notes state that both procedures were performed on the 4th metatarsal on the RT Foot, so I made an adjustment on the claim by adjusting off the charge as a bundled code.

** Key Point: Keeping good notes is another key factor in doing a great job. Putting in good notes will provide information as to what has been done or is being done to resolve the issue with that particular date of service. If someone decides to go into that particular claim, they will see your notes and will know exactly what is being done.

** Key point: Medicare will reimburse only for the lesser-valued of the two procedures.**

SITUATION 2

QUESTION: Were both procedures performed on the same toe?
ANSWER: The Op Notes state that the excision of the bone cyst was performed on the patient's RT Big Toe and the partial removal of the metatarsal head was performed on the 4th metatarsal (Diagnosis: 735.4 Hammer Toe), so both procedures were not performed on the same toe.

QUESTION: How is the claim corrected?
ANSWER: Per the CMS modifier indicator for Code pair Col 1/Col 2, CPT Code 28104/28288 has an indicator of "1." Indicator 1 states that the code pairs may be submitted separately for reimbursement as long as the two procedures were performed either in different anatomical sites, through separate incision/excision, or at a different session or patient encounter by the same physician on the same day. A modifier 59 may be attached (separate procedure) and medical documentation must support the use of this modifier.

Even though a code combination may be listed as a CCI Edit, CMS does allow for billing and payment of both codes identified in a Code pair edit under certain circumstances when submitted with the appropriate modifier. CCI identifies each code combination edit with a modifier indicator to identify which procedure code combination may be billed together with the use of a modifier. CMS utilizes three types of modifier indicators: 0, 1, and 9.

For help, go to: Area A4 Other Resources: http://www.cms.gov Select Medicare > Medicare Fee-For-Service. Select Physician Fee Schedule lookup for Payment Indicators.
A4 Other Resources: http://www.trailblazerhealth.com

RESOLUTION: Three steps to correct the claim
The Op Report states that the partial removal of the metatarsal head was performed on the 4th metatarsal, not the Big Toe. After identifying the code pair modifier indicator we need to correct the claim by adding the "59" modifier on the ticket/claim and refile or resubmit as a corrected claim.

Step 1. In the Main Menu, select COLLECTIONS, pull up PATIENT BILLING, then pull up the ticket. From the PATIENT ACCOUNT CLAIM DETAIL under "Billing," select MODIFY. Under Charge Entry on line 1, which lists CPT Code 28288, add 59 in the Modifier Column.

Step 2. Under Charge Entry, mark (X) File: HCFA Electronically so the claim can be billed.

Step 3: Now that you have resolved the claim issue, the next step is to add your notes on how you resolved the claim issue. Pull up PATIENT BILLING under the PATIENT ACCOUNT CLAIM DETAIL and select NOTES. Type in what the problem was and what you did to resolve the claim issue.

(**In every medical software there is a place to key in notes on what you did, either on that particular ticket or somewhere on that patient's account.**) An example of how you would type in your notes is as follows:

NOTE: Per the Medicare remittance dated 5/14/2008 denied CPT Code 28288 because per CCI Edits it is being bundled in with CPT Code 28104. The Op Notes state that CPT Code 28288 was performed on the RT Big Toe, not the 4th Metatarsal, so I added a 59 modifier and rebilled the corrected claim to Medicare.

** Key Point: Keeping good notes is another key factor in doing a great job. Putting in good notes will provide information as to what has been done or is being done to resolve the issue with that particular date of service. If someone decides to go into that particular claim, they will see your notes and will know exactly what is being done.

** Key point: Medicare will reimburse only for the lesser-valued of the two procedures.**

CASE O: SITUATION 1

MEDICARE PART B			(ERA) REMITTANCE ADVICE								
Provider#:											
Check/EFT (Electronic Fund Transfer) #:				Issue Date: 00/00/2008							
Name:		HIC	ACCT		ICN						

PROV #	DOS	POS	NOS	CPT	MOD	BILLED $	ALLOW	DEDUCT	COINS	GRP/RC	AMT	PAID PROV $
######	060208	11	1	73140		65.00	0.00	0.00	0.00	CO-16	65.00	0.00
				REM: MA63								
PT RESP	0.00			CLAIM TOTAL		65.00	0.00	0.00	0.00		65.00	0.00
											NET	0.00

Name:		HIC	ACCT		ICN						

PROV #	DOS	POS	NOS	CPT	MOD	BILLED $	ALLOW	DEDUCT	COINS	GRP/RC	AMT	PAID PROV $
######	060208	11	1	29065		128.00		0.00	0.00	CO-45		
######	060208	11	2	A4590		65.00	0.00	0.00	0.00	CO-16	65.00	0.00
				REM: M51								
PT RESP				CLAIM TOTAL			0.00	0.00	0.00		65.00	0.00
											NET	0.00

MESSAGE CODES: GROUP/CARC/RARC
CO   **Contractual Obligations**
16   **Claim/service lacks information which is needed for adjudication**
MA63   **Missing Principal Diagnosis**

CASE O: SITUATION 1

CODING ERROR: ANSI CARC/RARC CODES CO-16 MA63

QUESTION: When I pulled up the ticket/claim, a diagnosis was listed. Why would Medicare state the principal diagnosis is missing?
ANSWER: The ICD-9-CM that is listed, which is an E code, cannot be listed as a primary diagnosis. There has to be a primary diagnosis; then the E code can be listed as a secondary diagnosis. E codes, which are supplementary classifications of external causes of injury and poisoning, are used in addition to a code that indicates the nature of the patient condition.

For help, go to: Area A4 Resources: HCPCS Code book

QUESTION: What was the patient's primary condition?
ANSWER: After reviewing clinic notes, the doctor examined a scar from a prior surgery regarding infection due to a dog bite, but upon evaluation, today's visit was mainly regarding stiffness in fingers of patient's left hand.

QUESTION: What is the primary diagnosis?
ANSWER: Diagnosis for stiffness in joints of finger is 719.54.

RESOLUTION: Three steps to correct the claim

Step 1. Correct the claim by adding diagnosis 719.54 as the primary diagnosis, and listing diagnosis E906.0 (Dog bite) as the secondary diagnosis. In the Main Menu, select COLLECTIONS, pull up PATIENT BILLING, then pull up the ticket. From the PATIENT ACCOUNT CLAIM DETAIL under "Billing," select MODIFY. Under Charge Entry, locate the diagnosis section, change the E code from primary to secondary, and add diagnosis 719.54 as the primary diagnosis. On line 1, which lists CPT Code 73140 in the Diagnosis Column, link diagnoses 1 & 2 to line 1.

Step 2. Refile or resubmit corrected claim. Under Charge Entry, mark (X) File: HCFA Electronically so the claim can be batched and then billed to Medicare.

Step 3. Now that you have resolved the claim issue, the next step is to add your notes on how you resolved the claim issue. Pull up PATIENT BILLING under the PATIENT ACCOUNT CLAIM DETAIL and select NOTES. Type in what the problem was and what you did to resolve the claim issue.

(**In every medical software there is a place to key in notes on what you did, either on that particular ticket or somewhere on that patient's account.**) An example of how you would type in your notes is as follows:

NOTE: Per the Medicare remittance dated 5/14/2008 denied CPT Code 73140 because the primary diagnosis is missing. Made correction by changing diagnosis E906.0 to secondary diagnosis, then I added in 719.54 as primary diagnosis linking both to line 1 and refiled the corrected claim to Medicare.

** Key Point: Keeping good notes is another key factor in doing a great job. Putting in good notes will provide information as to what has been done or is being done to resolve the issue with that particular date of service. If someone decides to go into that particular claim, they will see your notes and will know exactly what is being done.

CASE P: SITUATION 1

MEDICARE PART B			(ERA) REMITTANCE ADVICE									
Provider#:												
Check/EFT (Electronic Fund Transfer) #:				Issue Date: 00/00/2008								
Name:		HIC	ACCT			ICN						
PROV #	DOS	POS	NOS	CPT	MOD	BILLED $	ALLOW	DEDUCT	COINS	GRP/RC	AMT	PAID PROV $
######	060208	11	1	73140		65.00	0.00	0.00	0.00	CO-16	65.00	0.00
				REM: MA63								
PT RESP	0.00			CLAIM TOTAL		65.00	0.00	0.00	0.00		65.00	0.00
										NET		0.00
Name:		HIC	ACCT			ICN						
PROV #	DOS	POS	NOS	CPT	MOD	BILLED $	ALLOW	DEDUCT	COINS	GRP/RC	AMT	PAID PROV $
######	060208	11	1	29065		128.00		0.00	0.00	CO-45		
######	060208	11	2	A4590		65.00	0.00	0.00	0.00	CO-16	65.00	0.00
				REM: M51								
PT RESP				CLAIM TOTAL			0.00	0.00	0.00		65.00	0.00
										NET		0.00

MESSAGE CODES: GROUP/CARC/RARC
CO   Contractual Obligations
16   Claim/service lacks information which is needed for adjudication
M51 Missing/Incomplete/Invalid Procedure code

CASE P: SITUATION 1

CODING ERROR: ANSI CARC/RARC CODES CO-16 M51

QUESTION: Medicare is denying the service because it is an invalid code. How do you know what the correct code is?
ANSWER: The A code is a Level II HCPCS code, so you will need to check the HCPCS code book. Locate A4590 in the code book. If the code is no longer a valid code, the HCPCS code book will provide you with the new code to use.

QUESTION: What is the correct code to use?
ANSWER: Per the HCPCS code book, under A4590, Special casting material (e.g., fiberglass), it states "See Q4001–Q4048." In this case, the correct code is Q4005.

QUESTION: What is the difference between the 29065 and HCPCS codes Q4001–Q4048?
ANSWER: CPT Code 29065 identifies the application, whereas the Q codes are for the casting material/supplies.

HCPCS CODE	DESCRIPTION	CPT CODES
Q4005	Cast Supplies, Long Arm Cast (LAC) adult, plaster (11 yrs +)	29065
Q4006	Cast Supplies, Long Arm Cast (LAC) adult, fiberglass	29065
Q4007	Cast Supplies, Long Arm Cast (LAC) pediatric, plaster (0-10 yrs)	29065
Q4008	Cast Supplies, Long Arm Cast (LAC) pediatric, fiberglass	29065

" Key Point: New and Deleted CPT/HCPCS codes

Providers should place orders for new code books sometime in June or July in order to have them delivered by the October/November time frame. New code books will provide you with the new and deleted codes for the new year. Websites will also have this information available as well.

" Key Point: Make sure the application matches with the materials. In this case, CPT Code 29065 is for the application for an Adult LAC, so you want to make sure to select the appropriate code for the materials for Adult Fiberglass for LAC.

" Key Point: Make sure to bill only 1 unit. Refer to Case T.

RESOLUTION: Three steps to correct the claim
Correct the claim by voiding A4590, then keying in the correct code Q4006, and billing out only 1 unit (add in the other unit but do not bill for it), then refile or resubmit the corrected claim to Medicare.

Step 1. In the Main Menu, select COLLECTIONS, pull up PATIENT BILLING, then pull up the ticket. From the PATIENT ACCOUNT CLAIM DETAIL under "Billing," select MODIFY. Under Charge Entry on line 2, which lists HCPCS Code A4590, void out the code by right-clicking, then key in the correct CPT Code, Q4006.

Step 2. Under Charge Entry, mark (X) File: HCFA Electronically so the claim can be resubmitted as a corrected claim.

Step 3. Now that you have resolved the claim issue, the next step is to add your notes on how you resolved the claim issue. Pull up PATIENT BILLING under the PATIENT ACCOUNT CLAIM DETAIL and select NOTES. Type in what the problem was and what you did to resolve the claim issue.

(**In every medical software there is a place to key in notes on what you did, either on that particular ticket or somewhere on that patient's account.**) An example of how you would type in your notes is as follows:

NOTE: Per the Medicare remittance dated 5/14/2008 denied the service because A4590 is an invalid code. The correct code is Q4006, so I voided A4590, keyed in the correct code, and resubmitted the corrected claim to Medicare.

" Key Point: Keeping good notes is another key factor in doing a great job. Putting in good notes will provide information as to what has been done or is being done to resolve the issue with that particular date of service. If someone decides to go into that particular claim, they will see your notes and will know exactly what is being done.

CASE Q: SITUATIONS 1 AND 2

MEDICARE PART B					**(ERA) REMITTANCE ADVICE**							

Provider#:
Check/EFT (Electronic Fund Transfer) #: Issue Date: 00/00/2008
Name: HIC ACCT ICN

PROV #	DOS	POS	NOS	CPT	MOD	BILLED $	ALLOW	DEDUCT	COINS	GRP/RC	AMT	PAID PROV $
######	052808	22	1	29881	RT	1950.00	549.50	0.00	110.30	CO-45	1400.50	439.20
######	052808	22	1	29877		1225.00	0.00	0.00	0.00	CO-125	1225.00	0.00
				REM:M15								
######	052808	22	1	29875		895.00	349.10	0.00	69.82	CO-45	545.90	279.28
PT RESP	180.12			CLAIM TOTAL		4070.00	898.60	0.00	180.12		3171.40	718.48
										NET		718.48

Name: HIC ACCT ICN

PROV #	DOS	POS	NOS	CPT	MOD	BILLED $	ALLOW	DEDUCT	COINS	GRP/RC	AMT	PAID PROV $
######	060208	21	4	15101		1358.00	0.00	0.00	0.00	CO-107	1358.00	0.00
				REM:N122								
PT RESP	0.00			CLAIM TOTAL		1358.00	0.00	0.00	0.00		1358.00	0.00
										NET		0.00

Name: HIC ACCT ICN

PROV #	DOS	POS	NOS	CPT	MOD	BILLED $	ALLOW	DEDUCT	COINS	GRP/RC	AMT	PAID PROV $
######	061208	11	1	99024		0.00	0.00	0.00	0.00	CO-45	0.00	0.00
######	061208	11	1	A6203		9.00	0.00	0.00	0.00	CO-A1	9.00	0.00
				REM:M15								
PT RESP	0.00			CLAIM TOTAL		9.00					9.00	0.00
										NET		0.00

Name: HIC ACCT ICN

PROV #	DOS	POS	NOS	CPT	MOD	BILLED $	ALLOW	DEDUCT	COINS	GRP/RC	AMT	PAID PROV $
######	052808	11	1	29405	RT	218.00	157.50	0.00	31.50	CO-45	60.50	126.00
######	052808	11	1	Q4038		48.00	26.50	0.00	5.30	CO-45	21.50	21.20
######	052808	11	2	Q4038		96.00	0.00	0.00	0.00	CO-97	96.00	0.00
				REM: M86								
PT RESP	36.80			CLAIM TOTAL			184.00	0.00	36.80		178.00	147.20
										NET		147.20

MESSAGE CODES: GROUP/CARC/RARC

CO Contractual Obligation
125 Submission/Billing Error
M15 Separately billed services/tests have been bundled as they are considered components of the same procedure

---

CASE Q: SITUATION #1 and #2

CODING ERROR: ANSI CARC/RARC CODES CO-125, M15

QUESTION: What code is CPT Code 29877 being bundled with and are the Code pairs actually bundled?
ANSWER: Per CCI Edit Table in the Medicare Correct Coding Guide Manual, CPT Code 29877 is being bundled with CPT Code 29881 (Column 1). CPT Code 29877 (Column 2) is identified by a ■ symbol that indicates "Misuse of Col 2 with Col 1."
For help, go to: Area A4 Other resources. http//www.trailblazerhealth.com

QUESTION: Is CPT Code 29877 and CPT Code 29881 considered components of the same procedure?
ANSWER: Yes, if both Arthroscopic Knee Procedures were performed in the same compartment, same session or encounter, by the same physician on the same day.

Reporting Arthroscopic Knee surgery can be a very challenging, especially if multiple arthroscopic knee procedures were performed in all three compartments on the same knee. The knee is divided up into Three Compartments; Medial, Lateral and Patella. When coding for Arthroscopic Knee surgery it is very important to review the Op notes carefully in order to identify were each procedure was performed, either in the same compartment or in other compartments of the knee.

When multiple Arthroscopic surgical procedures are performed in the same compartment of the same knee, only the more extensive or comprehensive procedure should be reported.

SITUATION 1

QUESTION: In this particular situation, were both arthroscopic surgical procedures performed in the same compartment?
ANSWER: No. The Op Notes state that chondroplasty (CPT Code 29877) was performed in the lateral compartment, whereas meniscectomy (CPT Code 29881) was performed in the medial compartment of the RT Knee.

You have learned that if a procedure was performed in a different anatomical area, you would be able to append a 59 modifier. The same applies to the knee. If the procedure was performed in different compartments, you would also append a 59 modifier. In the past and with some private insurers, this would and still may be correct, but Medicare will not accept the 59 modifier. Instead, CMS has given approval to report HCPCS code G0289 (loose-body and foreign-body removal as well as chondroplasty) when an orthopedic surgeon performs chondroplasty (CPT code 29877) and other arthroscopic surgical procedures in separate compartments of the same knee, such as meniscectomy (CPT Code 29881). It can be reported more than one time provided each time it is for a separate compartment, whereas CPT code 29877 can only be reported once, regardless of the number of compartments in which it was performed.

RESOLUTION: Three steps to correct the claim

Now we know that we can use G0289 in place of 29877. In order to correct the claim, we will need to void out CPT code 29877 and add in correct HCPCS Level II code G0289 and refile or resubmit the corrected claim.

Step 1. Pull up the original ticket/claim, then pull up the charge entry so you can make a correction and refile the claim. In the Main Menu, select COLLECTIONS, pull up PATIENT BILLING, then pull up the ticket. From the PATIENT ACCOUNT CLAIM DETAIL under "Billing," select MODIFY. In the Charge Entry screen on line 2, CPT Code 29877 is listed. Void out the charge and key in the correct HCPCS code G0289.

Step 2. Now that you have made the correction on the ticket/claim, you will need to refile or resubmit the claim electronically to Medicare. In the Charge Entry screen next to File: HCFA Electronically, mark (X) so the claim can be batched and billed.

Step 3: Now that you have resolved the claim issue, the next step is to add your notes on how you resolved the claim issue. Pull up PATIENT BILLING under the PATIENT ACCOUNT CLAIM DETAIL and select NOTES. Type in what the problem was and what you did to resolve the claim issue.

(**In every medical software there is a place to key in notes on what you did, either on that particular ticket or somewhere on that patient's account.**) An example of how you would type in your notes is as follows:

NOTE: Per the Medicare remittance dated 5/14/2008 denied the procedure code 29877 because it is being bundled with the more comprehensive procedure, CPT code 29881. The Op Notes state that the chondroplasty was performed in the lateral compartment, whereas the meniscectomy was performed in the medial compartment of the RT knee. Medicare does not accept the 59 modifier, but does accept HCPCS G0289 in the place of 29877, so I voided 29877. Then I keyed in the correct code G0289 on line 2 and refiled the corrected claim with Medicare.

** Key Point: Keeping good notes is another key factor in doing a great job. Putting in good notes will provide information as to what has been done or is being done to resolve the issue with that particular date of service. If someone decides to go into that particular claim, they will see your notes and will know exactly what is being done.

** Key point: Medicare will reimburse only for the lesser-valued of the two procedures.**

SITUATION 2

MEDICARE PART B   **(ERA) REMITTANCE ADVICE**

Provider#:

Check/EFT (Electronic Fund Transfer) #:   Issue Date: 00/00/2008

Name: HIC   ACCT   ICN

PROV #	DOS	POS	NOS	CPT	MOD	BILLED $	ALLOW	DEDUCT	COINS	GRP/RC	AMT	PAID PROV $
#######	052808	11	1	99213		74.00	54.00	0.00	10.80	CO-45	20.00	43.20
#######	052808	11	1	73600	LT	98.00	0.00	0.00	0.00	CO-125	98.00	0.00
				REM:M15								
#######	052808	11	1	73610		92.00	63.00	0.00	12.60	CO-45	35.00	50.40
				REM:M15								
PT RESP	23.40			CLAIM TOTAL		264.00	117.00	0.00	23.40		147.00	93.60
											NET	93.60

MESSAGE CODES: GROUP/CARC/RARC

CO   Contractual Obligation

125   Submission/Billing Error

M15   Separately billed services/tests have been bundled as they are considered components of the same procedure

CODING ERROR: ANSI CARC/RARC CODES CO-125, M15

Medicare is denying the first diagnostic test (CPT Code 73600: Radiologic Exam, Ankle: two views) because it is considered components of the same procedure.

QUESTION. Are the Code pairs actually bundled?

ANSWER: Per CCI Edit in the Medicare Correct Coding Guide Manual, CPT Code 73600 is being bundled with CPT Code 73610 (Column 1). CPT Code 73600 (Column 2) is identified by a diamond (◊) symbol that will help you on how to base your decision.

QUESTION: Looking at the charges under the description, what is the difference between the two X-rays?

ANSWER: Both X-ray's are related to the Ankle but the difference is in the description following the semicolon. CPT Code 73610 states, "Complete, minimum of three views," whereas CPT Code 73600 states, "Two views." The one is already included in the other. Both are considered within the same "Family of Codes", which describe redundant services.

QUESTION: Was there two x-rays taken and were they done on the same body part?

ANSWER: Per Encounter/Superbill, both CPT Codes were marked/circled but nothing else was hand written in. Per Clinic notes do state that both X-rays were done on LT ankle.

If clinic notes do not notate X-ray's were given, you will need to check with your X-ray Tech to see if x-rays were actually done. If they were, then the clinic notes will need to be corrected.

QUESTION: Is the patient condition the same on both hands?

ANSWER: Yes. Diagnosis 824.8 (Fracture of ankle) is the only diagnosis listed and both X-rays were linked to the one diagnosis.

RESOLUTION: Two steps to correct the claim
In this situation, because both are within the same Family of Codes, the next step is to adjust off the charge.

Step 1. In the Main Menu, select **COLLECTIONS**, pull up **PATIENT BILLING**, then pull up the ticket. From the PATIENT ACCOUNT CLAIM DETAIL under "Payment Type," select MODIFY. Under Payment Transaction post charges on line 2 in the Disallow/Adj Column and under the Disallow/Adj Type Column drop-down window, and select "Bundled." By posting your adjustment it will adjust off the charge.

Step 2. Now that you have resolved the claim issue, the next step is to add your notes on how you resolved the claim issue. Pull up PATIENT BILLING under the PATIENT ACCOUNT CLAIM DETAIL and select NOTES. Type in what the problem was and what you did to resolve the claim issue.

(**In every medical software there is a place to key in notes on what you did, either on that particular ticket or somewhere on that patient's account.**) An example of how you would type in your notes is as follows:

NOTE: Per the Medicare remittance dated 5/14/2008 denied the procedure code 73600 because it is being bundled with the more comprehensive procedure, CPT code 73610. Both are considered within the same Family of Codes, which describe redundant services, so I made an adjustment on the claim by bundling code 73600 with 73610.

** Key Point: Keeping good notes is another key factor in doing a great job. Putting in good notes will provide information as to what has been done or is being done to resolve the issue with that particular date of service. If someone decides to go into that particular claim, they will see your notes and will know exactly what is being done.

Another example: Different Diagnostic tests but same denial

MEDICARE PART B   (ERA) REMITTANCE ADVICE

Provider#:

Check/EFT (Electronic Fund Transfer) #:   Issue Date: 00/00/2008

Name: HIC   ACCT   ICN

PROV #	DOS	POS	NOS	CPT	MOD	BILLED $	ALLOW	DEDUCT	COINS	GRP/RC	AMT	PAID PROV $
######	052808	11	1	99213		74.00	54.00	0.00	10.80	CO-45	20.00	43.20
######	052808	11	1	73120	LT	98.00	0.00	0.00	0.00	CO-125	98.00	0.00
				REM:M15								
######	052808	11	1	73130		92.00	63.00	0.00	12.60	CO-45	35.00	50.40
				REM:M15								
PT RESP	23.40			CLAIM TOTAL		264.00	117.00	0.00	23.40		147.00	93.60
											NET	93.60

MESSAGE CODES: GROUP/CARC/RARC

CO   Contractual Obligation

125   Submission/Billing Error

M15   Separately billed services/tests have been bundled as they are considered components of the same procedure

CODING ERROR: ANSI CARC/RARC CODES CO-125, M15

Medicare is denying the first diagnostic test (CPT Code73120: Radiologic examination, hand: two views) because it is considered components of the same procedure.

QUESTION: Are the Code pairs actually bundled?

ANSWER: Per CCI Edit in the Medicare Correct Coding Guide Manual, CPT Code 73120 is being bundled with CPT Code 73130 (Column 1). CPT Code 73130 (Column 2) is identified by a diamond (◊) symbol that will help you on how to base your decision.

QUESTION: Looking at the charges under the description, what is the difference between the two X-rays?

ANSWER: Both X-ray's are related to the hand but the difference is in the description following the semicolon. CPT Code 73130 states, "Minimum of three views," whereas CPT Code 73120 states, "Two views." The one is already included in the other. Both are considered within the same "Family of Codes", which describe redundant services.

QUESTION: Was there two X-rays taken and were they done on the same body part?

ANSWER: Per Encounter/Superbill, both CPT Codes were marked or circled and RT and LT were hand written in. RT was marked next to CPT Code 73120 and LT was marked next to CPT Code 73130. Per Clinic notes do state that X-ray's were done on RT and LT hand.

QUESTION: Is the patient condition the same on both hands?

ANSWER: No, because per clinic notes state that patient diagnoses on RT hand is 716.94 and patient diagnosis on LT hand is 815.00. The problem here is that the CPT Codes were linking to both diagnoses, not separately.

RESOLUTION: Three steps to correct the claim

In this situation, because both diagnostic tests were done on separate hands, the next step is to correct and refile or resubmit as a corrected claim.

Step 1. In the Main Menu, select COLLECTIONS, pull up PATIENT BILLING, then pull up the ticket. From the PATIENT ACCOUNT CLAIM DETAIL under "Billing," select MODIFY. Under Charge Entry on line 3, which lists CPT code 73130, in the Modifier Column add RT, then add diagnosis 815.00 linking it to line 2, which lists CPT code 73120.

Step 2. Under Charge Entry, mark (X) File: HCFA Electronically so the claim can be billed.

Step 3. Now that you have resolved the claim issue, the next step is to add your notes on how you resolved the claim issue.

Pull up PATIENT BILLING under the PATIENT ACCOUNT CLAIM DETAIL and select NOTES. Type in what the problem was and what you did to resolve the claim issue.

(**In every medical software there is a place to key in notes on what you did, either on that particular ticket or somewhere on that patient's account.**) An example of how you would type in your notes is as follows:

** Key point: Medicare will reimburse only for the lesser-valued of the two procedures.**

CASE R: SITUATIONS 1 AND 2

MEDICARE PART B   (ERA) REMITTANCE ADVICE

Provider#:

Check/EFT (Electronic Fund Transfer) #:   Issue Date: 00/00/2008

Name: HIC   ACCT   ICN

PROV #	DOS	POS	NOS	CPT	MOD	BILLED $	ALLOW	DEDUCT	COINS	GRP/RC	AMT	PAID PROV $
######	052808	22	1	29881	RT	1950.00	549.50	0.00	110.30	CO-45	1400.50	439.20
######	052808	22	1	29877		1225.00	0.00	0.00	0.00	CO-125	1225.00	0.00
				REM:M15								
######	052808	22	1	29875		895.00	349.10	0.00	69.82	CO-45	545.90	279.28
PT RESP	180.12			CLAIM TOTAL		4070.00	898.60	0.00	180.12		3171.40	718.48
											NET	718.48

Name: HIC   ACCT   ICN

PROV #	DOS	POS	NOS	CPT	MOD	BILLED $	ALLOW	DEDUCT	COINS	GRP/RC	AMT	PAID PROV $
######	060208	21	4	15101		1358.00	0.00	0.00	0.00	CO-107	1358.00	0.00
				REM: N122								
PT RESP	0.00			CLAIM TOTAL		1358.00	0.00	0.00	0.00		1358.00	0.00
											NET	0.00

Name: HIC   ACCT   ICN

PROV #	DOS	POS	NOS	CPT	MOD	BILLED $	ALLOW	DEDUCT	COINS	GRP/RC	AMT	PAID PROV $
######	061208	11	1	99024		0.00	0.00	0.00	0.00	CO-45	0.00	0.00
######	061208	11	1	A6203		9.00	0.00	0.00	0.00	CO-A1	9.00	0.00
				REM:M15								
PT RESP	0.00			CLAIM TOTAL		9.00					9.00	0.00
											NET	0.00

Name: HIC   ACCT   ICN

PROV #	DOS	POS	NOS	CPT	MOD	BILLED $	ALLOW	DEDUCT	COINS	GRP/RC	AMT	PAID PROV $
######	052808	11	1	29405	RT	218.00	157.50	0.00	31.50	CO-45	60.50	126.00
######	052808	11	1	Q4038		48.00	26.50	0.00	5.30	CO 45	21.50	21.20
######	052808	11	2	Q4038		96.00	0.00	0.00	0.00	CO-97	96.00	0.00
				REM: M86								
PT RESP	36.80			CLAIM TOTAL			184.00	0.00	36.80		178.00	147.20
											NET	147.20

MESSAGE CODES: GROUP/CARC/RARC

CO   Contractual Obligation

107   Related or qualifying claim/service was not identified on this claim

N122   Add-on code cannot be billed by itself.

CASE R: SITUATIONS 1 AND 2

CODING ERROR: ANSI CARC/RARC CODES CO-107, N122

QUESTION: What is an Add-on code?
ANSWER: It is a service or procedure that can never stand alone. It is always reported in "addition to" or "conjunction with" the primary procedure.

An Add-on code allows the reporting of a significant supplemental/secondary service that describes additional intraservice work that is performed by the same physician that is related to the primary procedure.

It is not necessary to append a 51 (multiple procedure) modifier when reporting the Add-on code(s). They are not subject to "multiple procedures" fee reduction because they are already reduced to reflect a secondary procedure status.

QUESTION: How is an Add-on code identified?
ANSWER: Add-on codes are identified throughout the CPT code book with a plus (+) sign. Directly below the description in parenthesis ( ) it will state, e.g., "use 15101 in conjunction with 15100."

For help, go to: Area A4 Resources: CPT code book or Medicare Correct Coding Guide manual (also provides a description)

SITUATION 1

CODING ERROR: ANSI CARC/RARC CODES CO-107, N122

QUESTION: Is CPT code 15101 is to be used in addition to another service/procedure?
ANSWER: Yes.

Per the CPT code book, code 15101 is an Add-on code because it has a plus (+) sign next to it. Also, in the description of CPT code 15101 it states "each additional," which tells me this service/procedure is to be used in addition to another service/procedure.

Below the description (in parentheses) it states "use 15101 in conjunction with 15100," which means in order to report CPT code 15101 it has to be reported with the primary procedure, CPT code 15100.

QUESTION: In this situation, what is the Primary Procedure?
ANSWER: The Primary Procedure is CPT code 15100.

QUESTION: What type of procedure is CPT code 15100?
ANSWER: CPT code 15100 is a "Split-thickness Autograft, trunk, arms, legs; first 100 sq cm or less."

Per the Op Notes, patient sustained a gunshot wound to the left leg; therefore a "Split-thickness autograft" was performed.

QUESTION: What is the size of the skin graft?
ANSWER: Per the Op Notes, the procedure states "Split-thickness skin graft from right thigh to left leg medially and laterally, a total of 400 sq cm." The size is 400 square centimeters.

RESOLUTION: Three steps to correct the claim
Correct the claim, then refile or resubmit as a corrected claim.
(The correct way is to key in CPT code 15100 as the primary procedure (description states "first 100 sq cm,") then key in CPT Code 15101 on three separate lines appending 76 [repeated procedure] modifier to only the last two codes.)

Step 1. In the Main Menu, select COLLECTIONS, pull up PATIENT BILLING, then pull up the ticket. From the PATIENT ACCOUNT CLAIM DETAIL under "Billing," select MODIFY. Under Charge Entry, locate the Codes column. On line 1, void out 15101 and key in the correct code 15100. On lines 2, 3, and 4, add code 15101 and then locate the Modifiers column and add in the 76 modifier on lines 2, 3 and 4.

Step 2. Under Charge Entry, mark (X) File: HCFA Electronically so the claim can be batched and then billed to Medicare.

Step 3. Now that you have resolved the claim issue, the next step is to add your notes on how you resolved the claim issue. Pull up PATIENT BILLING under the PATIENT ACCOUNT CLAIM DETAIL and select NOTES. Type in what the problem was and what you did to resolve the claim issue.

(**In every medical software there is a place to key in notes on what you did, either on that particular ticket or somewhere on that patient's account.**) An example of how you would type in your notes is as follows:

NOTE: Per the Medicare remittance dated 5/14/2008 denied because .....

SITUATION 2

MEDICARE PART B (ERA) REMITTANCE ADVICE
Provider#:
Check/EFT (Electronic Fund Transfer) #: Issue Date: 00/00/2008
Name: HIC ACCT ICN

PROV #	DOS	POS	NOS	CPT	MOD	MOD	BILLED $	ALLOW	DEDUCT	COINS	GRP/RC	AMT	PAID PROV $
######	052808	21	1	15734			2750.00	1980.00	0.00	396.00	CO-45	770.00	1584.00
######	052808	21	1	15734	59	51	1377.00	425.00	0.00	85.00	CO-45	952.00	340.00
######	052808	21	1	44625	51		980.00	210.00	0.00	42.00	CO-45	770.00	168.00
######	052808	21	1	49568			820.00	0.00	0.00	0.00	CO-107	820.00	0.00
				REM: N122									
PT RESP	523.00			CLAIM TOTAL			5927.00	2615.00	0.00	523.00		3312.00	2092.00
												NET	2092.00

MESSAGE CODES: GROUP/CARC/RARC
CO Contractual Obligation
107 Related or qualifying claim/service was not identified on this claim
N122 Add-on code cannot be billed by itself.

CODING ERROR: ANSI CARC/RARC CODES CO-107, N122

QUESTION: In this situation, the related service was not identified, so is the claim missing the primary procedure?
ANSWER: Yes.
Per the CPT Code book code 49568 is an Add-on code and in parenthesis ( ) it states "use 49568 in conjunction with 11004-11006, 49560-49566," which means in order to report CPT Code 49568 it also has to be reported with one of the primary procedures, CPT Codes 11004-11006 and/or 49560-49566. In the description of CPT Code 49568 is states in parenthesis ( ) "List separately in addition to code for the incisional or ventral hernia repair."

QUESTION: What is the primary procedure?
ANSWER: Per Op notes state a "Repair of incisional hernia" so the primary procedure code is CPT Code 49560.

RESOLUTION: Steps to correct the claim

Correct the claim then refile or resubmit as a corrected claim.

(Correct the claim by adding in CPT code 49560 (description states "first 100 sq cm,") on line 4 because it needs to be primary to CPT Code 49568 and CPT Code 49568 needs to be entered in on line 5)

Step 1. Main Menu, select COLLECTIONS, pull up PATIENT BILLING, then pull up the ticket. From the PATIENT ACCOUNT CLAIM DETAIL under "Billing" select MODIFY then under Charge Entry locate column marked "Codes", under line 4 void out 49568 then key in correct code 49560, then on line 5 add code 49568.

Step 2. Under Charge Entry mark (X) File: HCFA Electronically so the claim can be batched and then billed out to Medicare.

Now that you have resolved the claim issue, the next step is to add in your notes on how you resolved the claim issue.

Step 3: Pull up PATIENT BILLING under the PATIENT ACCOUNT CLAIM DETAIL select NOTES. Type in what the problem was, how and what you did to resolve the claim issue.

(**Every Medical Software there is a place to key in notes on what you did either on that particular ticket or somewhere on that patients account as to what you did**) Example as to how you would type in your notes are as follows:

NOTE: Per the Medicare remittance dated 5/14/2008 denied because.…………………………………………

CASE S: SITUATION 1

MEDICARE PART B (ERA) REMITTANCE ADVICE

Provider#:

Check/EFT (Electronic Fund Transfer) #: Issue Date: 00/00/2008

Name: HIC ACCT ICN

PROV #	DOS	POS	NOS	CPT	MOD	BILLED $	ALLOW	DEDUCT	COINS	GRP/RC	AMT	PAID PROV $
#######	052808	22	1	29881	RT	1950.00	549.50	0.00	110.30	CO-45	1400.50	439.20
#######	052808	22	1	29877		1225.00	0.00	0.00	0.00	CO-125	1225.00	0.00
				REM:M15								
#######	052808	22	1	29875		895.00	349.10	0.00	69.82	CO-45	545.90	279.28
PT RESP	180.12			CLAIM TOTAL		4070.00	898.60	0.00	180.12		3171.40	718.48
										NET		718.48

Name: HIC ACCT ICN

PROV #	DOS	POS	NOS	CPT	MOD	BILLED $	ALLOW	DEDUCT	COINS	GRP/RC	AMT	PAID PROV $
#######	060208	21	4	15101		1358.00	0.00	0.00	0.00	CO-107	1358.00	0.00
				REM: N122								
PT RESP	0.00			CLAIM TOTAL		1358.00	0.00	0.00	0.00		1358.00	0.00
										NET		0.00

Name: HIC ACCT ICN

PROV #	DOS	POS	NOS	CPT	MOD	BILLED $	ALLOW	DEDUCT	COINS	GRP/RC	AMT	PAID PROV $
#######	061208	11	1	99024		0.00	0.00	0.00	0.00	CO-45	0.00	0.00
#######	061208	11	1	A6203		9.00	0.00	0.00	0.00	CO-A1	9.00	0.00
				REM:M15								
PT RESP	0.00			CLAIM TOTAL		9.00					9.00	0.00
										NET		0.00

Name: HIC ACCT ICN

PROV #	DOS	POS	NOS	CPT	MOD	BILLED $	ALLOW	DEDUCT	COINS	GRP/RC	AMT	PAID PROV $
#######	052808	11	1	29405	RT	218.00	157.50	0.00	31.50	CO-45	60.50	126.00
#######	052808	11	1	Q4038		48.00	26.50	0.00	5.30	CO-45	21.50	21.20
#######	052808	11	2	Q4038		96.00	0.00	0.00	0.00	CO-97	96.00	0.00
				REM: M86								
PT RESP	36.80			CLAIM TOTAL		184.00	0.00	36.80			178.00	147.20
										NET		147.20

MESSAGE CODES: GROUP/CARC/RARC

CO Contractual Obligation

A1 Claim/Service denied

M15 Separately billed services/tests have been bundled as they are considered components of the same procedure

CASE S: SITUATION 1

CODING ERROR: ANSI CARC/RARC CODES CO-A1, M15

QUESTION: What is HCPCS code A6203?
ANSWER: Description: Composite dressing, sterile, pad size 16 sq in or less, with any size adhesive border, each dressing

For help, go to: Area A4. Resources: HCPCS code book

QUESTION: What is it used for?
ANSWER: It is a wound cover dressing.

QUESTION: Is it considered a noncovered expense, and if so, can we bill the patient?
ANSWER: It is considered to be integral to or included in the Surgical Global Package of a surgical procedure and it cannot be billed to the patient. The Medicare Remittance does not state patient responsibility, so an adjustment will need to be made.

For help, go to: Area A4. Resources: Medicare Correct Coding Guide book for examples of services integral to a large number of procedures. List will include Surgical closure and dressing, Application, Management, and removal of post-operative dressings.

For help, go to: Area A4. Resources: http://www.cignagovernmentservices.com, DME Jurisdiction C/Publications/News/(Year) will provide a list of HCPCS that will inform you whether or not to submit to local carrier or DME MAC. This list is titled: "DMEPOS HCPCS Codes Jurisdiction List 20?? (year)."

Among the list of HCPCS codes A6154–A6411 (Surgical Dressings) states if "incident to" a physician's service, it not separately payable, but if supply for implanted prosthetic device or implanted DME or other, bill DME MAC Jurisdiction C (Colorado, New Mexico, Oklahoma, Texas and Virginia).

* Key Point: This would be a good tool to have on hand.*

RESOLUTION: Two steps to correct the claim
Correct the claim by adjusting off the charge.

Step 1. In the Main Menu, select **COLLECTIONS**, pull up **PATIENT BILLING**, and then pull up the ticket. From the PATIENT ACCOUNT CLAIM DETAIL under "Payment Type," select MODIFY. Under Payment Transaction, post charges on each line in the Disallow/Adj Column and under the Disallow/Adj Type Column drop-down window, select "Bundled." By posting your adjustment it will adjust off the charge.

Step 2: Now that you have resolved the claim issue, the next step is to add your notes on how you resolved the claim issue. Pull up PATIENT BILLING under the PATIENT ACCOUNT CLAIM DETAIL and select NOTES. Type in what the problem was and what you did to resolve the claim issue.

(**In every medical software there is a place to key in notes on what you did, either on that particular ticket or somewhere on that patient's account.**) An example of how you would type in your notes is as follows:

NOTE: Per the Medicare remittance dated 5/14/2008 denied A6203 because HCPCS codes A6154–A6411 (Surgical Dressings) are "incident to" a physician's service and not separately payable, so I made an adjustment on the claim by adjusting off the charge as a bundled code.

** Key Point: Keeping good notes is another key factor in doing a great job. Putting in good notes will provide information as to what has been done or is being done to resolve the issue with that particular date of service. If someone decides to go into that particular claim, they will see your notes and will know exactly what is being done.

CASE T: SITUATION 1

MEDICARE PART B   (ERA) REMITTANCE ADVICE

Provider#:

Check/EFT (Electronic Fund Transfer) #:   Issue Date: 00/00/2008

Name: HIC   ACCT   ICN

PROV #	DOS	POS	NOS	CPT	MOD	BILLED $	ALLOW	DEDUCT	COINS	GRP/RC	AMT	PAID PROV $
######	052808	22	1	29881	RT	1950.00	549.50	0.00	110.30	CO-45	1400.50	439.20
######	052808	22	1	29877		1225.00	0.00	0.00	0.00	CO-125	1225.00	0.00
				REM:M15								
######	052808	22	1	29875		895.00	349.10	0.00	69.82	CO-45	545.90	279.28
PT RESP	180.12			CLAIM TOTAL		4070.00	898.60	0.00	180.12		3171.40	718.48
										NET		718.48

Name: HIC   ACCT   ICN

PROV #	DOS	POS	NOS	CPT	MOD	BILLED $	ALLOW	DEDUCT	COINS	GRP/RC	AMT	PAID PROV $
######	060208	21	4	15101		1358.00	0.00	0.00	0.00	CO-107	1358.00	0.00
				REM:N122								
PT RESP	0.00			CLAIM TOTAL		1358.00	0.00	0.00	0.00		1358.00	0.00
										NET		0.00

Name: HIC   ACCT   ICN

PROV #	DOS	POS	NOS	CPT	MOD	BILLED $	ALLOW	DEDUCT	COINS	GRP/RC	AMT	PAID PROV $
######	061208	11	1	99024		0.00	0.00	0.00	0.00	CO-45	0.00	0.00
######	061208	11	1	A6203		9.00	0.00	0.00	0.00	CO-A1	9.00	0.00
				REM:M15								
PT RESP	0.00			CLAIM TOTAL		9.00					9.00	0.00
										NET		0.00

Name: HIC   ACCT   ICN

PROV #	DOS	POS	NOS	CPT	MOD	BILLED $	ALLOW	DEDUCT	COINS	GRP/RC	AMT	PAID PROV $
######	052808	11	1	29405	RT	218.00	157.50	0.00	31.50	CO-45	60.50	126.00
######	052808	11	1	Q4038		48.00	26.50	0.00	5.30	CO-45	21.50	21.20
######	052808	11	1	Q4038		96.00	0.00	0.00	0.00	CO-97	96.00	0.00
				REM: M86								
PT RESP	36.80			CLAIM TOTAL			184.00	0.00	36.80		178.00	147.20
										NET		147.20

MESSAGE CODES: GROUP/CARC/RARC

CO   Contractual Obligation

97   Payment is adjusted because the benefit for this service is included in the payment/allowance for another service/procedure that has been adjudicated

M86   Service denied because payment already made for same/similar procedure within set time frame

CASE T: SITUATION 1

CODING ERROR: ANSI CARC/RARC CODES CO-97, M86

QUESTION: Submission of the original claim we billed out 3 units all on one line, so why did Medicare split up Q4038 into two lines and why did they only pay for 1 unit?

ANSWER: Per Medicare Customer Service and was informed that for casting supplies Medicare will only allow 1 unit per 1 application. Even though we may apply 3 rolls of fiberglass, we only bill out 1 unit but still key in the other 2 with no fee. You still need to document a total of 3 were applied.

Submission of the original claim:

Claim # 123456   **CHARGE ENTRY**

Diagnosis: Patient Complaint:

1 726.72 (Description: Tibialis Tendinitis)

2_____ (Description:)   Date of Injury: ( ) File: HCFA Electronically

3_____ (Description:)   Date of Hospitalization: ( ) File: HCFA Paper

4_____ (Description:_____)   Discharge Date: ( )File: UB04

Facility: Office

Rendering Provider: Referring: Supervising/Ordering:

Line #	Date of Service	Code(s)	Diag	Modifier	POS	Unit(s)	$ Fee
(x) 1	From 05/28/08 To 05/28/08	29045	1		11		218.00
(x) 2	From 05/28/08 To 05/28/08	Q4038	1		11	3	144.00
(x) 3	From To						
(x) 4	From To						
(x) 5	From To						
(x) 6	From To						

QUESTION: How do you know if Medicare allowed the correct fee amount?
ANSWER: Pull up the fee schedule.

QUESTION: Is there a fee schedule for HCPCS codes?
ANSWER: Yes. You can locate the fee schedule in three ways:

For help, go to: Area A4. Resources: Website http://www.trailblazerhealth.com Fee Schedule, Medicare Fee Schedule, or http://www.cms.gov. Choose Medicare, Physician Fee Schedule Look-up, and search by "Payment Policy Indicator" or http://www.cignagovernmentservices.com DME MAC Jurisdiction C, Coverage & Pricing, Fee Schedule, DMEPOS Fee Schedule, Durable Medical Equipment and select Option 3: Search DataBase

QUESTION: If the database does not provide the fee for Q4038, where else can we go for help?
ANSWER: MLN Matters. It will provide you with the 2011 Splints & Casts Payment Limit amount.

For help, go to: Area A4. Resources: Website http://www.trailblazerhealth.com; 2011 Reasonable Charge for Splints and Casts. It pulls up MLN Matters Number MM 7225 Information for Medicare FFS for Health Care Professionals

* Key Point: This may not apply to all payers. In this situation we are following Medicare guidelines.*

RESOLUTION: Two steps to correct the claim

We still show a balance due because Medicare only allowed 1 unit, so we need to adjust off the other 2 units as being bundled into one unit.

Step 1. In the Main Menu, select COLLECTIONS, pull up PATIENT BILLING , then pull up the ticket. From the PATIENT ACCOUNT CLAIM DETAIL under "Payment Type," select MODIFY. Under Payment Transaction, post charges on each line in the Disallow/Adj Column and under the Disallow/Adj Type Column drop-down window select "bundled." By posting your adjustment it will adjust off the charge.

Step 2. Now that you have resolved the claim issue, the next step is to add your notes on how you resolved the claim issue.

Pull up PATIENT BILLING under the PATIENT ACCOUNT CLAIM DETAIL and select NOTES. Type in what the problem was and what you did to resolve the claim issue.

(**In every medical software there is a place to key in notes on what you did, either on that particular ticket or somewhere on that patient's account.**) An example of how you would type in your notes is as follows:

NOTE: Per the Medicare remittance dated 5/14/2008 denied the other 2 units because they only allow for one when billing casting supplies so I made an additional adjustment on the claim by bundling the other two units into the one unit.

CASE U: SITUATIONS 1, 2, AND 3

MEDICARE PART B   **(ERA) REMITTANCE ADVICE**

Provider#:

Check/EFT (Electronic Fund Transfer) #:   Issue Date: 00/00/2008

Name: HIC   ACCT   ICN

PROV #	DOS	POS	NOS	CPT	MOD	BILLED $	ALLOW	DEDUCT	COINS	GRP/RC	AMT	PAID PROV $
######	051408	11	1	20610	RT	158.00	98.00	0.00	19.60	CO-45	60.00	78.40
######	051408	11	1	J7324		394.00	0.00	0.00	0.00	CO-50	394.00	0.00
				REM: N25 N115								
PT RESP	19.60			CLAIM TOTAL		552.00	98.00	0.00	19.60			78.40
											NET	78.40

Name: HIC   ACCT   ICN

PROV #	DOS	POS	NOS	CPT	MOD	BILLED $	ALLOW	DEDUCT	COINS	GRP/RC	AMT	PAID PROV $
######	060208	22	1	76000	80	89.00	0.00	0.00	0.00	CO-4	89.00	0.00
PT RESP	0.00			CLAIM TOTAL		89.00	0.00	0.00	0.00		89.00	0.00
											NET	0.00

Name: HIC   ACCT   ICN

PROV #	DOS	POS	NOS	CPT	MOD	BILLED $	ALLOW	DEDUCT	COINS	GRP/RC	AMT	PAID PROV $
######	061208	22	1	11043		648.00	0.00	0.00	0.00	CO-151	648.00	0.00
				REM:M25								
######	061208	22	1	97605		165.00		0.00		C0-45		
######	061208	22	10				0.00	0.00	0.00	C0-45	0.00	0.00
PT RESP	1.20			CLAIM TOTAL		410.00	12.00	0.00	1.20		398.00	10.80
											NET	10.80

Name: HIC   ACCT   ICN

PROV #	DOS	POS	NOS	CPT	MOD	BILLED $	ALLOW	DEDUCT	COINS	GRP/RC	AMT	PAID PROV $
######	052808	22	1	29877	RT	1213.00	0.00	0.00	0.00	CO-11	1213.00	0.00
				REM: M81								
PT RESP	0.00			CLAIM TOTAL		1213.00	0.00	0.00	0.00		1213.00	0.00
											NET	0.00

MESSAGE CODES: GROUP/CARC/RARC

CO   Contractual Obligation

50   **Non-covered services because this is not deemed a 'medical necessity' by the payer**

CASE U: SITUATIONS 1, 2, AND 3

CODING ERROR: ANSI CARC/RARC CODES CO-50

QUESTION: The reason for denial states that the service/procedure provided was not deemed a "Medical Necessity." What does that mean?

ANSWER: The service/procedure that was provided to the patient was not reasonable, necessary, and appropriate based on the patient's diagnosis.

For help, go to: Area A4 Other Resources: http://www.trailblazerhealth.com

To help determine if a service/procedure is considered to be medically necessary as a covered benefit one must review the Medical Policy. A Medical Policy serves as a set of medical guidelines for coverage decisions that should include the following:

1. Indications and Limitations of Coverage and/or Medical Necessity
2. ICD-9-CM Codes that support Medical Necessity
3. Documentation Requirements
4. Utilization Guidelines

Medicare's Medical Policy is referred to as Local Coverage Determination or LCD. Each policy is assigned a Title as well as a determination number. If you are not able to locate a policy under the local carrier website in your jurisdiction, go to the CMS website and pull up the National Coverage Determination or NCD.

To help determine if a service/procedure is considered a covered benefit, ask yourself these questions: Would the procedure be considered cosmetic or reconstructive surgery? What is the reason for the procedure? Is the patient's complaint causing a medical problem or is it to improve the patient's looks? A couple of examples may be an upper eyelid lift or breast reduction. An upper eyelid lift is medically necessary because the excessive skin is causing a medical problem; it is obstructing the patient's vision. Breast reduction is medically necessary because large breasts have been causing the patient several medical conditions such as back pain. In order to perform a breast reduction, the LCD has specific limitations and guidelines that must be met to be considered a covered benefit. If the patient wanted a breast reduction because she feels her breasts are too big, this would not be covered because it would be considered cosmetic because the patient is not happy with her looks and her condition is not causing any medical problem.

SITUATION 1

CODING ERROR: ANSI CARC/RARC CODES CO-50
Based on the diagnosis, Medicare feels that it was not medically necessary that the patient be provided that particular service/procedure.

QUESTION: HCPCS Code J7324 (Orthovisc, Hyaluronan or derivative, for intra-articular injection). What is the diagnosis that is linked to the injection?
ANSWER: Diagnosis that is posted on the ticket/claim is 844.0 sprain/strain knee.

QUESTION: Is there an LCD for CPT Code J7324?
ANSWER: Yes.

For help, go to: Area A4: Resources: http://www.trailblazerhealth.com

Located LCD Title for HCPCS Code J7324 is listed under "Hyaluronate Polymers." The contractor determination number is 4I-87AB, effective date 3/1/2008. Locate "ICD-9-CM codes that support Medical Necessity." Check to see if the diagnosis that is linked to the service/procedure that was denied is listed in the LCD.

QUESTION: Is diagnosis 844.0 listed in the LCD?
ANSWER: No.

QUESTION: Diagnosis 844.0 was not listed. What do we need to do next?
ANSWER: View patient's medical records and see if you can use a different diagnosis that is listed in the LCD that can best describe the patient's current condition other than the diagnosis that was already used.

QUESTION: In clinic notes prior to this ticket/claim, the patient was diagnosed with osteoarthrosis of the RT knee, ICD-9-CM 715.96. Do we need to add 715.96 with diagnosis 844.0 or how do we correct the claim if Medicare already paid for the administration of the drug?
ANSWER: Add 715.96 and link it by itself to CPT Code J7324, leaving 844.0 linked to CPT Code 20610, and refile as a corrected claim.

** Key Note: If the diagnosis submitted on the claim is listed on the LCD, no correction can be made, and you believe that the service should be considered medically necessary, you may request a redetermination. Remember, you have only 120 days from the date of the RA to request a redetermination. A "Letter of Medical Necessity" dictated by yourself or the physician may be necessary in order for a claim to be reconsidered.

ADDITIONAL INFORMATION TO KNOW REGARDING MEDICATIONS:
LCD "Hyaluronate Polymers": HCPCS J7325 Synvisc or Synvisc-one, for intra-articular

1. Medication covered under patient insurance.
2. Some medications, depending on the payer, may provide coverage for the medication and the physician only bills for administration.
3. Some medications require authorization.
4. Some medications require specific guidelines that must be met prior to injection.
5. Some drug reps provide a support program to help with insurance verification, prior authorization assistance, and claims assistance for denied or unpaid claims. Synvisc provides physicians a support program called "Synvisc Connection," which is a personalized reimbursement solution. Drug J7323, Euflexxa, also provides a support program.

RESOLUTION: Three steps to correct the claim

Correct the claim by adding the correct diagnosis and refile or resubmit as a corrected claim.

Step 1. Pull up the ticket/claim and add in a diagnosis linking it to J7324. In the Main Menu, select **COLLECTIONS,** pull up **PATIENT BILLING**, then pull up the ticket. From the PATIENT ACCOUNT CLAIM DETAIL under "Billing," select MODIFY. In the Charge Entry screen under Diagnosis add 715.96, then link it by itself to CPT Code J7324, leaving 844.0 linked to CPT Code 20610.

Step 2. Now that you have made correction you will need to refile the claim electronically to Medicare. In the Charge Entry screen next to File: HCFA Electronically mark (X) so the claim can be batched and then billed.

Step 3. Now that you have resolved the claim issue, the next step is to add your notes on how you resolved the claim issue.

Pull up PATIENT BILLING under the PATIENT ACCOUNT CLAIM DETAIL and select NOTES. Type in what the problem was and what you did to resolve the claim issue.

(**In every medical software there is a place to key in notes on what you did, either on that particular ticket or somewhere on that patient's account.**) An example of how you would type in your notes is as follows:

NOTE: Per the Medicare remittance dated 5/14/2008 denied J7324 because it was not deemed medically necessary. Per LCD Title for HCPCS, Code J7324 is listed under "Hyaluronate Polymers." Diagnosis 844.0 is not listed in the ICD-9-CM codes that support Medical Necessity. In view of the patient's prior clinical notes, the patient was diagnosed with Osteoarthrosis of the RT knee, ICD-9-CM 715.96, which were the results from diagnostic testing. ICD-9-CM code 715.96 is listed in the LCD, so I made correction adding 715.96 and linking it to J7324 and rebilled the corrected claim to Medicare.

SITUATION 2

MEDICARE PART B   **(ERA) REMITTANCE ADVICE**

Provider#:

Check/EFT (Electronic Fund Transfer) #:   Issue Date: 00/00/2008

Name: HIC   ACCT   ICN

PROV #	DOS	POS	NOS	CPT	MOD	BILLED $	ALLOW	DEDUCT	COINS	GRP/RC	AMT	PAID PROV $
######	051408	22	1	28890		1930.00	0.00	0.00	0.00	CO-50	1930.00	0.00
				REM: N25 N115								
PT RESP	0.00			CLAIM TOTAL		1930.00	0.00	0.00	0.00		1930.00	0.00
											NET	0.00

MESSAGE CODES: GROUP/CARC/RARC

CO   Contractual Obligation

50   **Non-covered services because this is not deemed a 'medical necessity' by the payer**

CODING ERROR: ANSI CARC/RARC CODES CO-50

QUESTION: What is the diagnosis that is linked to CPT Code 28890?
ANSWER: Diagnosis 728.71 Plantar Fascial Fibromatosis

QUESTION: What is CPT Code 28890?
ANSWER: Type of procedure that was performed is an Orthotripsy.

QUESTION: What LCD is Orthotripsy listed under?
ANSWER: LCD Title: "Non-covered services" - 4Z-18AB-R19, Contractors Determination Number 4Z-18 (L26811)

QUESTION: Is diagnosis 728.71 listed in the LCD?
ANSWER: LCD for Non-Covered Services are listed by the type of service/procedure that was provided, not by diagnosis. Per LCD CPT Code 28890 is listed under "Not Medically Necessary."

QUESTION: Can we appeal their decision or do we adjust it off or bill the patient?
ANSWER: Since this is not a covered benefit for Plantar Fasciitis, you cannot appeal and per EOB because it doesn't state PR-50, you cannot bill the patient so the claim will need to be adjusted off.

** Key point: If you know that the service/procedure for patient condition will not be covered by insurance, do not bill insurance but collect money from the patient. If you bill the insurance they can deny it and if the EOB states that service/procedure needs to be adjusted off and cannot bill the patient, and your are contracted with that payer, you will have to adjust off the charge.**

RESOLUTION: Steps on how to correct the claim
Correct the claim by adjusting off the charge.

Step 1. Main Menu, select COLLECTIONS, pull up PATIENT BILLING , then pull up the ticket. From the PATIENT ACCOUNT CLAIM DETAIL under "Payment Type" select MODIFY then under Payment Transaction on each line in the Disallow/Adj Column post charges and under the Disallow/Adj Type Column drop down window and select "Not Med Nec." By posting your adjustment it will adjust off the charge.

Step 2. Now that you have resolved the claim issue, the next step is to add in your notes on how you resolved the claim issue.

Step 3. Pull up PATIENT BILLING under the PATIENT ACCOUNT CLAIM DETAIL select NOTES. Type in what the problem was, how and what you did to resolve the claim issue.

(**Every Medical Software there is a place to key in notes on what you did either on that particular ticket or somewhere on that patients account as to what you did**) Example as to how you would type in your notes are as follows:

NOTE: Per the Medicare remittance dated 5/14/2008 denied the procedure because Medicare felt it was not medically necessary. Per LCD does not list patient condition and the remittance does not state patient responsibility so I made adjustment on the claim by writing off the charge.

SITUATION 3

MEDICARE PART B   **(ERA) REMITTANCE ADVICE**

Provider#:

Check/EFT (Electronic Fund Transfer) #:   Issue Date: 00/00/2008

Name: HIC   ACCT   ICN

PROV #	DOS	POS	NOS	CPT	MOD	BILLED $	ALLOW	DEDUCT	COINS	GRP/RC	AMT	PAID PROV $
######	051408	11	1	64614		210.00	142.50	0.00	28.50	CO-45	67.50	114.00
######	051408	11	1	J0585		325.00	0.00	0.00	0.00	CO-50	325.00	0.00
				REM: N25 N115								
PT RESP	28.50			CLAIM TOTAL		535.00	0.00	0.00	28.50		392.50	114.00
											NET	114.00

MESSAGE CODES: GROUP/CARC/RARC

CO   Contractual Obligation

50   **Non-covered services because this is not deemed a 'medical necessity' by the payer**

CODING ERROR: ANSI CARC/RARC CODES CO-50

QUESTION: What type of drug is J0585?
ANSWER: HCPCS J0585 is Botulinum Toxin, known as Botox. This type of drug is usually used for cosmetic purposes to eliminate wrinkles but it also can be used for medical purposes as well.

Per LCD entitled: Botulinum Toxin Types A and B
Contractor's Determination Number: 4I-84 (L26765)

Indications and Limitations of Coverage and/or Medical Necessity per LCD states that Botulinum toxin injections are used to treat various muscle spastic disorders and contractions such as dystonias, spasms, and twitches and more. The drug produces some type of neuromuscular blockade that prevents acetylcholine from being released at the nerve endings which has a paralyzing affect. There are limitations that must be met in order for this type of drug to be used.

RESOLUTION: Steps on how to correct the claim
Correct the claim by adding the correct diagnosis that is listed in the LCD under "ICD-9-CM Codes that Support Medical Necessity."

Step 1. Pull up the ticket/claim and add the diagnosis linking it to J0585. In the Main Menu, select COLLECTIONS, pull up PATIENT BILLING, then pull up the ticket. From the PATIENT ACCOUNT CLAIM DETAIL under "Billing," select MODIFY, then in Charge Entry screen under Diagnosis add 351.8 then link it by itself to CPT Code J0585.

Step 2. Now that you have made the correction you will need to re-file the claim electronically to Medicare. In the Charge Entry screen next to "File:HCFA Electronically" mark (X) so the claim can be batched and then billed out.

Step 3. Now that you have resolved the claim issue, the next step is to add in your notes on how you resolved the claim issue. Pull up PATIENT BILLING under the PATIENT ACCOUNT CLAIM DETAIL, select NOTES. Type in what the problem was, and how and what you did to resolve the claim issue.
(**Every medical software has a place to key in notes on what you did, either on the particular ticket or somewhere on that patient's account.) Examples as to how you would type in your notes include

NOTE: Per the Medicare remittance dated 5/14/2008, denied J0585, because it was not considered medically necessary. Per LCD #L26765 entitled "Botulinum Toxin," diagnosis 844.0 that was keyed on the claim form is not listed under the list of ICD-9-CM codes that support medical necessity. In view of the patient clinical notes, patient was diagnosed with Facial Spasm. Diagnosis for facial spasm is 351.8 (other facial nerve disorder; facial spasm). Made correction on the claim by adding 351.8 and linking it to J0585 and re-billed out corrected claim to Medicare.

CASE V: SITUATIONS 1 AND 2

MEDICARE PART B					(ERA) REMITTANCE ADVICE						
Provider#:											
Check/EFT (Electronic Fund Transfer) #:					Issue Date: 00/00/2008						
Name:		HIC		ACCT		ICN					

PROV #	DOS	POS	NOS	CPT	MOD	BILLED $	ALLOW	DEDUCT	COINS	GRP/RC	AMT	PAID PROV $
######	051408	11	1	20610	RT	158.00	98.00	0.00	19.60	CO-45	60.00	78.40
######	051408	11	1	J7324		394.00	0.00	0.00	0.00	CO-50	394.00	0.00
				REM: N25 N115								
PT RESP	19.60			CLAIM TOTAL		552.00	98.00	0.00	19.60		454.00	78.40
											NET	78.40

Name:		HIC		ACCT		ICN					

PROV #	DOS	POS	NOS	CPT	MOD	BILLED $	ALLOW	DEDUCT	COINS	GRP/RC	AMT	PAID PROV $
######	060208	22	1	76000	80	89.00	0.00	0.00	0.00	CO-4	89.00	0.00
PT RESP	0.00					89.00	0.00	0.00	0.00		89.00	0.00
											NET	0.00

Name:		HIC		ACCT		ICN					

PROV #	DOS	POS	NOS	CPT	MOD	BILLED $	ALLOW	DEDUCT	COINS	GRP/RC	AMT	PAID PROV $
######	061208	22	1	11043		648.00	0.00	0.00	0.00	CO-151	648.00	0.00
				REM:M25								
######	061208	22	1	97605		165.00		0.00	1.20	C0-45		
######	061208	22				0.00	0.00	0.00	0.00	C0-45	0.00	0.00
PT RESP				CLAIM TOTAL					0.00			
											NET	

Name:		HIC		ACCT		ICN					

PROV #	DOS	POS	NOS	CPT	MOD	BILLED $	ALLOW	DEDUCT	COINS	GRP/RC	AMT	PAID PROV $
######	052808	22	1	29877	RT	1213.00	0.00	0.00	0.00	CO-11	1213.00	0.00
				REM: M81								
PT RESP	0.00			CLAIM TOTAL		1213.00	0.00	0.00	0.00		1213.00	0.00
											NET	0.00

MESSAGE CODES: GROUP/CARC/RARC

CO   Contractual Obligation

4   Procedure code is inconsistent with the modifier used or a required modifier is missing

---

CASE V: SITUATIONS 1 AND 2

CODING ERROR: ANSI CARC/RARC CODES CO-4
Based on the type of service that was provided, the CCI Edits are denying the claim because a modifier is not required or is missing.

QUESTION: How do we know if a modifier is required?
ANSWER: You can pull up the Fee Schedule and search for that particular CPT Code. Under Payment Indicators, look for "Assistant at Surgery." If the indicator has a "0" it states "Payment restrictions for assistant at surgery apply to this procedure unless supporting documentation is submitted to establish medical necessity." If medical documentation does not substantiate the need for an assistant, then reimbursement will be denied. If the indicator has "1" it states "Payment for an assistant surgeon may not be paid." Indicator "2" states "Payment for an assistant surgeon can be paid" and Indicator "9" states "Payment for an assistant surgeon does not apply."

For help, go to: Area A1. Guidebook: Refer to: Chapter 5, Unit II, Step 8, Part B, Section 5

For help, go to: Area A4. Resources: Website http://www.trailblazerhealth.com; Left-hand side under Quick Links, select Fee Schedule, then select Medicare Fee Schedule, select year, select locality, then do a search for that CPT Code.

QUESTION: Where can I go for a list of modifiers?
ANSWER: The Medicare website provides a "Modifier Manual."

For help, go to: Area A4 Resources: Website: http://www.trailblazerhealth.com. Publications: Modifier Manual

SITUATION 1

CODING ERROR: ANSI CARC/RARC CODES CO-4

QUESTION: What does the "80" modifier identify?
ANSWER: The "80" modifier identifies an assistant surgeon.

QUESTION: Is an assistant surgeon required for this type of service?
ANSWER: Per Medicare's Fee Schedule, listed under "Assistant at Surgery," the Payment Indicator for CPT Code 76000 is "0," which means payment will be issued only if we can supply medical documentation. Medicare feels in some cases that it is not necessary to have an assistant in order to perform a specific type of service or procedure.

QUESTION: Do the Op Notes provide enough documentation to support medical necessity?
ANSWER: No, they do not.

RESOLUTION: Two steps to correct the claim
In this situation, because an assistant surgeon was not necessary, the next step is to adjust off the charge.

Step 1. In the Main Menu, select COLLECTIONS, pull up PATIENT BILLING, then pull up the ticket. From the PATIENT ACCOUNT CLAIM DETAIL under "Payment Type," select MODIFY. Under Payment Transaction, post charges on each line in the Disallow/Adj Column and under the Disallow/Adj Type Column drop-down window, select "Assistant not covered." By posting your adjustment it will adjust off the charge.

Step 2: Now that you have resolved the claim issue, the next step is to add in your notes on how you resolved the claim issue. Pull up PATIENT BILLING under the PATIENT ACCOUNT CLAIM DETAIL and select NOTES. Type in what the problem was and what you did to resolve the claim issue.

(**In every medical software there is a place to key in notes on what you did, either on that particular ticket or somewhere on that patient's account.**) An example of how you would type in your notes is as follows:

NOTE: Per the Medicare remittance dated 5/14/2008 denied the procedure because MPFS states that in order for an assistant to be considered, medical documentation must support the need for an assistant. The Op Notes do not provide enough documentation to support medical necessity and therefore charges are being adjusted off.

** Key Point: Keeping good notes is another key factor in doing a great job. Putting in good notes will provide information as to what has been done or is being done to resolve the issue with that particular date of service. If someone decides to go into that particular claim, they will see your notes and will know exactly what is being done.

SITUATION 2

MEDICARE PART B   (ERA) REMITTANCE ADVICE

Provider#:

Check/EFT (Electronic Fund Transfer) #:   Issue Date: 00/00/2008

Name: HIC   ACCT   ICN

PROV #	DOS	POS	NOS	CPT	MOD	BILLED $	ALLOW	DEDUCT	COINS	GRP/RC	AMT	PAID PROV $
#######	060208	11	1	73500	50	95.00	0.00	0.00	0.00	CO-4	95.00	0.00
PT RESP	0.00					95.00	0.00	0.00	0.00		95.00	0.00
											NET	0.00

MESSAGE CODES: GROUP/CARC/RARC

CO   Contractual Obligation

4   Procedure code is inconsistent with the modifier used or a required modifier is missing

CODING ERROR: ANSI CARC/RARC CODES CO-4

Based on the type of service that was provided per the CCI Edits is denying the claim because a modifier is not required.

QUESTION: What does the "50" modifier identify?

ANSWER: The "50" modifier is used to identify bilateral service/procedure.

QUESTION: Is CPT Code 73500 a bilateral service/procedure?

ANSWER: No. Bilateral indicator for CPT Code 73500 indicates "0" which states that the bilateral adjustment is inappropriate for codes in this category because of (a) physiology or anatomy or (b) because the code descriptor specifically states that it is a unilateral procedure and there is an existing code for the bilateral procedure.

Description for CPT Code 73500 states "Radiologic exam of hip, unilateral; one view"

RESOLUTION: Three steps to correct the claim

Correct the claim by deleting the 50 modifier and then refile or resubmit as a corrected claim.

Step 1. In the Main Menu, select **COLLECTIONS,** pull up **PATIENT BILLING,** then pull up the ticket. From the PATIENT ACCOUNT CLAIM DETAIL under "Billing," select MODIFY. Under Charge Entry, locate the column marked "Modifier" and delete the 50 modifier.

Step 2. Under Charge Entry, mark (X) File: HCFA Electronically so the claim can be batched and then billed to Medicare

Step 3. Now that you have resolved the claim issue, the next step is to add your notes on how you resolved the claim issue.

Pull up **PATIENT BILLING** under the PATIENT ACCOUNT CLAIM DETAIL and select NOTES. Type in what the problem was and what you did to resolve the claim issue.

(**In every medical software there is a place to key in notes on what you did, either on that particular ticket or somewhere on that patient's account.**) An example of how you would type in your notes is as follows:

NOTE: Per the Medicare remittance dated 5/14/2008 denied because…………………………………

CASE W: SITUATION 1

MEDICARE PART B   **(ERA) REMITTANCE ADVICE**
Provider#:
Check/EFT (Electronic Fund Transfer) #:   Issue Date: 00/00/2008
Name: HIC   ACCT   ICN

PROV #	DOS	POS	NOS	CPT	MOD	BILLED $	ALLOW	DEDUCT	COINS	GRP/RC	AMT	PAID PROV $
######	051408	11	1	20610	RT	158.00	98.00	0.00	19.60	CO-45	60.00	78.40
######	051408	11	1	J7324		394.00	0.00	0.00	0.00	CO-50	394.00	0.00
				REM: N25 N115								
PT RESP	19.60			CLAIM TOTAL		552.00	98.00	0.00	19.60		454.00	78.40
											NET	78.40

Name: HIC   ACCT   ICN

PROV #	DOS	POS	NOS	CPT	MOD	BILLED $	ALLOW	DEDUCT	COINS	GRP/RC	AMT	PAID PROV $
######	060208	22	1	76000	80	89.00	0.00	0.00	0.00	CO-4	89.00	0.00
PT RESP	0.00			CLAIM TOTAL		89.00	0.00	0.00	0.00		89.00	0.00
											NET	0.00

Name: HIC   ACCT   ICN

PROV #	DOS	POS	NOS	CPT	MOD	BILLED $	ALLOW	DEDUCT	COINS	GRP/RC	AMT	PAID PROV $
######	061208	22	1	11043		648.00	0.00	0.00	0.00	CO-151	648.00	0.00
				REM: M25								
######	061208	22	1	97605		165.00		0.00		C0-45		
######	061208	22	10				0.00	0.00	0.00	C0-45	0.00	0.00
PT RESP	1.20			CLAIM TOTAL			12.00	0.00	1.20		398.00	10.80
											NET	10.80

Name: HIC   ACCT   ICN

PROV #	DOS	POS	NOS	CPT	MOD	BILLED $	ALLOW	DEDUCT	COINS	GRP/RC	AMT	PAID PROV $
######	052808	22	1	28238	RT	1213.00	0.00	0.00	0.00	CO-11	1213.00	0.00
				REM: M81								
PT RESP	0.00			CLAIM TOTAL		1213.00	0.00	0.00	0.00		1213.00	0.00
											NET	0.00

MESSAGE CODES: GROUP/CARC/RARC

CO   Contractual Obligation
151   Payment adjusted because the payer deems the information submitted does not support this many/frequency of services
M25   The information submitted does not substantiate the need for this level of service

---

CASE W: SITUATION 1

CODING ERROR: ANSI CARC/RARC CODES CO-151, M25
Payer determines that the information submitted doesn't support the need for this many services.

QUESTION: How many times can this type of service be billed?

For help, go to: Area A3, insurance company, and pull up their website and select "Medical Policy."

For the Medicare Part B Carrier in Oklahoma for 2010, the MAC website is http://www.trailblazerhealth.com. Select Local Coverage Determination (LCD); for other websites pull up Medical Policy. Do a search by entering CPT Code 11043 (debridement); it pulls up an LCD Titled "Wound Care." Once you have located the LCD, verify the effective date and what the "Limitations and Guidelines" are when billing for this type of service. Check the status of the policy to see if it is active. Also, check to make sure your diagnosis is listed on the policy by locating "ICD-9-CM Codes that support medical necessity." If your diagnosis code is not listed and you happen to resubmit the claim for some reason, it could come back as denied for medical necessity.

According to the "Limitations and Guidelines" the policy states, "Medicare will cover up to five surgical debridements, CPT Code 11043 and/or 11044, per patient, per year." The policy also states, "Services beyond the fifth surgical debridement, will be payable only upon medical review of records that demonstrate the medical reasonableness and necessity."

ANSWER: Apparently, this service has been billed out too many times.

QUESTION: How many times did we bill for a debridement?

For help, go to: Area A1, Guidebook and pull up PATIENT BILLING, pull up ALL billing, and verify how many times this procedure was billed. It can be identified by Place of Service 22 and Facility.

ANSWER: It looks like this procedure was billed out six times, which is over the limitation.

** Key point: If you are ever in doubt as to whether or not a review should be requested, you can contact provider relations and ask for help to determine if a review request would be acceptable or not.

The next step is to verify that the diagnosis code is listed under ICD-9-CM codes that support medical necessity.

Policy states "Services beyond the fifth surgical debridement, may be payable upon medical review," so the next step is to submit the claim for review to justify the medical need for exceeding five debridements per wound on the patient.

Level of Appeals: Reopenings, Redetermination, Reconsideration, Administrative Law Judge Hearing, Medicare Appeals Council Review, and Judicial Review in US District Court.

Reminder: An appeal must be submitted within 120 days from the initial denial determination date, which is the date on the EOB/RA.

For help, go to: Area A4 Other Resources: http://www.trailblazerhealth.com

---

RESOLUTION: Five steps to correct the claim
Submit in an Appeal

Step 1. Print out a Letter of Appeal. In the Main Menu, select the **COLLECTIONS** (CH 5, STEP 8) button, double-click in the box under LTR(Letters), mark (x) next to your Letter of Appeal, then select PRINT.

Step 2. Print out Clinic Notes, Op Notes, and a Letter of Medical Necessity (LMN). In the Main Menu, select the **MEDICAL RECORD** (CH 2, STEP 2) button, double-click in the box under DR (Doctors Notes), mark (x) next to date of service where initial first visit took place, then select PRINT. Double-click in the box under HOSP (Hospital Notes), mark (x) next to your date of service in question, then select PRINT. Double-click in the box under FORMS (Forms/Correspondence), mark (x) next to "Letter of Medical Necessity," then select PRINT.

Step 3. Mail the documentation and send via certified mail to the address on the form. Make a copy, have it scanned (if software is equipped) or place a copy in the patient chart.

Step 4. Follow up on your ticket/claim. In the Main Menu, select the **COLLECTIONS** (CH 5 STEP 8) button, double-click in the box under TCKLR (Tickler), mark (x) next to the month in which you want to follow up on your ticket/claim, then double-click on the day and add your message "Follow up on Appeal Ticket 123456."

Step 5. Now that you have resolved the claim issue, the next step is to add your notes on how you resolved the claim issue.

Pull up **PATIENT BILLING** under the PATIENT ACCOUNT CLAIM DETAIL and select NOTES. Type in what the problem was what you did to resolve the claim issue.

(**In every medical software there is a place to key in notes on what you did, either on that particular ticket or somewhere on that patient's account.**) An example of how you would type in your notes is as follows:

NOTE: Per the Medicare remittance dated 5/14/2008 denied CPT Code 11043 for the frequency that we billed for this type of service. The LCD states that MCR will cover up to 5 debridements per year per patient. Up to this date of service we have billed six. I am submitting a "Request for Review" attaching documentation to support the need for this many services. Copy is filed with my Daily Business. Also a copy of the appeal is filed in the patient chart. Setting a follow-up for 60 days.

** Key Point: Keeping good notes is another key factor in doing a great job. Putting in good notes will provide information as to what has been done or is being done to resolve the issue with that particular date of service. If someone decides to go into that particular claim, they will see your notes and will know exactly what is being done.

CASE X: SITUATION 1

MEDICARE PART B   **(ERA) REMITTANCE ADVICE**

Provider#:

Check/EFT (Electronic Fund Transfer) #:   Issue Date: 00/00/2008

Name: HIC   ACCT   ICN

PROV #	DOS	POS	NOS	CPT	MOD	BILLED $	ALLOW	DEDUCT	COINS	GRP/RC	AMT	PAID PROV $
######	051408	11	1	20610	RT	158.00	98.00	0.00	19.60	CO-45	60.00	78.40
######	051408	11	1	J7324		394.00	0.00	0.00	0.00	CO-50	394.00	0.00
				REM: N25 N115								
PT RESP	19.60			CLAIM TOTAL		552.00	98.00	0.00	19.60		454.00	78.40
											NET	78.40

Name: HIC   ACCT   ICN

PROV #	DOS	POS	NOS	CPT	MOD	BILLED $	ALLOW	DEDUCT	COINS	GRP/RC	AMT	PAID PROV $
######	060208	22	1	76000	80	89.00	0.00	0.00	0.00	CO-4	89.00	0.00
PT RESP	0.00			CLAIM TOTAL		89.00	0.00	0.00	0.00		89.00	0.00
											NET	0.00

Name: HIC   ACCT   ICN

PROV #	DOS	POS	NOS	CPT	MOD	BILLED $	ALLOW	DEDUCT	COINS	GRP/RC	AMT	PAID PROV $
######	061208	22	1	11043		648.00	0.00	0.00	0.00	CO-151		0.00
				REM:M25								
######	061208	22	1	97605		165.00		0.00		C0-45		
######	061208	22	10				0.00	0.00	0.00	C0-45	0.00	0.00
PT RESP	1.20			CLAIM TOTAL				0.00	1.20			
											NET	

Name: HIC   ACCT   ICN

PROV #	DOS	POS	NOS	CPT	MOD	BILLED $	ALLOW	DEDUCT	COINS	GRP/RC	AMT	PAID PROV $
######	052808	22	1	29877	RT	1213.00	0.00	0.00	0.00	CO-11	1213.00	0.00
				REM: M81								
PT RESP	0.00			CLAIM TOTAL		1213.00	0.00	0.00	0.00		1213.00	0.00
											NET	0.00

MESSAGE CODES: GROUP/CARC/RARC

CO   Contractual Obligation

11   Diagnosis is inconsistent with the procedure

M81   Required to code to the highest level of specificity.

CASE X: SITUATION 1

CODING ERROR: ANSI CARC/RARC CODES CO-11, M81

QUESTION: What does it mean to code to the highest level of specificity?
ANSWER: The patient diagnosis needs to be carried out to either a 4th or 5th digit.

For help, go to: Area A4. Resources: ICD-9-CM Code book.

In the code book on the left side of the diagnosis it will state whether that particular diagnosis requires a 4th or 5th digit. It will look like this: $\sqrt{}$ 5th, which means a 5th digit is required.

QUESTION: What is the patient diagnosis and does it require a 4th or 5th digit?
ANSWER: Patient diagnosis was keyed in as 719.4 (pain in joint). Next to the diagnosis in the ICD-9-CM code book it has $\sqrt{}$ 5th, so we need to add a 5th digit. The 5th digit will identify the area of the body in which the patient is having the joint pain. In this case, the procedure (CPT Code 29877) was an "Arthroscopic debridement/shaving of articular cartilage (chondroplasty) of knee, so the 5th digit for knee is 6.

> 0 site unspecified
>
> 1 shoulder region
>
> 2 upper arm
>
> 3 forearm
>
> 4 hand
>
> 5 pelvic region and thigh
>
> 6 lower leg
>
> 7 ankle and foot
>
> 8 other specified site
>
> 9 multiple sites
>
> YEAR 20?? ICD-9-CM CODE BOOK

RESOLUTION: Three steps to correct the claim
Correct the diagnosis and refile or resubmit as a corrected claim to Medicare.

Step 1. In the Main Menu, select **COLLECTIONS,** pull up **PATIENT BILLING,** then pull up the ticket. From the PATIENT ACCOUNT CLAIM DETAIL under "Billing," select MODIFY. Under Charge Entry, locate the diagnosis section and correct Primary Diagnosis 719.4 to Diagnosis 719.46 and make sure it is linked to CPT Code 29877 on line 1.

Step 2. Under Charge Entry, mark (X) File: HCFA Electronically so the claim can be batched and then billed to Medicare.

Step 3. Now that you have resolved the claim issue, the next step is to add your notes on how you resolved the claim issue.

Pull up **PATIENT BILLING** under the PATIENT ACCOUNT CLAIM DETAIL and select NOTES. Type in what the problem was and what you did to resolve the claim issue.

(**In every medical software there is a place to key in notes on what you did, either on that particular ticket or somewhere on that patient's account.**) An example of how you would type in your notes is as follows:

NOTE: Per the Medicare remittance dated 5/14/2008 denied because…

** Key Point: Keeping good notes is another key factor in doing a great job. Putting in good notes will provide information as to what has been done or is being done to resolve the issue with that particular date of service. If someone decides to go into that particular claim, they will see your notes and will know exactly what is being done.

CASE Y: SITUATION 1

MEDICARE PART B   **(ERA) REMITTANCE ADVICE**

Provider#:

Check/EFT (Electronic Fund Transfer) #:   Issue Date: 00/00/2008

Name: HIC   ACCT   ICN

PROV #	DOS	POS	NOS	CPT	MOD	BILLED $	ALLOW	DEDUCT	COINS	GRP/RC	AMT	PAID PROV $
######	060208	11	2	71100	50	60.00	0.00	0.00	0.00	CO-151	9.00	0.00
				REM: N362								
PT RESP	0.00			CLAIM TOTAL		60.00	0.00	0.00	0.00		9.00	0.00
											NET	0.00

Name: HIC   ACCT   ICN

PROV #	DOS	POS	NOS	CPT	MOD	BILLED $	ALLOW	DEDUCT	COINS	GRP/RC	AMT	PAID PROV $
######	061208	11	1	11750		390.00	0.00	0.00	0.00	CO-B9	390.00	0.00
PT RESP	1.20			CLAIM TOTAL		410.00	12.00	0.00	1.20		398.00	10.80
											NET	10.80

Name: HIC   ACCT   ICN

PROV #	DOS	POS	NOS	CPT	MOD	BILLED $	ALLOW	DEDUCT	COINS	GRP/RC	AMT	PAID PROV $
######	052808	11	1	99231	RT	190.00	0.00	0.00	0.00	OA-58	190.00	0.00
				REM: M77								
PT RESP	0.00			CLAIM TOTAL		190.00	0.00	0.00	0.00		190.00	0.00
											NET	0.00

Name: HIC   ACCT   ICN

PROV #	DOS	POS	NOS	CPT	MOD	BILLED $	ALLOW	DEDUCT	COINS	GRP/RC	AMT	PAID PROV $
######	060208	11	1	96372		75.00	60.00	0.00	12.00	CO-45	15.00	48.00
######	060208	11	1	J0170		23.00	0.00	0.00	0.00	CO-181	23.00	0.00
				REM:M56								
PT RESP	12.00			CLAIM TOTAL		9.00	0.00	0.00	12.00		38.00	48.00
											NET	48.00

MESSAGE CODES: GROUP/CARC/RARC

CO   **Contractual Obligation**

151   Payment adjusted because the payer deems the information submitted does not support this many/frequency of services.

N362   Number of Days or Units of Service exceeds our acceptable maximum

CASE Y: SITUATION 1

CODING ERROR: ANSI CARC/RARC CODES CO-151, N362

QUESTION: How many units did we bill?
ANSWER: A modifier is attached, which indicates a bilateral service, so the number of units is two.

QUESTION: Can we bill two units for CPT Code 71100?
ANSWER: No. Refer to the Medically Unlikely Edits (MUE) table, which indicates "1" unit.

For help, go to: Area A4 Other Resources: http://www.cms.gov Select Medicare >> Coding; National Correct Coding Initiative Edits, then select Medically Unlikely Edits (MUE).

QUESTION: Can we use a Bilateral (50) Modifier?
ANSWER: No. The Payment Indicator in the Fee Schedule indicates "0" (Description: Bilateral does not apply).

For help, go to: Area A4 Other Resources: http://www.cms.gov Select Medicare >> Medicare Fee-For-Service Payment; Physician Fee Schedule (Medicare Physician Fee Service Data Base, MPFSDB).

RESOLUTION: Three steps to correct the claim
Corrected claim by deleting the 50 modifier and correcting the number of units from 2 to 1 and rebilling the corrected claim to Medicare.

Step 1. In the Main Menu, select **COLLECTIONS,** pull up **PATIENT BILLING,** then pull up the ticket. From the PATIENT ACCOUNT CLAIM DETAIL under "Billing," select MODIFY. Under Charge Entry, locate the column marked "Modifier" and delete the 50 modifier, and then under column marked "Unit(s)" correct from 2 to 1.

Step 2. Under Charge Entry, mark (X) File: HCFA Electronically so the claim can be batched and then billed out to Medicare.

Step 3. Now that you have resolved the claim issue, the next step is to add your notes on how you resolved the claim issue.

Pull up **PATIENT BILLING** under the PATIENT ACCOUNT CLAIM DETAIL and select NOTES. Type in what the problem was and what you did to resolve the claim issue.

(**In every medical software there is a place to key in notes on what you did, either on that particular ticket or somewhere on that patient's account.**) An example of how you would type in your notes is as follows:

NOTE: Per the Medicare remittance dated 5/14/2008 denied the service because...

** Key Point: Keeping good notes is another key factor in doing a great job. Putting in good notes will provide information as to what has been done or is being done to resolve the issue with that particular date of service. If someone decides to go into that particular claim, they will see your notes and will know exactly what is being done.

CASE Z: SITUATION 1

MEDICARE PART B   **(ERA) REMITTANCE ADVICE**

Provider#:

Check/EFT (Electronic Fund Transfer) #:   Issue Date: 00/00/2008

Name: HIC   ACCT   ICN

PROV #	DOS	POS	NOS	CPT	MOD	BILLED $	ALLOW	DEDUCT	COINS	GRP/RC	AMT	PAID PROV $
######	060208	11	2	71100	50	60.00	0.00	0.00	0.00	CO-151	9.00	0.00
				REM: N362								
PT RESP	0.00			CLAIM TOTAL		60.00	0.00	0.00	0.00		9.00	0.00
											NET	0.00

Name: HIC   ACCT   ICN

PROV #	DOS	POS	NOS	CPT	MOD	BILLED $	ALLOW	DEDUCT	COINS	GRP/RC	AMT	PAID PROV $
######	061208	11	1	11750		390.00	0.00	0.00	0.00	CO-B9	390.00	0.00
PT RESP	1.20			CLAIM TOTAL		410.00	12.00	0.00	1.20		398.00	10.80
											NET	10.80

Name: HIC   ACCT   ICN

PROV #	DOS	POS	NOS	CPT	MOD	BILLED $	ALLOW	DEDUCT	COINS	GRP/RC	AMT	PAID PROV $
######	052808	11	1	99231	RT	190.00	0.00	0.00	0.00	OA-58	190.00	0.00
				REM: M77								
PT RESP	0.00			CLAIM TOTAL		190.00	0.00	0.00	0.00		0.00	0.00
											NET	0.00

Name: HIC   ACCT   ICN

PROV #	DOS	POS	NOS	CPT	MOD	BILLED $	ALLOW	DEDUCT	COINS	GRP/RC	AMT	PAID PROV $
######	060208	11	1	96372		75.00	60.00	0.00	12.00	CO-45	15.00	48.00
######	060208	11	1	J0170		23.00	0.00	0.00	0.00	CO-181	23.00	0.00
				REM:M56								
PT RESP	12.00			CLAIM TOTAL		9.00	0.00	0.00	12.00		38.00	48.00
											NET	48.00

MESSAGE CODES: GROUP/CARC/RARC

CO   **Contractual Obligation**

B9   **Patient is enrolled in a Hospice**

CASE Z: SITUATION 1

CODING ERROR: ANSI CARC/RARC CODES CO-B9

QUESTION: What is hospice care?

ANSWER: Hospice care provides humane and compassionate care for people who are in the last stages of a terminal illness, such as cancer or heart failure. Hospice care also provides emotional support to family members of a dying loved one. Medicare offers hospice care for those beneficiaries who are entitled to Hospital insurance (Part A).

For help, go to: Area A4 Other Resources: http://www.trailblazerhealth.com

QUESTION: Because our doctors are Orthopedic and Reconstructive specialists, and are not seeing the patient for their terminal illness, why would Medicare deny the claim?

ANSWER: The claims edit system is automatically denying the claim because in order for it to bypass the edit system, a modifier is required.

QUESTION: What modifier do we use?

ANSWER: Because we are billing under Medicare Part B, there are two hospice modifiers that we could use, GV or GW. In this case, we would append the GW modifier to our claim. The GW modifier states, "Service is not related to the hospice patient's terminal illness."

The service/procedure that was provided to the patient was Excision of nail (CPT Code 11750).

RESOLUTION: Three steps to correct the claim
Correct the claim by adding a modifier and refile or resubmit as a corrected claim.

Step 1. In the Main Menu, select **COLLECTIONS,** pull up **PATIENT BILLING,** then pull up the ticket. From the PATIENT ACCOUNT CLAIM DETAIL under "Billing," select MODIFY. Under Charge Entry on line 1, which lists CPT Code 11750, in the Modifier Column add the GW modifier.

Step 2. Under Charge Entry, mark (X) File: HCFA Electronically so the claim can be batched and billed to Medicare.

Step 3. Now that you have resolved the claim issue, the next step is to add your notes on how you resolved the claim issue.

Pull up **PATIENT BILLING** under the PATIENT ACCOUNT CLAIM DETAIL and select NOTES. Type in what the problem was and what you did to resolve the claim issue.

(**In every medical software there is a place to key in notes on what you did, either on that particular ticket or somewhere on that patient's account.**) An example of how you would type in your notes is as follows:

NOTE: Per the Medicare remittance dated 5/14/2008 denied the service because….

** Key Point: Keeping good notes is another key factor in doing a great job. Putting in good notes will provide information as to what has been done or is being done to resolve the issue with that particular date of service. If someone decides to go into that particular claim, they will see your notes and will know exactly what is being done.

CASE YY: SITUATIONS 1 AND 2

MEDICARE PART B   **(ERA) REMITTANCE ADVICE**

Provider#:

Check/EFT (Electronic Fund Transfer) #:   Issue Date: 00/00/2008

Name: HIC   ACCT   ICN

PROV #	DOS	POS	NOS	CPT	MOD	BILLED $	ALLOW	DEDUCT	COINS	GRP/RC	AMT	PAID PROV $
#######	060208	11	2	71100	50	60.00	0.00	0.00	0.00	CO-151	9.00	0.00
				REM: N362								
PT RESP	0.00			CLAIM TOTAL		60.00	0.00	0.00	0.00		9.00	0.00
											NET	0.00

Name: HIC   ACCT   ICN

PROV #	DOS	POS	NOS	CPT	MOD	BILLED $	ALLOW	DEDUCT	COINS	GRP/RC	AMT	PAID PROV $
#######	061208	11	1	11750		390.00	0.00	0.00	0.00	CO-B9	390.00	0.00
PT RESP	1.20			CLAIM TOTAL		410.00	12.00	0.00	1.20		398.00	10.80
											NET	10.80

Name: HIC   ACCT   ICN

PROV #	DOS	POS	NOS	CPT	MOD	BILLED $	ALLOW	DEDUCT	COINS	GRP/RC	AMT	PAID PROV $
#######	052808	11	1	99231	RT	190.00	0.00	0.00	0.00	OA-58	190.00	0.00
				REM: M77								
PT RESP	0.00			CLAIM TOTAL		190.00	0.00	0.00	0.00		190.00	0.00
											NET	0.00

Name: HIC   ACCT   ICN

PROV #	DOS	POS	NOS	CPT	MOD	BILLED $	ALLOW	DEDUCT	COINS	GRP/RC	AMT	PAID PROV $
#######	060208	11	1	96372		75.00	60.00	0.00	12.00	CO-45	15.00	48.00
#######	060208	11	1	J0170		23.00	0.00	0.00	0.00	CO-181	23.00	0.00
				REM:M56								
PT RESP	12.00			CLAIM TOTAL		9.00	0.00	0.00	12.00		38.00	48.00
											NET	48.00

MESSAGE CODES: GROUP/CARC/RARC

OA

58   Treatment was deemed by the payer to have been rendered in an inappropriate or invalid place of service

M77   Missing/incomplete/invalid place of service

CASE YY: SITUATIONS 1 AND 2

CODING ERROR: ANSI CARC/RARC CODES OA-58, M77

QUESTION: When they refer to Place of Service, to what are they referring?
ANSWER: Place of Service is the location where the service took place.

For help, go to: Area A1 Guidebook: Refer to: Chapter 3, Unit II, Step 4, Part A: Location

QUESTION: CPT Code 99231 is an E/M code. Is the correct place of service 11?
ANSWER: No. The correct place of service is 21 because the description states "Subsequent Hospital Care."

For help, go to: Area A4 Other Resources: CPT-4 Code book

CASE YY: SITUATION 1

CODING ERROR: ANSI CARC/RARC CODES OA-58, M77

QUESTION: What area do we look at?
ANSWER: Always verify that the correct code was selected by reviewing the Encounter/Superbill/Charge Sheet. Also, review clinic notes. In this situation, after reviewing the Encounter/Superbill/Charge Sheet and the clinic notes, the code was entered incorrectly; the numbers were transposed. The patient was seen in the office, not the hospital.

RESOLUTION: Three steps to correct the claim
Correct the claim by correcting the place of service and refile or resubmit as a corrected claim to Medicare.

Step 1. In the Main Menu, select **COLLECTIONS,** pull up **PATIENT BILLING,** then pull up the ticket. From the PATIENT ACCOUNT CLAIM DETAIL under "Billing," select MODIFY. Under Charge Entry locate the column marked "POS," correct the Place of Service 11 (Office) to Place of Service 21 (Inpatient Hospital).

Step 2. Under Charge Entry, mark (X) File: HCFA Electronically so the claim can be batched and then billed to Medicare.

Step 3. Now that you have resolved the claim issue, the next step is to add your notes on how you resolved the claim issue.

Pull up **PATIENT BILLING** under the PATIENT ACCOUNT CLAIM DETAIL and select NOTES. Type in what the problem was and what you did to resolve the claim issue.

(**In every medical software there is a place to key in notes on what you did, either on that particular ticket or somewhere on that patient's account.**) An example of how you would type in your notes is as follows:

NOTE: Per the Medicare remittance dated 5/14/2008 denied the service because...

** Key Point: Keeping good notes is another key factor in doing a great job. Putting in good notes will provide information as to what has been done or is being done to resolve the issue with that particular date of service. If someone decides to go into that particular claim, they will see your notes and will know exactly what is being done.

CASE YY: SITUATION 2

MEDICARE PART B (ERA) REMITTANCE ADVICE

Provider#:

Check/EFT (Electronic Fund Transfer) #: Issue Date: 00/00/2008

Name: HIC ACCT ICN

PROV #	DOS	POS	NOS	CPT	MOD	BILLED $	ALLOW	DEDUCT	COINS	GRP/RC	AMT	PAID PROV $
######	052808	22	1	25405	RT	2562.00	998.28	0.00	199.66	CO-45	1563.72	798.62
######	052808	22	1	76001		64.00	0.00	0.00	0.00	OA-58	64.00	0.00
				REM: M77								
PT RESP	199.66			CLAIM TOTAL		2626.00	998.28	0.00	199.66		1627.72	798.62
											NET	798.62

MESSAGE CODES: GROUP/CARC/RARC

OA

58 Treatment was deemed by the payer to have been rendered in an inappropriate or invalid place of service

M77 Missing/incomplete/invalid place of service

CODING ERROR: ANSI CARC/RARC CODES OA-58, M77

QUESTION: Was the service provided in the hospital?

ANSWER: Yes. After locating and reviewing the Op notes for this date of service the notes do indicate that fluoroscopic guidance (CPT Code 76001) was provided during the procedure.

Remember back in the beginning of the book we discussed how some codes can be billed out under professional components (physician) as well as the technical components (hospital), in this case is one of those times.

For help, go to: Area A1 Guidebook: Refer to: Chapter 5, Unit II, Step 8, Part B, Section 5

QUESTION: Where can we go to verify this?

ANSWER: You can pull up the Fee Schedule and search for that particular CPT Code and under Payment Indicators. Look for "Professional(PC)/Technical(TC) Component." The indicator has a "1" and it states "Diagnostic tests or radiology services." This indicator identifies codes that describe diagnostic tests, e.g., pulmonary function tests, therapeutic radiology procedures, radiation therapy. These codes generally have both a professional and technical component. Modifiers 26 and TC can be used with these codes.

The total RVUs for codes reported with a 26 modifier include values for physician work, practice expense, and malpractice expense.

The total RVUs for codes reported with a TC modifier include values for practice expense and malpractice expense only. The total RVUs for codes reported without a modifier equals the sum of the RVUs for both the professional and technical components.

For help, go to: Area A1. Guidebook: Refer to: Chapter 5, Unit II, Step 8, Part B, Section 5

For help, go to: Area A4. Resources: Website: http://www.trailblazerhealth.com. On the left-hand side under Quick Links, select Fee Schedule, then select Medicare Fee Schedule, select the year, the locality, and then search for that CPT Code.

RESOLUTION: Three steps to correct the claim

Correct the claim by adding a modifier and refile or resubmit as a corrected claim.

Step 1. In the Main Menu, select **COLLECTIONS,** pull up **PATIENT BILLING**, then pull up the ticket. From the PATIENT ACCOUNT CLAIM DETAIL under "Billing," select MODIFY. Under Charge Entry on line 2, which lists CPT Code 76001, in the Modifier Column add the 26 modifier.

Step 2. Under Charge Entry, mark (X) File: HCFA Electronically so the claim can be batched and billed out to Medicare.

Step 3. Now that you have resolved the claim issue, the next step is to add your notes on how you resolved the claim issue.

Pull up **PATIENT BILLING** under the PATIENT ACCOUNT CLAIM DETAIL and select NOTES. Type in what the problem was and what you did to resolve the claim issue.

(**In every medical software there is a place to key in notes on what you did, either on that particular ticket or somewhere on that patient's account.**) An example of how you would type in your notes is as follows:

NOTE: Per the Medicare remittance dated 5/14/2008 denied the service because …..

" Key Point: Keeping good notes is another key factor in doing a great job. Putting in good notes will provide information as to what has been done or is being done to resolve the issue with that particular date of service. If someone decides to go into that particular claim, they will see your notes and will know exactly what is being done.

CASE ZZ: SITUATION 1

MEDICARE PART B   **(ERA) REMITTANCE ADVICE**

Provider#:

Check/EFT (Electronic Fund Transfer) #:   Issue Date: 00/00/2008

Name: HIC   ACCT   ICN

PROV #	DOS	POS	NOS	CPT	MOD	BILLED $	ALLOW	DEDUCT	COINS	GRP/RC	AMT	PAID PROV $
######	060208	11	2	71100	50	60.00	0.00	0.00	0.00	CO-151	9.00	0.00
				REM: N362								
PT RESP	0.00			CLAIM TOTAL		60.00	0.00	0.00	0.00		9.00	0.00
											NET	0.00

Name: HIC   ACCT   ICN

PROV #	DOS	POS	NOS	CPT	MOD	BILLED $	ALLOW	DEDUCT	COINS	GRP/RC	AMT	PAID PROV $
######	061208	11	1	11750		390.00	0.00	0.00	0.00	CO-B9	390.00	0.00
PT RESP	1.20			CLAIM TOTAL		410.00	12.00	0.00	1.20		398.00	10.80
											NET	10.80

Name: HIC   ACCT   ICN

PROV #	DOS	POS	NOS	CPT	MOD	BILLED $	ALLOW	DEDUCT	COINS	GRP/RC	AMT	PAID PROV $
######	052808	22	1	99231	RT	190.00	0.00	0.00	0.00	OA-58	190.00	0.00
				REM: M77								
PT RESP	0.00			CLAIM TOTAL		190.00	0.00	0.00	0.00		190.00	0.00
											NET	0.00

Name: HIC   ACCT   ICN

PROV #	DOS	POS	NOS	CPT	MOD	BILLED $	ALLOW	DEDUCT	COINS	GRP/RC	AMT	PAID PROV $
######	060208	11	1	96372		75.00	60.00	0.00	12.00	CO-45	15.00	48.00
######	060208	11	1	J0170		23.00	0.00	0.00	0.00	CO-181	23.00	0.00
				REM:M56								
PT RESP	12.00			CLAIM TOTAL		9.00	0.00	0.00	12.00		38.00	48.00
											NET	48.00

MESSAGE CODES: GROUP/CARC/RARC

CO   Contractual Obligation

181   Procedure code was invalid on the date of service.

N56   Procedure code billed is not correct or valid for the services billed or the date of service billed

CASE ZZ: SITUATION 1

CODING ERROR: ANSI CARC/RARC CODES

QUESTION: Medicare is denying the service because it's an invalid code. How do you know what the correct code is?
ANSWER: Check the HCPCS code book. If it is no longer a valid code, the code book will provide you with the new code.

For help, go to: Area A4, Resources: HCPCS Code book

QUESTION: What is the new code?
ANSWER: Per the HCPCS code book, the new code is J0171. Per the HCPCS code book, J0170 is crossed out and directly underneath states "To report, see J0171."

¨ Key Point: New and Deleted CPT/HCPCS codes Providers should place orders for new code books sometime in June or July in order to have them delivered by the October/November time frame. New code books will provide you with the new and deleted codes for the new year. Websites will also have this information available.

Remember when adding new or deleting old CPT/HCPCS codes, corrections will need to be made: Update the medical software system (Coding System), the Encounter/Superbill/Charge sheet, and the Ticket/Claim.

RESOLUTION: Three steps to correct the claim
Correct the claim by voiding out the invalid code, J0170, and then add the new code, J0171, and refile or resubmit corrected claim.

Step 1. Pull up the original ticket/claim, then pull up the charge entry so you can make correction. In the Main Menu, select **COLLECTIONS,** pull up **PATIENT BILLING,** then pull up the ticket. From the PATIENT ACCOUNT CLAIM DETAIL under "Billing," select MODIFY. In the Charge Entry screen on line 2, which lists CPT Code J0170, void out the charge then key in the correct HCPCS code J0171.

Step 2. Now that you have made correction on ticket/claim, you will need to refile or resubmit the claim electronically to Medicare. In the Charge Entry screen mark (x) next to File: HCFA Electronically so the claim can be batched and then billed.

Step 3. Now that you have resolved the claim issue, the next step is to add your notes on how you resolved the claim issue.

Pull up **PATIENT BILLING** under the PATIENT ACCOUNT CLAIM DETAIL and select NOTES. Type in what the problem was and what you did to resolve the claim issue.

(**In every medical software there is a place to key in notes on what you did, either on that particular ticket or somewhere on that patient's account.**) An example of how you would type in your notes is as follows:

NOTE: Per the Medicare remittance dated 5/14/2008 denied the service because J0170 is an invalid code. The HCPCS code book states to report J0171 in place of J0170. Made correction voiding J0170 and keying in correct code J0171 and then billed the corrected claim to Medicare.

¨ Key Point: Keeping good notes is another key factor in doing a great job. Putting in good notes will provide information as to what has been done or is being done to resolve the issue with that particular date of service. If someone decides to go into that particular claim, they will see your notes and will know exactly what is being done.

Section 3: Other Claim Issues

I have provided you with four case examples (Cases Abc, Def, Ghi, Jkl), with one or two different situations regarding other claim issues. Some may have more than two. A step-by-step guide is provided for each case. I will provide you with questions then with the answers. Then, I will show how you how to resolve that particular issue on that claim.

CASE ABC: SITUATION 1

MEDICARE PART B   (ERA) REMITTANCE ADVICE

Provider#:

Check/EFT (Electronic Fund Transfer) #:   Issue Date: 00/00/2008

Name: HIC   ACCT   ICN

PROV #	DOS	POS	NOS	CPT	MOD	BILLED $	ALLOW	DEDUCT	COINS	GRP/RC	AMT	PAID PROV $
######	051408	11	1	99213		74.00	0.00	0.00	0.00	CO-29	74.00	0.00
PT RESP	0.00			CLAIM TOTAL		74.00	0.00	0.00	0.00		74.00	0.00
											NET	0.00

Name: HIC   ACCT   ICN

PROV #	DOS	POS	NOS	CPT	MOD	BILLED $	ALLOW	DEDUCT	COINS	GRP/RC	AMT	PAID PROV $
######	060208	11	1	A9300		9.00	0.00	0.00	0.00	PR-96	9.00	0.00
PT RESP	0.00			CLAIM TOTAL		9.00	0.00	0.00	0.00		9.00	0.00
											NET	0.00

Name: HIC   ACCT   ICN

PROV #	DOS	POS	NOS	CPT	MOD	BILLED $	ALLOW	DEDUCT	COINS	GRP/RC	AMT	PAID PROV $
######	061209	21	1	15830		3500.00	0.00	0.00	0.00	PR-96	3500.00	0.00
######	061209	21	1	15847		2900.00	0.00	0.00	0.00	PR-96	2900.00	0.00
PT RESP				CLAIM TOTAL		6400.00	0.00	0.00	0.00		6400.00	0.00
											NET	0.00

Name: HIC   ACCT   ICN

PROV #	DOS	POS	NOS	CPT	MOD	BILLED $	ALLOW	DEDUCT	COINS	GRP/RC	AMT	PAID PROV $
######	052808	11	1	99203		125.00	0.00	0.00	0.00	PR-204	125.00	0.00
######	052808	11	1	73620	RT	84.00	0.00	0.00	0.00	PR-204	84.00	0.00
PT RESP	209.00			CLAIM TOTAL		209.00	0.00	0.00	0.00		209.00	0.00
											NET	0.00

MESSAGE CODES: GROUP/CARC/RARC

CO   Contractual Obligation

29   Time limit for filing has expired

CASE ABC: SITUATION 1

CODING ERROR: ANSI CARC/RARC CODES CO-29

QUESTION: How long do we have to file a claim with Medicare?
ANSWER: You have 365 days from the date of service.

For help, go to: Area A4. Resources: Website: http://www.trailblazerhealth.com, Publications; select Manual, and under the Part B column select "Claim Submission."

NOTE: Other payers may be shorter. Some payers may have only 90 days to submit a claim, such as the Medicare Advantage HMO plan under Secure Horizon.

QUESTION: How do you know when the claim was first filed?
ANSWER: Pull up that individual ticket and on the Billing Screen locate where it states "File Date." The claim could have been submitted several times, if several file dates are posted.

QUESTION: Is it our fault that we didn't file the claim within the time frame or was the claim actually billed within the time allowed and the denial is an error on the payer's part?
ANSWER: In most cases, the error is on the payer's part. They use this as a way to stall payment. But if the error is our fault because we did not submit the claim within the time frame allowed, if the provider is contracted (in network) with that payer, charges will need to be adjusted off for "Untimely Filing." But if the claim was filed within the allowed time frame, you will need to submit an appeal.

QUESTION: What are some of the reasons a claim would have been billed past the timely filing period?
ANSWER: The claim was never billed and was submitted for the first time or the claim was originally billed to another payer in error and we were just informed. It is so important if you are billing a claim or resubmitting a claim to make sure you are within the time limit for filing a claim. If you have to resubmit a corrected claim, always attach the original identification number that is assigned by the payer. That will identify when the claim was originally received.

RESOLUTION: Six steps to correct the claim
Submit an appeal.

Step 1. Print a Letter of Appeal. In the Main Menu, select **COLLECTIONS** (Chapter 5, Step 8) button, double-click in the box under LTR (Letters), mark (x) next to your Letter of Appeal, then select PRINT.

Step 2. Print the screen of "File Date" from the billing. In the Main Menu, select **COLLECTIONS** (Chapter 5, Step 8) button, and select **PATIENT BILLING** button, under the PATIENT ACCOUNT CLAIM DETAIL select the Billing screen. Locate the "File Date" and double-click. This will pull up all dates when the claim was filed. Select PRINT to print the screen.

Step 3. Print the Electronic Clearinghouse Submission Report. In the Main Menu, select the **RECEIPTS** (Chapter 4, Step 7) button, double-click in the box under EDI RPT (Electronic Transmission Reports), mark (x) next to file date from the Billing in order to pull up the claims that were electronically transmitted. Locate your ticket/claim number and select PRINT to print the report.

Step 4. Mail the documentation via certified mail to address on the form. Make a copy, have it scanned (if software is equipped) or place a copy in the patient's chart.

Step 5. Follow up on your Ticket/Claim. In the Main Menu, select the **COLLECTIONS** (Chapter 5, Step 8) button, double-click in the box under TCKLR (Tickler), mark (x) next to the month in which you want to follow up on your ticket/claim. Double-click on the day and add your message "Follow up on Appeal Ticket 123456."

Step 6. Now that you have resolved the claim issue, the next step is to add your notes on how you resolved the claim issue. Pull up **PATIENT BILLING** under the PATIENT ACCOUNT CLAIM DETAIL and select NOTES. Type in what the problem was and what you did to resolve the claim issue.

(**In every medical software there is a place to key in notes on what you did, either on that particular ticket or somewhere on that patient's account.**) An example of how you would type in your notes is as follows:

NOTE: Per the Medicare remittance dated 5/14/2008 denied the service because claim was not submitted within the time allowed. I show the claim was filed within the proper time frame. Mailing proof that shows the file date when the claim was originally submitted electronically. Mailed out documentation certified to Trailblazer (address is listed on the redetermination request form) for redetermination. Placed copy in patient chart. Set follow up for 65 days.

" Key Point: Keeping good notes is another key factor in doing a great job. Putting in good notes will provide information as to what has been done or is being done to resolve the issue with that particular date of service. If someone decides to go into that particular claim, they will see your notes and will know exactly what is being done.

CASE DEF: SITUATION 1

MEDICARE PART B					(ERA) REMITTANCE ADVICE							
Provider#:												
Check/EFT (Electronic Fund Transfer) #:					Issue Date: 00/00/2008							
Name:		HIC		ACCT			ICN					

PROV #	DOS	POS	NOS	CPT	MOD	BILLED $	ALLOW	DEDUCT	COINS	GRP/RC	AMT	PAID PROV $
######	051408	11	1	99213		74.00	0.00	0.00	0.00	CO-29	74.00	0.00
PT RESP	0.00			CLAIM TOTAL		74.00	0.00	0.00	0.00		74.00	0.00
										NET		0.00

Name:		HIC		ACCT			ICN					

PROV #	DOS	POS	NOS	CPT	MOD	BILLED $	ALLOW	DEDUCT	COINS	GRP/RC	AMT	PAID PROV $
######	060208	11	1	A9300		9.00	0.00	0.00	0.00	PR-96	9.00	0.00
PT RESP	0.00			CLAIM TOTAL		9.00	0.00	0.00	0.00		9.00	0.00
										NET		0.00

Name:		HIC		ACCT			ICN					

PROV #	DOS	POS	NOS	CPT	MOD	BILLED $	ALLOW	DEDUCT	COINS	GRP/RC	AMT	PAID PROV $
######	061209	21	1	15830		3500.00	0.00	0.00	0.00	PR-96	3500.00	0.00
######	061209	21	1	15847		2900.00	0.00	0.00	0.00	PR-96	2900.00	0.00
PT RESP				CLAIM TOTAL		6400.00	0.00	0.00	0.00		6400.00	0.00
										NET		0.00

Name:		HIC		ACCT			ICN					

PROV #	DOS	POS	NOS	CPT	MOD	BILLED $	ALLOW	DEDUCT	COINS	GRP/RC	AMT	PAID PROV $
######	052808	11	1	99203		125.00	0.00	0.00	0.00	PR-204	125.00	0.00
######	052808	11	1	73620	RT	84.00	0.00	0.00	0.00	PR-204	84.00	0.00
PT RESP	209.00			CLAIM TOTAL		209.00	0.00	0.00	0.00		209.00	0.00
										NET		0.00

MESSAGE CODES: GROUP/CARC/RARC
PR Patient Responsibility
96 Non-covered charge

CASE DEF: SITUATION 1

CODING ERROR: ANSI CARC/RARC CODES CO-96

QUESTION: What is A9300?
ANSWER: It is exercise equipment.

For help, go to: Area A4 Resources: HCPCS Code book.

QUESTION: Why won't the insurer cover exercise equipment if it is provided by your doctor?
ANSWER: Medicare considers this a self-care product that is used at home. It is not primarily medical in nature. Bill the patient directly for the cost of the product. Do not bill insurance; collect at the time of service.

**Note: Home exercise programs for strengthening and stretching activities should be designated as therapeutic exercise. Physical Therapy training for home exercises involving functional activities should use code 97530, as long as PT is a covered benefit under the patient's insurance.

RESOLUTION: Three steps to correct the claim

Make an adjustment on the claim by transferring charges over to patient responsibility.

Step 1. In the Main Menu, select **COLLECTIONS**, pull up **PATIENT BILLING**, then pull up the ticket. From the PATIENT ACCOUNT CLAIM DETAIL under "Payment Type," select VIEW. Under the transfer column, key in charges on each line and select OK to save the transaction. This will transfer charges over to patient responsibility.

Step 2. In the Main Menu, select **REGISTRATION OF A PATIENT**, pull up the GT (Guarantor) tab, and under STATEMENT select PRINT and mail out a new statement.

Step 3. Now that you have resolved the claim issue, the next step is to add your notes on how you resolved the claim issue. Pull up **PATIENT BILLING** under the PATIENT ACCOUNT CLAIM DETAIL and select NOTES. Type in what the problem was and what you did to resolve the claim issue.

(**In every medical software there is a place to key in notes on what you did, either on that particular ticket or somewhere on that patient's account.**) An example of how you would type in your notes is as follows:

NOTE: Per the Medicare remittance dated 5/14/2008 denied the service because the service or item is not a covered benefit under his or her Part B Medicare plan. I transferred charges over to patient responsibility and mailed out a new statement.

** Key Point: Keeping good notes is another key factor in doing a great job. Putting in good notes will provide information as to what has been done or is being done to resolve the issue with that particular date of service. If someone decides to go into that particular claim, they will see your notes and will know exactly what is being done.

CASE GHI: SITUATION 1

MEDICARE PART B   **(ERA) REMITTANCE ADVICE**

Provider#:

Check/EFT (Electronic Fund Transfer) #:   Issue Date: 00/00/2008

Name: HIC   ACCT   ICN

PROV #	DOS	POS	NOS	CPT	MOD	BILLED $	ALLOW	DEDUCT	COINS	GRP/RC	AMT	PAID PROV $
######	051408	11	1	99213		74.00	0.00	0.00	0.00	CO-29	74.00	0.00
PT RESP	0.00			CLAIM TOTAL		74.00	0.00	0.00	0.00		74.00	0.00
											NET	0.00

Name: HIC   ACCT   ICN

PROV #	DOS	POS	NOS	CPT	MOD	BILLED $	ALLOW	DEDUCT	COINS	GRP/RC	AMT	PAID PROV $
######	060208	11	1	A9300		9.00	0.00	0.00	0.00	PR-96	9.00	0.00
PT RESP	0.00			CLAIM TOTAL		9.00	0.00	0.00	0.00		9.00	0.00
											NET	0.00

Name: HIC   ACCT 123456   ICN

PROV #	DOS	POS	NOS	CPT	MOD	BILLED $	ALLOW	DEDUCT	COINS	GRP/RC	AMT	PAID PROV $
######	061209	21	1	15830		3500.00	0.00	0.00	0.00	PR-96	3500.00	0.00
######	061209	21	1	15847		2900.00	0.00	0.00	0.00	PR-96	2900.00	0.00
PT RESP	1.20			CLAIM TOTAL		6400.00	0.00	0.00	0.00		6400.00	0.00
											NET	0.00

Name: HIC   ACCT   ICN

PROV #	DOS	POS	NOS	CPT	MOD	BILLED $	ALLOW	DEDUCT	COINS	GRP/RC	AMT	PAID PROV $
######	052808	11	1	99203		125.00	0.00	0.00	0.00	PR-204	125.00	0.00
######	052808	11	1	73620	RT	84.00	0.00	0.00	0.00	PR-204	84.00	0.00
PT RESP	209.00			CLAIM TOTAL		209.00	0.00	0.00	0.00		209.00	0.00
											NET	0.00

MESSAGE CODES: GROUP/CARC/RARC

PR   Patient Responsibility

96   Non-covered charge

CASE GHI: SITUATION 1

CODING ERROR: ANSI CARC/RARC CODES PR-96

QUESTION: Why would these types of procedures not be covered under the patients policy?
ANSWER: These types of procedures can be either considered cosmetic or reconstructive, depending on the patient's condition, what is being treated, and if the procedure is medically necessary or not.

QUESTION: What is the difference between cosmetic surgery and reconstructive surgery?
ANSWER: When a patient wants to enhance his or her looks because they don't like a particular part of their body, this would be considered a cosmetic procedure.

If the patient condition was caused by a birth defect, disease, infection, or traumatic injury OR if the patient condition is causing medical problems, the procedure would fall under reconstructive surgery.

Reconstructive surgery is done to repair and restore normalcy to a body part that has been altered by a birth defect (e.g., cleft lip or palate), disease (e.g., cancer), infection (e.g., ulcer), or traumatic injury (e.g., crushing injury to the nose).

Reconstructive surgery is covered by most payers whereas cosmetic is not.

For help, go to: Area A4 Other Resources: http://www.trailblazerhealth.com

QUESTION: Is the patient actually responsible?
ANSWER: Yes and no. It depends on if the procedure falls under cosmetic or reconstructive surgery.

In this case example, back in 2009 it was difficult to get Medicare to pay for a panniculectomy (CPT Code 15830) or abdominoplasty (CPT Code 15847). Panniculectomy/abdominoplasty and abdominal lipectomy (CPT Code 15877) were primarily cosmetic procedures, referred to as a "Tummy Tuck," but since that time many insurance companies, including Medicare, have changed their guidelines and policies to include this type of surgery as a reasonable and necessary medical procedure when certain medical conditions apply.

QUESTION: Should any type of procedure be preauthorized/precertified prior to surgery?
ANSWER: Yes.

Verification of coverage: This should always be done. Verify whether the patient's plan covers medical, outpatient/inpatient services, whether there is any exclusionary rider information, if they have a high deductible, and much more. Every medical office should supply some type of insurance "Verification of Coverage" form to capture information in order to know if services will be covered or not. Once you have verified coverage, locate the medical policy. A medical policy will provide you with detailed information on a particular service or procedure. It is a good tool to use. Keep these on hand to refer to whenever you come across the same case on another patient.

NOTE: Check the patient insurance card. Some will state if precertification is required.

QUESTION: If informed that the procedure is not a covered benefit, what steps should be taken?
ANSWER: Collect payment prior to surgery or set up payment arrangements.

QUESTION: There are cases where a procedure did not require preauthorization/precertification and may not be a covered benefit, but the patient and the doctor want to bill the insurance company anyway. What action should be taken?
ANSWER: If the doctor wants to take that chance on his/her services being denied, have the patient complete a Notice of Exclusions from Medicare Benefits (NEMB) and Advanced Beneficiary Notice (ABN) informing the patient that they may be responsible for the bill. In this type of situation a GA modifier will need to be appended to the claim prior to submission. Having the patient sign a waiver guarantees that the patient is aware of the situation that he or she may be responsible for the bill. That way they cannot come back and state they weren't aware it was a noncovered service/procedure.

For help, go to: Area A4. Resources: TrailBlazer website: http://www.trailblazerhealth.com Publications, Manual, Advanced Beneficiary Notice of Non-Coverage.

Today, if we were to correct the denied claim, the surgery would be considered as reconstructive, not cosmetic, and all we would need to do is resubmit a corrected claim listing ICD-9-CM 553.21 (Recurrent Incisional Hernia) as the primary diagnosis.

QUESTION: What LCD is a panniculectomy (CPT Code 15830) listed under now?
ANSWER: LCD Title: "Cosmetic and Reconstructive Surgery" - 4S-164AB-R2, Contractors Determination Number 4S-164AB (L30852).

Refer to the LCD "Indications and Limitations of Coverage and/or Medical Necessity" for the specifics. The LCD states that if the panniculus hangs below the pubis area and causes medical conditions such as chronic skin irritations, infection, or chafing of the skin that consistently recurs over a three-month period of time, it would fall under medical necessity. Check to see if the patient diagnosis is listed under the ICD-9-CM codes that support medical necessity.

CASE GHI SITUATION #1

CODING ERROR: ANSI CARC/RARC CODES PR-96

Claim # 123456   **CHARGE ENTRY**

Diagnosis: Patient Complaint: Pain in the right wrist

1 783.21   (Description: Abnormal loss of weight)

2 V85.3   (Description: BMI   Date of Injury: 02/08/06   ( ) File: HCFA Electronically

3 112.3   (Description: Candidiasis of skin)   Date of Hospitalization: 06/12/09   ( ) File: HCFA Paper

4 _____   (Description: _____)   Discharge Date: _____   ( ) File: UB04

Facility: Office

Rendering Provider: Jones   Referring: Supervising/Ordering:

Line #	Date of Service		Code(s)	Diag	Modifier	POS	Unit(s)	$ Fee
(x) 1	From 06/12/09	To 06/12/09	15830	1,2,3		21		3500.00
(x) 2	From 06/12/09	To 06/12/09	15847	1,2,3		21		2900.00
( ) 3	From 06/12/09	To 06/12/09	15877	1,2,3		21		1500.00
(x) 4	From	To						
(x) 5	From	To						
(x) 6	From	To						

Description: CPT Code 15830: "Panniculectomy" Removal of Pannus (excessive skin)

CPT Code 15847: "Abdominoplasty" Repair the abdominal wall.

Note: CPT Code 15847 is an Add-On code (refer back to Case P)

CPT Code 15877: "Lipectomy" Removal of fat

Note: CPT Code 15877 Collect from the patient, Do not bill insurance. Considered Cosmetic.

On our first submission of the above case example, the patient primary diagnosis was abnormal loss of weight, ICD-9-CM 783.21, secondary diagnosis was Body Mass Index (BMI), ICD-9-CM V85.36, and Candidiasis of skin, ICD-9-CM 112.3. Medicare denied the claim, stating it was a Non-Covered service. At that time, CPT Code 15830 was listed under LCD Titled: "Non-Covered Services" – 4Z-18AB-R19, Contractor's Determination Number 4Z-18 (L26811). Non-Covered Services are listed by the type of service/procedure that was provided, not by diagnosis.

Upon review of the patient H&P and clinical notes we learned that back in 2004 our patient was diagnosed with a tumor which led to a hysterectomy. Since the 2004 surgery patient was diagnosed with "Recurrent Ventral Incisional Hernia" (ICD-9-CM 553.21) and has dealt with this condition over several years, undergoing repeated surgery for hernia repair and due to that factor caused trauma to the abdomen. In between all that time up to the year 2009 the patient also had an excessive amount of weight loss and because of that weight loss developed the hanging skin which hung below the pubis area causing medical conditions such as recurrent skin infections. Due to several hernia repairs and excessive skin contributed to the patient condition.

QUESTION: Per the Remittance Advice (RA) the ANSI Reason Codes state that the service that was provided is the patient responsibility, do we go ahead and bill the patient or do we appeal Medicare's decision?
ANSWER: Leave claim pending insurance and appeal Medicare's decision based off the fact that Medicare should pay for the services that were provided due to the fact it was medically necessary.

QUESTION: How do you do an appeal?
ANSWER: Medicare has five levels of appeals: Redetermination, Reconsideration, Administrative Law Judge Hearing, Medicare Appeals Council Review, and Judicial Review in U.S. District Court.

For help, go to: Area A1. Refer to: Chapter 5, Unit II, Step 8, Part B: Daily Work, Section 5

You have 120 days from the original denial of the claim to submit in an appeal to Medicare.

First Level of Appeal: Redetermination request. Use the form Medicare provides.

For help, go to: Area A4. Resources: TrailBlazer Health website: http://www.trailblazerhealth.com Forms; Level I (Redetermination Request Form, Level II (Reconsideration Request Form), ReOpening Request Form (use when you need to resubmit a correction).

Attach a Letter of Appeal to the Redetermination form, a copy of the Medicare Remittance Advice notification, a Letter of Medical Necessity dictated by the doctor that provides a rationale for treatment, Clinical Notes and Operative Notes. Mail the medical documentation to the address on the redetermination form via certified mail so you have record that it was received.

For help, go to: Area A1 Guidebook: Refer to: Chapter 2, Unit II, Step 2, Part D: Forms/Correspondence (Letter of Medical Necessity

For a claim to be reviewed it takes 60 business days. Place a follow up at least 65 days out.

In this situation the claim came back denied. The letter was titled "Medicare Appeal Decision." If the provider and beneficiary do not agree with the redetermination, the next level is to submit a "Reconsideration Request Form" to a Qualified Independent Contractor (QIC). You have 180 days from the first level of appeal to submit a second appeal. At this level you may include any other supporting documentation that will assist you.

The next step is a **Second Level of Appeal**: "Reconsideration Request Form." In my whole career as a medical billing specialist, it took a second "Level of Appeal" in order for Medicare to reconsider reprocessing the claim. I got the patient involved by having the patient provide us with medical records from his/her primary care physician regarding prior surgeries for hysterectomy, hernia repair, and treatments for recurrent skin irritations.

We did receive confirmation that our reconsideration request was received and that Medicare hired a Q2 Administrator to review our appeal in order for a decision to be made. An Appeal Number is assigned and they do provide you with contact information if you have any questions or concerns. Q2 Administrators are hired by Medicare to review your file and make an independent decision.

After several weeks, the claim was reprocessed and an additional payment was issued. The claim issue was resolved.

RESOLUTION: Five steps to correct the claim
Submit an appeal.

Step 1. Print a Letter of Appeal. In the Main Menu, select the **COLLECTIONS** (Chapter 5, Step 8) button, double-click in the box under LTR (Letters), mark (x) next to your Letter of Appeal and select PRINT.

Step 2. Print the Clinic Notes, Op Notes, and a Letter of Medical Necessity (LMN). In the Main Menu, select the **MEDICAL RECORD** (Chapter 2, Step 2) button, double-click in the box under DR (Doctors Notes), mark (x) next to date of service when the first visit took place, then select PRINT. Double-click in the box under HOSP (Hospital Notes), mark (x) next to the date of service in question, and select PRINT. Double-click in the box under FORMS (Forms/Correspondence), mark an (x) next to "Letter of Medical Necessity," and select PRINT.

Step 3. Mail the documentation via certified mail to the address on the form. Make a copy and have it scanned (if software is equipped) or place a copy in the patient chart.

Step 4. Follow up on your Ticket/Claim. In the Main Menu, select **COLLECTIONS** (Chapter 5, Step 8) button, double-click in the box under TCKLR (Tickler), mark (x) next to the month in which you want to follow up on your ticket/claim, double-click on the day and add your message: "Follow up on Appeal Ticket 123456."

Step 5. Now that you have resolved the claim issue, the next step is to add your notes on how you resolved the claim issue.

Pull up **PATIENT BILLING** under the PATIENT ACCOUNT CLAIM DETAIL and select NOTES. Type in what the problem was and what you did to resolve the claim issue.

(**In every medical software there is a place to key in notes on what you did, either on that particular ticket or somewhere on that patient's account.**) An example of how you would type in your notes is as follows:

NOTE: Per Medicare Remit dated _/_/_ denied procedures because they were considered to be Non-Covered Benefits. This type of procedure is referred to as a "Tummy Tuck," which is considered cosmetic. Patient had undergone several surgeries for recurrent incisional hernia repair due to a hysterectomy for removal of a tumor. Patient also has lost an abnormal amount of weight, which has caused an excessive amount of skin that hangs below pubis causing irritation. With these factors in place, the doctor dictated a Letter of Medical Necessity stating the need for reconstructive surgery, not cosmetic. Mailed out medical documentation certified to Trailblazer (address is listed on the redetermination request form) for redetermination. Placed copy in patient chart and set a follow up for at least 65 days.

NOTE: Tickler: 65 day Follow-up Ticket/Claim # 123456.

We received Medicare's Appeal Decision letter which states "Unfavorable because procedure is cosmetic and patient is responsible for payment for these services." We are appealing their decision and leaving everything still pending insurance. We have been in contact with the patient, who has provided us with medical documentation from her primary care physician. We are attaching original documentation from our first appeal, additional documentation, and will mailing everything certified to Q2 Administrator (address is listed on the reconsideration request form) for a second level of appeal. Placed copy in patient chart and set follow up for at least another 65 days.

NOTE: Notification was received from Q2 Administrators informing us that our reconsideration (2nd Level of Appeal) was received, and assigning it an appeal number. Contact information was also provided if we had any questions or concerns. Medicare Appeal Number #######. Letter is in patient chart.

NOTE: After several weeks of reconsideration, the claim was reprocessed and an additional payment was received. The claim issue was resolved.

** Key Point: Keeping good notes is another key factor in doing a great job. Putting in good notes will provide information as to what has been done or is being done to resolve the issue with that particular date of service. If someone decides to go into that particular claim, they will see your notes and will know exactly what is being done.

CASE JKL: SITUATION 1

MEDICARE PART B					(ERA) REMITTANCE ADVICE							
Provider#:												
Check/EFT (Electronic Fund Transfer) #:					Issue Date: 00/00/2008							
Name:		HIC		ACCT			ICN					

PROV #	DOS	POS	NOS	CPT	MOD	BILLED $	ALLOW	DEDUCT	COINS	GRP/RC	AMT	PAID PROV $
######	051408	11	1	99213		74.00	0.00	0.00	0.00	CO-29	74.00	0.00
PT RESP	0.00			CLAIM TOTAL		74.00	0.00	0.00	0.00		74.00	0.00
											NET	0.00

Name:		HIC		ACCT			ICN					

PROV #	DOS	POS	NOS	CPT	MOD	BILLED $	ALLOW	DEDUCT	COINS	GRP/RC	AMT	PAID PROV $
######	060208	11	1	A9300		9.00	0.00	0.00	0.00	PR-96	9.00	0.00
PT RESP	0.00			CLAIM TOTAL		9.00	0.00	0.00	0.00		9.00	0.00
											NET	0.00

Name:		HIC		ACCT			ICN					

PROV #	DOS	POS	NOS	CPT	MOD	BILLED $	ALLOW	DEDUCT	COINS	GRP/RC	AMT	PAID PROV $
######	061209	21	1	15830		3500.00	0.00	0.00	0.00	PR-96	3500.00	0.00
######	061209	21	1	15847		2900.00	0.00	0.00	0.00	PR-96	2900.00	0.00
PT RESP				CLAIM TOTAL		6400.00	0.00	0.00	0.00		6400.00	0.00
											NET	0.00

Name:		HIC		ACCT			ICN					

PROV #	DOS	POS	NOS	CPT	MOD	BILLED $	ALLOW	DEDUCT	COINS	GRP/RC	AMT	PAID PROV $
######	052808	11	1	99203		125.00	0.00	0.00	0.00	PR-204	125.00	0.00
######	052808	11	1	73620	RT	84.00	0.00	0.00	0.00	PR-204	84.00	0.00
PT RESP	209.00			CLAIM TOTAL		209.00	0.00	0.00	0.00		209.00	0.00
											NET	0.00

MESSAGE CODES: GROUP/CARC/RARC
PR   Patient Responsibility
204   Service/equipment/drug is not covered under the patient's current benefit plan

---

CASE JKL: SITUATION 1

CODING ERROR: ANSI CARC/RARC CODES PR-204

QUESTION: Medicare's denial was based on what?
ANSWER: In this situation, services are not a covered benefit based on the patient diagnosis, not by the service or procedure that was provided.

QUESTION: In this case, what is the patient diagnosis?
ANSWER: In reviewing the ticket/claim as well as the clinic notes, the ICD-9-CM code is 754.61, "Congenital Pes Planus or "Flat Foot."

QUESTION: What LCD would list foot under?
ANSWER: LCD Title: "Routine Foot Care" 4P-11AB-R1, Contractors Determination Number 4P-11AB (L30848)

For help, go to: Area A4 Other Resources, http://www.trailblazerhealth.com

QUESTION: Is diagnosis 754.61 listed in the LCD?
ANSWER: No. The LCD states that the treatment or correction for Flat Foot is excluded from Medicare coverage.

QUESTION: Can we appeal their decision, do we adjust it off, or do we bill the patient?
ANSWER: Since this is not a covered benefit, you cannot appeal, and the RA states that the charges are the patient's responsibility. Transfer the charges to patient responsibility and send a bill.

It is the responsibility for the patient to know what type of coverage he or she has, but we should make every effort to verify that coverage as well so the patient is not surprised when they receive a bill.

RESOLUTION: Three steps to correct the claim
Make an adjustment on the claim by transferring charges to patient responsibility.

Step 1. In the Main Menu, select **COLLECTIONS**, pull up **PATIENT BILLING**, then pull up the ticket. From the PATIENT ACCOUNT CLAIM DETAIL under "Payment Type," select VIEW. Under the transfer column, key in charges on each line and select OK to save the transaction. This will transfer charges to patient responsibility.

Step 2. In the Main Menu select **REGISTRATION OF A PATIENT,** pull up the GT (Guarantor) tab and under STATEMENT, select PRINT and mail out a new statement.

Step 3. Now that you have resolved the claim issue, the next step is to add your notes on how you resolved the claim issue. Pull up **PATIENT BILLING** under the PATIENT ACCOUNT CLAIM DETAIL and select NOTES. Type in what the problem was and what you did to resolve the claim issue.

(**In every medical software there is a place to key in notes on what you did, either on that particular ticket or somewhere on that patient's account.**) An example of how you would type in your notes is as follows:

NOTE: Per the Medicare remittance dated 5/14/2008 denied the service because Flat Foot is excluded from Medicare coverage. I transferred charges over to patient responsibility, set the account to self-pay, and mailed out a new statement.

** Key Point: Keeping good notes is another key factor in doing a great job. Putting in good notes will provide information as to what has been done or is being done to resolve the issue with that particular date of service. If someone decides to go into that particular claim, they will see your notes and will know exactly what is being done.

1b. How to work OUTSTANDING CLAIMS (AGED)

Your objective is to find out why there is still a balance due on a ticket/claim that is sitting in the 45 to 120 and above (^) aging buckets. To work those claims pull up Aging Reports by Insurance.

COLLECTIONS

MEDICAL PRACTICE SOFTWARE

FILE EDIT VIEW TOOLS FORMAT

COLLECTIONS

UNPROCESSABLE OR DENIED CLAIM

STEP 8: COLLECTIONS

LTR (Letters)	TCKLR (Tickler)	RPT (Aging Report):
Double click in box to pull up letters	Double click in box to pull up tickler	Double click in box t pull up reports

SAVE

Reports:

(X) Accounts Receivable
( ) Active
( ) Administrative
( ) Financial
( ) Patients

( ) Aging by Doctor
( ) Aging by Financial Class
( ) Aging by Guarantor
(X) Aging by Insurance Carrier
( ) Aging by Patient Balance

Aging By Insurance Carrier Balance

Company Name: [   ]   SEARCH

Select: (x) ALL

Facility: [   ]   SEARCH

Select: (x) ALL

Doctor: [   ]   SEARCH

Select: (x) ALL

Aging Bucket: ( ) 45 ( ) 60 ( ) 90 ( )120 and ^

Date Type:

Sort by

INSURANCE CARRIER REPORT	Patient Name Patient Account #	0-30	31-60	61-90	91-120	121-150	150 ^	Total Balance
		I------------ AGING BUCKETS: 0-30 30-60 60-90------------I						
Medicare	Last Name, First #######	0.00	0.00	120.00	0.00	0.00	0.00	120.00
	Last Name, First #######	0.00	50.00	120.00	0.00	0.00	0.00	170.00
	Last Name, First #######	0.00	0.00	250.00	0.00	0.00	0.00	250.00
	Last Name, First #######	0.00	0.00	120.00	0.00	0.00	0.00	120.00
BCBS	Last Name, First #######	0.00	500.00	120.00	0.00	0.00	0.00	620.00
	Last Name, First #######	0.00	0.00	120.00	0.00	0.00	0.00	120.00
	Last Name, First #######	0.00	50.00	20.00	0.00	0.00	0.00	70.00
Aetna	Last Name, First #######	0.00	0.00	0.00	220.00	50.00	80.00	.00
	Last Name, First #######	0.00	0.00	120.00	0.00	0.00	0.00	120.00
	Last Name, First #######	0.00	0.00	120.00	0.00	0.00	0.00	120.00
Medicaid	Last Name, First #######	0.00	0.00	120.00	0.00	0.00	0.00	120.00
	Last Name, First #######	0.00	0.00	120.00	0.00	0.00	0.00	120.00

There may be a couple of reasons why there is a balance on a patient account:

1. Services were denied on a particular ticket/claim.
2. Balance on the ticket/claim is patient responsibility: Co-pay, co-ins, money applied toward patient deductible, or money that was actually sent to the beneficiary.
3. Contractual without or CPT code should have been adjusted off.

As a Medical Billing Specialist, it is my responsibility to see if we are still waiting for payment from the insurance carrier on a particular claim. Check file notes to see if the ticket/claim has been previously worked. If not, you will need to see if an EOB was received. If not, contact the insurance carrier to see if the claim was ever received. You need to see if services were denied, and if so, why and when? If informed by the insurance carrier that the ticket/claim was denied, you will need to request a duplicate EOB. If the ticket/claim was previously worked, check to see what was done and done correctly. In a way, you have to play detective. You have look here and look there for any clues as to what you need to do. The one thing I love about the job is once you have solved the ticket/claim issue, it is a very satisfying feeling.

How to work: Work the oldest first, as well as the ones with the highest dollar amount.

1c. How to FOLLOW UP on a claim

Go into Step 8 Collections   Select   [COLLECTIONS]   then pull up TCKLR (Tickler) or your Calendar.

Some software is not equipped with a tickler so in order to follow up on claims utilize your Calendar in Microsoft Outlook email Calendar.

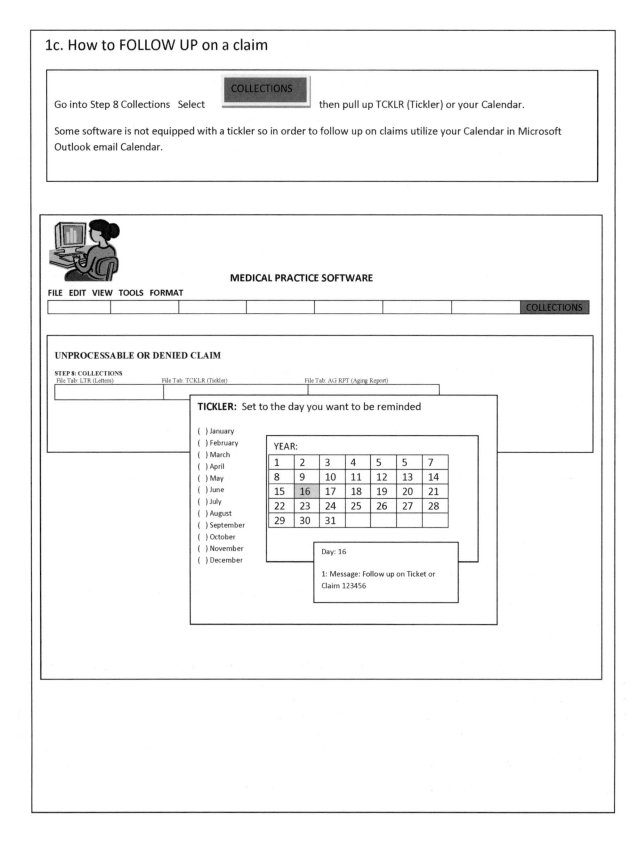

MEDICAL PRACTICE SOFTWARE

FILE   EDIT   VIEW   TOOLS   FORMAT

[COLLECTIONS]

UNPROCESSABLE OR DENIED CLAIM

STEP 8: COLLECTIONS
File Tab: LTR (Letters)   File Tab: TCKLR (Tickler)   File Tab: AG RPT (Aging Report)

TICKLER: Set to the day you want to be reminded

( ) January
( ) February
( ) March
( ) April
( ) May
( ) June
( ) July
( ) August
( ) September
( ) October
( ) November
( ) December

YEAR:

1	2	3	4	5	5	7
8	9	10	11	12	13	14
15	16	17	18	19	20	21
22	23	24	25	26	27	28
29	30	31				

Day: 16

1: Message: Follow up on Ticket or Claim 123456

1d. How to work PATIENT BALANCES

Run an Aging Report by Patient Balance only.

Go into Step 8 Collections   Select   [COLLECTIONS]   then pull up AG RPT (Aging Reports)

MEDICAL PRACTICE SOFTWARE

FILE   EDIT   VIEW   TOOLS   FORMAT

COLLECTIONS

UNPROCESSABLE OR DENIED CLAIM

STEP 8: COLLECTIONS
File Tab: LTR (Letters)   File Tab: TCKLR (Tickler)   File Tab: AG RPT (Aging Report)

Reports:

(X) Accounts Receivable
( ) Active
( ) Administrative
( ) Financial
( ) Patients

OPEN

( ) Aging by Doctor
( ) Aging by Financial Class
( ) Aging by Guarantor
( ) Aging by Insurance Carrier
(X) Aging by Patient Balance

OPEN

Aging By Patient Balance

Company Name

Facility

Doctor

Aging Bucket   60 days – 90 days

Date Type

Sort by   Patient Name

PRINT

| PATIENT REPORT | | I------------ AGING BUCKETS: 0-30 30-60 60-90------------I | | | | | Total |
Patient Name Patient Account #	0-30	31-60	61-90	91-120	121-150	150 ^	Balance
Last Name, First #######	0.00	0.00	120.00	0.00	0.00	0.00	120.00
Last Name, First #######	0.00	50.00	120.00	0.00	0.00	0.00	170.00
Last Name, First #######	0.00	0.00	250.00	0.00	0.00	0.00	250.00
Last Name, First #######	0.00	0.00	120.00	0.00	0.00	0.00	120.00
Last Name, First #######	0.00	500.00	120.00	0.00	0.00	0.00	620.00
Last Name, First #######	0.00	0.00	120.00	0.00	0.00	0.00	120.00
Last Name, First #######	0.00	50.00	20.00	0.00	0.00	0.00	70.00
Last Name, First #######	0.00	0.00	0.00	220.00	50.00	80.00	.00
Last Name, First #######	0.00	0.00	120.00	0.00	0.00	0.00	120.00
Last Name, First #######	0.00	0.00	120.00	0.00	0.00	0.00	120.00
Last Name, First #######	0.00	0.00	120.00	0.00	0.00	0.00	120.00
Last Name, First #######	0.00	0.00	120.00	0.00	0.00	0.00	120.00

Unit IV, Step 8

Part A: Eliminate Losses and Increase Revenue

To run a successful medical office it takes excellent practice management skills. You must have a complete understanding of the revenue cycle and how it functions. By developing departmental skills, from managing the front end (front office) as well as the back end (business office) of a medical office will help you ensure that certain steps are taken so that physicians will be paid. Following my eight-step guidebook will give you a complete understanding of how a revenue cycle works. By following these steps, you will help eliminate claim issues and prevent accounts receivables loss.

A revenue cycle begins when the patient calls to set up an appointment. The scheduler will schedule that patient and will collect information such as insurance coverage. That patient insurance information is forwarded to the front office clerk for verification of coverage and benefits. It is a good idea to always verify coverage and benefits before the patient is even seen. This ensures that when that patient comes in for his or her first visit, you already know if they have medical coverage or not. If you are informed that the patient does not have any medical coverage, you have time to contact the patient and inform him or her that their account will have to be set up as self-pay and what the doctor's fee will be at the time of the visit.

Once this has been completed and the patient comes in for his or her appointment, the rest of the patient information is gathered when the patient fills out the Patient Registration form. That form is forwarded to the patient data entry clerk, where that information is transferred into the patient account that has been created in the medical software.

Next part of the revenue cycle occurs, after a patient is registered and seen by the doctor, is the posting of the doctor's fees. Once charges have been posted, the claim is submitted to the payer. From there, the claim will be paid, denied, or placed on hold for further information. If a claim is paid, a check will be issued and attached to the Explanation of Benefits. Once payment is received, it is posted to the patient's account for the date the patient was seen. If there is a balance due, a statement will go out to collect the patient's portion. Checks received will then go to the accounting department and will then be forwarded to the bank for deposit. Expenses are deducted in order to run the office and then the doctor is paid for services provided to patients.

As long as everything keeps flowing properly, there will be no problems; but once a problem occurs, things become very intense and that's when the office may experience financial distress. The doctor will start asking questions as to why money is down. That's why it is so important to keep the cycle flowing.

Figure 5.22 is a diagram I put together to give you an example of what a revenue cycle looks like. It is based on this book.

Eliminate Front-End Errors

Problems can begin from the very first time the patient is seen. Information is gathered and keyed in, but nothing is verified. When the patient comes in, they fill out the Patient

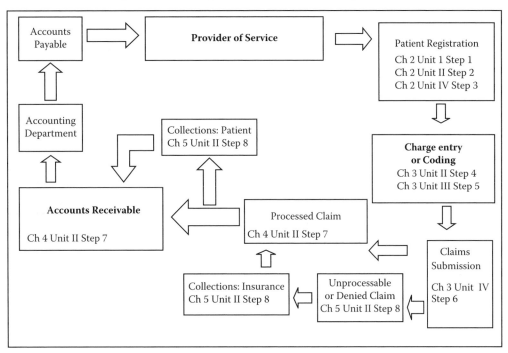

Figure 5.22 Revenue cycle.

Registration form, but by the time that information is keyed in, you notice the form is not complete. Without the right information, you are already starting off with a problem.

Patient Data

Managing the revenue cycle begins at the time that patient information is gathered. It is vital to key in correct information at the beginning, because if not, it will slow down the whole process.

Patient Information

Always review the Patient Registration form to make sure everything is complete. Two other important items are needed:

1. A copy of the patient's insurance card. Compare the information on the card to the patient information form.
2. A copy of the patient's driver's license. Make sure the patient is who they say they are. Match up names and information to the insurance card as well. This will help avoid insurance card fraud. It is a good idea to train yourself and the staff to recognize false information.

Insurance Verification

Patients will often present an expired insurance card or will present the wrong insurance card by mistake at the time of registration. To avoid a claim going out with wrong information and having to go back and collect correct insurance information, a key factor is to do a preregistration at the time the patient calls to set up an appointment. Have the patient provide you with their insurance information so that you can verify coverage and benefits before he or she walks in the door.

If a patient has a primary insurance as well as a secondary payer, and that patient doesn't know who is primary and who is secondary, it is best to verify both, unless the patient is employed and the primary payer is her group health insurance. If that's the case, the group health insurance would be primary. People have a hard time when a patient has Medicare and is also covered under another plan. In this case, it's always best to verify both. The biggest problem is that one will state that Medicare is primary, but Medicare shows that the patient has other primary coverage. This will need to be straightened out before the patient arrives for his or her appointment.

Another way to avoid claims going out with front-end errors is to review the claim by "scrubbing" it first. Before a claim is billed, check everything over. Make sure the ID number is correct. Is the claim being sent to the correct payer? Is the patient's name spelled correctly? Is there anything else wrong with the claim that could cause the claim to be denied? Asking these questions will help eliminate denial of the claim.

To avoid wrong addresses or wrong insurance information, every time a patient comes into the office, have them sign a slip that asks them if anything has changed, such as their address or insurance information. This will help eliminate front-end errors from happening as well.

Eliminate Denied claims

Eliminating the codes that you know are not payable will help eliminate a denied claim. In order for a service or procedure to be paid, does a modifier need to be attached? Denied claims can mean a hold up of reimbursement. Too many denied claims can set off a flag to the carrier that can result in an audit. These things make it look as if the provider's office staff doesn't know what it is doing. That is why it is so important to let the charge entry and coders know when a service is not billable so they do not bill for that code. Duplicate billing is another thing that sets off a flag. It looks like the office is trying to collect more money, even if it's an error on our part. It may be important to run a Daily Charge Report to go over issues like this. A Daily Charge Report will provide a list of all the charges that have been keyed in that are ready to be billed. By going over such a report, you may catch duplicate charges and catch those codes that should not be billed. It is best to try to eliminate denied claims as much as possible.

Knowing What to Bill and What Not to Bill

Knowing the difference between unbundled codes and bundled codes will help you know what codes to bill and what codes not to bill with certain services or procedures. Knowing the difference between cosmetic services and services that are considered medically necessary will also help you know what to bill and what not to bill.

Can a modifier be attached? Knowing the different modifiers and what modifiers can be used for what types of service will help you to know what to bill and what not to bill.

Go back and review Unit II, Step 8, Part B, Section 5. It will provide you with all the information you need to help you know what to bill and what not to bill.

Loss of Revenue: Common Causes

Here are some situations identified through my experience that have or would have caused a loss in revenue if not caught.

Missed Charges

In a clinic there is always a chance that an encounter/superbill or charge sheet will be misplaced or lost. That is why it is important to always cross-reference the appointment sign-in sheet with the encounter/superbills or charge sheets. That way, if you see that a patient signed in but you're not able to locate an encounter/superbill or charge sheet, you will be able to investigate why it is missing. You can also run a Charge Report once all charges are posted and compare it against the appointment sign-in sheet. There have been some instances where a patient signed in but left before even being seen, so that maybe a reason for a missing encounter/superbill or charge sheet. Another reason could be that the patient did not turn in the encounter/superbill or charge sheet when checking out. Another reason for a missing encounter/superbill or charge sheet is that the patient was a "No Show" or rescheduled their appointment. Pull up the patient account to see under Appointments if the appointment type has changed. It is a good idea to run another report that will provide you a list of all the encounter/superbills or charge sheets that were created that day. Once you have determined that the patient was not actually seen that day, you can go back and delete that encounter/superbill or charge sheet.

Under Coding E/M Visits

Doctors have a tendency to cheat themselves out of revenue by not properly selecting the correct level of complexity, which means they are cheating themselves out of billing a higher level of E/M code. A doctor may be seeing a patient who has a chronic disease, hypertension (HTN) and diabetes, but the patient's chief complaint for the visit was knee pain. The physician checks the patient's vitals and does a glucose reading and determines everything is within normal range, so the physician states there is no need to change the patient's regimen as far as meds, but then goes on to examine the patient and diagnosis the patient with a sprain/strain of the knee. Before the physician even examines that patient, he or she may not realize that the patient is already be at a Level 3 visit.

The physician notes the exam, but doesn't even consider noting the decision to not treat for HTN and diabetes.

Nontreatment is part of medical decision making. The visit could have been coded at 99214 but instead it was coded at 99213, and because it was undercoded the physician lost out on a higher reimbursement.

Patient History is one of the major parts in an evaluation and management code. The more detailed the history, the more likely a physician can justify a higher-level code. The physical exam is also considered to be another major part of the evaluation and management code. The more areas that a physician examines, the more thorough and detailed the exam becomes, the higher the level and the more the physician can be reimbursed.

Physicians lose a lot of money because they end up going over the scheduled time. For example, at the end of an exam, when the physician has documented his last note and is ready to exit the room, the patient may ask a question that is totally unrelated to their initial complaint. When a physician is forced into a more lengthy exam or counseling session, there is no time to go back and redo his or her notes or reevaluate the level of complexity for the visit because they are trying to move on to their next patient. When this happens, physicians will usually go ahead and code the one code they use the most. In this situation, if the additional question does not involve a medical emergency, it is best for the physician to inform the patient that he or she doesn't have the time at present to give that patient the full attention needed, and that the patient should schedule another appointment.

A couple of suggestions can help eliminate this problem. They are as follows:

1. Provide the physician with templates instead of an encounter/superbill or charge sheets. A template can be set up by the doctor's specialty; it's compiled with a number of questions, concerns, and diagrams. With a template, all a physician has to do is check a box, which means they are less likely to miss anything. Once the physician has the time to go back over the template it can be used as a means to determine at what level the E/M needs to be coded.
2. Have a certified coder perform an internal chart review. They can provide information to the physician on how to code to the highest level. This will help eliminate undercoding.

Accepting What the RA/EOB States

Review the RA/EOB to make sure there was no reduction in payment or that a service/procedure was denied in error.

When services are being paid under the out-of-network versus in-network portion of the plan, make sure the payer is paying what the contracted fee schedule states. There have been several cases I have come across where the allowed fee amount was not the correct amount. It was based on the previous year's fee or the claim was paid out-of-network. It is important to have a copy of a contracted fee schedule for comparison. If you do not have one, contact the insurer and request a copy of the fee schedule. You have a right to have this information because you have a contract with them.

I work off of the Medicare ERA because by doing this I catch a lot of problems before they actually become a bill problem. By reviewing an RA I happened to come across a problem where an ERA was set up to automatically post payments as well as other adjustments. I came across an ANSI CARC denial code CO-97 that, for some reason, was automatically adjusting off the charge in error. So any service or procedure that had a CO-97 was being adjusted off. When we originally set up the system for ERAs, we were able to set up the system to automatically adjust off a charge that was identified by a specific ANSI CARC code. As an example, if a service or procedure that is provided by a physician's assistant (PA) is denied by Medicare, an ANSI CARC code of CO-54 is used. When the ERA is posted and the system recognizes the CO-54 code, it was supposed to automatically adjust the charge off. Apparently when the system was originally set up, we must have set it up to adjust off charges when it recognized the CO-97 instead. Somewhere along the line, Medicare started using the ANSI CARC code CO-97 along with an ANSI RARC code denying services and procedures that where within the global period of a surgery. Therefore, when the system recognized the CO-97 code it was still reading it and automatically adjusting it off. If I had not caught and fixed the problem, the system would have continued adjusting off a service that should not have been adjusted, which would have resulted in loss in revenue.

Do not always accept a denied code. Don't write it off just because the EOB states that it's bundled, or a duplicate. Always investigate.

Slow Reimbursement Time

Can the claim be billed electronically? You will need the Payer ID and CPID number of the insurance company, payer, or carrier. The Payer ID can be located on the insurance card.

Bill all claims electronically for quicker turnaround time (Medicare 15–20 days).

Insurance stall tactics—know them and understand how to handle them, including "No claim on file" or claim is on hold because the payer is "Waiting for additional Information." What can you do in these situations?

For "No claim on File," ask the insurer what their timely filing period is and see if you can fax the claim to them if it is within the timely filing period. For some reason, they always manage to lose your claims. That is why I recommend filing all claims electronically. Make sure you receive confirmation that the claim was faxed. Most faxes are equipped with some type of confirmation. If not, call the insurer back to make sure the claim was received.

If the insurer states that they are "waiting for additional information," ask what the insurer needs to process the claim. Do they need information from the doctor's office or from the patient? Did the office receive a notification?

If the insurer needs information from the patient, contact the patient. Find out if they sent in the requested information. If so, find out when. Just like claims, they have a tendency to lose things. The best thing to do is to get a copy of the filled-out request form and fax it to the insurer yourself.

In this profession you have to always be one step ahead of the insurance company. If not, things can become a mess. Know the "prompt pay" law. The Oklahoma Statute Code §36-1219.12 regarding prompt payment, Title 36, Chapter 1, Art. 12, Section 1219 states that the healthcare provider shall be notified in writing within 45 calendar days, and if no such notification is issued regarding the reason for the delay in payment, the claim will be paid in accordance with the terms of the policy.

If you are having a problem with an insurer, you can file a formal complaint with the Insurance Commissioner's office. Make sure before you do this that you have all your ducks in a row. Compile your documentation to show proof as to why you are filing a formal complaint. A "Prompt Pay" form or a "Request for Assistance" form must be completed when submitting your documentation.

These two steps will help your company to avoid losing money.

Not Collecting at the Time of the Service

It is always best to collect at the time of the visit. Once a patient walks out the door, it can be very difficult to collect money.

At the time of the appointment, collect the patient's out-of-pocket expenses—the co-pay, co-insurance, and deductible. The patient may have a high deductible. If so, and the patient is scheduled for surgery, collect payment prior to any surgery. Also collect on those services, procedures (forthcoming surgery), or supplies (exercise equipment) that are not a covered benefit.

In a large clinic it is best to have someone, like a financial representative, who does nothing but collect money from patients at the time of their appointments. Provide those patients who are in a financial bind with an in-house Financial Payment Plan. There are also companies that can provide them with healthcare financing, such as CareCredit. Offering them choices will show that you care and are willing to help patients out.

Insurer Requesting a Refund

How can you make sure that paid claims stay that way? For example, two years after payment your office receives a notification from an insurer asking for their money back because they found out the patient didn't have coverage at time of the service. By the time the provider receives a request for a refund it may be too late for the provider to seek payment from any other payer, including the patient, if the patient is not around. It may also be too late to collect from the patient because the statute of limitations for collecting payment may have run.

Can an insurer request an overpayment refund any time, or is there a time limit? Is the insurer legally entitled to the refund? There are some states that have a time limitation under specific laws. For the state of Oklahoma, under the Statute code §36-1250.5 (Title 36, Chapter 1, Art. 12-A 1, Section 1205.5) there is an Insurance Refund Recoupment Law that provides a 24-month limitation under specific requirements. To qualify for reimbursement the payment made by the insurer must be truly erroneous under one of the following conditions: (1) the patient was uninsured at the time of service, (2) the services were not a covered benefit under the plan, (3) the payment was greater than the amount actually owed, or (4) the insurer was not the primary payer. If payment did not fall under any of these four circumstances, the payment was not erroneous and therefore a refund is not owed.

It has been my experience that the insurer must provide us proof as to why they want a refund request, such as a letter or document stating what the error was and when it was discovered in order to forward that information on to a secondary payer, so we can provide that party with proof as to why we are now seeking payment from them.

Further research on this topic may be necessary in order to determine the law and whether a provider can legally decline a request. This is where you want to get an attorney involved.

Revenue Opportunities: Other Ways to Increase Revenue

There may be some things of which your office may not be aware that can enable you to actually collect money, but make sure that everything is documented.

Reimbursement for Unbillable Services

No Shows
Your office loses money every time a patient fails to keep an appointment. I have seen instances where patients have not kept up to two or more appointments. It is very frustrating, especially if you are the one doing all the work preparing for that patient's arrival by pulling the patient chart, and the time spent when that patient calls the office to reschedule his or her appointment over and over again. This takes up a lot of staff time and the doctor is losing money because that time slot could have filled with another patient.

A medical office can put in place a "Clinic Cancellation Policy" that states that if a patient is a "no show" a second time, charges can be billed as if services were provided. This is one way to handle chronic offenders, but make sure you provided the patient with enough information about his or her appointment. You can do this by providing patients with

an appointment card, and call the patient as a reminder of his or her appointment.

A sign may be on display or a brochure that's available in the waiting area that states what the clinic's policy is for no shows so that patients are aware.

Forms
It takes time for a doctor to fill out a form or put together a letter for schools. Charge a $10 fee for this service. The doctor needs to be paid for his or her time spent on providing that information.

Improve Customer Service

Availability
Today, everyone is so busy. Making things more available and convenient will make things run so much smoother.

Provide Several Options
The more you offer to your patients, the better off you will be in collecting payment. Offer your patients things like financial help such as monthly payment arrangements (provide a coupon book), CareCredit (financing), and prompt pay discounts.

Automate by offering online bill pay (credit cards, transfer of payment, financial assistant), e-statements (viewing and retrieval), preregistration (adding or updating patient information).

Inform your patients that you offer these things so they are aware that they have options.

Third-Party Collection Agency (Outside Source)

Patient Balance
You have tried every avenue possible but are having no luck collecting the balance on a patient account. You don't have the time to spend on trying to collect on uncollectable accounts. You want to spend that time collecting on those accounts you know you will be paid.

It is best to have a collection policy in place so that you know exactly which accounts are uncollectable and you can turn them over to your third-party collection agency.

Trauma Fund

In 1999, Senate Bill 290 established the Trauma Care Assistance Revolving Fund (Trauma Fund) which provides reimbursement of uncompensated costs associated with the care of injuries that were provided by facilities and emergency medical providers that fall under major trauma clinical criteria. In 2004, House Bill 1554 added physicians to the list of providers as well. For hospitals and physicians to be eligible for reimbursement from the Trauma Fund, cases must meet clinical criteria and must meet specific requirements, among them the patient diagnosis (ICD-9 code), must fall between 800.0 and 959.9. All efforts to collect from the patient must be exhausted as well. To learn more for the state of Oklahoma, go to the Oklahoma State Department of Health, http://www.ok.gov/health.com and click "T" to search for Trauma Registry. Then click Trauma Registry and on the right-hand side of the screen, click "Trauma Fund." The contact number for the Trauma Division is (405) 271-2657 or 4027. Make a note that there is a timeline when reporting your cases to the State Trauma Registry.

Victim of a Crime

If a doctor specializes in plastic surgery, he or she may have treated a patient who was a victim in a crime, and the patient was robbed and beaten in the face. The doctor provided his or her services by doing reconstructive surgery on the patient's nose. You have discovered that the patient has no insurance. You may ask if this patient filed a claim for compensation. If a report was filed, he or she may also file a claim to the Crime Victims Compensation Program in your area. A claim must be turned in at least one year from the day the incident occurred. For the state of Oklahoma, contact Oklahoma District Attorneys Council at 421 NW 13th, Ste 290, Oklahoma City, OK 73103; phone 800-745-6098. Website: http://www.okgov/dac/victims_services.

You have access to review the claim status by pulling up their website or you can email them at victimservices@dac.state.ok.us or fax your request to 405-264-5097.

Invest in Proper Equipment

For any office to run smoothly, it is important to have the proper equipment, especially in a large clinic. You may need to invest in the beginning, but in the long run it will save you time and money and will increase productivity.

Software products: There are so many out there, how do you know which one is the best? When it comes to selecting the right equipment, you have to decide what is going to make the job easier and more efficient from the front end to the back end. From the front end, what will help make patient registration easier and more efficient? A Patient Portal Solution that offers preregistration (add and update patient information), online bill pay (offers discounts, financial assistant, virtual terminal for instant credit card approval), e-statements (view and retrieve statements), and health forms (patient medical history and medications).

On the back end, what will produce the quickest and most accurate way to do charge entry? Does the program have a way to capture charges electronically but also includes a pre-edit coding system? It must be set up to do electronic billing (submitting claims electronically).

Is it capable of scanning in medical documents, or have an electronic medical record (EMR) system? Does it have some way to pull up delinquent accounts (Collection Module) or a Missing Charge Report (cross-reference the appointments schedule with encounters/superbills)?

When purchasing new products, remember that they have to be compatible with the software. Another thing to remember when purchasing these products is that they will require a provider license. Costs may vary.

INDEX

Page numbers followed by f indicate figure
Page number followed by t indicate table